LANGUAGE AND IMAGES OF RENAISSANCE ITALY

Language and Images of Renaissance Italy

edited by
ALISON BROWN

CLARENDON PRESS · OXFORD

*This book has been printed digitally and produced in a standard specification
in order to ensure its continuing availability*

OXFORD
UNIVERSITY PRESS

Great Clarendon Street, Oxford OX2 6DP

Oxford University Press is a department of the University of Oxford.
It furthers the University@ objective of excellence in research, scholarship,
and education by publishing worldwide in

Oxford New York

Auckland Bangkok Buenos Aires Cape Town Chennai
Dar es Salaam Delhi Hong Kong Istanbul Karachi Kolkata
Kuala Lumpur Madrid Melbourne Mexico City Mumbai Nairobi
Sₒo Paulo Shanghai Taipei Tokyo Toronto

Oxford is a registered trade mark of Oxford University Press
in the UK and in certain other countries

Published in the United States
by Oxford University Press Inc., New York

ISBN 0-19-820318-7

Jacket illustration: Poggio a Caiano, last panel of the frieze. Courtesy of the Sopraintendenza
per I Beni Ambientali e Architettonici, Palazzo Pitti, Florence.

Printed in Great Britain by

Antony Rowe Ltd., Eastbourne

Preface

THIS book originated in the papers delivered at a conference on 'Cultural Definition and the Renaissance', which was held at the Courtauld Institute, University of London, in June 1990. The idea for such a colloquium came from Patricia Rubin and it was she who was largely responsible for its successful organization and funding. It was from the start intended to be interdisciplinary, the speakers being asked to reconsider problems raised by Jacob Burckhardt's model—particularly the individualism and modernity he claimed for the Renaissance—in the light of recent emphasis on family and gender history. Sir Ernst Gombrich opened the conference (at 6.30 p.m.), as he opens this book, with his customary wit and incision; and of the original papers we have been able to include all but five, with new papers being contributed by Professor Patricia Fortini Brown and Professor Lauro Martines, who was one of the chairpersons and interlocutors at the conference.

Both the conference and the publication of this book were made possible through the generosity of the Samuel II Kress Foundation, the Latsis Foundation, the Nuffield Foundation, Dr Gert Flick, Lord Forte, the British Academy, Christie's and the Hon. Charles Allsop, to all of whom we are greatly indebted. We are also grateful to Tony Morris of the Oxford University Press for his encouragement and help in publishing the book; to Malcolm Forbes for his copy-editing; and to Shayne Mitchell for her careful indexing of the volume. Royalties will be used in helping to fund future seminars in London University on Renaissance history and culture.

A. M. B.
P. R.

Acknowledgements

THE contributors and publishers thank the following for permission to reproduce figures: Staatliche Museen, Berlin; Musée Condé, Chantilly; National Museum, Cracow; Gisela Fittschen-Badura; Palazzo Pitti, Florence; Staedel Institute, Frankfurt am Main; Museu Regional, Lagos; Pinacoteca del Castello Sforzesco, Milan; Princeton University Library, New Jersey; Capitoline Museum, Rome; Museo Nazionale Romano, Rome; Osvaldo Böhm, Venice; Biblioteca Nazionale Marciana, Venice; Kunsthistorisches Museum, Vienna.

Contents

PART III   Rereading the Renaissance Body

List of Illustrations

List of Contributors

ROBERT BLACK is Senior Lecturer in Modern History at the University of Leeds. He is author of *Benedetto Accolti and the Florentine Renaissance* (Cambridge, 1985) and, together with Louise George Clubb, of *Romance and Aretine Humanism in Sienese Comedy, 1516: Pollastra's* Parthenio *at the Studio di Siena* (Siena, 1993). He is editing a book of unpublished documents on medieval and Renaissance Aretine education, to be published by the Accademia Petrarca di Arezzo, and completing a book entitled *Humanism and Education in Medieval and Renaissance Tuscany*, to be published by the Cambridge University Press.

ALISON BROWN is Reader in Italian Renaissance Studies at the University of London. Her published work includes a biography, *Bartolomeo Scala, Chancellor of Florence* (Princeton, 1979, Ital. tr. Florence, 1990), a volume of collected essays, *The Medici in Florence* (Florence, 1992), and a translation of Guicciardini's *Dialogue on the Government of Florence* (Cambridge, 1994). She is at present working on a study of the Florentine élite from 1480 to 1502.

PATRICIA FORTINI BROWN is Associate Professor of Art and Archaeology at Princeton University where she teaches Italian Renaissance Art. Her published work includes *Venetian Narrative Painting in the Age of Carpaccio* (New Haven, Conn., 1988) and numerous articles on Venetian art and society. She is at present completing a book entitled *Venice and Antiquity: The Venetian Sense of the Past*.

SAMUEL K. COHN, Jr. is Professor of History of Brandeis University and received his Ph.D. from Harvard University in 1978. His major publications are *The Laboring Classes in Renaissance Florence* (New York, 1980); *Death and Property in Siena: Strategies for the Afterlife* (Baltimore, 1988); and *The Cult of Remembrance: Six Renaissance Cities in Central Italy* (Baltimore, 1992), and *Women in the Streets and Other Essays* (Johns Hopkins, Baltimore, Italian tr. Giunti,

Florence), forthcoming. He is now studying mountain civilization after the Black Death.

SIR ERNST H. GOMBRICH, O.M. former Director of the Warburg Institute of the University of London.

WILLIAM HOOD has been Professor of Art History at Oberlin College since 1974. He has written on Titian and on aspects of Dominican art and liturgy. He has recently published a critical study of Fra Angelico, *Fra Angelico at San Marco* (London, 1993).

BILL KENT holds a personal chair in History at Monash University, where he has taught for 25 years. He has been several times Visiting Professor at Villa I Tatti, Florence. He is a specialist in the cultural, social, and political history of Renaissance Florence. His publications include *Household and Lineage in Renaissance Florence* (Princeton, 1977), and he is at present writing a biographical study of Lorenzo de' Medici.

AMANDA LILLIE is lecturer in the History of Art at the University of York. She is at present writing a book on Florentine villas in the fifteenth century.

LAURO MARTINES is former Professor of History at the University of California, Los Angeles. His publications include *The Social World of the Florentine Humanists, 1390–1460* (London, 1963), *Lawyers and Statecraft in Renaissance Florence* (Princeton, 1968) and *Power and Imagination: City States in Renaissance Italy* (London, 1979). He has published *An Italian Renaissance sextet: Six Tales in Historical Context* (New York, 1994).

JOHN M. NAJEMY is Professor of History at Cornell University. His work on Florentine politics includes essays on the guilds and a study of elections and office-holding, *Corporatism and Consensus in Florentine Electoral Politics, 1280–1400* (Chapel Hill, 1982). He has also written on Machiavelli and political thought and recently published *Between Friends: Discourses of Power and Desire in the Machiavelli–Vettori Letters of 1513–1515* (Princeton, 1993).

JESSIE ANN OWENS is Professor of Music and former Dean of the College at Brandeis University. Her work centres on sixteenth-century music: the Italian madrigal, the life and work of Cipriano de Rore, approaches to musical analysis (with particular attention to mode and tonal structures), history of theory, and music historiography. She has recently completed a book entitled *Composers at Work: The Craft of Musical Composition, 1450–1600*, to be published by the Oxford University Press, 1996.

SALVATORE SETTIS is Professor of History of Classical Art and Archaeology at the Scuola Normale Superiore in Pisa, Italy and Director of the Getty Center for the History of Art and the Humanities, Santa Monica, California. His books include *La 'Tempesta' interpretata* (Turin, 1978), with English translation as *Giorgione's Tempest: Interpreting the Hidden Subject* (Cambridge, 1990); and *La Colonna Traiana* (1988). He has been editor of *Memoria dell'antico nell'arte italiana* (1984–6).

PATRICIA SIMONS is an Associate Professor in History of Art and Women's Studies at the University of Michigan, Ann Arbor, having held positions in Melbourne and Sydney Universities. Her research concentrates on the gendered construction of authority and identity in Renaissance Italy, particularly in relation to patronage and to portraiture.

QUENTIN SKINNER is Professor of Political Science in the University of Cambridge and a Fellow of Christ's College. He has co-edited and contributed to several volumes on the Renaissance, including *The Cambridge History of Renaissance Philosophy* (Cambridge, 1988) and *Machiavelli and Republicanism* (Cambridge, 1991). Among his other publications on Renaissance thought are *The Foundations of Modern Political Thought*, 2 volumes (Cambridge, 1978) and *Machiavelli* (Oxford, 1981).

Prolusion

E. H. GOMBRICH

IT being now 5.30, the time has come for me to make the introductory remarks with which you have been threatened on the programme. No, it was not a slip of the tongue when I said 5.30, despite what your watch and the programme says. We have all set our watches to British summer time which is an hour ahead of sun time, to bamboozle us to get up earlier and to enjoy as much daylight as possible in the evening.

I often think of this simple example when I hear historians debate what they call periodization. It illustrates, does it not, that it is we who impose an arbitrary network on the flux of events, but having imposed it we accept it as something real, part of the nature of things. To be sure, the nature of things comes in: day and night are natural phenomena, due to the rotation of the earth, at least beneath the polar circle. We can count these days from any arbitrary point, so that the assertion that today is 28 June refers to a general agreement but not to the nature of things.

The Greeks who liked to reflect on these questions made a distinction between matters which are due to social convention, *thesis*, and others which are due to nature, *physis*. It is always a challenging exercise to reflect on the share these factors have in our behaviour and in our languages. If you do, you will discover that these two factors are best visualized not so much as mutually exclusive categories, than as the two opposite ends of a continuous spectrum. Months and years, like the days, are based on facts of nature, but slightly tidied up by convention; centuries are purely conventional, except that the habit of counting in multiples of ten derives from the fact of nature that we have ten fingers on our two hands—not really a good reason, I sometimes think, for making such a fuss about centenaries, or the year 2,000, which will surely be celebrated as an event, while it is only a notch on an arbitrary measuring rod.

One of the many important reasons for learning languages is that they should make us realize the extent to which languages chop up

reality into manageable bits which may or may not be grounded in
the nature of things. When Nikolaus Pevsner wanted to launch a
series of books corresponding to the German *Handbuch für
Kunstwissenschaft*, he found that he had to label certain volumes not
as French Art or Japanese Art, but as 'The Art and Architecture of
France' or 'of Japan' because in German the term *Kunst* comprises
architecture while the English word art does so less obviously. Even
without this particular experience we should all become wise to the
fact that our notions have fuzzy edges. It is for this reason that we
are so frequently exhorted to define our terms, as in this meeting on
'Cultural definitions'. But there are two contrasting ideas about definition. One that derives from the philosophy of Aristotle tells us
that definitions must and will capture the essence of the concept, the
other, to which I incline, insists that definitions are a matter of linguistic conventions. In taking this line I am taking sides in a philosophical quarrel that engaged the minds of medieval schoolmen; the
quarrel between the nominalists and the realists. The nominalists
stressed that names or words are human artifacts while the realists
insisted that they denote metaphysical realities which have a prior
existence. *Universalia sunt ante rem.* Those of our colleagues who
agonise about the essence of art still live in an Aristotelean universe
which has long been discarded by scientists and by our legislators.
We remember the recent debates in Parliament about the moment
when life can be said to begin. It was decided by a majority vote.

Shelley called poets the unacknowledged legislators of the world,
but he might have said the same of the great historians who have
imposed their vision on our past. Burckhardt, of course, was one of
them, and since the year 1860, when he published his great book on
the *Civilization of the Renaissance in Italy*, the debate has not ceased
whether or not he had discovered the essence of that period or had
failed to do so.

Let me say at once that any such criticism of Burckhardt misses
the point. In its original German the book is subtitled *Ein Versuch*,
which means literally an attempt, an experiment, a try-out. It is one
of the devilish accidents of language that this simple notion cannot
be transferred into our linguistic network because the nearest equivalent is the French term *Essay*, which Burckhardt must also have had
in mind. 'Essay', of course, derives from *essayer*, to try, but this
original meaning of the term has faded with use, so that nobody who
is asked to write an essay realizes that he should be aware of the

tentative nature of what he writes. Burckhardt was. He wrote in his introduction, which I hope every member of this conference has taken to heart, that to every eye that views the outline of a period it may present a different picture, and that was especially true in the case of an age that had given birth to our own civilization. Here, as he insists, subjective opinions and emotions will inevitably influence both the author and the reader. Thus, he emphasizes, the researches he undertook for the work in question might have led others to very different conclusions.

Burckhardt's reference to the Renaissance as the parent of his own age is of course significant. Writing in 1860 he lived at a time that witnessed the most dizzy development of technology and of science ever experienced by mankind. This progress was a fact, but it also led to a conventional belief only partly based on fact, the ideology which postulated progress everywhere. However critical Burckhardt himself may have been of this ideology, he could not but impose this all-encompassing notion on his narrative, even using, as I have tried to show elsewhere,[1] the seductive creed of Hegelian metaphysics to give meaning to the events of the period.

It was of course the very cult of progress that also provoked the strongest reaction, in the political sense of the term, the great cleavage of the intellectual world between those who looked upon the Middle Ages as a time of darkness and those who exalted them as the Age of Faith. This had been the context in which the great French historian of the progressive wing, Michelet, in his volume on the Renaissance[2] rounded on the Romantics, accusing them of having forgotten or neglected two achievements which, in his words, 'belonged to the Renaissance to a larger extent than to all previous ages, the discovery of the world and the discovery of man'.

It was a stroke of genius for Burckhardt to use this memorable phrase as the leading theme of his subjective picture, though remember that Michelet had merely claimed that these achievements belonged to that age 'to a larger extent than to earlier ones'—and Burckhardt would hardly have claimed anything else. Yet the phrase solidified into a conventional cliché that soon lost all contact with any possible reality. It is hard to imagine what people did, who had not yet 'discovered man'. I once shocked an audience by asserting

---

[1] E. H. Gombrich, *In Search of Cultural History* (Oxford, 1969), 14–25, repr. in E. H. Gombrich, *Ideals and Idols* (Oxford, 1979), 34–42.

[2] Jules Michelet, *Histoire de France*, VIII, *La Renaissance* (Paris, 1855).

that I had saved a good deal of time in my life, because whenever I saw the word Man in a book on the Renaissance, I knew I didn't have to read it.

I am happy to say that on reading the summaries of the papers to be presented here, I found that that hoary old cliché did not raise its head. Maybe the talk about man has now been replaced by talk about women. In any case the papers show that our own age, like that of Burckhardt, has generated enough questions and issues that have given rise to new research—after all, research merely means 'new search', search for the evidence which supports a new vision or interpretation.

I hope I have made it clear that I believe in the reality of such evidence. However we divide and articulate what I have called the flux of events, we must not fall into the trap of believing that the past can ever be wholly our own creation, any more than the days are, or the years. Many of the things Burckhardt described, and many others you will hear described in the conference, really happened to people like you and me.

Perhaps I may take an example from the field for which I was officially responsible in this university, the History of the Classical Tradition. It is a fact that the poet Petrarch developed a burning enthusiasm for the ancient world and that he passed on this enthusiasm to Boccaccio and Salutati who, in their turn, infected others. If we think in terms of human beings, it is of course immensely interesting to ask how this infection spread, and to whom, and in what way, it may have influenced the life and outlook of individuals and ultimately of groups. But in my view we spoil the problem if we use such blanket terms as the Dawn of the Renaissance or the Spirit of the Age. It was a Renaissance man, Leonardo da Vinci, who wrote that abbreviators harm both knowledge and love. Aby Warburg liked to say: 'Der liebe Gott steckt im Detail' (God dwells in the detail). Maybe, therefore, his adversary is lurking in unsupported generalizations. I hope that many of them will be exorcized during this conference.

An exorcist must not be a respector of persons or of authority. I trust I yield to nobody in my admiration for Erwin Panofsky, but maybe he, too, was a slight case of possession. I remember a lecture he gave at the Art Historical Congress in Amsterdam in 1952 when he rallied to the defence of the traditional interpretation of the Renaissance as a unified age. Contrasting a church by Sangallo with a Gothic building, he kept repeating that surely 'something must have happened.' At least one of his listeners muttered to himself: 'Of course something happened, a new style of architecture was adopted.'

I was all the more interested when in 1960 Panofsky's book *Renaissance and Renascences in Western Art* came out, which opens with the splendidly-named chapter ' "Renaissance"—Self-definition or Self-Deception', a chapter which I recommend to anyone interested in this topic for its erudition and for its wit.

I also commend it for the discussion you find on page 3 on the problem of method, which is my concern. It shows the author somewhat ill at ease about the issue of periodization, which should not, as he admits, lead to our turning ages into 'quasi-metaphysical entities'. He adds a significant footnote in which the great historian of art defends himself against George Boas, the great historian of ideas, who had accused him of having done precisely this. If you pay attention to that note you will discover behind the banter the old issues of nominalism versus realism. Pan conceded to his opponent that it would not be helpful, for instance, to speak of a spirit of cathood as opposed to that of doghood, but he pleads that it would be quite innocuous to enumerate the features which turn cats into cats rather than dogs, such as the possession of retractable claws and the inability to swim, which in the aggregate describe the *genus Felis* as opposed to the *genus Canis*. I am afraid Panofsky was here giving hostages to fortune, for I have pasted into my copy of the book a cutting from *The Times* of December 1964 with the headline: 'Turkish Cats with a passion for swimming.'

Admittedly our notions of cats and dogs are somehow rooted in the order of nature, but do not let us forget that science could only advance when the entrenched belief in the immutable character of species was swept away by Darwin. I think that the same is true of our work. I do not believe that there ever was such a species as 'Renaissance Man'. I think we shall make better progress in our debates if we forget about cats and dogs and rather remember summer-time.

Introduction

ALISON BROWN

IT is high time to re-evaluate the Renaissance. Everyone agrees that the Burckhardtian paradigm is outmoded, with its emphasis on individualism and progress and—far worse in the eyes of some—its bold attempt to characterize the period as a whole. But without Burckhardt's belief in a unifying *Zeitgeist*, it has been difficult to find an alternative and less deterministic way of discussing Renaissance culture in its historical context. As a result, Renaissance studies have gone in many different directions, so that art, music, literature, and history are now normally treated as separate disciplines. The period itself has become progressively indistinct, overlapped on one side by the later Middle Ages, which it is claimed anticipated Renaissance individualism and artistic culture, and on the other by the early modern period, with its scientific discoveries and inventions. At the same time as these local frontier disputes have been taking place, the barbarians have been foregathering to assault the foundations of this highbrow territory in the name of 'the New History': history from below, quantitative history, history of the body—and of the silent voices missing from traditional history.[1]

Nothing is new for long, however, and already this history is being displaced by the recent return to cultural history, called in its turn 'the new cultural history'.[2] Influenced by the theories and techniques of literary criticism as well as anthropology, its novelty is to give

---

[1] See Peter Burke (ed.), *New Perspectives on Historical Writing* (Oxford, 1991), esp. 2–23: 'What is the New History?' On the two dominating paradigms of historical explanation in the 1960s and 1970s, Marxism and the 'Annales' school, see Lynn Hunt (ed.), *The New Cultural History* (Berkeley, Calif., 1989), 1–6.

[2] See n. 1 above. The inspiration of the volume, as Lynn Hunt explains (p. ix), occurred at a conference on French early modern history; nevertheless the problem it confronts is identical to that facing historians of the Renaissance. She cites as examples of recent challenges to the Marxist and Annales paradigms the work of Gareth Stedman Jones, *Languages of Class: Studies in English Working Class History, 1832–1982* (Cambridge, 1983), and Roger Chartier, 'Intellectual History or Sociocultural History', now repr. as 'Intellectual History/History of *Mentalités*' in his *Cultural History: Between Practices and Representations* (Oxford, 1988), 6–7.

language and art an important role in actively creating social reality instead of passively reflecting it, as Marx had earlier suggested they did. The language we use and the symbols and social practices we adopt not only structure our world but provide the means through which power is exercised. Together they form competing systems of 'representation', which are rarely politically neutral.[3] To interpret them is not so easy, however, and requires a variety of skills, literary and visual as well as historical—which is why it is a good moment to return to Burckhardt. For the diversity and pluralism of this 'remarkable new phase' of cultural history[4] provide exactly the interdisciplinary environment we need for re-assessing his similarly all-embracing work, with its description of popular fêtes and festivals as well as of the élite culture of courts. Whether we define the Renaissance as an intellectual movement or more widely as a system of social relationships within a defined period (say, from the mid-fourteenth to mid-sixteenth century in Italy, later elsewhere), language and image-making are central to it.

Written in 1860 and first translated into English in 1878, Burckhardt's *Civilization [Kultur] of the Renaissance in Italy* is divided into six sections, 'The State as a Work of Art', 'The Development of the Individual', 'The Revival of Antiquity', 'The Discovery of the World and of Man', 'Society and Festivals' and 'Morality and Religion'. Its ambition was to create 'as complete a picture as possible of the continuous process in which the world develops'.[5] The breadth of his approach makes the book difficult to

---

[3] Chartier, *Cultural History*, 7–10: the 'three modes' by which representation relates to the social world are intellectual classification, symbolic representation of rank or status, and institutional practices.

[4] Hunt, *New Cultural History*, 22.

[5] Quoted by Joseph Mali, who contrasts Burckhardt's conservative view of the Renaissance as a *grosses geistiges Kontinuum* with the discontinuity Nietzsche found in it, in 'Jacob Burckhardt: Myth, History and Mythistory', *History and Memory*, 3 (1991): 86–118, quoting from 112, cf. 108. On Burckhardt, see also F. Gilbert, *History: Politics or Culture? Reflections on Ranke and Burckhardt* (Princeton, 1990), 46–105; P. Gay, 'Burckhardt's *Renaissance*: Between Responsibility and Power', in L. Kreiger and F. Stern (eds.), *The Responsibility of Power: Historical Essays in Honor of H. Holborn* (New York, 1967), 183–98 (cf. his *Style in History: Gibbon, Ranke, Macaulay, Burckhardt* (New York, 1988), 141–82); Hans Baron, 'The Limits of the Notion of "Renaissance Individualism": Burckhardt After a Century (1960)', in his *In Search of Florentine Civic Humanism: Essays on the Transition from Medieval to Modern Thought* (Princeton, 1988), ii. 155–81. I quote subsequently from the Phaidon Press edition of Jacob Burckhardt, *The Civilization of the Renaissance in Italy* (London, 1950; first pub. 1860).

ignore even today, and it seems valid to ask—as we asked the participants in the conference at which this book took shape—how far contemporary scholarship has modified Burckhardt's picture. Ernst Gombrich rightly reminds us that his book was subtitled 'an attempt' or 'try-out': a subjective interpretation based on one man's period eye, which others might see very differently. And, as he also reminds us, one mote in this period eye is Burckhardt's belief in progress. Burckhardt's belief in 'continuous development' and the hegemonizing influence of a single spirit or nation now marks his book as a child of its time, opposed to our present outlook.

So, too, is his emphasis on the individualism and modernity of the Renaissance, which seems to stem from the same Enlightenment view of progress. Both medievalists and historians of Renaissance religion and family have understandably attacked his famous description of the Middle Ages as a time when men 'lay dreaming or half awake beneath a common veil', conscious of themselves only as members of 'a race, people, party, family or corporation'.[6] But far from sharing the Enlightenment moralism of his fellow Swiss historian, J. C. L. de Sismondi, who (like Hans Baron later) attributed Italy's cultural achievements to the republicanism of its city states, Burckhardt was in fact reacting against it. He was more influenced by the ideas of Goethe and Schopenhauer than Sismondi in attributing the growth of individualism to the agonistic struggles of Italy's developing despotisms.[7] Here Burckhardt may be closer than he might appear to present-day critics of the republican myth (represented in this

---

[6] Burckhardt, *Civilisation*, 81. Renaissance historians of the family include F. W. Kent, *Household and Lineage in Renaissance Florence* (Princeton, 1977); C. Klapisch-Zuber, *Women, Family and Ritual in Renaissance Italy* (Chicago, 1985); and T. J. Kuehn, *Law, Family and Women: Toward a Legal Anthropology of Renaissance Italy* (Chicago, 1991); see also the bibliography in Lauro Martines's essay, p. 315, n. 5. On Burckhardt and religion, see Timothy Verdon, 'Christianity, the Renaissance and the Study of History: Environments of Experience and Imagination', in T. Verdon and J. Henderson (eds.), *Christianity and the Renaissance: Image and Religious Imagination in the Quattrocento* (Syracuse, 1990), 1–2.

[7] See David Norbrook, 'Life and Death of Renaissance Man', *Raritan*, 8 (1989), 89–110, esp. 93–100, and Baron, 'Limits of the Notion', esp. 161–2; both refer to Burckhardt's appeal to Nietzsche, but this is assessed more critically by Baron, 157–8, n. 4. For a fuller bibliography on individualism, see Patricia Simons's essay (pp. 263–4, n. 2). On 12th-c. individualism, see J. F. Benton, 'Consciousness of Self and Perceptions of Individuality', in R. L. Benson and G. Constable (eds.), *Renaissance and Renewal in the Twelfth Century* (Oxford, 1985), 263–95, and Caroline W. Bynum, 'Did the Twelfth-Century Discover the Individual?' in id., *Jesus as Mother: Studies in the Spirituality of the High Middle Ages* (Berkeley, 1982), 82–109.

book by the essays of Black and Skinner), and there is even room for individualism within the family and corporate patronage of art described in the essays of Kent and Cohn.

Another way of re-assessing Burckhardt's Renaissance is to distance ourselves from it by becoming anthropologists and viewing it as 'an alien . . . or half-alien' culture that is 'receding from us, becoming more alien every year'.[8] Thanks to the work of Richard Trexler, Bill Kent, Peter Burke, and others, Renaissance studies are already moving in this direction, studying concepts of identity through changing attitudes to life and death,[9] or, as in Kent's and Cohn's essays in this volume, through family patronage patterns.[10] But there is as yet no overall study of these categories to show 'culture as process of change' and to integrate familiar Renaissance highbrow images of time, space, macro- and microcosm, with more popular outlooks and mentalities—although Lauro Martines's essay in this volume provides a model of how this could be done.

Such a study might provide the best way forward for Renaissance studies today if we interpret the Renaissance simply as a given period of time, and adopt as our criterion of culture the wide Geertzian definition of it as 'a system of inherited conceptions expressed in symbolic forms by means of which men communicate, perpetuate, and develop their knowledge about and attitudes toward life'.[11] However, this begs serious questions about the Renaissance if we see it less as a contained system of largely inherited concepts than as a period characterized by change and conflicting (though often concealed) ideas. Here the new literary techniques may be especially useful in 'rereading' texts to elicit missing voices from dialogues and fables and to investigate the Renaissance's self-image.

---

[8] See Peter Burke, 'Anthropology of the Italian Renaissance', *Journal of the Institute of Romance Studies*, 1 (1992), 210. The model he suggests is A. J. Gurevich, *Categories of Medieval Culture* (Moscow, 1972; tr. London, 1985).

[9] Following Alberto Tenenti's *Il senso della morte e l'amore della vita nel Rinascimento* (Turin, 1957) and Philippe Ariès' *L'Homme devant la mort* (Paris, 1977; tr. New York, 1981), recent studies include J. R. Banker, *Death in the Community* (Athens, Ga., 1988); M. Tetel, R. G. Witt, and R. Goffen (eds.), *Life and Death in Fifteenth-Century Florence* (Durham, NC, 1989); and S. T. Strocchia, *Death and Ritual in Renaissance Florence* (Baltimore, Md., 1992). Peter Burke, *The Historical Anthropology of Early Modern Italy* (Cambridge, 1987), contains studies of other new areas.

[10] See also Kent, *Household and Lineage*, and S. K. Cohn, Jr., *The Cult of Remembrance and the Black Death* (Baltimore, Md., 1992).

[11] Clifford Geertz, *The Interpretation of Cultures: Selected Essays* (New York, 1973), 89.

An example of a text that provides a bridge between tradition and novelty is Francesco Vettori's diary of his *German Travels*, which includes the stories, plays, and conversations that he heard during his travels.[12] Criticized by his brother for writing about such frivolous things, Vettori responded by reflecting that all writings are harmful, beginning with those of theologians, and continuing with the writings of lawyers, orators (who seduce the ignorant plebs), and poets, to end with historians—including in his list, among the poets, certain 'ambiguous' writers like Pliny, Aulus Gellius, Macrobius, Apuleius, and, among the new, Poliziano, Pontano, and Crinito, who seem very learned and were read willingly and with approval, and yet contained many 'weak points and falsities and vulgar things'.[13] The relativism and scepticism encouraged by his travels is reflected in a debate about gambling with which the diary ends, its proponent concluding that all pleasures, such as wine, love-making and eating, are the cause of good as well as evil, it's all a matter of degree.[14]

Far from contrasting with the learned culture of his day, the popular culture that Vettori describes in his diary is in fact very closely linked to the humanist milieu. Both were influenced by travel and by the discovery of new lands and frontiers that encouraged the relativism of Vettori's outlook.[15] This relativism in turn influenced Renaissance rhetoric and Valla's new theory of language,[16] as well as the novel humanist genres. The new histories, biographies, letter-collections, ambiguous fables, and dialogues could all be used to conceal potentially dangerous political and moral arguments and they undoubtedly helped to undermine respect for the 'hard' and 'difficult'

[12] Vettori, 'Viaggio in Alamagna' in his *Scritti storici e politici*, ed. E. Niccolini (Bari, 1972), 122; 'né può essere perfettamente prudente chi non ha conosciuto molti uomini e veduto molte città'; see now J. Najemy, *Between Friends. Discourses of Power and Desire in the Machiavelli–Vettori Letters of 1513–1515* (Princeton, 1993), 248–52.

[13] Vettori, 'Viaggio in Alemagna', 40–2: 'certi scrittori che si possono chiamare di titolo ambiguo,' 'molte cose debole e false e basse.'

[14] Ibid. 130–2.

[15] See esp. Amerigo Vespucci's *Mundus novus*, 1503–4, facsimile reprinted in L. Firpo (ed.), *Prime relazioni di navigatori italiani sulla scoperta dell' America: Colombo, Vespucci, Verazzano* (Turin, 1966). On Columbus and changing attitudes to travel and discovery, see S. Greenblatt, *Marvelous Possessions: The Wonder of the New World* (Chicago, 1991).

[16] Quentin Skinner, *Thomas Hobbes: Rhetoric and the Construction of Morality*, The British Academy, London, 1991, and id., *Renaissance Rhetoric and the Dilemmas of Moral Argument*, annual lecture to the Renaissance Society, May 1993 (forthcoming); R. Waswo, *Language and Meaning in the Renaissance* (Princeton, 1987).

established canon of authorities approved by the Church.[17] In them we can follow a train of thought that acquires coherence through the opposition they aroused at the time. Is this the sense in which we can talk of antiquity as 'the other', not because it was so remote but because it was a threat to the hegemonizing Christian culture of the day?[18]

A recent reassessment of the role of Christianity in the Renaissance has treated Christianity and Renaissance as 'equal coefficients'.[19] As Verdon says, it is crucial to get the balance between tradition and innovation right, since both precariously co-existed as the source of the dynamic tension that encouraged the Renaissance explosion of artistic and literary creativity. In the essays that follow, religion is not treated as a separate topic, why should it be? But it plays an important role in Renaissance patronage, as the essays of Hood, Kent, and Cohn demonstrate, and it provided the cement that helped to bind Renaissance society together.

A starting point for defining the Renaissance has always been the period's self-image of itself as a rebirth, or *rinascita*: a new period of light detached from the dark or 'middle' period between the end of antiquity and the present. Once seen as evidence of progress and more recently as myth-making,[20] the Renaissance can be better understood as one of a number of sequential periods that move ('progress') by changing their attitude to the past, or 'the other.' Such periods reorganize themselves by selecting what is to be remembered

---

[17] See Riccardo Fubini, 'L'umanista: Ritorno di un paradigma? Saggio per un profilo storico da Petrarca ad Erasmo', *Archivio storico italiano*, 147 (1989): 435–508 at 469, and id., 'All'uscita dalla Scolastica medievale: Salutati, Bruni, e i "Dialogi ad Petrum Histrum" ', *Archivio storico italiano*, 150 (1992): 1065–103. On histories, N. Struever, *The Language of History in the Renaissance* (Princeton, 1970) and Robert Black, 'The new laws of history', *Renaissance Studies*, 1 (1987): 126–56; on letter-writing as a 'Proteus among Renaissance literary genres', John Najemy, in id., *Between Friends*, 57; on fables, J. H. Whitfield, '*Momus* and the Language of Irony' in *The Languages of Literature in Renaissance Italy* (Oxford, 1988), 31–43; and on the dialogue, David Marsh, *The Quattrocento Dialogue* (Cambridge, Mass., 1980), Virginia Cox, *The Renaissance Dialogue* (Cambridge, 1992), and Alison Brown, introd. to Francesco Guicciardini, *Dialogue on the Government of Florence*, tr. A. Brown (Cambridge, 1994), pp. xviii–xx.

[18] What Michel de Certeau calls 'a *reconquista* of the believers', *The Mystic Fable* (Chicago, 1992), 86. I am grateful to Lyndal Roper for directing me to de Certeau's writings.

[19] Verdon, 'Christianity, the Renaissance and the Study of History', 2.

[20] Waswo, *Language and Meaning*, 62, quoting C. S. Lewis, 'Our legend of the Renaissance is a Renaissance legend . . . we have simply inherited it from the people we are studying.'

and what discarded, as the Renaissance period did in labelling itself new and the preceding period dead.[21] By re-establishing a close bond with antiquity, the Renaissance legitimized its own novelty in offering continuity with a past. At the same time, in adopting the language and images of antiquity as its artistic and cultural model, it established a new system of representation that acted as a form of power.

This way of looking at the Renaissance provides a useful introduction to Part I on the Ancient Model. In order to understand the role of antiquity in the idea of revival, Salvatore Settis investigates the model's role in antiquity itself: did the ancients, he asks, have an antiquity? Here the crucial text is a passage from Pliny's *Natural History* (XXXIV. 52), in which Pliny describes the loss and 'revival' of the technique of bronze castings. By quoting and mistranslating technique, *techne*, as art, Settis suggests that Lorenzo Ghiberti may have helped to create the Renaissance model of the decline and revival of the arts: 'indeed, modern Art History could be described as the revival of a literary genre invented by the Greeks'. The literary genre consisted of writings on artistic techniques which provided the Romans with the language and vocabulary of art criticism. It also supplied them with the idea of needing to return to a distant past for authenticity. This helped to distance them and us from ancient art and also to provide this art, and those who invoked it, with a special exalted status, since the various ways of invoking it became the privilege of the educated classes. These ideas developed quite independently of contemporary artistic developments and had more to do with political power and legitimization than cultural awakening.

In this account, Settis demonstrates how the revival model developed out of an existing literary tradition and was used both as a link to 'an extremely remote past of which all sure evidence . . . had been lost', as Burckhardt put it,[22] and as a new beginning, authenticating political regimes and new cultural movements. As well as emphasizing the importance of the literary tradition and how it was established, Settis highlights the two other topics that are important for our discussion of later revivals: the definition of antiquity with its related pattern of death and revival, and the use made of the revival model for authentication.

---

[21] See Michel de Certeau, *The Writing of History* (New York, 1988), esp. 3–6.

[22] Cited by Settis (see p. 49, n. 28).

It is the first of these that Robert Black deals with in proposing 'a new source for the concept of Renaissance'. Ghiberti's reference to Pliny demonstrates the influence of the ancient model on the language of the fifteenth-century artistic revival, but for his framework of decline and revival Ghiberti was also indebted to another literary tradition that according to Black played an equally important part in influencing the language of revival in the fifteenth century. As Black says, 'For there to be rebirth, there must have been birth followed by death', and in the scheme he proposes it was the supposed Donation of Constantine (legitimizing the papacy's temporal power in Italy after Constantine's departure in AD 330) that constituted the death of an era in the medieval mentality. The debate between the papalists who supported the Donation and those who criticized it raged most intensely in the first half of the fourteenth century. Since this was exactly the time when Petrarch was shaping 'the programme of the nascent humanist movement', the Donation may well have provided his framework of renewal, making the boundaries he drew between ancient, medieval, and modern history much less clear-cut and original than has been argued. For instead of describing a transition from an ancient pagan to a Christian Dark Ages and hence to a secular rebirth in the Renaissance, he was novel only in applying a long-established scheme of church history to secular culture as well.

Black's revised scheme accords well with Quentin Skinner's in reducing the significance of republicanism as the point both of the death (in 29 BC) and the revival of antiquity in the fourteenth century. Petrarch was not a republican himself, as his friends complained, but by correlating 'the freedom of our era' with the birth of the Roman republic and establishing an intimate relationship with ancient republicans like Cicero, he encouraged Leonardo Bruni's later political interpretation of rebirth and his 'new' Cicero, *Cicero novus*.[23] According to Bruni, the death of antiquity and its rebirth at the time of Petrarch was brought about by the loss of political free-

---

[23] See Hans Baron, *Crisis of the Early Italian Renaissance*, rev. edn. (Princeton, 1966), esp. 55–6, quoting from Petrarch's *Africa*; id., *In Search of Florentine Civic Humanism*, i. 24–8, 29. Cf. M. Lorch, 'Petrarch, Cicero, and the Classical Pagan Tradition,' in A. Rabil (ed.), *Renaissance Humanism: Foundations, Forms and Legacy* (Philadelphia, 1990), i. 71–94, esp. 81. On Bruni's *Cicero novus*, partly ed. Baron in *Leonardo Bruni Aretino, Humanistisch-philosophische Schriften* (Berlin, 1928), 113–20, see Baron, *In Search*, 121–2, and E. Fryde, *Humanism and Renaissance Historiography* (London, 1983), 33–53; G. Griffiths in *The Humanism of Leonardo Bruni* (Binghamton, 1987), 177–8, 184–90.

dom at the end of the Roman republic and its recovery with the rise of the Italian communes.[24] In this interpretation, the link with antiquity served the political purpose of authenticating the newly independent city-states, as it did later for Machiavelli—and more recently for Hans Baron, though not for Burckhardt. For although Burckhardt did relate Florence's modernity 'as the first modern State in the world' to the city's 'intellectual freedom and independence',[25] it was Baron who emphasized the role first of Petrarch and then Bruni in bringing about 'the decisive break with medieval thinking' in the quattrocento.[26]

Quentin Skinner attacks this account of Renaissance republicanism in reminding us of the *longue-durée* of republican vocabulary. Far from originating with Petrarch and Bruni, or even earlier with the revival of Aristotle in the mid-thirteenth century, this vocabulary goes back to the early days of the Italian communes in the twelfth and early thirteenth century. The key republican concepts were drawn, he argues, not from newly-discovered texts or from avant-garde humanist writings, but from familiar works of Cicero and Sallust diffused in grammatical and rhetorical handbooks and in practical advice-books for magistrates. Long before Petrarch rediscovered Cicero, citizens were being taught that elective government was better than monarchy in providing equality and a free way of life, and that only free communes could achieve true glory and greatness. The resonant political concepts of liberty, equality, glory, and *grandezza* thus began their new life long before Bruni and Machiavelli revived them, suggesting that if republicanism is to mark the beginning of the revival, the period must predate Petrarch and the quattrocento Renaissance. And if this frontier is shifted, maybe the earlier frontier needs shifting too, since republican idealism may have been less important as a marker for the death as well as for the revival of antiquity. More important, perhaps, was its value as an authentic alternative voice in the conflictual politics of the day.

Although Burckhardt briefly included 'a few words on music . . . as not out of place', he knew nothing of Italian music before Palestrina in the mid-sixteenth century and so confined himself to

---

[24] See Bruni's *Lives of Dante and Petrarch*, cited by Black (see p. 53, n. 3), in Alison Brown, *The Renaissance* (London, 1988), doc. 3.

[25] Burckhardt, *Civilization*, 48–50, 'The State as a Work of Art'.

[26] See n. 23 above.

discussing music's position in the social life of the day.[27] The explanation for this, Jessie Ann Owens tells us, was that music survived
only as long as it continued to be performed or as long as its notation could be read, so it lacked both an antiquity and a tradition of
revival. For this reason, it was alone among the arts in disparaging
antiquity, as a sixteenth-century German humanist commented. Not
only were songs fresh from the copyist preferred to ancient compositions but there was ignorance about the age of surviving practices.
The 'rediscovery of its musical past' came with the recovery of lost
repertories, which coincided with the development of music as an
academic discipline towards the end of the eighteenth century. It was
not until 1868 that the word Renaissance was first applied to
music—significantly, by a friend of Burckhardt's, August Wilhelm
Ambros, who used it in the third volume of his *History of Music*,
published eight years after *The Civilization of the Renaissance*. Of
the different meanings he gives to the word, Owens accepts as valid
only its use to describe the revival of interest in classical music theory, not its use to describe a period, since in terms of notation or
musical language the period would have to start much earlier and
continue longer. What the word did instead was to provide music
belatedly with a birth—or rebirth—certificate to provide it with its
missing parentage.

The same problem of lacking an ancient past was experienced by
Venice, although for different reasons. So Patricia Fortini Brown's
account of 'how Renaissances happened in Venice' provides valuable
comparative evidence of the function of revivals as authentication.
Founded in the sixth century, when refugees from Aquileia fled there,
Venice provided herself with a missing past by claiming parentage
not from ancient Greece and Rome (despite the claims made by
Marin Sanudo (1466–1536) and later humanist historians), but from
two other cities, Byzantine Constantinople and Aquileia. As 'a
reborn Aquileia', where St Mark had preached, Venice could, like
Rome, lay claim to apostolic succession, while by modelling St
Mark's and its surrounding buildings on Justinian's Church of the
Holy Apostles and on imperial palatine architecture in Constantinople (reinforced after 1204 by relics of St Mark and spoils from
the sacked city), Venice acquired the imperial legitimacy she lacked.
Since the city drew eclectically from a variety of disparate architec-

---

[27] Burckhardt, *Civilization*, 237–40.

tural and literary models, oriental and Byzantine as well as Roman, to renovate herself from the ninth century onwards, it is impossible to apply Renaissance periodization to Venice, any more than to the history of music. As with music, her very lack of antiquity serves to highlight the role played by revivals in legitimizing novelty by offering continuity with a past.

The redrawing of frontiers in these essays not only revises our periodization of the Renaissance but also how we interpret it in terms of what was included as new (the rebirth of early Christianity as well as of political independence) and rejected as old (papal as well as imperial hegemonizing). Studying revivals diachronically, as they developed over time, only gets us so far in understanding the Renaissance as a cultural revival, however. To go further, we need to see how these ideas came together in the particular context of fifteenth-century Italy, the subject of Part II. The emphasis here is particularly on religious and social history, where the thrust of recent work challenges Burckhardt's original paradigm most directly and offers new ways of interpreting it. For if we define culture as widely as possible, we can see that the achievements he attributed to gifted individuals were produced by them as members of interacting groups and corporate bodies—whether they are the religious orders discussed by William Hood, the guilds discussed in a paper (not able to be included here) by Diane Zervas,[28] or the families discussed in differing ways by Bill Kent, Amanda Lillie and Samuel Cohn. As Kent and Cohn also show, these corporate bonds do not preclude egoism and 'a growing sense of exclusiveness' as spurs to patronage. Neither go as far as Richard Goldthwaite in attributing the new culture to the growth of individual consumerism, what Goldthwaite describes as 'an interactive process between consumer and goods by which culture itself was generated'.[29] But like him they describe this culture as the product of interacting social forces.

In the first essay, it is the friars and clergy of the observant reform movement, interacting with their secular patrons and supporters, who contributed to the Renaissance by their innovative cloister painting programmes. As William Hood suggests in his title, the observants, as a new movement, lacked a history or 'memory', and

---

[28] Her conference paper on the art patronage of Orsanmichele will now form part of a book, Diane F. Zervas, *Orsanmichele* (Modena, forthcoming).

[29] Richard Goldthwaite, *Wealth and the Demand for Art in Italy, 1300–1600* (Baltimore, 1993), introd., 5.

their attempt at self-definition by providing themselves with ancient roots nicely illustrates one of the functions of the Ancient Model discussed already. Between 1420 and 1450 as many as seven monastic cloisters in Florence were decorated with unified mural cycles. Only one of these was a conventual, or unreformed, church, S. Maria Novella, and here the cloister murals are not historical but illustrate the universalist ministry of the Dominican Order. By contrast the others, with one exception, attempted to reinforce their claims to authenticity by illustrating the lives of their monastic founders in Christian antiquity. The exception, San Marco, lacked an ancient history, but instead of following the model of its parent house, S. Maria Novella, it attempted to achieve the same ends as the other observants by quoting instead from an early ascetic text of the Dominican order, *De modo orandi*. Painted within a time-span of thirty years, these innovative mural cycles illustrate the practical function of ancient models and also the close relationship enjoyed by the artists, patrons, and audience in creating this innovative art.

The same is true of the cultural patronage described by Bill Kent, which owed more to family and religious bonds than to the 'individuals' in his title—even though, as he recognizes, the two are not incompatible. His composite model patron, Giovanni X, combines family building (chapels, palaces, and villas) with ecclesiastical or charitable patronage, all of which can be defined as collective. When non-typical patrons departed from the model by patronizing churches outside their parishes and excluding more distant kin from their tombs, the explanation is probably either social (new men substituting family with friends or patrons), or political (allegiance to a Big Man or boss). This second reason points to an interesting development in the later fifteenth century, when the Medici seem to have intentionally fostered, for political reasons, 'a sense of exclusiveness' among their intimates, which is demonstrated by the use of personal instead of family insignia on buildings and private chapels. This is also perhaps the context for understanding the use made of the antique in palace building. If not supplying these palace builders with a missing history, it certainly made a public statement about their exclusive status within the ruling group, easily understandable by 'the tide of civic life' that washed around their palaces.[30]

---

[30] Discussed by F. W. Kent in his essay, 'Palaces, Politics and Society', *I Tatti Studies*, 2 (1987), 41–70, esp. 51–5 on the antique, and 58–60 on palaces as social centres.

Is the same true of the Renaissance villa, discussed by Amanda Lillie? Because the villa's antique pedigree was impeccable, having enjoyed a continuous history in classical literature from Hesiod's *Works and Days* in the 8th century BC onwards, it offered an obvious model for imitation. As a result, not only were rich urban patrons like 'Giovanni X' seduced by the pastoral idea of a country retreat, where they could admire nature and cultivate their souls; so too were generations of scholars, who have described the Renaissance villa as 'a fantasy which is impervious to reality.' This fantasy has in its turn mythologized the form and function of such villas, Lillie argues, since far from representing the romantic Other, fifteenth-century villas were nearly all strongholds providing food, wine, and defence for their owners. Usually retaining their traditional castellated form associated with ancestral power, they served as agricultural centres (and also, one could add, as hotels and stables, too, where clothes could be changed and horses stabled before arriving in the city). If the antique has a message in this context, it must surely be contained in the classicizing frescoes and the splendid frieze at Poggio a Caiano, which terminates in Apollo, the sun god (with whom Lorenzo was often identified), riding triumphantly out in his chariot to greet the day. It was perhaps only in the antique setting of a country villa that such a scene could safely be portrayed.

Moving farther from the walls of urban Florence, Samuel Cohn adopts a comparative approach to reassess Burckhardt's individualism. Using some 3,400 last wills and testaments in six central Italian towns—Florence, Siena, Pisa and Arezzo in Tuscany, and Perugia and Assisi in Umbria—he is able to base his comparison on testators who are not only geographically diverse but come from very different social classes, since they include peasants and artisans, as well as lowly woolworkers. Interesting contrasts emerge, for whereas by the 1270s, influenced by the preaching of the friars, all the testators began to fragment their patrimonies by bequeathing numerous but small monetized bequests, later this pattern was pronounced only in Siena, Pisa and Assisi—towns where women retained stronger control over their dowries and patrimonies. In the remaining three towns—Florence, Arezzo and Perugia—testators early on and with greater frequency left less numerous but more substantial bequests (often with fideicommission clauses and restrictions attached) to memorialize themselves with burial chapels, tombstones, painting and other art works. This pattern was not restricted to the rich, since even modest testators—such as blacksmiths—bequeathed money for self-memorialization. Nor does Florence emerge as an exception. The only common factor that can account for these contrasts, Cohn suggests, is family structure, since mendicant values proved less powerful when patrilines were strong and the desire for self-memorialization was greatest. But far from representing modern individualism, this desire to perpetuate themselves, as Kent also suggests, stemmed from archaic family pride: 'Renaissance fame . . . ran down the veins of male blood lines.'

Placed in its social context, Renaissance patronage of art and architecture cannot be explained by a single formula, for as we have seen it reflected archaic family sentiments, new political bonding, and religious piety. The patronage of most Renaissance art, these essays suggest, was corporate and was addressed to a wide audience. Who this audience was and at what level it participated in Renaissance culture remains as yet unclear. Many would have been women or illiterates who have left no record in history. The artisans and peasants represented in Cohn's sample of testaments are exceptional, or have seemed so up to now. Women present particular difficulty in being both idealized and treated as silent, so that Burckhardt could famously claim that 'women stood on a footing of perfect equality with men' and had no need of 'women's rights' or female emancipation, because 'the thing itself was a matter of course'.[31] So, too, do homosexuals. Despite Florence's widely-diffused reputation for sodomy and the known homosexuality of a few outstanding artists and writers, the importance of homoerotic relationships in its society and culture is only now beginning to be recognized.[32] The techniques of literary theory, psychology, and anthropology make it possible to recover some of these missing voices to provide a new account of gender and the body in Renaissance culture, which is explored in the essays in Part III.

The Renaissance body in its public presentation was predominantly male, reflecting the patriarchalism of its society as well as its homoeroticism. In the phrase quoted by Kent and Cohn, the blood-lines coursed through 'masculine veins' in this body, which was idealized in Leonardo's visual image of man as the measure of all things,

[31] Burckhardt, *Civilization*, 240–1.
[32] See M. J. Rocke, 'Male Homosexuality and its Regulation in Late Medieval Florence', Ph.D. thesis (Binghamton, 1989), University Microfilms, Ann Arbor; shortly to be published by the Oxford University Press (New York).

or in Pico della Mirandola's *Oration* as the central link in the universe. As the boundary between inside and outside, the body is a sensitive indicator of cultural values and change, but historians have been slow to follow the lead of Stephen Greenblatt and others in investigating the ambiguity of the protean Renaissance body.[33]

In his essay on 'Body Metaphors in Italian Renaissance Political Thought' John Najemy does just this, in probing the ambivalence at the heart of the body metaphor as it was used by political writers in order to throw light on the Renaissance natural body. The metaphor itself is dialectical in being used simultaneously to unify a collection of disparate elements—a corporation, a state or 'body politic', a 'body' of laws—and also to acknowledge the disunity it seeks to exclude, as Marsilius of Padua seems to understand in his description of the 'contrariety' of the body politic. But whereas humanist writers from Petrarch to Alberti attempted to suppress the body's dangerous nature, only Machiavelli seemed prepared to accept it—both in his political model of mixed government (and, one could add, of the centaur as a model for princes) and in his descriptions of natural bodies. In this way, contradictions in the political metaphor provide Najemy with the means to uncover the proto-Freudian conflicts hidden in the natural Renaissance body, which the humanists had been so successful in concealing.

Even more than men, women have been subjected to oversimplified and idealized readings of their visual image. Writing as an art historian, Patricia Simons continues Najemy's deconstruction to provide a sustained rereading of the Renaissance portrait, and through it, of Renaissance attitudes to women. Far from being emblematic of 'individualism' and 'naturalism', portraits are both difficult to read as texts and multifunctional. Like written texts, they are distorted by rhetorical devices to eulogize and memorialize sitters and artists, as well as by the purposes they were intended to serve. Since these included not only flattery, propaganda, and family bonding but also self-presentation or fashioning, the portrait must additionally be viewed as a mask that concealed complex anxieties and fantasies behind its seeming naturalism. This is especially true of female portraits, which present a series of unresolved dichotomies: commissioned by husbands, male lovers, and courtesans themselves (to adorn their walls), are they real-life, idealized, safely anonymous, or

[33] See most recently S. Greenblatt, *Shakespearean Negotiations* (Oxford, 1988), and his better-known *Renaissance Self-Fashioning* (Chicago, 1980).

dangerously pornographic, do they memorialize or titillate? If their role as masks intentionally prevents us from answering these questions, we can now at least understand how multivalent the portraits are. Like so many other artefacts, they are better at providing evidence of Renaissance masculinity than evidence of women's equality with men.

It is perhaps easier to deconstruct Renaissance bodies than it is to reassemble them to understand how they moved, where, and with whom, and what they ate. In the final essay Lauro Martines employs the new literary genre of the *novella*, or short story, to reconstruct the social life of Renaissance people. The problem lies in knowing how far the storytellers are merely telling a good story or are 'acting as reporters' in chronicling an outlook and a reality. It is the dynamic cut and thrust between opposing points of view, the 'contradictory play of acceptance and censure' of friars' lasciviousness and cuckolds' credulity in the stories, and the contradiction between friendship and hostility in the Florentine *beffa*, Martines argues, that reveal their reality and enable us to enter the popular mentality. Other clues, such as dress and the use of 'tu' or 'voi' serve to reveal the social distinctions of this agonistic society, while the use and gendering of city space and movement provide us with other ways of recreating city culture (squares, cathedrals, and possibly even markets were male spaces, whereas local churches were female space, and indoors the window space was female, a hole onto the outside world). For someone's trade, family, streets, and shops defined who that person was—hence Grasso the woodcarver's loss of self when these props were removed. The stories also define this elusive sense of being a city man by describing its 'other', the boorish contadino who is everything the citizen isn't; and for the same reason even their flights of imaginative fantasy tell us a lot about the problem of the real world they are fleeing from. As Martines says, a wealth of historical experience is needed to negotiate their secrets, but his essay shows how the 'social buzz' of city life can be re-evoked as the voices of a lively oral culture, the 'gossip' that citizens fear will bring them shame.

The question to return to in conclusion is how far the arguments presented in these essays constitute, not a new Renaissance—since this would run counter to the multiple and open interpretations these essays exemplify—but an account of a mixed culture that characterizes the society producing it. Connecting links do emerge in the dialogic play and counterpoint of its social buzz and its body language; also in the disjunction between real life and its appearance, expressed by Grasso's lost self, the ambivalent portraits of women, and the conflicted body, which can be summed up in the view of the world as a stage or 'as a confidence trick', as Francesco Vettori called it.[34] Aware of the divorce between the republican idealism and political reality of Medicean Florence, Guicciardini too talked of politics as role-playing and of liberty as only a 'name', a 'show' or an 'image'.[35] This view of 'the world as representation' is not only fashionable now but it also reflects some aspects of Burckhardt's agonistic and self-aware Renaissance society. The essays that follow provide us with both the critical tools and the research to destroy old generalizations about the Renaissance without losing a sense of its coherence as a period.

[34] Quoted by W. Rebhorn, *Lions and Foxes* (Ithaca, NY, 1988), 12: 'in effetto tutto il mondo è ciurmeria, e comincia ai religiosi e va discorrendo ne' giusconsulti, ne' medici, negli astrologi, ne' principi secolari, in quelli che sono loro intorno, in tutte l'arti ed esercizii . . .', tr. by Rebhorn as 'arts and disciplines.'

[35] F. Guicciardini, *Maxim*, no. 216, tr. in the *Dialogue*, p. 174, and *Dialogue*, 23, 35–6, 97; discussed in a conference paper by A. Brown, ' "The Name, the Show, the Image of Liberty": Revising Renaissance Republicanism', Hobart, February 1994.

PART I

The Ancient Model

1. Did the Ancients have an Antiquity? The Idea of Renaissance in the History of Classical Art

SALVATORE SETTIS

FEW passages in Western art literature can have been more influential than Pliny the Elder's celebrated remark in his *Natural History* (XXXIV. 52): '*Cessavit* deinde ars, ac rursus Olympiade CLVI *revixit*' [my emphasis]: ('In the 121st Olympiad [i.e. 296–293 BC] art ceased to exist, to revive again in the 156th Olympiad [i.e. 156–153 BC]'). According to one current interpretation,[1] Pliny points here to a period of stasis in the history of ancient art lasting 140 years, from about 296 to about 156 BC. Curiously enough, this is precisely the period in which the Pergamum school of sculpture flourished, which he nevertheless goes on to mention (XXXIV. 84).

Still more significant, however, is the fact that in this passage, as in the whole of Pliny and Latin literature, the word *ars* cannot be translated simply as 'art'. For there is no equivalent for our sense of the word in the classical languages. Neither the Latin *ars* nor the Greek *techne* (τέχνη) refers to the quality of an artifact, but is an absolutely neutral means of designating some particular artistic, or indeed non-artistic, technique. It is always clear from the context what technique is meant in any given passage. Thus, since Book XXXIV is dedicated to the *techne* of bronze-work, it is clear that the 'ars' which 'cessavit', 'ac rursus revixit' was simply that of casting in bronze. This celebrated remark of Pliny's, then, needs to be seen in connection with complaints he makes elsewhere of the falling off of this or that technique. As far as the art of bronze-work is concerned,

I wish to thank Paul Tucker for his help in drafting the English text of this paper.

[1] See e.g. R. Bianchi Bandinelli, in *Enciclopedia dell'arte antica* (1959), ii. 703.

it is sufficient to recall that at the start of this same book (XXXIV. 5) Pliny says that in his time 'auctoritas artis extincta est' ('the glorious art [of casting in bronze] has died out'), going on to explain that 'exolevit fundendi aeris praetiosi ratio' ('the technique of casting in precious bronze [that is, in bronze with the addition of silver and gold] is no longer practised').

The fact that the meaning of this famous passage in Pliny is so clear makes it still more remarkable that it should continue to be misinterpreted as a sort of forewarning of the decline of classical art. When, as here, a totally unwarranted interpretation becomes widely accepted, it is clearly providing a focus for certain *contemporary* historiographical problems and tendencies which look to ancient literature for support and points of reference. In the present instance the following two points at least are to be borne in mind:

1. The claim, referred to above, that the Latin *ars* may be given the same meaning as our modern 'art'.
2. The attempt to locate hiatuses within the history of ancient art, where possible with the aid of the sources.

This passage in Pliny ('cessavit ars, ac rursus revixit') has played a relevant role in forming the idea of a Renaissance of the arts, especially in Italy. Emblematic of its importance in this context is its quotation by Lorenzo Ghiberti in his *Commentarii*, where 'revixit' is translated as 'rinacque',[2] thus introducing the idea of a 'Rinascimento dell'antichità'. This provided a model not only for the enduring idea that (especially in Italy) artists had managed to bring about a 'revival' of classical art, but for all attempts to see the history of European art in terms of the eclipse or revival of a 'classical' vision of the world and a 'classical' form of art.

That his cyclical model prevailed for so long is entirely due to Winckelmann, whose *Geschichte der Kunst des Alterthums* (1764) presents a pattern of development (based upon the biological/biographical sequence of birth–infancy–youth–maturity–senility and death), derived from ancient sources—primarily Pliny the Elder. This is superimposed on a comprehensive picture of ancient art, fully consistent with trends which had their roots in the artistic taste of Winckelmann's own time. As we will see, this pattern is strongly connected with the very idea of a Renaissance, or rebirth, of art and culture in modern Europe.

[2] J. Schlosser, *La letteratura artistica*, 3rd Italian edn. (Florence, 1977), 152.

Implicit in terms like Rinascimento, Renaissance, or rebirth, is a central *topos* of European history, the 'end of the ancient world'— given that a new birth is possible only after death and gives rise to a new biological cycle. The image which the Italian Renaissance painted of itself as the very re-embodiment of the classical world thus became a lasting paradigm for art historians. A second *topos*, namely, the opposition between continuity and discontinuity as con-flicting patterns in the interpretation of history, is no less significant in the present context. Every model based on the 'death' and 'rebirth' of antiquity is, of course, one of discontinuity; but a picture centred on *the* Renaissance spreading from Italy throughout Europe was dra-matically weakened as, in the course of time, 'new' renascences emerged from the art-historical workshops. Thus we have not only the Italian proto-Renaissance of the fourteenth century, but also the Renaissance of the Twelfth Century (very popular thanks to Haskins's famous book of 1927); the Carolingian Renaissance (in western Europe), the Macedonian Renaissance (in the east), the Northumbrian Renaissance (in England) and, more recently, the Liutprandic Renaissance in Longobardic Italy.[3] This proliferation of renaissances is still more noticeable when we come to consider spe-cific periods of history. For example, Alexander Kazdhan has recently remarked that

Byzantine cultural history is seen as a continuous Renaissance divided into several phases: the historical definitions 'Macedonian Renaissance', 'Comnenian Renaissance' or 'Palaeologue Renaissance' are not uncommonly found among book-titles. Paul Spek has added the expression 'Pre-Macedonian' or iconoclastic Renaissance to the list. Taken together, these various Renaissances cover the entire Byzantine millenium. But do not the ideas of continuity and rebirth contradict one another?[4]

Though written in 1988, this comment of Kazdhan's, together with his attempt to distinguish the 'true' Renaissances in Byzantine cul-tural history from the rest, immediately recall Erwin Panofsky's famous *Renaissance and Renascences in the Western World* (1960), which set out to find a suitable formula for distinguishing *the* 'true' Renaissance (with a capital R) from mere 'renascences' (with a small r). In order to single out the Italian Renaissance as the actual

---

[3] A. M. Romanini, 'Il concetto di classico e l'alto Medio Evo', in *Magistra Barbaritas* (Milan, 1984), 665–78.

[4] A. Kazdhan, 'L'eredità antica a Bisanzio', *Studi Classici e Orientali*, 38 (1988), 139–53, esp. 144–8.

inception of the modern age and of modern self-awareness, the well-known principle of disjunction of form and content was introduced by him as a distinctive feature of the Middle Ages when it comes into contact with classical antiquity. According to Panofsky, this disjunction would eventually be reversed by being overcome in the reunion of classical form and classical subject-matter in the Renaissance.[5]

The very idea of Renaissance, therefore, and not only its limits and use(s), is a problem in itself, and a long-debated one. For historians of classical art and culture in our century, on the other hand, it has been possible to take for granted the concept of 'Renaissance', as it was used to describe what happened in Europe between the fifteenth and sixteenth centuries, as a formula to clarify a historical phenomenon of the Roman epoch. Indeed, they do frequently make use of the word 'Renaissance', primarily as a sort of shorthand for the revival of Greek elements and models in Roman time. Examples could range from W. Schmid (1898) to the Tenth Classical Colloquium of the British Museum (1989), actually entitled *The Greek Renaissance in the Roman Empire*.[6]

The history of the word 'Renaissance' as used by historians of classical art and culture, as well as the full range of the issues involved, cannot be discussed here. I merely wish to concentrate on a very influential article by Gerhart Rodenwaldt, one of the major German archaeologists of this century, 'Über das Problem der Renaissancen' (1931).[7] It appeared prior to Panofsky's book, but is

---

[5] For a discussion of this principle, see my article 'Von *auctoritas* zu *vetustas*: die antike Kunst in mittelalterlicher Sicht', *Zeitschrift für Kunstgeschichte*, 51 (1988), 157–79.

[6] W. Schmid, *Über den kulturgeschichtlichen Zusammenhang und die Bedeutung der griechischen Renaissance in der Römerzeit* (Leipzig, 1898); S. Walker and A. Cameron (eds.), *The Greek Renaissance in the Roman Empire* (London, 1989), *Bulletin of the Institute of Classical Studies*, suppl. 55. A different, and somewhat extreme, use of this word is found in P. N. Ure, *The Greek Renaissance* (London, 1921), which deals, in fact, with 'what the Greeks achieved in the first two centuries of their recorded history', i.e. after the 'Hellenic Middle Age', a 'Dark Age' which included Homer and his poems.

[7] In *Archaeologischer Anzeiger* (1931), 318–38. Rodenwaldt's starting point was A. Alföldi, 'Die Vorherrschaft der Pannoner in Römerreich und die Reaktion des Hellenentums unter Gallienus', in *25 Jahre Römisch-germanische Kommission* (Berlin, 1930), 11 ff. On Rodenwaldt's view of Roman art, see A. H. Borbein, 'Gerhart Rodenwaldts Bild der römischen Kunst', in E. Gabba and K. Christ (eds.), *Römische Geschichte und Zeitgeschichte in der deutschen und italienischen Altertumswissenschaft während des 19. und 20. Jahrhunderts*, ii. *L'impero romano fra storia generale e storia locale* (Como, 1991), 175–200.

still relatively unfamiliar to non-specialists (partly because Panofsky failed to cite it). Rodenwaldt clearly states from the outset that he has consciously adopted the Renaissance *par excellence* and its meaning as a model for determining and defining other, earlier Renaissances. But the most interesting problem he raises is the existence of Renaissances *within* the history of Graeco-Roman art and culture itself. Thus, he distinguishes the following series of 'Renaissances' within ancient art:

1. The classicism of the Hellenistic age.
2. The Augustan era, in which by its contribution to ancient visual art the Roman spirit comes of age, and which also sees the onset of Rome's humanistic mission to hand on the art of the classical age to all subsequent periods of European history.
3. The classicism of the reign of Hadrian, in which the balance between the Greek East and the Roman West is redefined and the foundations are laid of the future dualism between the art of the Eastern and that of the Western empire.
4. The neo-Augustan Renaissance of late antiquity.
5. The archaism of the age of Justinian, characterized as a *renovatio* of the Empire (clearly the backward projection of a model employed by the medievalist P. E. Schramm, in his book *Kaiser, Rom und renovatio*, published in 1929), as well as a *Byzantinische Antike*, named after the book by Matzulevitsch, also published in 1929. This was followed by a Byzantine Renaissance in the ninth and tenth centuries.

According to Rodenwaldt, each of these Renaissances must have had 'its own specific character'. To this already lengthy list of Renaissances he suggests adding that of the age of Gallienus. This 'Gallienic Renaissance' is still a subject of debate, and deserves to be examined in some detail for two reasons. First, there have been attempts to link the stylistic trends of the age of Gallienus with the aesthetic thought of the contemporary philosopher Plotinus. If this proved to be true, it would give us textual and theoretical evidence for at least one of the renaissances within classical antiquity. Secondly, what we call the Gallienic Renaissance was in any case extremely brief, given that this emperor's reign lasted only fourteen years (for seven of which he ruled jointly with his father).[8] Thus this

[8] L. de Blois, *The Policy of the Emperor Gallienus* (Leiden, 1976); W. Kuhoff, *Herrschertum und Reichskrise: die Regierungszeit der römischen Kaiser Valerianus und Gallienus (253–68 n. Chr.)* (Bochum, 1979).

particular 'renaissance', postulated in the 1930s, will provide a perfect means of testing both the retroactive influence of the concept of
Renaissance on the study of the history of ancient art, and also its
validity.

It is typical that studies of the Gallienic Renaissance should concentrate on portraits of this emperor.[9] In a first type (FIG. 1.1),
belonging to the period in which Gallienus still shared the throne
with his father Valerianus (AD 253–60), the sculptural treatment of
the hair on the forehead is evidently intended as a sort of 'quotation'
of the dynastic portraits of the early imperial period, especially those
of Augustus. Still more striking is the 'classicism' of the second type
among portraits of Gallienus, from the years in which he reigned
alone (260–68). In the Museo delle Terme portrait (FIG. 1.2) as well
as in the less well-known one from the Museu Regional of Lagos in
Portugal (FIG. 1.3) the fine features and the richly-worked hair recall
models from the Julio-Claudian period, confirming the idea of 'quotation' from early imperial portraiture.[10] It is sufficient to compare
these portraits with those of an immediate predecessor of Gallienus,
Decius (249–51) (FIG. 1.4), or with those of a successor such as
Probus (276–82) (FIG. 1.5), or again with what is probably a portrait
of Carinus (282–85) (FIG. 1.6).[11] These correspond perfectly to the
cliché of the *Soldatenkaiser*, from which it is true that Gallienus' are
utterly different. The models for his portrait are rather to be found
in those of Augustus (FIG. 1.7), or possibly in those of Hadrian (FIG.
1.8). The important question here, it seems to me, is not so much
whether Gallienus' contemporaries recognized the 'quotation' in the
same way as we do (that is, in terms of artistic taste and style), as
what its function was, or might have been, at least so far as the intentions of the emperor or of his court-sculptor were concerned. Did
reference to a portrait of Augustus or Hadrian imply a deliberate
wish to revive the art of the past, its style and achievements? Or
might it not rather be understood as a dynastically-flavoured

[9] Recent studies on the portraits of Gallienus' time include M. Bergmann, *Studien
zum römischen Porträt des 3. Jahrhunderts n. Chr.* (Bonn, 1977); A. M. McCann,
'Beyond the Classical in Third Century Portraiture', in *Aufstieg und Niedergang der
römischen Welt*, II, 12, 2 (1982), 623 ff.

[10] See K. Fittschen and P. Zanker, *Katalog der römischen Porträts in den
Capitolinischen Museen und den anderen kommunalen Sammlungen der Stadt Rom*
(Mainz am Rhein, 1985), i. 134–7, nos. 112 and 113 (first type); i. 137–9, nos. 114 and
115 (second type).

[11] Fittschen and Zanker, *Katalog der römischen Porträts*, i. 130, no. 110 (Decius); i.
139, no. 116 (Probus); i. 141, no. 117 (Carinus?).

FIG. 1.1 Portrait bust of the emperor Gallienus, Capitoline Museum, Rome

FIG. 1.2 Portrait bust of the emperor Gallienus, Museo delle Terme, Rome

FIG. 1.3 Portrait bust of the emperor Gallienus, Museu Regional, Lagos, Portugal

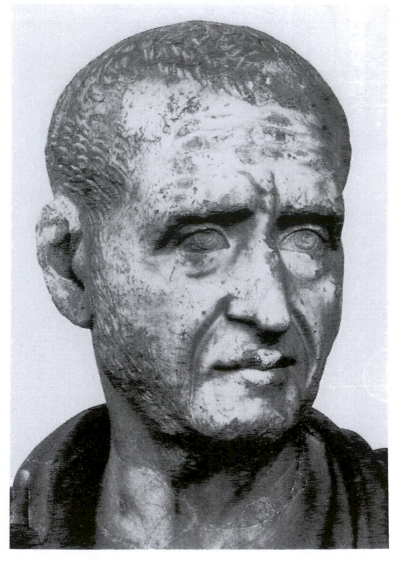

FIG. 1.4 Portrait bust of the emperor Decius, Capitoline Museum, Rome

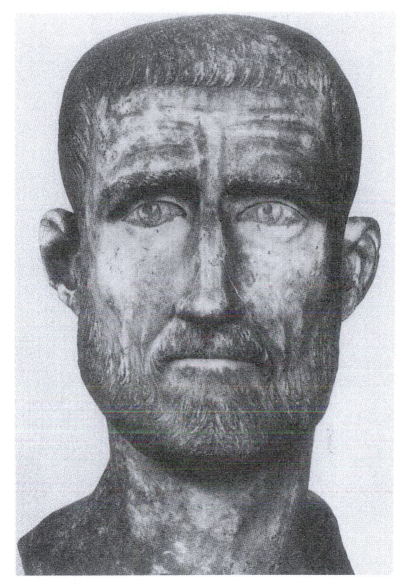

Fig. 1.5 Portrait bust of the emperor Probus, Capitoline Museum, Rome

Salvatore Settis

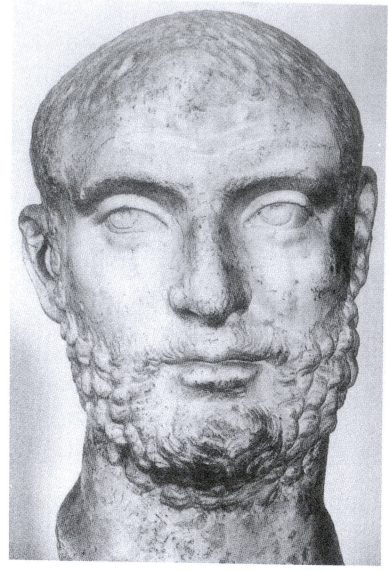

Fɪɢ. 1.6 Portrait bust of the emperor Carinus [?], Capitoline Museum, Rome

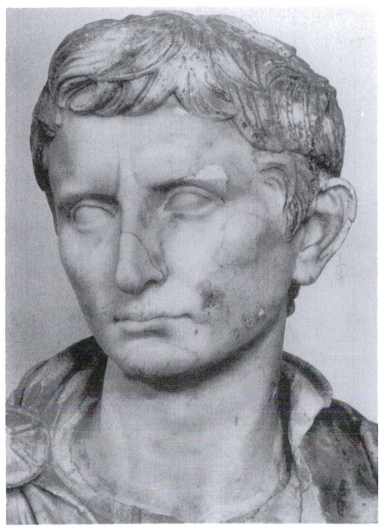

FIG. 1.7 Portrait bust of the emperor Augustus, Museo Nazionale, Rome

FIG. 1.8 Portrait bust of the emperor Hadrian, Capitoline Museum, Rome

reminiscence of the emperors of the olden days and so have a legit-imizing and celebratory function with regard to Gallienus, if not the force of a political manifesto?

At first, the reference to Plotinus seems to complicate things. Porphirius links Gallienus with the philosopher twice: 'From about the first year of Gallienus, Plotinus had begun to write upon such subjects as had arisen in his lectures. When I first came to know him in the tenth year of the reign he had composed 21 treatises' (*Vita Plotini*, 4); 'The Emperor Gallienus and his wife greatly honoured and venerated him' (*Vita Plotini*, 12). This personal contact is frequently seen as very important, and Plotinus' aesthetic theories are thought of as having influenced Gallienus' taste and his patronizing of the arts. Thus, trea-tises by Plotinus such as *On Intelligible Beauty* or *On Beauty*, as well as several passages from other works contained in the *Enneads*, have been interpreted as mirroring the taste of the Gallienic Renaissance. For instance, according to Gervase Mathew,[12]

a passage in the sixth *Ennead* of Plotinus is perhaps our best gloss on the aesthetic standard that seems to underlie Gallienic sculpture: 'We have to recognize that beauty is that which irradiates symmetry rather than symme-try itself and it is that which truly calls out love. Why else is there more of the glory of beauty upon the living and only some faint trace of it upon the dead, even though the face still retains its fullness and symmetry? Why are the most living portraits the most beautiful, even though others seem to be more symmetric?' (vii. 22).

In Mathew's view, this passage, like the sculpture of the Gallienic age, 'is consciously classical in much of its inspiration, and very clearly marked by its attempts at a renewal or a re-birth'. But Gallienic art shows a peculiar trend: 'it is consciously Graeco-Roman, but it is moving perhaps unconsciously on to a new phase of expression, . . . an essentially romantic rendering of life in transience which has no known first- or second-century source.' In other words, Gallienic classicism, very much like its Hadrianic coun-terpart, was chiefly marked by a 'romantic' attitude towards a 'clas-sical' past. The subtle interplay in Plotinus' passage between symmetry and beauty is interpreted as a desire for a 'romantic ren-dering of life in transience'.

It is interesting that, in these same years, the link between

---

[12] G. Mathew, 'The Character of the Gallienic Renaissance', *Journal of Roman Studies*, 33 (1943), 65–70.

Gallienus and Plotinus (or rather their contemporaneity) having been established, the above passage from the *Enneads* was interpreted in exactly the opposite sense. Silvio Ferri[13] claimed that, precisely because symmetry is not the only criterion of aesthetic judgement adduced by Plotinus, 'the existence and creation of what the ignorant call ugly [thus not only of Gallienus' portrait but also of those of his predecessors and successors] is legitimated by him'. He goes on: 'There is no substantial difference between Gallienic, semi-Gallienic and non-Gallienic heads; the principles of art set out by Plotinus may serve to characterize all three.' This is not the proper place for a detailed discussion of the passages in question. I merely wish to say that if we consider this and other statements in Plotinus' *On Beauty* in the context of his work as a whole, it becomes quite clear that there is no precise correspondence between his writings and the art of his time.

Plotinus' conception of Beauty, which he defines as intelligible and refers to the supersensible, is essentially philosophical-cum-textual in scope. He makes no contemporary references, nor does he seem to aim at influencing the art of his time. He addresses Plato, rather than Gallienus, but compared with Plato, whose doctrine was centred on the idea of *mimesis* (μίμησις), Plotinus distinctly revaluates sensible beauty, allotting it a place in the progress towards the supersensible. For him, sensible beauty as conveyed by artists in their works is, in fact, the first step (the second step being Love, the third Philosophy) in the way from the earthly world to intelligible Beauty, which partakes in *eidos* (Form) and belongs to the supreme world of the ideas and of Goodness. However, sensible beauty as seen in Nature is conceived by him as substantially higher than that represented in Art.

Accordingly, Plotinus' remarks on the beauty of things devoid of symmetry are clearly meant to deny that sensible beauty can be described in terms of precise rules (for example, those relating to *symmetria* (συμμετρία), or a proper interrelation of the parts, a favourite precept of the Stoics). Thus, the form enclosed within the mind of the artist and imposed by him on raw matter is exempted from the rules governing the art in question, and the primacy of natural beauty over that of the art-work with its 'rules' is averred. The most interesting point, which I cannot go into here, is that Plotinus *assumes*, or presupposes, the theoretical and prescriptive literature

[13] 'Plotino e l'arte del III secolo', *Critica d'arte*, 1 (1935–6), 166–71 (repr. in S. Ferri, *Opuscula Studi Classici e Orientali*, 11, 1962) (Florence, 1962), 112–21.

on art that had arisen since Plato's time. He distinctly parts from Plato's contempt of *mimesis* and artistic *techne* as inferior to Nature, since for him the mimetic activities of artists are based upon the same ideas from which Nature itself derives, and which are present in their minds. For example, Phidias' statue of Zeus in Olympia was not made from a sensible model, but the sculptor succeeded in catching the god's likeness 'as it would appear to mortals, if the god were to manifest himself to our eyes'.[14] The artist's imaginative power is therefore given a higher status. Nevertheless, Plotinus reaffirms one essential aspect of the Platonic doctrine, the idea that the Ideal was superior to the Sensible, against the 'rules' which aimed at giving art the status of truth.

This is the only warrantable reading of Plotinus: others (including those that see him as foreshadowing medieval aesthetics[15]) simply take too much for granted. The art of the age of Gallienus, or rather his portrait, has to be interpreted without direct reference to the writings of Plotinus. On the very subject of Gallienus Alföldi had written that 'art is the thermometer of history, and the portrait is where it is most sensitive'.[16] The re-use of dynastic models from the golden period of the Empire had the same programmatic meaning for Gallienus as the slogans featured on his coins, with their keywords *Virtus Gallieni Augusti, Securitas Orbis, Securitas Perpetua, Aeternitas Augusti, Felicitas Aeterna, Clementia temporum*, and so on.[17] And it is no coincidence that first Alföldi and then Rodenwaldt should have defined this backward-looking programme of Gallienus as a 'Renaissance', despite his short reign. Indeed, for both these scholars the operative model of the Italian Renaissance was that found in the then recently-published book by Konrad Burdach, *Reformation, Renaissance, Humanismus* (1918; 2nd edn., 1926),

[14] Plotinus, *On Intelligible Beauty*, v. viii. 1.

[15] A. Grabar, 'Plotin et les origines de l'esthétique médiévale', in id., *L'Art de la fin de l'antiquité et du moyen âge*, i (Paris, 1968), 15–29. On Plotinus' aesthetic theories, see E. de Keyser, *La Signification de l'art dans les Enneades de Plotin* (Louvain, 1955); F. Bourbon di Petrella, *Il problema dell'arte e della bellezza in Plotino* (Florence, 1956); A. N. M. Rich, 'Plotinus and the Theory of Artistic Imitation', *Mnemosyne*, 4/13 (1960), 233–9.

[16] Alföldi, 'Die Vorherrschaft'; 'Art the thermometer of history' is quoted by F. Haskell, in É. Pommier (ed.), *Winckelmann: La naissance de l'histoire de l'art à l'époque des Lumières* (Paris, 1991), 90.

[17] O. Voetter, 'Die Münzen des Kaisers Gallienus und seiner Familie', *Numismatische Zeitschrift*, 32 (1900), 117–47 and 33 (1901), 73–110; H. Mattingly and E. A. Sydenham, *The Roman Imperial Coinage* (London, 1927), v. i. 129–90.

where the rebirth of the arts and letters was seen in a predominantly historico-political context.

The 'renaissance' of Roman art at the time of Gallienus thus turns out to be a rather arbitrary description, in stylistic terms, of what was a specifically *political* attitude. But the fact that Gallienus and/or his court-sculptors looked to the portraits of past emperors for their models suggests a further train of thought. For Gallienus (as for the cultivated men of his age), the art of the past represented a sort of standardized (and easily available, because visible) repertory of forms, to which corresponded certain values. In this, the art of his time followed the example set by Augustus: just as for Gallienus Augustus' portrait was associated with the stability and security which he sought to enforce within the Empire, for Augustus similar values were identified with forms borrowed from classical Greek art (for example, from Policletus). Indeed Augustus was the originator of this procedure, which has recently been encapsulated in Hölscher's formula in *Römische Bildsprache als semantisches System* and analysed by P. Zanker in his *Augustus und die Macht der Bilder*.[18]

This re-use of forms as corresponding to certain ethical values is unthinkable without a widely-circulated, specialized literature on art (and in particular on painting and sculpture),[19] in which such a correspondence between forms and values might be rehearsed. Indeed one might claim that writing on art was founded in Greece as a result of the self-awareness and self-assertion of the architects first, then of the sculptors and later on of the painters. The first corpus of 'specialized' literature grew up in the course of a few generations (from the end of the fifth to the middle of the third century BC). It comprised technical reports ('How the Heraion of Samos was Built', mid-sixth century BC), collections of rules (Policletus' *Canon*), anecdotes, biographies, lists of artists (arranged by 'genres') and of their works (*nobilia opera*, 'masterpieces'), guidebooks or *periegeseis* (περιηγήσεις), and descriptions of works of art or *ekphraseis* (ἐκφράσεις). An entire vocabulary of 'technical' terms was developed

---

[18] T. Hölscher, *Römische Bildsprache als semantisches System* (Heidelberg, 1987) [=*Abhandl. der Heidelberger Akademie der Wissenschaften, Philos.-histor. Klasse*, 1987, 2]; P. Zanker, *Augustus und die Macht der Bilder* (Munich, 1987).

[19] For a general survey, see E. Pernice and W. H. Gross, 'Die griechischen und römischen literarischen Zeugnisse', in U. Hausmann (ed.), *Handbuch der Archäologie: Allgemeine Grundlagen der Archäologie* (Munich, 1969), 395–496.

(mainly borrowed from the longer-established field of Rhetoric), and the four main aims of art criticism were fixed:

1. Refining a verbal definition of artistic achievement, with words such as *decor, lumen, symmetria*.
2. Defining the development of individual styles, centred on the *floruit*, or mature period, of the artist and on his chronology.
3. Classifying the artists according to specific regional or workshop traditions (such as the famous Sicyonian school of painting, culminating in Apelles, pupil of Pamphilus and master of Perseus).
4. Elaborating the idea of artistic development or 'progress' itself, with the evolutionary model involved.

In late Hellenistic and Roman times, this art-historical literature was translated into summaries for the use of the new wave of collectors—in Alexandria, Antioch, Pergamum, and eventually Rome—far away from the old centres of Greek art. It is in this literature that a system of values, both aesthetical and ethical, was firmly associated with artistic forms, and used as a means of describing and evaluating them.

We usually think of the ancients as being fortunate in not having had an antiquity.[20] And yet writings on art from the Hellenistic and early Roman age show that they *did* have one. A new outlook on the 'high classical' period (from, say, the fifth to the middle of the third century BC) was firmly established in literary works on sculpture and painting. This is the view handed down to us in the only surviving compendium of ancient art history, compiled by Pliny the Elder;[21] and it is only in this context that his (or others') complaints on the decline of the arts (such as that of casting in bronze) make sense. Pliny's text counted (and still counts) as a substitute, or epitome, of an entire corpus of lost art-historical works, from which it inherited the biological pattern of evolution through the sequence of birth–infancy–youth–maturity–senility and death. Pliny's text in turn provided the scheme for all future histories of art, whether of classical antiquity or of post-classical Europe, from Ghiberti to Winckelmann and onwards. Modern art history could indeed be described as the revival of a literary genre invented by the Greeks.

Thus the choice of models extracted from the art of the past, seen

---

[20] N. Himmelmann, 'Das Altertum keine Antike hatte', *Utopische Vergangenheit: Archäologie und moderne Kultur* (Berlin, 1976), 41.
[21] J. Isager, *Pliny on Art and Society* (Odense, 1991), with earlier literature.

as a repertory of forms, was directed by a set of ethical and/or aesthetic values, endorsed by the language of art-criticism and acting as a sort of filter. For example Policletus' *decor* was perfectly suited to the likeness of an emperor, but at the same time the *veritas* of Hellenistic art was *de rigueur* when it came to representing men, beasts, battles, and landscapes. This gave rise to the curious paradox whereby those critical judgements aiming at tracing a diachronic process of rise and fall lost their historical character in the Roman period, when they settled into a series of standard formulas, and so ended up translating the historical development of Greek art into what was virtually a synchronic repertory of forms and values, in which the ethical came to dominate the historical and aesthetic.

The crucial (and entirely novel) point is that late Hellenistic and still more Roman art actually coexisted with a literature on art entailing both the awareness of a historical development and the effort to describe it, and for this very reason producing a new sense of the *distance* of the art of the past. Of course, this literature circulated much less widely than the actual art objects. The Romans, furthermore, produced practically no written criticism of contemporary art. Consequently the art of the past, above all that of Greece, came to acquire a special, exalted status and the various modes of retrospectively invoking it (collecting, copying or 'quoting' it) became the privilege of the educated classes: 'To the educated, the very foreignness of this imagery became a mirror of human destiny which the past held up to the present: the message of the myth [and, more in general, the message of "ancient art"] came from beyond the bounds of the contemporary society.'[22]

On the other hand, as is well known, the continuous presence of Greek elements (with regard both to iconography and style) in Roman art has been, and remains, a major problem for its definition. It is precisely here that a sharp distinction must be made between the Renaissance(s) (however defined) of modern Europe and the 'Renaissance(s)' occurring within Graeco-Roman antiquity. For the former regarded classical antiquity as a whole, taking its (relative) continuity for granted; while, if we wish to analyse the latter, it is essential first to distinguish what is classical and what is not within the civilization and art of antiquity itself.[23]

[22] O. J. Brendel, *Prolegomena to the Study of Roman Art* (New Haven, Conn., 1979), 180.
[23] In a leaflet presented to visitors to a recent exhibition of Greek bronzes in

In Winckelmann's view, there was no such thing as 'Roman art', but only 'Greek Art under Roman rule'; and, needless to say, it was placed at the very end of the art-historical life cycle, towards the point of 'senility and death'.[24] This view of Roman art has its roots in the absence of a specifically Roman art-historical tradition. Indeed, our almost entire ignorance even of the names of the Roman artists has always posed a problem. The revaluation of Roman art begun by Wickhoff and Riegl in Vienna around 1900 was based on a very different set of assumptions. It viewed Roman art as the foundation of that of the Middle Ages (itself the object of revaluation) and as a testing-ground for critical and aesthetic categories that had emerged in the *fin de siècle* period. In the 1930s, thanks to Rodenwaldt himself, historians of classical art began to distinguish two contrasting but coexisting branches or tendencies within Roman art, one of which was on a 'higher' level than the other and closer to the Greek tradition, while the other was 'lower' because further removed from this.[25]

In its best-known form this dual character of Roman art has been defined (by Ranuccio Bianchi Bandinelli) as the opposition between *arte aulica* ('high art') and *arte plebea* ('plebeian art').[26] For those holding such a view, it is no longer a question either of a 'decline' of the Greek style during the Roman period, or of a 'typically Roman' style, to be singled out and identified as the 'root' of medieval art. Instead, two main art traditions are seen as co-existent—interwoven with one other—defining different stylistic levels and employed according to the purpose, context, training or

American collections (Cleveland, Los Angeles, and Boston, 1989), two meanings of the word 'classical' are distinguished: 'The term *classical* is used broadly to describe the Greek, Etruscan, and Roman cultures from about 1200 BC to AD 476, while *Classical* refers strictly to Greece from 490 to 320 BC'.

[24] Recent literature on Winckelmann includes T. Gaehtgens (ed.), *Johann Joachim Winckelmann, 1717–1768* (Hamburg, 1986) and E. Pommier (ed.), *Winckelmann: La naissance de l'histoire de l'art à l'époque des Lumières* (Paris, 1991).

[25] See Brendel, *Prolegomena*.

[26] Ranuccio Bianchi Bandinelli first put forward this formula in his famous article 'Arte plebea', *Dialoghi di Archeologia*, 1 (1967), 7–19. Cf. G. Agosti, 'Ranuccio Bianchi Bandinelli dall'invenzione del "Maestro delle Imprese di Traiano" alla scoperta dell' "arte plebea" ', *Annali della Scuola Normale Superiore di Pisa*, 3/16 (1986), 307–29. Bianchi Bandinelli's formula is in turn derived from Rodenwaldt's chapter on 'The Transition to Late-Classical Art', in *Cambridge Art History*, xii (Cambridge, 1939), 547, where he introduced the English terms *popular* and *great* art, to become Bianchi Bandinelli's *in arte plebea* and *arte aulica* respectively (see Brendel, *Prolegomena*, 119–21).

inclination of the artists and/or their patrons. The periodic revival of 'classicizing' styles (or 'Renaissances'), as evidenced by Rodenwaldt, belongs to this trend: 'neo-classical' periods (like the Augustan, Hadrianic, or Gallienic age) are seen as a recurrent feature of Roman art history.

But these two opposed theories of Roman art (as a period of 'decadence', and as the expression of a new *Kunstwollen*) share at least one very important trait: both evaluate Roman art by referring it to that of Greece. Both acknowledge the coexistence in Roman art of 'Roman' *and* 'Greek' elements (however the former are defined). Indeed it has even been said that 'the history of this dualism would itself provide the best possible history of Roman art'.[27] The final preponderance of the 'Roman elements' in the art of late Antiquity is what binds this historiographical process together in all its various forms. In the view of 'decadence' theories, this age sees the irremediable decline of those classical forms which the Romans had taken over from *Graecia capta*, and casts a denigratory shadow backwards over all its formal precedents. Similarly, those tending to look in the direction of the Middle Ages and to re-evaluate late Roman art as the formative period of medieval art consider its 'purely Roman elements' as a bridge towards medieval art; while the classical forms the Romans had taken over from *Graecia capta* may be conceived as a storehouse for later classicizing styles, or 'renaissances'.

And in fact, while Winckelmann's new picture of ancient art was dominated, as in the sources, by the Greeks, his Greek art could not be fashioned out of a fresh corpus of statues, but only out of the familiar set of those to be seen in Rome ('le statue di Roma'), or from the 'Greek' element in them. It was, so to speak, distilled by dint of inspiration from Roman art (including copies of Greek masterworks), without going back to the lost originals (as the archaeologists were later to do) by way of a 'philological' analysis of the surviving copies, but rather attempting to extract the essence of the statues of Athens from those in Rome. Winckelmann considered the *Apollo Belvedere* an original, indeed the quintessence of Greek art, and not, as we now know, a late Roman copy. And yet without his prophet's insight into Greek art (and the *Apollo*) we should never have learned to distinguish the originals from the copies. Following

---

[27] R. Bianchi Bandinelli, *Archeologia e cultura* (Milan–Naples, 1961), 235–6. I have commented on this point in my essay at the end of the Italian translation of O. J. Brendel, *Introduzione all'arte romana* (Turin, 1982), 161–200, esp. 169–76.

in his footsteps, the nineteenth century was to see the true rediscovery of the art of Greece, thanks to the bringing of the marbles of Aegina to Munich and those of the Parthenon to London. And if the Musée Napoléon was the last substantially Roman museum, the first museum of the new era, the British Museum, was more Greek than Roman.

Problems in defining Roman art, essentially 'dual', are, then, largely dependent upon the presence of classical Greek elements in it; and those elements, in turn, foster every subsequent 'renaissance', as they did for Winckelmann's view of Greek art. But at the back of each period of 'rebirth' (whether the Carolingian, the Macedonian or that of the Renaissance itself) there is this abiding and possibly unique peculiarity of the Western tradition, the living presence, and *auctoritas*, of antiquity, almost like a sort of land unto itself, out of which all influence and models, as well as projects for the renewal of art, came. This peculiarity was stressed in 1856 in a text by Jakob Burckhardt, first published in 1991: according to him,

The awakening (*renaître*) of a past civilization or of its forms alone. . . . is possibly unique in world history, and it is one of the essential characteristics of recent centuries that they could link themselves to an extremely remote past, of which all sure evidence, both with regard to its art and to its civilization, had been lost; and they did it of their own will, showing an even arbitrary preference.[28]

It is important to emphasize that this line of *auctoritas* links up with Greek culture itself. For the latter had canonized itself, promoting the cult of the past which had then been translated into the twin tradition of art history and the practice of making copies. The main difficulty in defining Roman art is precisely that it is for us two very different if not contradictory things. On the one hand it formed the basis for the development of medieval art by ensuring the continuity of artistic techniques and social practices. On the other, it has repeatedly been seen (for instance by Wiligelmus, Mantegna,

---

[28] The complete passage runs as follows: 'Der Begriff: Die Wiedererweckung (*renaître*) einer untergegangenen Welt der Civilisation oder der Formen alleine. . . . Dieses Factum steht beinahe einzig in der Weltgeschichte da, ja es ist ein wesentlicher Charakterzug der letzten Jahrhunderte, daß sie sich mit Willen—ja mit freister Wählerei—an irgend ein Längstvergangenes abschließen können, und daß ihnen darob die sichere Überzeugung—nicht bloß in der Kunst sondern in allen Zweigen der Zivilisation—abhanden kommt.' The text was published by M. Ghelardi, *La scoperta del Rinascimento: L' "Età di Raffaello" di Jakob Burckhardt* (Turin, 1991), 147 n. 10.

Thorwaldsen) as *the* origin of all possible 'renascences'. It has thus given us the idea of the classical as a whole, an antiquity *en bloc*, an idea from which, since Winckelmann's work, and time, Greek art has gradually disentangled itself.

Matrix of the Middle Ages and matrix of the Renaissance: for this reason we necessarily see Roman art as internally (but not unfathomably) flawed. Its notorious and perhaps unresolved dualism reflects and perpetuates the historiographical opposition between the Middle Ages and the Renaissance: a self-warranted opposition first set up on the stage of the Renaissance and entailing an all-inclusive idea of Graeco-Roman antiquity as a whole, to be likened to the present and distinguished from the medieval past: therefore, the Middle Ages had to be separated from antiquity by means of some form of 'cessavit ars'. Winckelmann's interpretative model—highly influential on art-historical thought and practice ever since—also combined both Greek and Roman elements. But he redistributed the roles, placing the Greeks on one side (the same as that of Raphael and Michelangelo) and the Romans on the other (the same as that of medieval art).[29]

This is, basically, the idea of antiquity we inherited and are still making use of, an idea which includes both the 'high classic' and its counterpart, the 'decadence(s)' that followed, and, then, the corresponding Renaissance(s). It was the antiquity of the ancients that gave rise to our own idea of antiquity: something which could die, but also be reborn, again and again.

---

[29] For a broader discussion, see my 'Un'arte al plurale: L'impero romano, i Greci e i posteri', in E. Gabba and A. Schiavone (eds.), *Storia di Roma*, iv, *Caratteri e morfologie* (Turin, 1989), 827–78.

2.   The Donation of Constantine: A New Source for the Concept of the Renaissance?

ROBERT BLACK

THE concept of the Renaissance presupposes a vision of history, a historical scheme. For there to be rebirth, there must have been birth followed by death—or, to change the metaphor, a period of light must have been followed by a time of darkness: the Renaissance was, then, renewing this original time of light. During the Renaissance, these historical concepts were repeatedly and explicitly discussed by humanists and others, who spoke of a revival of the arts achieved in their own or recent times after a long period of decay.[1] The idea of

---

[1] Frate Guido da Pisa, in his 'capitoli dichiarativi' to the *Inferno*, with a continual Latin gloss by him, cited by Orazio Bacci, *La critica letteraria* (Milan, 1910), 163 (which is quoted below, p. 83; see P. O. Kristeller in *Renaissance Thought and its Sources*, ed. M. Mooney (New York, 1979), 273). Boccaccio, *Decameron*, vi. 5, ed. V. Branca (Milan, 1976), 550–1; id., 'Della origine, vita . . . di Dante', in A. Solerti (ed.), *Le vite di Dante, Petrarca e Boccaccio* (Milan, 1904), 13; id., *Opere latine minori*, ed. A. F. Massera (Bari, 1928), 194–7. C. Salutati, *Epistolario*, ed. F. Novati (Rome, 1891–1911), iii. 82–4. L. Bruni, *Vita del Petrarca*, in Solerti (ed.), *Le vite*, 289–90. Guarino Veronese, *Epistolario*, ed. R. Sabbadini (Venice, 1916), ii. 587–8. Poggio Bracciolini, 'Oratio ad . . . Nycholaum V', in *Opera* (Basel, 1538), 291–2 (also *Opera* (Strassburg, 1513) fos. 109ᵛ–110ʳ). Sicco Polenton, *Scriptorum illustrium latinae linguae libri XVIII*, ed. B. L. Ullman (Rome, 1928), 125, 128–9, 139, 163. Flavio Biondo, *Italia illustrata*, in id., *De Roma triumphante libri X* (Basel, 1531), 293, 346–7. Lorenzo Valla, *Sex elegantiarum libri*, in E. Garin (ed.), *Prosatori latini del Quattrocento* (Milan, 1952), 598. Matteo Palmieri, *Vita civile*, ed. G. Belloni (Florence, 1982), 43–6 (also ed. F. Battaglia (Bologna, 1944), 36–7). Aeneas Sylvius, *Opera omnia* (Basel, 1551), 600, 646. L. B. Alberti, *On Painting and On Sculpture: The Latin Texts of De Pictura and De Statua*, ed. C. Grayson (London, 1972), 32. Benedetto Accolti, *Dialogus*, in *Philippi Villani liber de civitate Florentiae famosis civibus*, ed. G. Galletti (Florence, 1848), 121–2. Alamanno Rinuccini, *Lettere ed orazioni*,

Robert Black

an earlier decline, therefore, is inherent in the concept of the Renaissance. Moreover, this notion of an earlier decline seems to have been an actual source for the concept of the Renaissance as it developed in the fourteenth century and afterwards. Indeed, the idea of the decline of the ancient world was not a concept which was born in the Renaissance itself; as early as the third century and increasingly during the Middle Ages, historical theories were put forward to clarify and explain the end of antiquity. These visions of history—powerfully suggestive not only of decline but also of eventual renewal—were a precedent for the humanists' concept of the death and rebirth of the ancient world; indeed, the humanists' idea of the Renaissance apparently developed, at least in part, out of one of these medieval traditions of historical thinking about decline and possible revival. How, when, and why this decay began were questions sometimes ignored in discussions of the revival of the arts or comparisons of the ancients and moderns; on the other hand, authors frequently put forward theories for the decline of the ancient

ed. V. R. Giustiniani (Florence, 1953), 107–8. Cristoforo Landino, *Scritti crittici e teorici*, ed. R. Cardini (Rome, 1974), i. 118–19, 123–4. Vespasiano da Bisticci, *Le vite*, ed. A. Greco (Florence, 1970–6), i. 32, ii. 502–3. Marcantonio Sabellico, *De latinae linguae reparatione*, in *Opera omnia*, iii (Basel, 1560), cols. 319–20. Marsilio Ficino, *Opera omnia* (Basel, 1561), 944 (see P. O. Kristeller, *The Philosophy of Marsilio Ficino* (New York, 1943), 22–3). Paolo Cortesi, *De hominibus doctis*, ed. G. Ferraù (Messina, 1977), 101, 107, 111 ff. Erasmus, *Opus Epistolarum*, ed. P. S. Allen (Oxford, 1906), i. 107–8; (Oxford, 1910) ii. 488 ff. (tr. R. A. B. Mynors and D. F. S. Thomson, *The Correspondence of Erasmus* (Toronto, 1974), i. 39–40; (Toronto, 1977), iv. 463 ff.). Machiavelli, *Arte della guerra*, ed. S. Bertelli (Milan, 1961), 519. Carlo Sigonio, *Historiarum de Regno Italiae libri quindecim* (Basel, 1575), dedicatory epistle, fos. 3ᵛ–4ʳ nn.; *Historiarum de occidentali imperio libri XX* (Basel, 1579), 5. Some fundamental secondary works on this theme are: F. Simone, 'La conoscenza della rinascita negli umanisti', *La rinascita*, 2 (1939), 838–71; 3 (1940), 164–86. W. K. Ferguson, 'Humanist views of the Renaissance', *American Historical Review*, 45 (1939), 1–28 (repr. in his *Renaissance Studies* (New York, 1963), 31–54); *The Renaissance in Historical Thought* (New York, 1948), 1 ff. H. Weisinger, 'Renaissance Theories of the Revival of the Fine Arts,' *Italica*, 20 (1943), 163–70; 'The Self-Awareness of the Renaissance as a Criterion of the Renaissance,' *Papers of the Michigan Academy of Science, Arts and Letters*, 29 (1943), 561–7; 'Who Began the Revival of Learning? The Renaissance Point of View', *Papers of the Michigan Academy of Science, Arts and Letters*, 30 (1944), 625–38; 'The Renaissance Theory of the Reaction against the Middle Ages as a Cause of the Renaissance', *Speculum*, 20 (1945), 461–7; 'Ideas of History during the Renaissance', *Journal of the History of Ideas*, 6 (1945), 415–35; 'Renaissance Accounts of the Revival of Learning', *Studies in Philology*, 45 (1948), 105–18. B. L. Ullman, 'Renaissance: The Word and the Underlying Concept', in id., *Studies in the Italian Renaissance* (Rome, 1955), 11–25.

world—the barbarian invasions[2] or the loss of republican liberty[3] are only two of the favoured arguments. What I should like to examine is perhaps a less familiar but in fact equally, if not more, significant Renaissance historical theory—that the crucial decay set in with the conversion of the Roman Empire to Christianity and with the famous so-called Donation of Constantine.[4]

By this name is now understood a forged privilege, probably emanating from the papal chancery in the eighth century, which conferred extensive rights and possessions on the Pope and the Roman church. The text, often identified as the 'Constitutum domini

[2] L. Bruni, *Historiae florentini populi*, ed. E. Santini, *Rerum italicarum scriptores* (2nd Ser.), vol. xix, sect. 3 (Città di Castello, 1914), 14–15. Flavio Biondo, *Historiarum ab inclinato Romano imperio decades*, in *De Roma triumphante* (Basel, 1531), 4. Valla, *Elegantiae*, in Garin (ed.), *Prosatori*, 610. Accolti, *Dialogus*, 111. Landino, *Scritti*, i. 118, 123–4. Bartolommeo della Fonte, in C. Trinkhaus, 'A Humanist's Image of Humanism: The Inaugural Orations of Bartolommeo della Fonte', *Studies in the Renaissance*, 7 (1960), 96, 101–3, 120. Cortesi, *De hominibus doctis*, 108. Sabellico, *Opera omnia*, iii (Basel, 1560), cols. 323–4. Bernardo Corio, *Istoria di Milano*, ed. E. De Magri (Milan, 1855–7), i. 13. Machiavelli, *Istorie fiorentine*, bk. I, ch. 1, ed. F. Gaeta (Milan, 1962), 72–5. Ph. Melanchton, *Declamationes*, ed. Hartfelden (1891), ii. 14 (cited by G. Gordon, '*Medium aevum* and the Middle Ages,' *Society for Pure English, Tract XIX* (1925), 18). Erasmus, *Opus Epistolarum*, i. 108 (tr. Mynors and Thomson, i. 40). See also Weisinger, 'Renaissance theory . . . as a cause', 462–6; 'Renaissance accounts', 112–15. An important secondary work on this theme is S. D'Elia, *Il Basso Imperio nella cultura moderna dal Quattrocento ad oggi* (Naples, 1967).

[3] Bruni, *Historiae*, 14–15; *La vita di Messer Francesco Petrarca*, in Solerti (ed.), *Le vite*, 289–90. Poggio, *Opera* (Basel, 1538) 365, 371. Biondo, *Decades*, 4. Vespasiano, *Le vite*, ii. 502–3. For Le Roy, see Weisinger, 'Renaissance accounts', 115. See H. Baron, *The Crisis of the Early Italian Renaissance* (Princeton, 1966), rev. edn., *passim*.

[4] The text of the Donation has been given a critical edition by Horst Fuhrman, *Das Constitutum Constantini (Konstantinische Schenkung)*, in *Fontes iuris Germanici in usum scholarum ex Monumentis Germanicae Historicis separatim editi*, x (Hanover, 1968). The fundamental work on the afterlife of the Donation in the Middle Ages and Renaissance was done by Gerhard Laehr, *Die Konstantinische Schenkung in der abendländischen Literatur des Mittelalters bis zur Mitte des 14. Jahrhunderts* (Berlin, 1926) (hereafter, Laehr I) and 'Die Konstantinische Schenkung in der abendländischen Literatur des ausgehenden Mittelalters', *Quellen und Forschungen aus italienischen Archiven und Bibliotheken*, 23 (1932), 120–81 (hereafter, Laehr II). Wolfram Setz has made a further invaluable contribution to the understanding of the Donation's afterlife in his *Lorenzo Vallas Schrift gegen die Konstantinische Schenkung, De falso credita et ementita Constantini donatione: Zur Interpretation und Wirkungsgeschichte* (Tübingen, 1975), including a full bibliography of primary and secondary sources on pp. ix–xviii. See also G. Antonazzi, *Lorenzo Valla e la polemica sulla Donazione di Costantino* (Rome, 1985). The best discussion of the medieval afterlife of the Donation in English is I. von Döllinger, *Fables Respecting the Popes of the Middle Ages*, tr. A. Plummer (London, 1871), 133–78 (in the rev. German edn. of this fundamental work, *Die Papstfabeln des Mittelalters*, ed. J. Friedrich (Stuttgart, 1890), 72–125).

Constantini imperatoris', was addressed to Pope Sylvester I. In the first part (called 'Confessio') Constantine told of his instruction in the Christian religion by Sylvester, made a profession of his new faith, and related his baptism in Rome by Sylvester, who thereby cured him of leprosy. In the 'Donatio' or second part, Constantine gratefully conferred upon the pope primacy over the other patriarchs and bishops; he gave the pope the same honorary rights and insignia as the emperor; he presented the pope and his successors with the Lateran palace, Rome and the provinces, districts and towns of Italy, and all the Western regions. Constantine, it says, led the horse upon which the pope rode; for himself, the emperor established in the East a new capital to bear his name and he now betook himself and his administration there, since it was inappropriate for a secular ruler to have power where God had established the residence of the head of the Christian church.

It has long been recognized that the Donation of Constantine was a text of fundamental importance in medieval political and historical thought. It could—depending on the perspective—be cited as evidence for the spiritual primacy of the Roman see or indeed serve as the basis for a theory of papal world rule; it could be seen as the triumph of the church militant or alternatively as the cause of its fall from evangelical purity; it could signify the beginning or the end of legitimately-sanctioned secular rule.[5] But the idea that the Donation exercised a formative influence on Renaissance thought has usually been dismissed on the grounds that it was supposedly in the Renaissance that the document was definitively discredited as a forgery. However, far from being relegated to the status of quaint medieval fable, the Donation continued to enjoy the limelight of controversy well into the sixteenth century; the refutations by Nicholas of Cusa, Valla, and Reginald Pecock did not prevent the Donation from becoming a bulwark of orthodoxy for reformed Catholicism, nor from being one of the *bêtes noires* of Protestantism. Moreover, the Donation had always been a controversial document: denials of its authenticity—for example by Otto III[6] or by Arnold of Brescia's revolutionary followers in twelfth-century Rome[7]—not to mention

---

[5] See Laehr II, 120.

[6] *Monumenta Germaniae Historica. Legum sectio IV. Constitutiones et acta publica imperatorum et regum*, i (Hanover, 1893), Otto III, Constitutiones, n. 26 (a. 1001), p. 56. See Laehr I, 22, 183–4.

[7] *Bibliotheca rerum Germanicarum*, i, ed. Philipp Jaffé (Berlin, 1864), 542. See Döllinger, *Fables*, 141–2; Laehr I, 67; Setz, *Lorenzo Vallas Schrift*, 24.

repeated rejections of its legitimacy, especially by civil lawyers,[8] served only to enhance the preoccupation with the Donation in the Middle Ages, and the same was true of Valla's declamation, which, ironically, gave new life to the document beginning in the later fifteenth century. What is particularly suggestive is that the Donation reached the climax of its power to provoke intellectual ferment in the first half of the fourteenth century[9]—precisely the time when the programme of the nascent humanist movement was being shaped by Petrarch. Therefore, it would seem worthwhile to consider some of the Donation's reverberations in the realm of historical thought and in particular what effect these may have had on the emerging concept of the Renaissance.

To understand the significance of the Donation, it is necessary to start with the idea of the primitive church, a concept which goes back at least to the church fathers.[10] Although St Jerome contrasted the austere pre-Constantinian church with its subsequent greater wealth but lesser virtue,[11] until the twelfth century the term *ecclesia primitiva* more often referred to the apostolic church of the New Testament or less chronologically to the ideals of the common and apostolic life:[12] this historical vagueness is clear from the accusation by one twelfth-century preacher that the Cathars did not even know under which pope the interruption of the apostolic succession, and hence the decline from apostolic purity, had allegedly begun.[13] But

---

[8] See Domenico Maffei, *La donazione di Costantino nei giuristi medievali* (Milan, 1964).

[9] Laehr II, 120.

[10] Glenn Olsen, 'The Idea of the *ecclesia primitiva* in the Writings of the Twelfth-Century Canonists', *Traditio*, 25 (1969), 66–7, suggested that the 'writings of John Cassian . . . seem to contain the earliest references to the idea of the primitive church', but Peter Stockmeier, 'Causa Reformationis und Alte Kirche. Zum Geschichte der Reformbewegungen', in R. Bäumer (ed.), *Von Konstanz nach Trient* (Munich, 1972), 1 n. 1, writes, 'Bereits Origenes, hom. in Jes. 4, 2 (GCS 3, 259) kritisiert die kirchliche Gegenwart am Ideal der "ersten Liebe"; der Hinweis von Glenn Olson [*sic*] . . . ist also zu berichtigen.'

[11] *Vita Malchi Monachi, Patrilogia latina*, ed. J. P. Migne (Paris, 1883), xxiii, col. 55: 'Scribere enim disposui . . . ab adventu salvatoris usque ad nostram aetatem, id est, ab apostolis, usque ad nostri temporis faecem, quomodo et per quos Christi Ecclesia nata sit, et adulta, persecutionibus creverit, et martyriis coronata sit; et postquam ad Christianos principes venerit, potentia quidem et divitiis major, sed virtutibus minor facta sit.' See Olsen, 83.

[12] Olsen, 85–6.

[13] Eckberti Abbatis Schonaugiensis, *Sermones contra Catharos*, x. 3 (*Patrilogia latina*, col. 195, p. 71): 'Si nunc dicitis quod sacerdotalis ordo defecerit in Romana

during the twelfth century, it became gradually more usual for the idea of the primitive church to be conceived historically: Otto of Freising, for example, contrasted the poverty and humility of the church before Constantine with its temporal power thereafter,[14] while a later twelfth-century Florentine heretic called Diotisalvi declared that all popes from the time of Sylvester I were in hell.[15] Important in this change to a more historical view of the early church were the twelfth-century canonists. Gratian associated the *ecclesia primitiva* with the pre-Constantinian church: the apostles had foreseen the expansion of the church and so did not bother to amass property; after Constantine's conversion, the church was richly endowed and allowed to have possessions. Gratian thus betrayed a concern for growing ecclesiastical materialism after the Donation, and other canonists of the time similarly stressed the differences in the church before and after Constantine: for example, according to Stephen of Tournai, the essential change from simplicity to complexity and involvement in the world took place under Sylvester I.[16] The most influential figure in the transition to this historical view of the *ecclesia primitiva* was St Bernard; in the early church evangelical poverty prevailed because martyrs refused to be associated with the powers of this world; under Constantine, as the church made its peace with the secular authorities and became wealthy, it ceased to struggle against the forces of corruption, by which it had been contaminated ever since. Bernard clearly traced the worldliness of his own day back to the new, non-scriptural principles introduced into the church by the Donation.[17]

Ecclesia, oportet ut nobis hoc demonstretis, sub quo papa acciderit iste defectus . . . Dicitis forte: Nescimus sub quo papa acciderit iste defectus, sed hoc scimus, quod ex multis temporibus omnes, qui dicebantur Romani pontifices et cardinales, semper avari fuerunt et superbi, et multis ex causis indigni sacerdotio Christi, et ex hoc certi sumus, quoniam verum sacerdotium apud istos non est.' See Laehr I, 176.

[14] Otto of Freising, *Chronica sive historia de duabus civitatibus*, ed. A. Hofmeister (Hanover and Leipzig, 1912) (*Scriptores rerum germanicarum in usum scholarum*), prologue to bk. 4, pp. 182–3. See Olsen, 83 n. 59.

[15] *Acta Sanctorum*, vol. 18, May, V (Paris and Rome, 1866), 21 May, col. 86: 'quidam Florentinus . . . nomine Diotesalvi . . . doctrinam Manichaeorum pessimam in Urbeveteri seminavit; asserens . . . Beatum Silvestrum et omnes suos successores aeternae poenae cruciatibus alligatos . . .' See Olsen, 83 n. 59.

[16] Olsen, 81–2, 85.

[17] *De consideratione*, in *S. Bernardi Opera: Tractatus et opuscula*, ed. J. Leclercq and H. M. Rochais (Rome, 1963), iii. 453–4: 'Petrus hic est, qui nescitur processisse aliquando vel gemmis orantus, vel sericis, non tectus auro, non vectus equo albo, nec stipatus milite, nec circumstrepentibus saeptus ministris. Absque his tamen credidit

Bernard's contribution was to sharpen the historical focus; he helped to establish a consensus in the thirteenth century that the Donation represented a great historical turning point, although not everyone was agreed that it was necessarily a change for the worse. For the author of the anti-imperial pamphlet of 1245–6, *Eger cui lenia*, the change brought about by the Donation marked the transition from illegitimate tyranny to divinely-ordained government, by which the wicked would be punished and the good praised.[18] Ptolemy of Lucca developed this high papalist view of the pre-Constantinian empire as a tyranny and of the Donation not as a gift but as a return to what Christ had originally given to Peter. He argued that four monarchies had preceded Christ, who inaugurated the fifth and last monarchy, but as an example of humility Christ preferred to live in poverty and to conceal his reign; although in possession of the true imperial title, Christ allowed the pagans to retain power. Christ's kingdom grew through the martyrdom of his followers and when it was perfected, he struck Constantine down with leprosy; when the cured emperor ceded dominion to the pope, spiritual and worldly power were at last united and the Christian monarchy, hitherto hidden, was now disclosed for all to behold.[19] Other

satis posse impleri salutare mandatum: Si amas me, pasce oves meas. In his successisti, non Petro, sed Constantino. Consulo toleranda pro tempore, non affectanda pro debito ... Etsi purpuratus, etsi deauratus incedens, non est tamen quod horreas operam curamve pastoralem ... non est quod erubescas Evangelium.' For the interpretation of this passage and its effect, see Paul de Vooght, 'Du "De consideratione" de Saint Bernard au "De potestate Papae" de Wiclif', *Irénikon*, 26 (1953), 114–32. See Olsen, 82–4, for an admirable discussion of Bernard, the Donation and the primitive church, and 83 n. 59 for further references to the literature on the *De consideratione* and the Donation; see also Setz, *Lorenzo Vallas Schrift*, 20–1. For the influence of the Bernardine texts on Luther, see Scott Hendrix, 'In Quest of *Vera Ecclesia*: The Crises of Late Medieval Ecclesiology', *Viator*, 7 (1976), 355–6.

[18] Peter Herde, 'Ein Pamphlet der päpstlichen Kurie gegen Kaiser Friedrich II von 1245/46 ("Eger cui lenia")', *Deutsches Archiv für Erforschung des Mittelalters*, 23 (1967), 473–5; see the text on 521–2: 'Verum idem Constantinus per fidem Christi catholice incorporatus ecclesie illam inordinatam tyrampnidem, qua foris antea illegitime utebatur, humiliter ecclesie resignavit ... et recepit intus a Christi vicario, successore videlicet Petri, ordinatam divinitus imperii potestatem, qua deinceps ad vindictam malorum laudem vero bonorum uteretur, ut qui prius abutebatur potestate permissa, deinde fungeretur auctoritate concessa.' See also Charles Davis, 'Ptolemy of Lucca and the Roman Republic', *Proceedings of the American Philosophical Society*, 118 (1974), 43–4; repr. in id. *Dante's Italy* (Philadelphia, 1984), 277–8, cf. 240.

[19] *Determinatio compendiosa de iurisdictione imperii auctore anonymo ut videtur Tholomeo Lucensi ... accedit Tractatus anonymus de origine ac translatione et statu romani imperii*, ed. Marius Krammer (Hanover and Leipzig, 1909) (*Fontes iuris germanici antiqui in usum scholarum*), 6, 7, 14, 20, 21, 25, 46, 48, 50–1, 64, 73–4. See also

pro-papalists emphasized not so much the changed status of the Roman church as the material benefits of the Donation. For Pope Nicholas III in 1278, the Roman church had been strengthened through Constantine's affliction; the church gained the freedom of action which was essential for its future development.[20] Pietro Olivi, the Franciscan theologian and preacher, went further: as a result of the Donation, Satan had been expelled from Rome. The gross manners of the gentiles were counteracted, a new age was inaugurated, and the church began finally 'utiliter et rationaliter' to own temporalities.[21]

Others in the thirteenth century emphasized the gloomier historical results of Constantine's gift. A favourite *topos* of these deprecators of the Donation was the story that when Sylvester had received his rewards a heavenly voice was heard to declare, 'Hodie infusum est venenum ecclesie' ('Today the church has been suffused with poison').[22] This tale is found in the letter directed to the Roman

Ptolemy's *Ecclesiastica historia nova*, *Rerum italicarum scriptores*, ed. L. Muratori (Milan, 1727), vol. xi, col. 823 ff. See Laehr I, 106–10. Davis, *Dante's Italy*, 216, 230, 246, 277–8. Bruno Nardi, 'La "Donatio Constantini" e Dante', in id., *Nel mondo di Dante* (Rome, 1944), 117–19.

[20] Bull of 18 July 1278 (VI. i. vi. 17), in *Corpus iuris canonici*, ed. E. Friedberg (Leipzig, 1879–81), vol. ii, col. 957: 'Ne autem ipsa mater ecclesia in congregatione et pastura fidelium temporalibus careret auxiliis, quin potius ipsis-adiuta spiritualibus semper proficeret incrementis: non absque miraculo factum esse concipitur, ut occasionaliter Constantini monarchae a Deo provisa, sed curata baptismalibus fomentis infirmitas, quandam quasi adiiceret ipsi ecclesiae firmitatem, qui quarto die sui baptismatis una cum omnibus satrapis et universo senatu, optimatibus etiam et cuncto populo, in persona beati Silvestri, sibi Romanam concedendo urbem relinquens, ab eo et successoribus eius per pragmaticum constitutum disponendam esse, decernens in ipsa Urbe utriusque potestatis monarchiam Romanis Pontificibus, declaret, non iustum arbitrans, ut, ubi sacerdotii principatum et Christianae religionis caput imperator coelestis instituit, illic imperator terrenus habeat potestatem; quin magis ipsa Petri sedes in Romano iam proprio solio collocata, libertate plena in suis agendis per omnia potiretur, nec ulli subesset homini, quae ore divino cunctis dignoscitur esse prelata.' See Laehr I, 105.

[21] Charles Davis, 'Rome and Babylon in Dante', in P. A. Ramsey (ed.), *Rome in the Renaissance: The City and the Myth* (Binghamton, 1982), 31–2.

[22] This story goes back at least to Gerald of Wales, who mentions it first in his *Gemma ecclesiastica* in 1197 and then in three other works: for the citations see Laehr I, 72 n. 61; for the date of this work, see R. Bartlett, *Gerald of Wales* (Oxford, 1982), 218. Its next appearance seems to have been in a poem of Walther von der Vogelweide (Lachmann edn. no. 25; for the text see H. Protze, *Sprüche und Lieder* (Halle, 1963) or W. Wilmanns (ed.), *Walther von der Vogelweide* (Halle, 1912), rev. edn., 161) which is generally dated to 1213 (see G. F. Jones, *Walther von der Vogelweide* (New York, 1968), 109, who also gives an English prose translation on 109–10). Beryl Smalley, *English Friars and Antiquity in the Early Fourteenth Century* (Oxford, 1960), 195, was therefore probably wrong to say that Walther was the 'first' to tell this tale,

citizenry in 1265 by Manfred, Frederick II's illegitimate son and successor, who also declared that Constantine, unlike Augustus, had improvidently diminished, not enhanced, the empire with the Donation.[23] It is also repeated by the Dominican preacher in Florence, Remigio Girolami, who stressed the ill effects of the Donation not only on the empire but also on the church: Constantine's and Sylvester's actions had brought corruption into the spiritual world; the modern church now suffered more from anxiety to preserve its temporal wealth than the primitive church had endured from persecution at the hands of pagan tyrants.[24]

The most extreme interpretation of the Donation's historical results was found in heretical circles: the Donation marked the end of the Christian church: Sylvester was either the last pope or even the Prince of Darkness himself; after the Donation the church had

---

but he may have been the first to say that a good angel spoke these words, because in Gerald's version it was the devil who declared he had given this poison to the church. Walther's version became the generally-accepted form of the legend in the Middle Ages: it was cited in a thirteenth-century marginalium to a Viennese manuscript (see G. H. Pertz, in *Archiv der Gesellschaft für ältere deutsche Geschichtskunde*, 7 (1939), 475, quoted by F. Tamburini in his edition of Remigio dei Girolami, *Contra falsos ecclesie professores* (Rome, 1981), 58; the same gloss is quoted by Willmanns, *Walther*, 161, without, however, giving the location or folio reference). For further discussion of the development of this legend in Germany in the later Middle Ages, see Döllinger, *Fables*, 167–70; Remigio, *Contra falsos*, 58; G. Prochnow, *Mittelhochdeutsche Silverlegenden und ihre Quellen* (Marburg, 1901); K. Burdach, *Rienzo und die geistige Wandlung seiner Zeit*, Erste Hälfte (Berlin, 1913) (= *Briefwechsel des Cola di Rienzo*, ed. K. Burdach and P. Piur, Erster Teil = K. Burdach, *Von Mittelalter zur Reformation. Forschungen zur Geschichte der deutschen Bildung*, Zweiter Band), 226–7 n. 2. See below, 60, 70 n. 66, 74 for its development.

[23] E. Dupré Theseider (ed.), *L'idea imperiale di Roma nella tradizione del medioevo* (Milan, 1942), 223–4: 'Nam ille inprovidus Constantinus [sacerdotibus] submictere alienum, nullius servitutis caracterem inponere potuit futuris imperatoribus . . . Praeterea cum Augustum ab augendo dici mandaverit legislator, iam dicto Constantino donante fuit, donacio illa nulla . . . Vere quippe velocitati ventorum tradiderunt Romane prelati ecclesie, cum prefate donacionis, invalide ipso iure, transgressio aspiravit vocem ancelicam tunc dicentem: "hodie diffusum est venenum in ecclesia sancta Dei." ' Theseider, p. 224, n. 1, points out that this is a pun on the name Augustus also found in the gloss to *Cod.* I, 1, 1: 'Augusti ab augeo, quia semper huius propositi debet esse ut augeat imperium.' See also Davis, *Dante's Italy*, 47; Nardi, 'La "Donatio Constantini" ', 130–1.

[24] Remigio, *Contra falsos*, 58–9; the story is also referred to but not cited on 237. Remigio also repeats it almost verbatim in *De misericordia*, ed. A. Samaritani, 'La misericordia in Remigio de' Girolami e in Dante nel passagio tra la teologia patristico-monastica e la scolastica', *Analecta Pomposiana*, 2 (1966), 196. See also Charles Davis, *Dante and the Idea of Rome* (Oxford, 1957) 84–5; id., *Dante's Italy*, 165, 220.

become a whore who had traded riches for spirituality; the true church was now only represented by the elect.[25] Thus a Dolcinist, Pietro of Lucca, declared in 1321 that 'when poverty was removed from the church by Saint Sylvester, sanctity of life was taken from it and the devil entered into this world'.[26] Among the Spiritualist followers of Angelo of Clareno near Tivoli in 1334, 'Brother Francesco ... said ... that Sylvester's and Constantine's bones should be burnt', because 'they enriched the church and from riches of the churches wars have arisen'.[27] Wyclif repeated the story about the angel's voice and the deadly poison, declaring that 'from the time of the Donation to the church the Roman empire was gradually torn by dissention' and that the church became not Christ's but Antichrist's.[28] Hus too referred to the heavenly voice and the deadly poison, which he maintained had spiritually murdered innumerable souls.[29]

This controversy over the historical implications of the Donation reached its climax in the earlier fourteenth century. An anonymous

[25] Laehr I, 175–9. On the Donation as a historical turning point for the Spirituals and the Waldensians, see Hendrix, 'In quest of Vera Ecclesia', 356; G. Leff, 'The Making of the Myth of a True Church in the Later Middle Ages', *Journal of Medieval and Renaissance Studies*, 1 (1971), 14–15; id., 'The Apostolic Ideal in Later Medieval Ecclesiology', *Journal of Theological Studies*, NS, 18 (1967), 75; M. Reeves, *The Influence of Prophecy in the Later Middle Ages: A Study in Joachimism* (Oxford, 1969), 411; I. von Döllinger, *Beiträge zur Sektengeschichte des Mittelalters* (Munich, 1890), i. 187–8 and ii. 40, 252, 306, 320, 352, 356. For the Waldensians, see also G. Leff, *Heresy in the Later Middle Ages* (Manchester, 1967), ii. 457–9; J. Gonnet and A. Molnar, *Les vaudois au moyen âge* (Turin, 1974), 406 ff.

[26] Döllinger, *Fables*, 173 n. 1: 'Quando paupertas fuit mutata ab ecclesia per S. Sylvestrum, tunc sanctitas vitae fuit subtracta ecclesiae et diabolus intravit—in hunc mundum.' See Laehr I, 177.

[27] Burdach, *Cola und die Wandlung*, 230 n. 1: 'frater Franciscus ... dixit ... quod ossa sancti Silvestri et Constantini deberent comburi, qui dictaverant [= ditaverant] ecclesiam et ex divitiis ecclesiarum fiebant guerre.'

[28] *De ecclesia*, ed. J. Loserth (London, 1886), 369, for the angel and the poison; *De veritate sacrae scripturae*, ed. R. Buddensieg, iii (London, 1907), 239: 'a tempore dotacionis ecclesie scissum est per dissensiones paulative Romanum imperium.' The Donation and its historical effects were a constant theme in *De ecclesia*. In the *Trialogus*, Wyclif said that Antichrist was produced by the Donation and from this proceeded the fall of the Roman Empire: see Döllinger, *Fables*, 173. See also Laehr II, 140–8; Leff, *Heresy*, ii. 528; G. A. Benrath, 'Traditionsbewusstsein, Schriftverständnis und Schriftprinzip bei Wyclif', in A. Zimmermann (ed.), *Antiqui und Moderni: Traditionsbewusstsein und Fortschrittsbewusstsein im späten Mittelalter*, *Miscellanea Mediaevalia*, ix (Berlin, 1974), 365–6.

[29] H. Kaminsky, *A History of the Hussite Revolution* (Berkeley, Calif., 1967), 52–5; see also 40–8 for the views of Nicholas of Dresden. For Lollards and other heretics in the Empire in the 15th c., see Laehr II, 148–9.

papal publicist at the time of Henry of Luxemburg's expedition to Italy claimed that, since the time of Constantine, Rome, Tuscany, and Sicily had belonged to the pope.[30] Henry of Cremona, another curialist, also emphasized actual papal temporal rule: for him, the Donation did not remedy the church's lack of title but of power[31]— and indeed, as has already been seen with Ptolemy of Lucca, the Donation as *restitutio* was a common view among papal publicists.[32] Egidius Spiritalis of Perugia, writing in 1328, staunchly upheld the Donation's significance, maintaining that although the pope had always had ownership of temporalities, it was through the Donation that his possession was recognized.[33] Lambertus Guerrici of Hoy, also writing in 1328, drew a sharp contrast between the primitive and modern churches, emphasizing the simplicity of the former and the complex needs of the latter and suggesting that the crucial dividing line between them was the Donation.[34] James of Viterbo, in *De regimine christiano*, emphasized the positive side of the church's temporal authority too: worldly might, he maintained, gave power and

[30] *Notitia de iuramentis ab imperatore praestitis et ordo quaestionum*, in *Monumenta Germaniae Historica, Constitutiones* (Hanover and Leipzig, 1909–11), IV. ii. 1330, 1332, 1339. See Laehr I, 125, 127.

[31] *De potestate papae*, in R. Scholz (ed.), *Die Publizistik zur Zeit Philipps des Schönen und Bonifaz' VIII* (Stuttgart, 1903), 467–8: 'ante Constantinum . . . non erat deffectus iuris, sed potencie . . . Et ideo dominus voluit fidei subvenire et hoc [aliter] bene fieri non poterat . . . nisi potestatem ecclesie dando. Quare inspiravit Constantinum, ut renunciaret imperio et confiteretur se ab ecclesia illud tenere, nec tunc . . . fuit dotata primo de iure, sed de facto . . .' See ibid. 162; Laehr I, 114–15; Nardi, 'La "Donatio Constantini" ', 118.

[32] e.g. Augustinus Triumphus, *Summa de ecclesiastica potestate*, Aug. Vind. 1473, not foliated, 43. 3: 'Constantinus autem reddit ecclesie et vicario Christi illa que ab ipso receperat cum dictum sit supra omnia esse dei et per consequens papae vicarius [*sic*] eius quantum ad honoris venerationem et dominii recognitionem.' See W. D. McCready, 'The Problem of the Empire in Augustinus Triumphus and Late Medieval Hierocratic Theory', *Traditio*, 30 (1974), 335–6 n. 31 for *restitutio* in Aegidius Spiritalis, Augustinus Triumphus, Alexander de S. Elpidio, Alvarus Pelagius, Conrad of Megenberg, François de Meyronnes, James of Viterbo, Henry of Cremona, Lambertus Guerrici de Hoyo and Ptolemy of Lucca. See also M. Wilks, *The Problem of Sovereignty in the Later Middle Ages: The Papal Monarchy with Augustinus Triumphus and the Publicists* (Cambridge, 1963), 543 n. 1.

[33] R. Scholz, *Unbekannte kirchen-politische Streitsschriften aus der Zeit Ludwigs des Bayerns (1327–1354)* (Rome, 1911–14), ii. 127: 'proprietas potuit dari a Constantino, sed maius dominium fuit semper a Deo, licet de facto non semper fuerit recognitum.' See Laehr I, 145–6.

[34] Scholz, *Streitsschriften*, ii. 160–1 for the abridged text and i. 60 ff. for the analysis. See also Laehr I, 143–4.

honour to divine rule; the rights which Sylvester had as Christ's vicar could be better exercised after the Donation.[35]

Particularly interesting are the views of Augustinus Triumphus of Ancona: he accepted that there was a decline from imperial unity after Constantine but he turned this fact, usually considered prejudicial to the papal cause, against his adversaries, arguing that, in order to preserve peace, temporal administration in Italy was, following the Donation, committed to the empire only to a limited extent. Although aware of the dangers for the church of mixing too much in secular affairs, he maintained that the Donation provided legitimate wealth, pointing out that Abraham had been rich yet pious and untainted by avarice.[36] It was for the empire and particularly in Italy that the Donation had the greatest practical historical effects according to Augustinus. Elsewhere in Europe the pope's overlordship was limited by the fact that rulers derived their power not only by divine right and hence from the pope but also from the people; by prescription, the Donation no longer applied here, nor in Germany, moreover, since the Germans could be trusted to respect the church because of their indigenous piety. In Italy, however, the Donation meant, according to Augustinus, that the pope's direct administration was not only theory but fact; his remarkably realistic treatment was fine-tuned to the contemporary Italian political world and particularly to the ambitions of the church party, wishing to restore the papacy's temporal role after the debacle of Boniface VIII and Philip the Fair and the threats posed by the emperors Henry VII and Lewis of Bavaria.[37]

Such concrete and threatening ambitions from the church were bound to provoke extreme reactions. For example, the French publicist Pierre Dubois, writing at the turn of the fourteenth century,

---

[35] See Scholz, *Publizistik*, 148; Laehr I, 115.

[36] *De ecclesiastica potestate*, 43. 2: 'temporalium administratio non auget cupiditatem nisi per inordinatam et affectionum et spiritualibus bonis retractionem. Nam abraham multorum bonorum temporalium administrationem habuit et tamen primo ipse de salute humani generis promissionem recipere meruit.' See Laehr I, 147, 186.

[37] See McCready, 'The Problem of the Empire', 333 n. 26, and 339, 341, 342, 344–9. McCready's reading of Augustinus not only shows much greater sensitivity to political realities and their influence on Augustinus but also much greater accuracy than that of Wilks, who frequently ignores the textual context of the quotations he extracts from Augustinus in an attempt to see him as a completely hierocratic theorist. A particularly powerful defence of the Donation, emphasizing its decisive effects, was also made by Konrad von Megenberg in 1354: see Scholz, *Streitschriften*, ii. 312–20; Laehr I, 153 ff.

asserted that the Donation had been the foundation of the church's secularization; the post-Sylvestran papacy would be better advised to imitate the poverty of the pre-Constantinian church.[38] According to King Robert of Anjou's letter to Pope Clement V (ca. 24 August 1313), the *respublica romana* was effectively dissolved by the Donation; once the emperor had been *dominus quasi omnium*, but now the earth was filled with independent principalities.[39] However, two critics of the Donation's historical effects rose above all others at the beginning of the fourteenth century: the imperial theorist, Marsilius of Padua, and Dante. Marsilius declared that, since Sylvester, the popes had usurped jurisdiction over the spiritual and secular worlds on the basis of the Donation: Christ and the apostles had not given the papacy any particular spiritual or temporal pre-eminence. It was Constantine, so maintained Marsilius, who gave the popes authority over the church as well as the state. Previous critics had accepted that Christ had at least given the popes spiritual supremacy, but for Marsilius the Donation was the greatest historical turning point in world history: from mere priests the popes had become usurpers of world monarchy through Constantine's and Sylvester's pact.[40]

If Marsilius's analysis revealed in the starkest terms the profound historical consequences of the Donation, it was left for Dante to depict its results with the most emotive and powerful language and imagery. In his eyes, it would have been better if Constantine had never been born: he was a good Christian who had made a catastrophic error. The first disaster had been for the empire: the seamless tunic of world monarchy had been rent.[41] By removing the imperial capital to the East, he had become a Greek and turned back the flight of the imperial eagle against the course of the sky;[42] no

---

[38] Scholz, *Publizistik*, 400. Another important pro-French critic of the Donation is John of Paris, whose *Tractatus de regia potestate* (1302) originated during the quarrel of Boniface VIII and Philip the Fair: see Johannes Quidort von Paris, ed. F. Bleienstein, *Über königliche und päpstliche Gewalt* (*De regia potestate et papali*) (Stuttgart, 1969), proemium and ch. 21, pp. 69 ff., 185–96. For the date, see ibid. 13–14. There is an English tr. by J. A. Watt, John of Paris, *On Royal and Papal Power* (Toronto, 1971). He also repeats the story about the voice and the poison: see Johannes Quidort, *Über königliche*, ch. 21, p. 187.

[39] Davis, *Dante and the Idea of Rome*, 184–5.

[40] Marsilius, *Defensor pacis*, ed. R. Scholz (*Fontes iuris germanici antiqui in usum scholarum*) (Hanover, 1933), II. xi–xiv. 262 ff.; II. xvi. 345; II. xviii. 380–1; II. xxii. 429 ff., 437 ff.; II. xxix. 585 ff. See Laehr I, 137–9; Leff, 'Apostolic ideal', 69, 72; G. Piaia, ' "Antiqui", "moderni" e "via moderna" in Marsilio da Padova', in A. Zimmermann (ed.), *Antiqui und Moderni*, 333–5.

[41] *De monarchia*, i. 16; ii. 12; iii. 10.   [42] *Paradiso*, vi. 1–6.

longer could the all-powerful Augustus maintain peace, as arrogant popes undid the work of good rulers such as Justinian or Charlemagne.[43] The second disaster had been for the church: ecclesiastics could now mix in worldly affairs and ignore their spiritual callings. Constantine's pious intentions could not protect the demon of avarice and worldly power from possessing the church. The gift of the Western half of the empire to the church is depicted as the dropping of the eagle's feathers on the chariot, with the consequent growth of weeds covering its wheels and pole and the appearance of its seven heads and of the whore as its passengers.[44] The cupidity of the church, excited by the Donation, led to ever more outrageous ecclesiastical usurpations; a rich church could no longer imitate Christ. The final but not least of the disasters was for Rome and Italy. Constantine had brought unmentionable grief to a rich land. God had destined the Roman people for rule, but since the Donation Italy's worst enemy had been resident in Rome itself. Italy, deprived of her true lords, was now prey to the illicit temporal desires of the popes. It is hard to know which historical consequence of the Donation was most lamented by Dante.[45]

It is important to have dwelt on the interpretations of the Donation in the Middle Ages, because the Renaissance humanists were heirs to the deep sense of history displayed by medieval authors when faced with the Donation. Thus Petrarch followed in the footsteps of the medieval critics from St Bernard to Dante. In *Epistola sine nomine* 17, he addresses Constantine as a wrecker who threw away an empire which had been built up with great effort over the centuries— the popes before the Donation were humble; now they are haughty.[46]

---

[43] *Paradiso*, vi. 22–7, 94–6.   [44] *Purgatorio*, xxxii. 112 ff.

[45] See *Paradiso*, xx. 60; *Inferno*, xix. 106–17. Also Nardi, 'La "Donatio Constantini" '; Davis, *Dante and the Idea of Rome*, 195 n. 1; id., *Dante's Italy*, 17, 22–4, 30, 45, 47, 59, 61–2; Leff, 'Apostolic ideal', 76–7; Laehr I, 128–9. For Rienzo's view of Constantine's reign as a turning point in history, see Burdach, *Rienzo und die Wandlung*, 221–2. See also P. G. Ricci, 'Il commento di Cola di Rienzo alla *Monarchia* di Dante', *Studi medievali*, ser. 3, 6/2 (1965), 674, 701–2, 706–7, who repeats on p. 702 the story about the voices and the poison, attributing it to Gregory the Great ('refert— credo—Gregorius').

[46] Paul Piur (ed.), *Petrarcas 'Buch ohne Namen' und die Päpstliche Kurie. Ein Beitrag zur Geistesgeschichte der Frührenaissance* (Halle, 1925), 222: 'O inconsulte princeps ac prodige! Nesciebas quantis laboribus constaret imperium, quod tam facile disperge- bas? Solent stulti adolescentes a patribus quesita prodigere, nempe ignari unde vel qualiter parta sint, si quidem indigentie ac laborum recordatio magnum prodigalitati ac lascivie frenum ponit. At tu senex, quid agebas? ubi eras? Si videri munificum

In another letter he does not go so far as some medieval critics in condemning Sylvester, whom he regards as pious both before and after Constantine's endowment, but he remains firm in his conviction that the Donation was the turning point for the church and the papacy: 'that generosity injured and perhaps will continue to injure his successors'.[47] In one of the three sonnets directed against Avignon and the so-called Babylonian Captivity of the church, he contrasts the humble and pure poverty of the early church, established by Christ and the apostles, with modern riches and corruption: Constantine will not return to help again, he declares ironically, but let him remain in hell where he belongs: 'Founded in pure and humble poverty, against your founders you raise your horns, shameless whore: and where have you put your hope? In your adulteries, in so many ill-born riches? Now Constantine does not return, but let the sad world which upheld him take him.'[48] Petrarch's fullest treatment of the Donation and its consequences occurs in his sixth *Eclogue*, which is a dialogue between two shepherds, Pamphilus, representing St Peter, and Mitio, standing for Pope Clement V. The contrast is again between the severity, chastity, and poverty of the *ecclesia primitiva* and the corruption, wealth, and licence of the modern church: Christendom is in ruins; the church has gained riches, of which Constantine (Corydon bizantius) is the donor—'This mirror I treasure | Byzantine Corydon gave me.' Keep the gifts of Corydon—the fiend—and let him suffer forever who first gave the popes the fatal gift of secular lordship: 'cling to Corydon's mirror! | Oh, may he

delectabat, de proprio largireris, tuam donasses, Imperii hereditatem quam curator acceperas, successoribus integram reliquisses. Nescio quidem an potueris, sed fecisti ut ad has tunc humiles, nunc superbas manus heu longe aliis manibus fundati status administratio pervenerit.' The best discussion of Petrarch and the Donation is found in Paul Piur, 'Paupertas evangelica und Constantinische Schenkung', in id., *Petrarcas*, 57–77; see also 42, 44, 51 for more citations of Petrarchan texts on the return to the early church (Sonnet 137; *Sen.* vii. 1; *Sen.* ix. 1) as well as *Fam.* vi. 1 and vi. 3, cited and discussed by Piur, *Petrarcas*, 61, 62, 70. See also H. Baron, 'Franciscan Poverty and Civic Wealth', *Speculum*, 13 (1938), 6–11, revised in id. *In Search of Florentine Civic Humanism* (Princeton, 1988), i. 158–225.

[47] 'Nocuit successoribus suis forsitan ea largitas nocebitque': *Sen.* ii. 2, cited by Piur, *Petrarcas*, 66–7.

[48] Rime 138, in *Rime, trionfi e poesie latine*, ed. F. Neri, G. Martellotti, E. Bianchi and N. Sapegno (Milan, 1961), 203: 'Fondata in casta e umil povertate | contra tuoi fondatori alzi le corna, | putta sfacciata: e dove ai posto spene? | Negli adulteri tuoi, ne le mal nate | ricchezze tante? Or Constantin non torna, | ma tolga il mondo tristo che'l sostene.'

suffer forever, the wretch who first gave the shepherds | Fatal endowment of lordship!'[49]

Now what is significant for the emergence of the concept of the Renaissance is that Petrarch in adopting this historical outlook—indeed this particular historical scheme—actually took it beyond the history of the church and applied it to secular culture and history. This intellectual transition is documented in his famous *epistola familiaris* vi. 2, describing his tour of the sites of ancient Rome with his friend Giovanni Colonna.[50] He cites the archaeological remains of classical and early Christian Rome to evoke the memory of past greatness—both secular and spiritual. Both are fused together by Petrarch to represent what for him is worth studying—that is, ancient history—and the dividing line he takes between ancient and modern times is the Donation of Constantine: 'Our conversation often turned on history, which we appeared to have divided up between us in such a fashion that in modern history you, in ancient history I, seemed to be more expert; and ancient were called those events which took place before the name of Christ was celebrated in Rome and adored by the Roman emperors, modern, however, the events from that time to the present.'[51] This scheme is reinforced by his archaeological picture of ancient Rome: this is presented not in topographical but in chronological order—first of classical, then of Christian sites; his account goes up to Sylvester and Constantine and then abruptly breaks off. The Donation for Petrarch becomes the fundamental turning point in the history of civilization—the end of antiquity—and hence it represents a crucial defining feature of his concept of the Renaissance.

It is possible that Petrarch's move beyond ecclesiology to embrace secular culture may have been influenced by the view that the decline of ancient culture had set in, indeed had been deliberately caused by, the rise of Christianity. Often in the Middle Ages this anti-pagan

---

[49] *Petrarch's Bucolicum Carmen*, ed. and tr. by T. G. Bergin (New Haven, Conn., 1974), 74–97: 'Speculum Coridon bizantius istud, | Quo michi complaceo, dono dedit . . . fruere et speculum Coridonis habeto. | Eternum gemat ille miser, pastoribus aule | Qui primus mala dona dedit!'

[50] Petrarch, *Le familiari*, ed. V. Rossi (Florence, 1934), ii. 55–60.

[51] Ibid. 58: 'Multus de historiis sermo erat, quas ita partiti videbamur, ut in novis tu, in antiquis ego viderer expertior, et dicantur antique quecunque ante celebratum Rome et veneratum romanis principibus Cristi nomen, nove autem ex illo usque ad hanc etatem.' The translation used here is by Theodor Mommsen, 'Petrarch's Conception of the "Dark Ages" ', in id., *Medieval and Renaissance Studies* (Ithaca, NY, 1959) 115–16.

iconoclasm was seen to have been the work of Gregory the Great, but there are instances where the destruction of ancient art was pushed back to the reign of Constantine. Thus in some versions of the *Mirabilia urbis Romae*, the statue of Sol erected by Nero at the Colosseum was said to have been destroyed by Sylvester, and in the *Canones Conciliorum*, a ninth-century manuscript at Vercelli, pagan books were burned on the orders of Constantine (and Theodosius).[52] Petrarch, unlike his contemporary Boccaccio,[53] made no explicit reference to this view that the legacy of pagan antiquity had been destroyed by Christianity, but both this secular perspective and the ecclesiological scheme of the Donation placed the end of antiquity in the reign of Constantine. The influence of the secular view on Petrarch must remain speculative, in the absence of positive documentation; but on the explicit evidence of his letter to Colonna,[54] it is clear that the historical vision which lay behind Petrarch's concept of the Renaissance derived in large part from the medieval view of church history, in which the Donation of Constantine represented the crucial dividing line.

The nature of Petrarch's crucial role in the adoption and transformation of medieval ecclesiology in the Renaissance has not hitherto been clearly understood, mainly because of the distorted picture of Petrarch's historical ideas presented in an influential article by Theodor Mommsen.[55] Mommsen believed that *epistola familiaris* vi. 2 marked a transition from a medieval and Christian to a Renaissance and secular view of the Dark Ages: 'with this change of emphasis from things religious to things secular, the significance of the old metaphor became reversed: Antiquity, so long considered as the "Dark Age", now became the time of "light" which had to be "restored"; the era following Antiquity, on the other hand, was submerged in obscurity.'[56] He claimed that in this letter Petrarch 'ventured to state explicitly that his primary interest was in the history of pagan rather than Christian Rome, thus drawing a sharp boundary-line between "ancient" and "modern" history.'[57] Mommsen was saying that, for Petrarch, ancient history was above all pagan

---

[52] T. Buddensieg, 'Gregory the Great, the Destroyer of Pagan Idols,' *Journal of the Warburg and Courtauld Institutes*, 28 (1965), 47 and n. 10; *Codice topografico della città di Roma*, ed. R. Valentini and G. Zucchetti (Rome, 1946), iii. 150 n. 1.

[53] See below, 78.   [54] See above, 66.   [55] Mommsen, 'Petrarch's Conception'.
[56] Ibid. 109.   [57] Ibid. 117.

whereas modern history was Christian: with his preference for antiquity over modern times, Mommsen was therefore suggesting that
Petrarch was moving from a medieval Christian to a secular, modern historical perspective.

Mommsen based his interpretation on the alleged extent to which
epistola familiaris vi. 2 was devoted to the sites of pagan Rome: 'it
is to be noted that for the most part Petrarch recalls spots which
were connected with the great figures and events of the history of
pagan Rome, especially of the times of the Roman republic, whereas
only a very small part of the enumeration is devoted to the scenes of
Christian Rome: the proportion shows where Petrarch's main interest lay . . . he puts an almost exclusive emphasis on the history of
pagan Rome and neglects the Christian aspects of the eternal city.'[58]
The proportion Mommsen referred to is 'about ten to one: lines 47
to 105 are devoted to the description of pagan Rome, lines 106 to
111 to that of Christian Rome.'[59] But in fact lines 89 to 105 give both
Christian and pagan associations of sites, acting as a kind of transition from pagan to Christian Roman history; moreover, Mommsen
neglected the climax achieved by Petrarch when he ends the description of memories evoked by sites: the rhetorical emphasis is on the
end of the passage. In minimizing the fact that Petrarch had previously listed Christian as well as pagan sites and associations in his
topographical sketch of ancient Roman history, Mommsen over-
looked that, as for other humanists, antiquity for Petrarch consisted
of both classical pagan and primitive Christian history.

In reading this text, Mommsen seems to have been dazzled by a
Burckhardtian–Hegelian preconception of the Renaissance as the
birth of modern secular history in contrast to the more Christian
Middle Ages. It is significant how prominent citations of Burckhardt
and Hegelians such as Croce are in Mommsen's article.[60] Moreover,
Mommsen oversimplified the medieval historical outlook, following
Comparetti's erroneous reduction of the medieval view 'into two distinct periods—a long period of error and darkness, and then a period
of purification and truth, while midway between the two stood the
Cross of Calvary'.[61] It is no wonder that to Mommsen the beginning
of vi. 2 appeared inconsistent, with its denial of 'the intrinsic value

---

[58] Mommsen, 'Petrarch's Conception', 114–15.
[59] Ibid.   [60] Ibid., nn. 63, 65, 66, 67, 73, 84.
[61] Ibid., 124, citing D. Comparetti, *Vergil in the Middle Ages*, tr. E. Benecke
(London, 1908), 174.

of secular knowledge' and declaration 'that everything must be referred to eternal religious truth'.[62] In fact, the letter's structure and contents are perfectly harmonious: just as knowledge moves from secular arts to Christian truth, so history has moved from the pagan heroes to Christian saints and martyrs.

Petrarch's humanist successors, not to mention other writers not associated with the revival of letters, continued to focus on the Donation and its historical effects. For Salutati in *De seculo et religione*, the primitive church succeeded in establishing and extending Christianity for more than two hundred and thirty years from Nero to Diocletian, but then Constantine 'non dotavit sed ditavit ecclesiam') ('did not endow but enriched the church'). As a result, ecclesiastical princes were now rich, but much of Christendom had been lost to the Saracens, the Greek church no longer recognized the primacy of Rome and the Latin church was divided by schism. While poor, Christianity had grown; since the Donation, almost all had been lost.[63] Boccaccio, in *De casibus illustrium virorum*, declared that the poison of Constantine's gift had filled the church with greed,[64] while Giovanni de' Mussi, in his *Chronicon placentinum*, writing of the year 1376 declared that it would be better if the church renounced its worldly inheritance, on account of the 'innumerable wars, death and destruction' that had affected one or other part of

---

[62] Mommsen, 'Petrarch's Conception', 115.

[63] Salutati, *De seculo et religione*, ed. B. L. Ullman (Florence, 1957), ii. ix. 129–30: 'si respiciamus morem et institutionem ecclesie primitive, . . . appareat illos primos in renovatione temporum celestis civitatis et ecclesie catholice fundatores aut pauperes extitisse aut . . . paupertatem voluntariam elegisse. Hi fuerunt qui . . . adeo vite integritate . . . claruerunt quod in omnem terram exivit sonus eorum et in fines orbis terre verba eorum. Hi pauperes et humiles infinitis martiriis per ducentos triginta et amplius annos ab Nerone . . . usque in Dyoclitianum et Maximum imperatores . . . ecclesiam catholicam fundaverunt. Quam post Constantinum, qui non dotavit sed ditavit ecclesiam et superba sibi tradidit imperialis apicis ornamenta . . . hi nostri presules, quibus . . . primo pecunie, deinde imperio cupido crevit . . . illam civitatem gloriosam abomabilem reddiderunt . . . et bonos mores plene cuncta cum sua gloriosa rerum omnium opulentia destruxerunt.' This passage is translated by C. Trinkaus, *In Our Image and Likeness* (London, 1970), ii. 668. See also Baron, 'Franciscan poverty', 16.

[64] Giovanni Boccaccio, *De casibus illustrium virorum*, ed. P. G. Ricci and V. Zaccaria (Milan, 1983), ix. vii. 780: 'Attamen postquam virus largitionis magnifice Costantini Augusti, per sacram piorum congregationem dispersum, ceca cupidine corda cepit inficere, onus quod tanquam non omnibus humeris portabile, non nunquam ab aliquibus fugiebatur, vesana presumptione ambiri atque occupari et a non nullis minus sancte teneri ceptum est.' See Laehr II, 122.

Italy, 'from about the time of pope St Sylvester in AD 307'.[65] Particularly sharp was the historical focus of the conciliarist Jean Gerson, who contrasted the simple and poor *ecclesia primitiva* with the endowed post-Constantinian church. Although believing the Donation resulted in declining spirituality and increasing legalism, Gerson's historical perspective did not lead him to accept the views of Wyclif and Hus, whom he was at pains to refute. Times and circumstances had changed since the early church; the *ecclesia primitiva* had recruited from the poor and uneducated classes, while the post-Constantinian church looked to the rich and learned; endowment had enhanced the church's appeal to a wider population; these new circumstances required changes in the church's legal apparatus as reflected in the growth of canon law.[66]

What is interesting is that even after the Donation's authenticity had been called into doubt in the 1430s and 1440s, the reign of Constantine was still seen as a crucial turning point in history. After Nicholas of Cusa's exhaustive demonstration of the Donation's fraudulence before the Council of Basle in 1433, Leonardo Teronda of Verona composed two *Memoirs* in 1435 and 1436 which echo Cusa's critique: Teronda denied the Donation's actual authenticity, but nev-

---

[65] Giovanni de' Mussi, *Chronicon placentinum*, L. Muratori (ed.), *Rerum italicarum scriptores* (Milan, 1723–51), vol. xvi, col. 528: 'Et etiam melius esset et quantum ad Deum, et quantum ad Mundum, quod dicti Pastores dimitterent in totum dominia temporalia, propter innumerabiles guerras, et mortalitates, et destructiones, quae subsequutae sunt propter dicta moninia continue vel ab una parte Italiae, vel ab alia, a tempore, quo ipsi habuerunt, scilicet a tempore Sancti Sylvestri Papae circa, quod fuit anno Christi CCCVII.' See Laehr II, 128–9.

[66] L. B. Pascoe, 'Gerson and the Donation of Constantine: growth and development within the church', *Viator*, 5 (1974), 469–85; Gerson also cites the story about the voice and the poison (p. 476), which he declares by his day had become proverbial: 'ab omnibus recitatur' (see Döllinger, *Fables*, 169 n. 4). Indeed, not only had it become a commonplace among lawyers (see Maffei, *La donazione di Constantino*, 154–5, 181, 284), among heretics in France, (see Smalley, *Friars*, 196 n. 2 for a sermon of Durand de Saint-Pourçain)and especially in Germany (see pp. 58–60 above), but also in England: Ranulf Higden gave Gerald of Wales's version with the 'hostis antiquus' as the speaker (see *Polychronicon*, ed. J. R. Lumby, Rolls series (London, 1874), v. 130), drawing the conventional contrast before and after the Donation between a spiritual and a worldly church. The Dominican Robert Holcot also told the tale, making the same conventional contrast between the thriving, poor early church before the Donation and wealthy, secularized Christianity afterwards. Interestingly, his emphasis on the Donation as a cause of ecclesiastical legalism paralleled Gerson's view, but unlike Gerson, Holcot saw no positive changes as a result: see Smalley, *Friars*, 194–7, 336–7. The story, in Gerald's version, appears in Reginald Pecock's *Repressor*, who says that other chroniclers merely copied Gerald: see Döllinger, *Fables*, 169–70.

ertheless he saw the beginning of decline with Sylvester's acceptance of small gifts from Constantine; these were the seeds of the papacy's greed.[67] It is true that Valla denied that such a monumental change in the relations of church and state as implied by the 'Constitutum Constantini' could have taken place in the time of Pope Sylvester; nevertheless, he too clung to the idea that somehow the reign of Constantine marked a turning point. He accepted the historicity of the tract *De primitiva ecclesia*, spuriously attributed to Sylvester's predecessor Melchiades and saw the historical core of the false Donation in Constantine's gifts to him; as for Teronda, these apparently represented the seeds of the later secularization of the church.[68] Even more important was Valla's historical assessment of the actual Donation. He never specified when the 'constitutum' was forged, but, whenever this occurred, it represented the decisive moment in history: the Donation for Valla constituted a monumental historical change not because it was actually made by Constantine but because of its effects. The false Donation, he declared, was the *patrocinium* (the beginning of patronage), the *principium potentie papalis*; it led to *cupiditas*, the *radix . . . omnium malorum*,[69] and to *avaritia* and *imperandi vanitas*.[70] As for his medieval and early Renaissance predecessors who recognized the Donation's historicity, for Valla it still was the cause and foundation of the worldly and corrupted Roman church under the misguided leadership of a Boniface VIII or a Eugenius IV.[71]

[67] F. Gaeta (ed.), in app. to his *Lorenzo Valla* (Naples, 1955), 241–2: 'Fuerit autem bonus aut ideo non malus Silvester sanctus sentiens . . . Iacombum et Philippum apostolos . . . nihil amplius quam paternum hereditarium agellum . . . quem propriis colerent manibus possessiones habere confessos. Credideritque ideo Silvester sibi licere accipere quod apostolis habere licuisset . . . utinam autem peiora alii postea non fecissent. Nam quales, o Deum, clerici, quales successere pontifices egressi iam limites quoad mallent progredi licuit. Confortati sunt in terra quia de malo ad malum egressi sunt . . . Cum iam agros et predia possiderent, mox sibi regnum et imperium concupiverunt sibi iam divinis subactis legibus licentiam arrogantes occupandi omnia per omnes artes quesiverunt occasiones.' See Setz, *Lorenzo Vallas Schrift*, 25–32.

[68] W. Setz (ed.), *Monumenta Germaniae Historica: Quellen zur geistesgeschichte des Mittelalters* (Weimar, 1976), 93 ff.

[69] Ibid. 61, 80, 173.

[70] Ibid. 60. Valla's accusation that papal temporal power, grown from the seed of the Donation, was the cause of all Italy's troubles (ibid. p. 172) is almost identical to Marsilius's claim (*Defensor pacis* ed. R. Scholz), II. xxiii. 11, p. 449: 'Hec enim pestilencie Ytalici regni radix est et origo, ex qua cuncta scandala germinaverunt et proderunt.'

[71] For recent analyses of and further bibliography on Valla's text, see Setz, *Lorenzo Vallas Schrift*; Antonazzi, *Lorenzo Valla e la polemica*, 49–104, and S. Camporeale, 'Lorenzo Valla e il "De falso credita donatione" ', *Memorie domenicane*, NS, 19 (1988), 191–293.

It has been asserted that after Cusa, Valla, and Pecock, 'the role of the Donation of Constantine was played out,'[72] but such a simplistic view is hardly acceptable in view of recent research on the Donation's influence after Valla.[73] His attack inspired a succession of writers to champion the church's temporal role, and belief in the Donation continued until the eighteenth century, notwithstanding the *Declamatio*. What is particularly significant is that over and above the debate on the Donation, another series of polemics emerged directed against Valla's work. Although other authors had attacked the authenticity of the Donation, their works were hardly referred to, while in refutation of Valla special treatises were written.[74] Evidence has been advanced to show that the pontificate of Paul II represented 'a true and proper Constantinian revival',[75] and it was particularly at the end of the fifteenth century, during the pontificate of Alexander VI, with his hierocratic ideology of Christ's vicariate on earth, that the Donation became especially topical.[76] The Donation may indeed have been of relevance for the papal bull of 1493 granting jurisdiction over Columbus's discoveries, in that islands were said to pertain to the Roman church by virtue of the Donation.[77] More generally, it has been shown that the legend of Sylvester continued to exercise an influence on *communis opinio* in the late fifteenth and early sixteenth centuries; particularly interesting was the insertion of the Donation story into later fifteenth-

[72] Laehr II, 166.

[73] See Setz, *Lorenzo Vallas Schrift*, 90–194; and Antonazzi, *Lorenzo Valla e la polemica*, 105–14. C. L. Stinger, *The Renaissance in Rome* (Bloomington, 1985), 248–54, is a summary in English of some of the recent literature.

[74] See G. Antonazzi, 'Lorenzo Valla e la Donazione di Costantino nel secolo XV con un testo inedito di Antonio Cortesi', *Rivista della storia della chiesa in Italia*, 4 (1950), 205–6.

[75] R. Fubini, 'Papato e storiografia nel Quattrocento', *Studi medievali*, 3/18 (1977), 341–3.

[76] M. Miglio, 'L'umanista Pietro Edo e la polemica sulla Donazione di Costantino', *Bulletino dell'Istituto storico italiano per il medioevo*, 79 (1968), 175–8, 216, 220–9.

[77] Ibid. 228–9. On the Donation and papal sovereignty over islands, see Döllinger, *Fables*, 136–8, who cites the Bull of 1155 conferring dominion of Ireland to Henry II on the grounds that all Christian islands belonged to St Peter and the Roman Church. Although the Pope does not mention the Donation in his Bull, Hadrian IV's friend and adviser John of Salisbury takes credit for having the idea of using the Donation in this context; ibid. p. 138, quoting *Metalogicon*, 4. 42: 'Ad preces meas illustri regi Anglorum, Henrico II., concessit et dedit Hiberniam jure haereditario possidendam, sicut literae ipsius testantur in hodiernum diem. Nam omnes insulae, de jure antiquo, ex donatione Constantini, qui eam fundavit et dotavit, dicuntur ad Romanam Ecclesiam pertinere.'

century translations of the Golden Legend (an omission which Valla had used to attack the Donation in his *Declamatio*).[78]

Regardless of its authenticity, the Donation remained an admirably convenient *topos* to justify or condemn the church's temporal jurisdiction and power, and as in the Middle Ages, the Donation, not surprisingly, continued to be seen as a fundamental turning point in history. St Antoninus, Archbishop of Florence, regarded the Donation as a restitution of the church's rightful worldly position,[79] whereas Aeneas Sylvius Piccolomini in *Germania* contrasted the poverty of the *ecclesia primitiva* with the wealth of the modern church; for him the turning point was the reign of Constantine, whose donations laid the foundations of contemporary Christianity.[80] In reaction to the conspiracy of Stefano Porcari, the humanist Giuseppe Brivio wrote a Latin poem defending the Donation and asserting its historical significance,[81] while according

---

[78] Miglio, 'L'umanista Pietro Edo', 221–2, 229–32.

[79] *Chronicorum opus* (Lyon, 1586), tit. VIII, cap. ii, par. 8, vol. I, p. 577: 'non fuit simplex donatio: sed potius restitutio ecclesiae facta iuris sui, cum omnia sint de Christi dominio, cuius papa est vicarius in terris, caetera vero dimisit dominis temporalibus.' See Setz, *Lorenzo Vallas Schrift*, 108; Laehr II, 174, 178; Giorgio Falco, *La polemica sul medioevo* (Turin, 1933), 31. The passage is translated by J. B. Walker, *The 'Chronicles' of Saint Antoninus: A Study in Historiography* (Washington, 1933), 137; Walker discusses Antoninus and the Donation on 131–9, 147.

[80] Piccolomini, *Germania*, ed. A. Schmidt (Cologne, 1962), 101: 'Quodsi dixeris priores ecclesie nostre duces usque ad Constantini tempora inopes fuisse et modico contentos suis plebibus salubriter prefuisse, respondebimus eo tempore parvas fuisse christianorum plebes et latenter coluisse Christum. Nam Constantino primum imperante publice christianis ecclesie concesse sunt'; 102: 'Ex inopibus enim religionis nostre principium est'; 105: 'Quod nisi divina providentia Constantinus et qui postea secuti sunt cesares Romanam ditassent ecclesiam, profecto vix hodie fundamenta eius inveniremus . . . Habuimus ecclesiam primitivam inopem, sed tunc Christi nomen occultum fuit et non nisi in martyrio vocabatur. Postea vero laus fuit nominare Christum'; 111–12: 'At vero, cum inter turbines et adversa mundi succresceret ecclesia, ad hoc usque pervenit, ut non solum gentes, sed etiam principes Romani, qui totius orbis monarchiam tenebant, ad fidem Christi et baptismi sacramenta concurrerent, ex quibus vir religiosissimus Constantinus primus fidem veritatis potenter adeptus licentiam dedit per universum orbem suo degentibus imperio non solum fieri christianos, sed etiam fabricandi ecclesias et predia tribuendi constituit et donaria immensa ipse contulit . . . Quodsi non deberent ecclesie bonis abundare, male fecissent Constantinus imperator, qui Romanam tantopere ditavit, qui, ut Damasus ait ad Hieronymum, multa illi bona concessit. Nec dubium est, quin princeps ille Silvestro multa contulerit.' On Aeneas Sylvius's *Dialogus pro donatione Constantini*, ed. J. Cugnoni, *Opera inedita* (Rome, 1883), 234–99, see Setz, 101–7. It is interesting that, although in this latter work Aeneas denied the validity of the Donation, he nevertheless saw Constantine's endowment of the church as a turning point in ecclesiastical history.

[81] 'O gentem fatuam, subvertere velle quod annis | mille sit ecclesie donatum': cited by Miglio, 'L'umanista Pietro Edo', 171 n. 1.

to the fifteenth-century *Storia di San Silvestro*, the pope gained *regno del mondo* from the Donation, including direct rule over the empire and the Roman patrimony; in a curious adaptation of the legend of the heavenly voice, the text relates that following the Donation a cry in the air was heard throughout Rome: 'Today the holy spirit has descended over the church.'[82] In 1496, the humanist Pietro Edo maintained that the empire was recreated after the Donation before which it had been illegal,[83] while the philosopher Agostino Steuco, in 1547, revived yet again the time-honoured medieval *topos* of the Donation as restitution.[84] Nor was its defence moribund in the papal states during the later sixteenth century, when the censors of the humanist Carlo Sigonio (who, as an outstanding historical critic, of course had rejected its historicity) wanted to continue to see the Donation as a fundamental turning point: 'he [the censor] wished to have the papacy elevated since the moment of the donation of Constantine ... From the time of the donation the popes had had supreme authority in the Occident, exercised through the mediation of kings and emperors in most of Europe, but without intermediation in the lands of the Papal State in Italy.'[85]

On the other hand, critics of the Roman church often continued to regard the Donation as a negative turning point. The canonist Antonio Roselli's picture of the disastrous results of the Donation in his poem 'Quelli or veggiam che si dirieno in sorte' recalled the fiery

---

[82] *Storia di S. Silvestro: testo di lingua inedito, pubblicato secondo la lezione di un codice proprio da Michele Melga* (Naples, 1859), 52–3: 'E allora si gridò una voce per l'aire, e fu udita per tutta Roma, e disse così: è sparto el Spirito Santo nella chiesa di Dio.' See Laehr I, 180; Miglio, 'L'umanista Pietro Edo', 222 n. 1.

[83] Pietro Edo, *Antidotum*, cited by Setz, *Lorenzo Vallas Schrift*, 147, and now published by Antonazzi, *Lorenzo Valla e la polemica*, 234: 'Constantinus suscepta fide non tam est a Silvestro confirmatus imperator quam denuo creatus, quandoquidem nullum iure fuit imperium ante habitum'; on this passage, see also Miglio, 'Pietro Edo', 198. On this work in general, see Miglio; Setz, *Lorenzo Vallas Schrift*, 145–51.

[84] Steuco, *Contra Laurentium Vallam De falsa Donatione Constantini libri duo* (Lyon, 1547), 21–2: 'Nec ea Sylvestro, a Constantino sed Petro, et Christo donabantur ... Quocirca donatio Constantini, fuit restitutio ...' On this text, see T. Freudenberger, *Augustinus Steuchus aus Gubbio* (Münster, 1935), esp. 306–47; Setz, *Lorenzo Vallas Schrift*, 183–8; Laehr II, 177 ff. For this passage, see Setz, 187; Freudenberger, 345. See also Freudenberger, 282 ff. for Steucho's treatment of the Donation in his *Pro religione christiana*. For the medieval idea of the Donation as restitution, see 61, 73, above. For Cardinal Giovanni Antonio Sangiorgi's (d. 1509) view that the Donation was not a 'nova acquisitio' but 'potius restitutio' and 'recognitio debita', see Maffei, 322, n. 2. On Steuco's *Antivalla*, see also M. T. Graziosi, 'Agostino Steuco e il suo *Antivalla*', *L'umanesimo umbro: Atti del IX Convegno di studi umbri*, Gubbio, 23–25 September 1974 (publ. Perugia, 1977), 511–23.

[85] W. McCaig, *Carlo Sigonio* (Princeton, 1989), 278.

invectives of Dante and Petrarch; for him Constantine inaugurated a new age of ecclesiastical greed and corruption, whose ill effects even Saints Ambrose, Jerome, and Francis were unable to mitigate.[86] Exactly the same periodization of church history was explicitly adopted by Roselli's nephew, the lawyer Francesco Accolti, in his canzone 'Tenebrosa, Crudel, avara e lorda', written 'in detestazione e biasimo della Corte Romana e di tutti i preti': for Accolti, the Donation remained the decisive turning point.[87] From a slightly

[86] *Scritti letterari*, ed. A. Lumini, ser. 1 (Arezzo, 1884), 59–63: 'La mirabile vita santa e buona | Perseverò infin che fu confitto | Quel mendace sermon che ancor risuona, | Che Cesar Costantino l'amplo profitto | Desse del magno dono a santa madre | Pel qual n'ha oggi il ciel quasi in dispitto, | Perché da poi le istituzion leggiadre | Sempre son state strette dalla soga | De' temporali e loro opere ladre. | Diventata è la nova Sinagoga, | Madre di fornicar, Babilon magna | Che fra miseri avari cieca s'affoga. | Puttaneggia costei bramosa cagna | Oggi coi regi e l'idolatria face | Che disfè degli ebrei sì gran compagna. | Per por rimedio a tale ardente face | La divina giustizia Ambrogio santo | E me mandò a ricordar la pace | Già predicata nel suo primo canto | Con Girolamo pio, che, tal ricordi | Per far con noi, durò fatica tanta. | Ma poco valse, che (e') più vi son sordi | E sutrati da dolci ben terreni | Nei qual lassando Iddio son vissi ingordi. | Né c'è valuto emendati sereni | Per quel che tutto arse de caritate | Che ancor Dio fe' per spenger tal veleni. | Né del consorte suo pien di pietade | Tutto divin serafico Francesco, | Che volson rinnovar la prima etate. | Che quasi ciascun oggi lieto e fresco, | Clerica non per Dio né per virtute, | Ma per oro e per argento aver grand'esco.' This poem is attributed in one manuscript to Francesco Accolti, but F. Flamini, *La lirica toscana del Rinascimento* (Pisa, 1891), 724–5 n. 6, shows on the basis of manuscript evidence that the author was Roselli. G. Mancini, *Vita di Lorenzo Valla* (Florence, 1891), 157 n. 1 and following him, Laehr II, 128 n. 1, attribute the poem to Accolti. On Roselli and the Donation, see also now J. H. Burns, 'The "Monarchia" of Antonio Roselli (1380–1466): Text, Context and Controversy', *Monumenta iuris canonici*, ser. 6/9 (1992), 344–5.

[87] 'Le rime di Francesco Accolti d'Arezzo', ed. M. Messina, *Giornale storico della letteratura italiana*, 122 (1955), 211–15: 'El successor del Sacerdote eterno, | che la nova famiglia in terra resse, | come la gloria sua mostra nel cielo, | poi che le chiavi in man gli fur concesse | del divin ministerio e del governo | che volse il cieco mondo a miglior telo, | prigion, morte angosciosa, fame e gelo, | con que' che'eran disposti a simil sorte, | per dar conforto al suo popol, sostenne; | onde le pecorelle bene scorte | l'inveterato error, l'antico velo | rupper, che prima'l mondo cieco tenne, | infin che'l secol venne | sotto il giogo cristian quasi del tutto, | poscia che Costantino a Dio si volse. | Da' veraci pastor sì dolce frutto | la santa fede colse, | non da vostro tesoro o viver brutto. | Così, senza temer, diritta corse | per virtù de' rettor fra gran tempeste, | la sacrosanta inviolabil barca; | né per cose terrene al Ciel moleste, | povera e nuda, mai la mente torse | dal glorioso suo sommo Monarca. | Oh, sinagoga ria! come se' carca | di miseria trista, e del tuo bene | ingratissima, cieca e sconoscente. | Già gli usati flagelli e l'aspre pene | non fur tolti da te per farti un'arca | anzi un inferno di perduta gente, | ma perché, pienamente, | si rivolgesse il mondo al sacro Lume, | e tu fossi ver Dio levata in pace. | Segui le vane pompe e'l tuo gran sume | infin che l'ira tace | che si nutrica nel divin volume. | Per te ogni virtù vie più si sprezza | che per la disperata iniqua gregge, | che'l furor di Satan tormenta e preme. | Qual barbarica gente mai si legge, | vota più di costume e peggio avvezza, | aver sì spento di virtute'l seme? | Miser chi s'argomenta o prende speme | del suo

different perspective, Poggio Bracciolini, writing in the mid-1450s, saw Constantine as a plague on the empire, having deserted Rome as a stepmother and moved to Thrace,[88] while Marsilio Ficino regarded 'the domination and administration of earthly affairs attached to the popes as accidental, not in their capacity as vicars of God but inasmuch as they were heirs of Constantine Caesar.'[89] At the beginning of the sixteenth century the humanist Giles of Viterbo viewed the second age of church history—the first of eight periods of progressive decline—as beginning when the pious Constantine gave riches to the church, which thereby abandoned the eremitic life.[90] Ariosto also accepted the Donation's authenticity,[91] reiterating the conventional historical contrast between the pre-Constantinian 'sweet scent' and the post-Sylvestran 'stench'.[92] Protestant reformers were eager to follow Valla's lead in regarding the forgery as the basis for the disastrous and illicit temporal rule of the papacy in the Middle Ages: 'The Donation of Constantine therefore is a great lie', wrote Luther, 'by which the pope usurped for himself half of the Roman empire.'[93] But sixteenth-century Italians did not always

ben'operar, se mai si fida | nella tua pravità, maligna setta, | perché l'empia tua gola altro non grida | che posseder tesoro, e tristo geme | chi tra voi dignità sanz'oro aspetta. | La santa Sposa, eletta | a trionfar nel Ciel beata e bella, | per ricchezze terrene in voi si strazia | si che'l Verbo divin par che divella | tanto da te sua grazia, | quanto tu pe'l mal far gli se' ribella.'

[88] Bracciolini, *De miseria humanae conditionis*, in *Opera* (Strasburg, 1513), fo. 47ᵛ. See Laehr II, 121 n. 4; E. Walser, *Poggius Florentinus* (Leipzig, 1914), 306 n. 2.

[89] Ficino, *De christiana religione*, 28, in *Opera omnia* (Basel, 1561–76), i. 50: 'Tale fuit Iesu Nazareni regnum, quale a Prophetis Christo promittitur, ideo ipse ait: regnum meum non est huius mundi. Pontificibusque eius successoribus in spiritualibus rebus proprie reliquit imperium, nec usque ad mundi finem substantialis, et praecipua Pontificum in quantum Pontifices sunt, et Christi vicarii, iurisdictio ulterius se extendit. Rerum vero terrenarum dominatio et administratio pontificibus accessoria est, tanquam accidens, non in quantum vicarii Dei, sed in quantum Constantini Caesaris sunt Haeredes. Haec autem dicta sunt, non ut authoritatem rerum temporalium Pontifici adimamus, habet enim re vera, quamvis tamquam accidens quoddam, sine quo trecentos annos olim Pontifex verus fuit, atque esse potest, sed ut tela Iudaeorum hac veritate facilius devitemus.'

[90] J. W. O'Malley, *Giles of Viterbo on Church and Reform* (Leiden, 1968), 105–7, 130, 145.

[91] Ariosto, *Orlando furioso*, XVII. 78 (ed. E. Bigi (Milan, 1982), i. 707): 'là [sc. in Constantinople] le richezze sono, | che vi portò da Roma Constantino: | portonne il meglio, e fe' del resto dono.'

[92] Ibid. XXXIV. 80 (ed. Bigi, ii. 1456): 'Di varii fiori ad un gran monte passa, | ch'ebbe gia buono odore, or putia forte. | Questo era il dono (se però dir lece) | che Constantino al buon Silvestro fece.'

[93] Luther, *Werke. Kritische Gesamtausgabe. Tischreden* (Weimar, 1919), v. 456 n. 6043: 'Magnum igitur mendacium est donatio Constantini, qua papa dimidium de

lag behind northerners in anticlericalism: like Luther, Francesco Guicciardini denied the historical truth of the Donation but still saw the reign of Constantine as the point of change from sanctity, spirituality, and poverty to secularism and wealth.[94] A kind of compromise between the two extreme interpretations of the Donation was offered by Pierfrancesco Giambullari in his *Istoria dell'Europa*, left incomplete on his death in 1555; he saw the Donation as a double-edged change: from the religious point of view 'such an alteration was the work of the Holy Spirit, leaving Rome to Christ in the person of his vicar Sylvester', but speaking 'as a worldly historian' it was a disaster, especially for Italy.[95]

For all these writers the Donation remained a live issue, serving to make the reign of Constantine a historical dividing line; although not all saw the conversion to Christianity as crucial,[96] there were

imperio Roman sibi arrogat. Etiamsi factum esset, tamen non fuisset in potestate imperatoris, neque convenit papae iuxta dictum Christi: Vos autem non sic' [Luke, 22, 26]. See 675 n. 6562 for an almost identical statement. See Setz, *Lorenzo Vallas Schrift*, 168–9.

[94] F. Guicciardini, *Storia d'Italia*, ed. C. Panigada (Bari, 1929), i. 371 ff.

[95] P. Giambullari, *Istoria dell'Europa* (Livorno, 1831), 1–3: 'La veneranda maestà dello imperio . . . si mantenne in somma grandezza, ed in reverenzia dello universo sino a tanto che Costantino, di che sempre dolere si debbe la bella Italia (parlo come istorico mondano, perchè considerando le grazie che ebbe Costantino, fu opera dello Spirito Santo tale mutazione, con lasciar Roma a Cristo nel suo Vicario Silvestro) . . . abbandonò la universal regina del mondo, e . . . trasferì la sedia in Bisanzio ed agli ultimi confini della Grecia se ne portò tutto quello, che la già gloriosa Roma, con tanta virtù, e con si onorate fatiche, lungamente aveva acquistato. Il che di quanto momento fusse alla rovina della Occidente assai chiaro ce lo dimostrano i tanti diluvj delle barbare nazioni, che non solamente inondarono nella Europa, ma e nella Affrica ancora, con sommo danno dello universo, e massimamente della imperio stesso romano. Il quale . . . venne finalmente a una debolezza tale e sì fatta, che la poverella Italia a tanti Barbari lasciata in preda, non perdè solamente la gloria e la onoratissima fama sua, ma la virtuosa semenza ancora di quegli animi chiari ed illustri, che l'avevano fatta sì grande.'

[96] Bruni, *Historiae florentini populi*, 15. For Biglia, see D. Webb, 'The Decline and Fall of Eastern Christianity', *Bulletin of the Institute of Historical Research*, 49 (1975), 207. Such a division may be suggested in Andrea da Barberino's *I reali di Francia*, which begins with Constantine and Sylvester: see P. Grendler, 'Chivalric Romances in the Italian Renaissance,' *Studies in Medieval and Renaissance History*, 10 (1988), 68. For Bernardo Giustiniani, see P. Labalme, *Bernardo Giustiniani* (Rome, 1969), 275. Cortesi, *De hominibus doctis*, 108. Sabellico, *De latinae linguae reparatione*, 323: 'Ademerat Romanae urbi multum splendoris et dignitatis imperii sedes Byzantium translata.' Machiavelli *Istorie fiorentine*, I. i. 72. For Melanchton, see Falco, *La polemica*, 51–3. Sigonio, *De occidentali imperio* (Bologna, 1578), 3–4, 109. This became the dividing line between antiquity and the Middle Ages for Christoph Keller (Cellarius), 'the first historian to make practical use of the division of history into three periods

several Renaissance authors for whom, as for Petrarch, it was the Christianization of Rome which marked a cultural turning point, signalling the end of antiquity and which was connected with an eventual revival of the arts. In the preface to his *Genealogie deorum gentilium*, Boccaccio considered why so many ancient texts dealing with the subject had been destroyed: 'with the growing power of the most glorious name of Christ, and with his splendid teaching of sincere truth removing the shadows of deadly error and especially paganism; and also with the declining glory of the Greeks for some time, while the champions of Christ were clamouring against the unfortunate [previous] religion and driving it into destruction, there is no doubt but they destroyed at the same time many books laden with this material.'[97] Filippo Villani also attributed the decline of poetry to the rise of Christianity, 'which began to abhor the figments of poetic imagination as a pernicious and a vain thing.'[98] Similarly Albrecht Dürer deplored the loss of the 'noble books . . . of the old pagan painters and sculptors', suggesting that they 'were misunderstood and destroyed as idolatrous in the early days of the church'.[99]

. . . as a principle of organization. . . . To him must be accorded the credit for introducing this formula into the system of academic instruction' (Ferguson, *Renaissance in Historical Thought*, 75–7); see also Falco, *La polemica*, 90; A. Pertusi, *Storiografia umanistica e mondo bizantino* (Palermo, 1967), 113–14.

[97] Boccaccio, *Genealogie deorum gentilium libri*, ed. V. Romano (Bari, 1951), i. 6: 'Preterea invalescente gloriossimo christi nomine eiusque doctrina sincere veritatis perlucida letiferi erroris et potissime gentilitii tenebras amovente, ac etiam iam diu Grecorum declinante fulgore, clamantibus in infaustam religionem Christi nuntiis ac eam in exterminium pellentibus, nulli dubitandum est quin secum multos deleverint libros huius materiei refertissimos.' See Buddensieg, 'Gregory the Great', 49.

[98] Filippo Villani, *De vita et moribus Dantis Poetae comici insignis*, in Solerti (ed.), *Le vite*, 82: 'Post Claudianum, quem fere poetarum illustrium ultimum antiqua tempora protulerunt, Caesarum pusillanimitate et avaritia omnis pene consenuit poesis eo etiam fortasse quod ars non esset in pretio, cum fides catholica coepisset figmenta poetarum, ut rem pernitiosam et vanissimam, abhorrere. Ea igitur iacente sine cultu, sine decore, vir maximus Dantes Allegherii, quasi ex abisso tenebrarum erutam evocavit in lucem, dataque manu prostratam erexit in pedes . . .' See also Domenico di Bandino, ibid. 92: 'Reversus [Dante] ad poetica post Anticlaudianum, quem poetarum ultimum antiqua tempora protulerunt, iam perditam poesim ad lucem erexit Fidei.' 'Anticlaudianum' should probably be emended to 'Claudianum'. Villani's is the earlier text and provided the source for Bandini's life: see A. F. Messera, 'Le più antiche biografie del Boccaccio', *Zeitschrift für romische Philologie*, 27 (1903), 299 ff., 323. I find Eugenio Garin's attempt to distinguish between the two texts oversubtle and unconvincing: see his 'Dante nel Rinascimento', in id., *L'età nuova* (Naples, 1969), 183–4.

[99] Albrecht Dürer, *Treatise on Painting*, in E. G. Holt, *A Documentary History of Art* (Garden City, NY, 1957), i. 314–15, and in Buddensieg, 'Gregory the Great', 57.

Machiavelli blamed the early 'heads of the Christian religion', declaring 'with what stubbornness they persecuted all ancient memories, burning the works of poets and historians and wrecking everything else which would preserve any sign of antiquity.'[100] One speaker in Erasmus's dialogue *Antibarbari* 'attempted to prove that the death of letters was to be laid at the door of the Christian religion', arguing, among other things, 'now that Christianity had spread everywhere and the use of these books [of pre-Christian writers] was not greatly needed for the confutation of opponents, they were inclined to think that, the superstition of the Jews and pagans having been destroyed, their literature and language should also be abolished.'[101] Giovambattista Gelli declared that, in addition to the barbarian invasions, 'not inconsiderable damage was also added by the foolish opinion of some popes living at the time, who, guided by a vain superstition and not by the true love of the Christian religion, sought themselves to remove the statues and other works of the pagans'.[102] Indeed according to Montaigne, 'It is certain that in those early times when our religion began to gain authority with the laws, zeal armed many believers against every sort of pagan books, thus causing men of letters to suffer an extraordinary loss. I consider that this excess did more harm to letters than all the bonfires of the barbarians.'[103]

More explicitly reminiscent of the Donation is the opening of Lorenzo Ghiberti's *Second Commentary*:

The Christian faith was victorious in the time of Emperor Constantine and Pope Sylvester. Idolatry was persecuted in such a way that all the statues and pictures of such nobility, antiquity and perfection were destroyed and

[100] Machiavelli, *Discorsi*, ed. S. Bertelli (Milan, 1960), II. v. 292: 'E chi legge i modi tenuti da San Gregorio e dagli altri capi della religione cristiana, vedrà con quanta ostinazione e' perseguitarono tutte le memorie antiche, ardendo le opere de' poeti e degli istorici, ruinando le imagini e guastando ogni altra cosa che rendesse alcun segno della antichità.' See also ibid. II. ii. 282–3; *Istorie fiorentine*, I. v. 82.

[101] Erasmus, *Antibarbarorum liber*, tr. M. M. Phillips, in *Collected Works of Erasmus*, xxiii (Toronto, 1978), Literary and Educational Writings, ed. C. R. Thompson, i. 24–5. This particular passage on the specific effect of Christianity's triumph on the decline of pagan letters is not found in the first version of the text: see Erasmus, *Opera omnia* (Amsterdam, 1969), I. i. 46–7.

[102] G. Mancini (ed.), 'Vite d'artisti di Giovanni Battista Gelli', *Archivio storico italiano*, 4/17 (1896), 35: 'Aggiunse non poco danno . . . la stolta oppinione di alcuni pontefici, che furono in que' tempi, che, guidati da una vana superstizione et non da il vero amore della cristiana religione . . . cercarono ancora eglino di levare via le statue et le altre opere dei gentili.' See Buddensieg, 'Gregory the Great', 58–9, n. 42.

[103] Montaigne, *Essai*, tr. D. R. Frame, *The Complete Essays of Montaigne* (Stanford, Calif., 1958), II. xix. 506.

broken to pieces. And with the statues and pictures, the theoretical writings, the commentaries, the drawing and the rules for teaching such eminent and noble arts were destroyed. In order to abolish every ancient custom of idolatry it was decreed that all the temples should be white. At this time the most severe penalty was ordered for anyone who made any statue or picture. Thus ended the art of sculpture and painting and all the teaching that had been done about it. Art was ended and the temples remained white for about six hundred years.[104]

Vasari echoed this view when he blamed Christianity for the decline of ancient art, and he too explicitly saw in the time of Constantine and Sylvester the end of antiquity: 'ancient works of art of antiquity are those which were produced in Corinth, Athens, Rome, and other famous cities, before the time of Constantine . . . old works of art are those which were produced from the time of St Sylvester.'[105] Just as explicit in linking the destruction of the antique heritage to the rise of Christianity under Constantine was Bernardo Gamucci, who wrote in 1565: 'Beginning with Saint Sylvester, in order to remove the grandeur of such buildings from the eyes of the simple flock of pilgrims, who, coming to Rome inspired by holy feelings, were stupefied in admiration and sometimes were induced to scandalous behaviour, these most holy men wanted to destroy their impact and convert the rest from false idolatrous practice to the true worship of our catholic faith.'[106]

---

[104] *Lorenzo Ghibertis Denkwürdigkeiten (I Commentarii)*, ed. J. von Schlosser (Berlin, 1912), i. 35: 'Adunche al tempo di Constantino imperadore et di Silvestro papa sormonto su la fede christiana. Ebbe la ydolatria grandissima persecutione in modo tale, tutte le statue et le picture furon disfatte et lacerate di tanta nobiltà et anticha et perfetta dignità et così si consumaron colle statue et picture et vilumi et comentarij et liniamenti et regole davano amaestramento a tanta et egregia et gentile arte. Et poi levare via ogni anticho costume di ydolatria constituirono i templi tutti essere bianchi. In questo tempo ordinorono grandissima pena a chi facesse alcuna statua o alcuna pictura et cosi finì l'arte statuaria et la pictura et ogni doctrina che in essa fosse fatta. Finita che fu l'arte stettero e templi bianchi circa d'anni 600.' Tr. Holt, *Documentary History of Art*, i. 152–3.

[105] G. Vasari, *Le vite*, ed. P. Barocchi and R. Bettarini (Florence, 1967), ii. 29: 'antiche furono le cose, innanzi a Costantino, di Corinto, d'Atene e di Roma e d'altre famosissime città, fatte fino a sotto Nerone, ai Vespasiani, Traiano, Adriano et Antonino, perciò che l'altre si chiamano vec[c]chie che da S. Salvestro in qua furono poste in opera . . .' For the role of triumphant Christianity in destroying ancient art, see ibid. 19–20, tr. G. Bull (London, 1965), 37, 45–6.

[106] Gamucci, *Le antichità della Città di Roma* (Venice, 1565), cited by Buddensieg, 'Gregory the Great', 60: 'cominciando da santo Silvestro, quei santissimi huomini per levar la grandezza di così fatti edificij dinanzi a gli occhi a quelle semplici pecorelle, che venendo a Roma mosse da santo affetto, con stupore le ammiravano, e talvolta generavano scandolo in loro, volsero parte ruinarle, et il restante ridurre dalla falsa idolatria a' veri sacrificij della nostra catholica fede.'

But Francesco Maria Molza (d. 1543) went further, linking the triumph of Christianity under Constantine not only with barbarous iconoclasm but with the decline of language and civilization in general.[107] A fully-articulated scheme of decline and rebirth, with the reign of Constantine cited explicitly as the *coup de grâce* to the ancient world, was given by Lefevre d'Etaples:

Why may we not aspire to see our age restored to the likeness of the primitive church, when Christ received a purer veneration, and the splendour of his name shone forth more widely? ... As the light of the Gospel returns, may He who is blessed above all grant also to us this increase of faith, this purity of worship: as the light of the Gospel returns, I say, which at this time begins to shine again. By this divine light many have been so greatly illuminated that, not to speak of other benefits, from the time of Constantine, when the primitive Church, which had little by little declined came to an end, there has not been greater knowledge of languages, more extensive discovery of new lands, of wider diffusion of the name of Christ in the more distant parts of the earth than in these times.[108]

---

[107] *Orazione di M. Francesco Maria Molza contro Lorenzino de' Medici recata dal latino in italiano da Giulio Bernardino Tomitano Accademico fiorentino* (Treviso, 1809), 11–12: 'in que' primi tempi, ne' quali per benefizio di Costantino dai nascondigli uscita questa stessa nostra Religione cominciò a comparire alla luce, da ppoichè pigliato ebbe piede intieramente, in quella stagione vi furono più uomini di tal maniera animosi, che non si confidavano di dover abbastanza piacere a loro concittadini che s'erano dati a Cristo, se non avessero dato bruttamente il guasto a' monumenti de' loro antenati, dalle massime de' quali erano apertamente discordi: quinci si videro rubati gli ornamenti della Città, quinci i sacri, e profani edifizi col foco, e col ferro disfatti, sviati gli Acquidotti, profanati i Templi, quinci i laqueati tetti, quinci i marmi, quinci i bronzi spezzati e consunti: di maniera che non maggior danneggiamento alla Repubblica le irruzion de' barbari, a mio avviso abbiano apportato, che lo spirito di partito, e la dissomiglianza delle nostre opinioni, e de' nostri riti religiosi: al che s'aggiunga la crudeltà, ed il furore de' Principi, sotto il di cui dominio gli uomini di cristiano nome con vari tormenti erano stati lacerati. Il perchè essi pensavansi di perseguir le ingiurie, e vendicarsi di molto, se ne avessero in qualche modo oscurata la rimembranza: sembrami eziandio che a questa pazzia desse qualche luogo lo stimar eglino giovar gran fatto e ad avvalorare le forze della nuova Religione, e ad indebolire le antiche cerimonie, che convinta l'antica Setta, ed in tutte le guise sconciamente sembrasse di leggiata. In quale densa caligine poi di mente uomini di goffo e stupido ingegno erano avvolti, quanto dell'arti squisite degli antichi erano lungi, Dei immortali! nella lingua s'era insinuata la barbarie, tutta la purezza del dire offuscata vergognosamente era andata in disuso: trucidata la Repubblica erano di squallidezza ricoperte tutte le cose, e spento quasi il nome Romano, erano già perite.'

[108] *The Prefatory Epistles of Jacques Lefèvre d'Etaples and Related Texts*, ed. Eugene F. Rice, Jr. (New York, 1972), 427–8 (prefatory *epistle* to his *Commentaries on the Four Gospels*, 1522): 'Et quidni saecula nostra ad primigeniae illius ecclesiae effigiem redigi optaremus, cum tunc et purius Christus coleretur et nomen eius latius effulgeret ... Quam fidei amplitudinem, quem puritatis cultum redeunte evangelii luce nobis quoque annuat ille qui est super omnia benedictus. Redeunte inquam evangelii

The historical view of the Donation of Constantine—with its image of decline and its vision of eventual renewal—seems therefore to have been one source of the humanists' concept of the Renaissance.[109] This was not just an intellectual *topos* but a genuine programme of revival. If Gombrich is right to see the Renaissance as a movement,[110] then that movement was not fully born until its adherents had a programme to follow. It is important here to realize that proto-Renaissance and proto-humanist activities—antiquarianism, classicized rhetoric and grammar, copying of antique models, and so on—all of which of course existed before the fourteenth century, did not of themselves add up to a fully-fledged manifesto. Weiss has demonstrated 'that Italian humanism was already in existence before Petrarch and Boccaccio were born', suggesting 'that this early humanism was not the result . . . of a conscious desire for a "renovatio studiorum" and hopes of a new golden age, but that it was a spontaneous and natural development of classical studies as pursued during the later middle ages.'[111] Weiss may have been unaware that

luce quae sese tandem mundo rursum hac tempestate insinuat, qua plerique divina luce illustrati sunt, adeo ut praeter alia multa a tempore Constantini, quo primitiva illa quae paulatim declinabat desiit ecclesia, non fuerit maior linguarum cognitio, non maior orbis defectio, non ad longinquiora terrarum spatia quam temporibus istis nominis Christi propagatio', tr. in J. B. Ross and M. M. McLaughlin (eds.), *The Portable Renaissance Reader* (New York, 1953), 85–6.

[109] Konrad Burdach groped his way towards articulating a connection between the concept of the Renaissance and the Donation (*Cola und die Wandlung*, 213–33), but Burckhardt, with his notoriously anachronistic emphasis on Italian nationalism in the Renaissance, led him astray. Thus, according to Burdach the Donation and the Renaissance were linked by an Italian patriotic strand leading from Boniface VIII's political purification of Rome, through Rienzo, and up to the iconography of the 'Sala di Costantino' in the Vatican (see esp. 218); however, this tends to overlook the influence of the negative views of Constantine's legacy on the emerging concept of the Renaissance. Burdach, with his tendency to view the Renaissance as emanating from medieval eschatology and spiritual revival, was aware of the vast amount of condemnation which Constantine had received in the Middle Ages and early Renaissance, but he saw this as ultimately producing a shift from the cult of Constantine to the cult of Augustus, which he felt was characteristic of the Renaissance; this tendency was allegedly supported by the increasingly influential papal doctrine of *restitutio* which itself lessened the historical role of Constantine, since *de iure* the empire always had belonged to Peter's successors (see esp. 229–33). It became particularly clear after the publication of Burdach's work that the idea of *restitutio* was equally powerful to the Middle Ages, but it should also be noted that Burdach was contradicting himself, asserting the continued influence of Constantine in the Renaissance, on the one hand, and denying it, on the other. The fact is that the Donation remained a powerful force until the end of the 16th c., both for its supporters and its critics.

[110] E. H. Gombrich, *In Search of Cultural History* (Oxford, 1969), 35–8.

[111] R. Weiss, 'The Dawn of Humanism in Italy,' *Bulletin of the Institute of Historical Research*, 42 (1969), 14.

pre-humanist classicism was accompanied by praise for the revival of letters after a long period of decay, anticipating the claims of humanism in full bloom. Thus, before Petrarch, Frate Guido of Pisa had declared of Dante: 'By this poet, dead poetry was resuscitated . . . he revived poetic knowledge and made the ancient poets live again in our minds.'[112] Frate Guido's encomium of Dante was part of a long and copious rhetorical tradition whereby authors were praised by comparing them to the ancients;[113] indeed, one particular *topos* within this tradition was to praise writers because they had revived poetry or eloquence. Thus Augustine had declared that Ambrose had initiated in his age a rebirth of eloquence and knowledge, hitherto moribund.[114] Similarly, Milo Crispinus emphasized learning's debt to Lanfranc, 'whom latinity, having been revived by him to its ancient state of knowledge, recognized as its supreme master with due love and honour.'[115] But more was needed for such comments as Frate Guido's to stand out from the mass of medieval formulaic panegyric and become the effective rallying cry for a new intellectual movement.

This further dimension in the emergence of the programme for the Renaissance was a sharper and wider historical perspective, a profound sense of belonging to a new time: in Mommsen's words, 'the whole idea of the Italian "rinascita" is inseparably connected with

---

[112] In an unedited poem from the third decade of the fourteenth century, Frate Guido of Pisa gave his 'capitoli dichiarativi' to the *Inferno* together with a continual Latin gloss: 'l'alta Comedia | ch'è fabricata dal grande doctor | per cu' vive la morta poesia.' To these verses correspond the following gloss: 'Per istum enim poetam resuscitata est mortua poesis. Nam oblivioni iam tradita erat ipsa scientia et summi philosophi qui studuerunt vel floruerunt in ea. Et ad hoc demonstrandum dicit ipse auctor in primo cantu primae canticae ubi loquitur de Vergilio: *chi per lungo silenzio parea fioco.* Ipse vero poeticam scientiam suscitavit et antiquos poetas in mentibus nostris reminiscere fecit.' Cited by Bacci, *La critica letteraria,* 162–3; see Kristeller, *Renaissance Thought,* 273.

[113] E. R. Curtius, *European Literature and the Latin Middle Ages,* tr. W. R. Trask (New York, 1953), esp. 162 ff.; R. Black, *Benedetto Accolti and the Florentine Renaissance* (Cambridge, 1985), 194 ff.

[114] Augustine, *Soliloquiorum libri duo,* II. xiv. 26: 'Nam et multos [sc. libros] ante nostram aetatem scriptos esse arbitror, quos non legimus: et nunc, ut nihil quod nescimus opinemur, manifestum habemus, et carmine . . . et soluta oratione; et ab iis viris quorum nec scripta latere nos possunt, et eorum ingenia talia novimus, ut nos in eorum litteris quod volumus, inventuros desperare non possimus: praesertim cum hic ante oculos nostros sit ille [sc. Ambrosius], in quo ipsam eloquentiam quam mortuam dolebamus, perfectam revixisse cognovimus.' See Kristeller, *Renaissance Thought,* 273.

[115] Cited ibid. from *Patrilogia latina,* 150, 29, *Vita Beati Lanfranci,* by Milo Crispinus.

the notion of the preceding era as an age of obscurity. The people living in that "renascence" thought of it as a time of revolution. They wanted to break away from the medieval past and all its traditions and they were convinced that they had effected such a break.' He went on to suggest that this 'notion of belonging to a new time . . . was peculiar to the Italian Renaissance and it found its expression in the condemnation of the medieval epoch as an era of "darkness".'[116] Mommsen here placed particular emphasis on the shift from a religious historical view in the Middle Ages to a secular perspective in the Renaissance, on a reversal of the old metaphor of the dark ages which had contrasted pagan obscurity with Christian light.

However, the opposite vision of a transition from light to darkness in the passage from antiquity to the following period was a fully developed historical perspective throughout the Middle Ages. It is now clear that this historical self-consciousness, this vision of a historical break between antiquity and subsequent ages, was not a distinctive feature of the Italian Renaissance. The ecclesiological scheme, as implicit in the Donation of Constantine and the idea of the primitive church, was a fully mature, widely accepted and deeply felt manifesto of revival during the Middle Ages. Mommsen was right to stress Petrarch's central role in the development of the Renaissance vision of history, but he was hasty to claim Petrarch as 'the father of the concept or attitude which regards the Middle Ages as the "Dark Ages" '.[117] In fact, as early as 1330 Frate Guido da Pisa had written of Dante: 'He himself brought dead poetry back from the shadows to light.'[118] Moreover, Mommsen was wrong to argue that 'by passing over the traditional marks either of the foundation of the Empire or of the birth of Christ Petrarch introduced a new chronological demarcation in history . . . distinguished from older medieval . . . ones by the name "humanistic", for it formed the underlying principle of most of the historical works written by Italian humanists.'[119] Petrarch's contribution was not so much to break with previous historical perspectives as to adapt and broaden medieval views. It was Petrarch's great achievement to join together several hitherto separate strands of historical thinking—

---

[116] Mommsen, 'Petrarch's Conception', 129. [117] Ibid. 129.
[118] Guido da Pisa, *Expositiones et glose super Comediam Dantis*, ed. V. Cioffari (Albany, NY, 1974), 4: 'Ipse enim mortuam poesiam de tenebris reduxit ad lucem.' See Kristeller, *Renaissance Thought*, 273.
[119] Mommsen, 'Petrarch's Conception' 125.

proto-humanist classicism accompanied by encomia for the revival of letters, laments for the destruction of pagan Rome by Christian zealots, and, above all, calls for Christian and Roman renewal—to create a compelling and effective programme for the Renaissance. It was not so much a change from a religious to a secular interpretation of history, but rather the broadening of a religious vision to encompass all types of achievement, including secular culture.

3. The Vocabulary of Renaissance Republicanism: A Cultural *longue-durée*?

QUENTIN SKINNER

THIS paper seeks critically to examine one of the ways in which the concept of the Renaissance has been used to refer not merely to a historical period but to a category of thought.[1]

Within the history of moral and political thought, the period conventionally treated as central to the Renaissance—that is, quattrocento Italy—has often been seen as an era of decisive intellectual change. For example, Hans Baron, and more recently John Pocock, have both found in this period a new vocabulary of politics, one centred on the figure of the *civis* and on his capacity to secure his *libertas* by way of participating in a *res publica*, an elective system of republican government.[2]

Of late this thesis has been criticized, I think justly, by scholars such as Nicolai Rubinstein,[3] for failing to take account of the extent to which a similar vocabulary had already been put into circulation with the recovery and dissemination of Aristotle's moral and political theory in Latin by the time of the early trecento. But what I want to argue in this paper is that we need to reckon with an even longer *durée*, one that links the duecento with the cinquecento in Italy, and thereby casts what seems to me decisive doubt on the usefulness of the Renaissance as a heuristic category at least for the historian of moral and political thought.

---

[1] A slightly different version of the paper I delivered at the Conference was subsequently published in G. Bock, Q. Skinner and M. Viroli (eds.), *Machiavelli and Republicanism* (Cambridge, 1990), 121–41. I am grateful to the Cambridge University Press for permission to republish it here.

[2] See J. G. A. Pocock, *The Machiavellian Moment* (Princeton, 1975), ch. 3; H. Baron, *The Crisis of the Early Italian Renaissance* (Princeton, 1966), 29, 49, 121.

[3] N. Rubinstein, 'Political Theories in the Renaissance', in A. Chastel (ed.), *The Renaissance: Essays in Interpretation* (London, 1982), 153.

The articulation of an ideology of self-governing republicanism can in fact be traced to a period scarcely later than the emergence of the communes themselves. The writers of this pre-humanist era had virtually no access to Greek philosophy, but they were able to draw on a number of Roman moralists and historians who had written with scarcely less eloquence about the ideals of freedom and citizenship. By basing themselves on these authorities—and in particular on Sallust and Cicero—I want to show that they were able to construct a full-scale defence of the special virtues of republican rule.

To Cicero they were especially indebted for his analysis of the civic virtues in the *De Officiis*. But they owed an even deeper debt to Sallust's histories, and in particular to the opening of the *Bellum Catilinae* with its explanation of the rise and fall of republican Rome. The importance of Sallust in the evolution of republican political theory in Italy has not been much emphasized, except by Rubinstein in his important discussion of Mussato.[4] But one of my aims will be to show that Sallust exercised an overwhelming influence on pre-humanist debates about city government, an influence that can still be discerned in the most sophisticated of the later humanist treatises on republican rule.

To recover the outlook of the earliest spokesmen for the communes, we have to concentrate on two closely related bodies of literature. First, we need to consider the numerous treatises on the *Ars dictaminis* issued by the *Dictatores* or teachers of rhetoric associated with the law schools of medieval Italy.[5] These treatises generally comprised a set of model speeches and letters, often preceded by a theoretical discussion of the rhetorical arts.[6] The value of these sources

---

[4] N. Rubinstein, 'Some Ideas on Municipal Progress and Decline in Italy of the Communes,' in D. J. Gordon (ed.), *Fritz Saxl, 1890–1948. A Volume of Memorial Essays* (London, 1957), 165–83. On the use of Sallust by medieval writers, see B. Smalley, 'Sallust in the Middle Ages,' in R. R. Bolgar (ed.), *Classical Influences on European Culture AD 500–1500* (Cambridge, 1971), 165–75.

[5] On these writers the classic study remains P. O. Kristeller, 'Humanism and Scholasticism in the Italian Renaissance', in M. Mooney (ed.), *Renaissance Thought and its Sources* (New York, 1979), 85–105. But for a different approach see the admirably documented discussion in R. Witt, 'Medieval "Ars dictaminis" and the Beginnings of Humanism: A New Construction of the Problem', *Renaissance Quarterly*, 35 (1982), 1–35. For an excellent recent survey, citing many of the writers I discuss, see also E. Artifoni, 'I podestà professionali e la fondazione retorica della politica communale', *Quaderni storici*, 63 (1986), 687–719.

[6] See J. J. Murphy, *Rhetoric in the Middle Ages* (Berkeley, Calif., 1974), esp. 218–20 on Hugh of Bologna's early distinction between the introductory theoretical treatise (the *Ars*) and the ensuing model examples (the *dictamina*).

derives from the fact that a large number of the speeches and letters they contain were specifically designed for use on public occasions by such officials as ambassadors and city magistrates. As a result, they commonly include a great deal of information about the values and attitudes informing the conduct of city government in the pre-Renaissance period.[7]

A number of these writings survive from as early as the start of the twelfth century. Hugh of Bologna's *Rationes dictandi*, for instance, appears to have been produced around the year 1120.[8] For the most part, however, the earliest surviving examples date from the opening decades of the next century, by which time the genre had become well established, not to say highly repetitious in content.[9] Among the more important examples from this era are Raniero da Perugia's *Ars notaria* of *c*.1215,[10] Thomas of Capua's *Ars dictandi* of *c*.1230,[11] Boncompagno da Signa's *Rhetorica novissima* of 1235,[12] and above all, Guido Faba's numerous writings of the same period,[13] including his *Dictamina rhetorica* of 1226–8,[14] his *Epistole* of 1239–41[15] and his *Parlamenti ed Epistole* of 1242–3.[16] Finally, by the

[7] A point excellently brought out in H. Wieruszowski, '*Ars dictaminis* in the Time of Dante', in id., *Politics and Culture in Medieval Spain and Italy* (Rome, 1971), 589–627.

[8] See Murphy, *Rhetoric in the Middle Ages*, and for an edition see Hugh of Bologna, *Rationes dictandi*, in *Briefsteller und Formelbücher des Elften bis Vierzehnten Jahrhunderts*, ed. L. Rockinger, 2 vols. (Munich, 1863), i. 53–94.

[9] For a survey of the literature of this period see Murphy, *Rhetoric in the Middle Ages*, 194–268.

[10] E. Monaci, 'Sulle formole volgari dell' *Ars notaria* di Raniero di Perugia', in *Rendiconti della Reale Accademia dei Lincei*, 14 (1905), 268–81, discusses Raniero's *Dictamina* and republishes a number of fragments. For the suggested date see G. Bertoni, *Il duecento* (Milan, 1947), 253.

[11] For an edition, and for the suggested date, see Thomas of Capua, *Ars dictandi*, ed. E. Heller (Heidelberg, 1929).

[12] See Boncompagno da Signa, *Rhetorica novissima*, ed. A. Gaudenzi, in *Bibliotheca Juridica Medii Aevi* (Bologna, 1892), 247–97. For the suggested date see A. Gaudenzi, 'Sulla cronologia delle opere dei dettatori Bolognesi', *Bullettino dell' istituto storico italiano*, 14 (1895), 85–174, at 112.

[13] For a full list of Faba's rhetorical writings see V. Pina, 'La *Summa de vitiis et virtutibus* di Guido Faba', *Quadrivium*, 1 (1956), 41–152, at 42–3 and nn.

[14] G. Faba, *Dictamina Rhetorica*, ed. A. Gaudenzi, in *Il propugnatore* (1892–3), repr. in G. Vecchi (ed.), *Medium Aevum* (Bologna, 1971). For the date of the *Dictamina Rhetorica* see Gaudenzi, 'Sulla cronologia', 133.

[15] G. Faba, *Epistole*, ed. A. Gaudenzi, in *Il propugnatore* (1892–3), repr. in G. Vecchi (ed.), *Medium Aevum* (Bologna, 1971). For the date of the *Epistole* see Gaudenzi, 'Sulla cronologia', 145.

[16] G. Faba, *Parlamenti ed Epistole*, in A. Gaudenzi, *I suoni, le forme e le parole dell' odierno dialetto della città di Bologna* (Turin, 1889), 127–60. For the date of the *Parlamenti* see Gaudenzi, 'Sulla cronologia', 148.

end of the thirteenth century a number of similar treatises began to appear in the *volgare*.[17] Matteo de' Libri's vernacular *Arringhe* dates from c.1275,[18] Giovanni da Vignano's *Flore de parlare* from c.1290,[19] Filippo Ceffi's *Dicerie* from c.1330.[20]

The other body of writings we need to consider are the treatises on city government designed specifically for the guidance of *podestà* and other magistrates. This genre was originally an offshoot of the *Ars dictaminis*, with most of the early treatises still containing model letters and speeches in addition to general advice on how to manage city affairs.[21] The earliest surviving work of this description is the anonymous 'Oculus pastoralis', which has usually been dated to the early 1220s.[22] This was shortly followed by Orfino da Lodi's *De sapientia potestatis*, an advice book composed in leonine verse during the 1240s.[23] The next such work—the fullest and most important from this pre-humanist period—was Giovanni da Viterbo's *Liber de regimine civitatum*, which was probably completed in 1253.[24] This was in turn followed—and to some degree plagiarized—by Brunetto Latini in his *Livres dou Trésor* of 1266, a widely-used encyclopedia

[17] Note, however, that Faba had pioneered the production of vernacular *Dictamina* a generation earlier. See A. Castellani, 'Le formule volgari di Guido Faba', *Studi di filologia italiana*, 13 (1955), 5–78.

[18] Matteo de' Libri, *Arringhe*, ed. E. Vincenti (Milan, 1974), 3–227. For the date of the *Arringhe* see P. O. Kristeller, 'Matteo de' Libri, Bolognese Notary of the Thirteenth Century, and his *Artes Dictaminis*', in *Miscellanea Giovanni Galbiati, ii* (*Fontes Ambrosiani* 26) (Milan, 1951), 283–320, at 285 n.

[19] Giovanni da Vignano, *Flore de parlare*, ed. E. Vincenti, in Matteo de' Libri, *Arringhe* (Milan, 1974), 229–325. For the date of the *Flore* see C. Frati, ' "Flore de parlare" o "Somma d'arengare" attribuita a Ser Giovanni Fiorentino da Vignano', *Giornale storico della letteratura italiana*, 61 (1913), 1–31 and 228–65, at 265.

[20] F. Ceffi, *Dicerie*, ed. G. Giannardi in *Studi di filologia italiana*, 6 (1942), 27–63. For the date of the *Dicerie* see S. Giannardi, 'Le "Dicerie" di Filippo Ceffi', *Studi di filologia italiana*, 6 (1942), 5–63, at 5, 19.

[21] For this connection between rhetoric and politics—between the rhetor and the rector—see Artifoni, 'I podestà professionali'.

[22] D. Franceschi, 'Oculus pastoralis', in *Memorie dell'accademia delle scienze di Torino*, 11 (1966), 3–70. For the suggested date of 1222 see ibid. 3. But A. Sorbelli, 'I teorici del reggimento comunale', *Bullettino dell' istituto storico italiano per il medio evo*, 59 (1944), 31–136, at 74, suggests 1242.

[23] Orfino da Lodi, *De regimine et sapientia potestatis*, ed. A. Ceruti, in *Miscellanea di storia italiana*, 7 (1869), 33–94. For the suggested date see Sorbelli, 'I teorici', 61.

[24] Giovanni da Viterbo, *Liber de regimine civitatum*, ed. C. Salvemini, in *Bibliotheca juridica medii aevi*, iii (Bologna, 1901), 215–80. For the suggested date see G. Folena, ' "Parlamenti" podestarili di Giovanni da Viterbo', *Lingua Nostra*, 20 (1959), 97–105, at 97. But F. Hertter, *Die Podestaliteratur italiens im 12. und 13. Jahrhundert* (Leipzig, 1910), 52–3 suggests 1228, while Sorbelli, 'I teorici', 94–6, suggests 1263.

which concludes with a section entitled 'On the Government of Cities'.[25]

These writers are all fully committed to the view that the best form of constitution for a *commune* or *civitas* must be of an elective as opposed to a monarchical character. If a city is to have any hope of attaining its highest goals, it is indispensable that its administration should remain in the hands of officials whose conduct can in turn be regulated by established customs and laws. To understand how this conclusion was reached, we accordingly need to begin by asking what these writers had in mind when they spoke about the goals or ends of communities, and in particular about the highest goal to which a city can aspire.

The goal they emphasize above all is that of attaining greatness—greatness of standing, greatness of power, greatness of wealth. This preoccupation is in part expressed in a distinctive literature devoted to celebrating the *magnalia* or signs of greatness in cities. The most famous contribution to this genre, Leonardo Bruni's *Laudatio Florentinae Urbis*, is of course a much later work, composed in 1403–4 in the highest humanist style.[26] But there are several examples dating from the period when the ideology of the city-republics was first being formulated. One of the earliest is the anonymous poem in praise of the city of Lodi, 'De laude Civitatis Laudae', probably written in the 1250s;[27] perhaps the best-known is Bonvesin della Riva's panegyric on Milan, *De magnalibus Mediolani*, which was completed in 1288.[28]

The same preoccupation with glory and greatness suffuses the

---

[25] B. Latini, *Li Livres dou Trésor*, ed. F. Carmody (Berkeley, Calif., 1948). On the date and sources of the *Trésor* see Sorbelli, 'I teorici', 99–104 and F. Carmody, 'Introduction' to Brunetto Latini, *Li Livres dou Trésor* (Berkeley, Calif., 1948), pp. xiii–xx, xxii–xxxii.

[26] For an edition see Hans Baron, *From Petrarch to Leonardo Bruni* (Chicago, 1968), 217–63. The classic analysis is given in Baron, *Crisis*, 191–224. But Baron, as often, marks too sharp a break with pre-humanist discussions, especially when he speaks of 'a new ideal of "greatness" ' in the *Laudatio*. See Baron, *Crisis*, pp. xvii, 202–4. For a contrasting appraisal see J. E. Seigel, ' "Civic humanism" or Ciceronian rhetoric? The culture of Petrarch and Bruni', *Past and Present*, 34 (1966), 3–48.

[27] G. Waitz, 'De Laude civitatis Laudae', in *Monumenta Germaniae Historica* (Hanover, 1872), xxii. 372–3. For the suggested date see J. K. Hyde, 'Medieval Descriptions of Cities', *Bulletin of the John Rylands Library*, 48 (1965), 308–40, at 340.

[28] Bonvesin della Riva, *De Magnalibus Mediolani*, Italian tr. G. Pontiggia, ed. M. Corti (Milan, 1974). For a later celebration of Milan (dated *c*.1316 in Hyde, 'Medieval descriptions', 340) see Benzo d'Alessandria, *De Mediolano Civitate*, ed. L. A. Ferrai in *Bullettino dell' istituto storico italiano*, 9 (1890), 15–36.

pre-humanist treatises on city government. The main inspiration for their claim that these are the highest ends of civil life derives of course from the Roman historians and moralists, with the most influential statements of the belief being due to Sallust. Not only do they draw on his account in the *Bellum Catilinae* of how the Roman republic grew to greatness—how the 'respublica crevit'.[29] They also like to quote the passage from the *Bellum Iugurthinum* in which the king of Numidia congratulates Jugurtha on the honour and glory brought by his deeds, while adjuring him at the same time to remember how small communities succeed in rising to greatness—how 'parvae res crescunt'.[30]

All the pre-humanist writers speak in similar terms. The 'Oculus pastoralis', which opens with a set of model speeches designed for incoming *podestà*, particularly advises them to promise that their rule will conduce 'to increase both glory and honour', and will thereby ensure 'that the city grows to greatness'.[31] The model speeches included in Giovanni da Viterbo's *Liber de regimine civitatum* similarly emphasize the value of 'increase', as well as the importance of ensuring that cities are able to grow and flourish.[32] By the end of the thirteenth century, we find the same ideas beginning to be expressed in the vernacular. Matteo de' Libri advises both ambassadors and *podestà* to promise that they will ensure increase and growth,[33] while Giovanni da Vignano's model speech for outgoing *podestà* bids them express the hope that the city they have been administering 'will at all times grow and increase', above all in prosperity.[34]

At the same time, the vernacular writers of this period begin to invoke a new concept to describe their vision of the proper ends of civic life. They begin to speak of *grandezza*, using a term evidently coined to supply the lack, in classical Latin, of an expression at once denoting grandeur and magnitude. We already find Guido Faba

---

[29] Sallust, *Bellum Catilinae*, tr. J. C. Rolfe (London, 1921), x. 1, p. 16.

[30] Sallust, *Bellum Iugurthinum*, tr. J. C. Rolfe (London, 1921), x. 6, p. 148.

[31] See Franceschi 'Oculus pastoralis', 25, on conducing 'ad incrementum et gloriam et honorem', and 27, on the hope that 'excrescit civitas'.

[32] See Viterbo, *Liber de regimine civitatum*, 231 col. 2, on the importance of ensuring that 'civitates crescunt'. Cf. also 232 col. 1, on the value of 'incrementum' and 'maximum incrementum'.

[33] See Libri, *Arringhe*, 10, on the duty to bring 'acresimento de ben en meglo', and 70, on the duty to assure 'bon stato, gradeça et acresemento'.

[34] See Vignano *Flore de parlare*, 286, for the wish 'che questa terra sempre acresca'.

speaking in this fashion in his *Parlamenti ed Epistole* of the early 1240s. In his model speech for the use of newly-elected *podestà*, Faba advises them to promise 'to do whatever may be necessary for the maintenance of the standing and the *grandeça* of the commune, and for the increase of the honour and glory of those friendly to it'.[35] Shortly afterwards the same terminology recurs in the vernacular passages of Giovanni da Viterbo's *Liber de regimine civitatum*. An incoming *podestà*, he advises, must vow to uphold 'the honour and *grandecça* and welfare' of the city given into his charge.[36] By the next generation, we find the same terminology in standard use among the writers of vernacular *Dictamina*. Matteo de' Libri suggests that city magistrates should promise at the time of their election to uphold 'the good standing, repose and *grandeça* of the city';[37] outgoing magistrates should proclaim that they have in fact upheld its '*grandeça*, honour, good standing and repose'.[38] Giovanni da Vignano echoes the same sentiments in virtually the same phraseology, continually urging ambassadors and magistrates alike to speak of their city's 'exaltation, *grandeça* and honour',[39] of its 'good standing, *grandeça* and repose'[40] and at the same time of 'the honour, *grandeça*, unity and repose' of all its citizens.[41]

Given this emphasis on *grandezza*, it is not surprising that these writers are especially concerned to establish what policies need to be pursued if this goal is to be achieved. Initially they simply tend to reiterate the familiar Augustinian assumption that no community can hope to flourish unless it lives in perfect peace. The 'Oculus', for example, contains a model speech for chief magistrates to deliver in the face of warring factions, warning them that 'only through quiet and tranquillity and peace can a city grow great'.[42] Latini similarly

[35] See Faba, *Parlamenti ed Epistole*, 156 on the need 'de fare quelle cose . . . che pertegnano ad statum et a grandeça di questo communo, et ad acresamento de gloria e d'onore de tuti quilli c'ameno questa citade'. Cf. the very similar formula at 143.

[36] See Viterbo, *Liber de regimine civitatum*, 234 col. 2 on the need to act 'ad honore et grandecça, et utilitate de questu communu'. Cf. also 231, col. 1 on the need to promote 'grandeça'.

[37] Libri, *Arringhe*, 105: 'buono stato, riposo et grandecça.'

[38] Ibid. 99: 'grandecça, honori, bon stato e bon reposo'. For further references to the ideal of *grandezza* in Libri, see 12, 28, 53, 69–70, 93, 110, 112, 114.

[39] Vignano, *Flore de parlare*, 237: 'exaltamento, grandeça et honore'.

[40] Ibid., 289: 'bom stato, grandeça e reposo'.

[41] Ibid., 251: 'honore, grandeça e unità e reposo'. For similar formulas see 237, 239, 245, 251, 286–7.

[42] Franceschi, 'Oculus pastoralis', 27: 'Per quietam autem tranquilitatem et pacem ipsius excrescit civitas.' Cf. also 53, 59.

lays it down in his chapter on the virtue of concord that 'peace brings very great good, while war lays it waste'.[43] The same argument was subsequently reiterated by numerous writers of vernacular *Dictamina*. Matteo de' Libri strongly associates the rule of those who enable their communities 'to live in total tranquillity' with the attainment of 'honour and good standing'.[44] Filippo Ceffi writes even more emphatically, offering repeated assurances that if a city 'can manage to maintain itself in a good and peaceable state', this will always conduce 'to your honour and your *grandezza*'.[45]

Soon after the start of the fourteenth century, however, a number of writers began to voice a certain anxiety about such unqualified celebrations of peace.[46] Sallust was again their main authority at this point. As he had emphasized at the start of the *Bellum Catilinae*, it was during the period when Rome had been forced to wage continual wars against savage neighbouring peoples, and subsequently against the invading Carthaginians, that the republic had originally grown to greatness. By contrast, it was when this period was followed by an era of peace and plenty that the Roman civic spirit had begun to decline. The fruits of peace proved to be avarice and self-interest, and with the resulting loss of civic virtue the free and self-governing republic eventually collapsed.[47]

With the traditional systems of communal government everywhere falling prey to the rise of *Signori* in the early fourteenth century,[48] a number of Italian historical and political writers began to express similar doubts. Albertino Mussato, for example, prefaces his history of the collapse of civic liberty in his native Padua with an explanation taken almost word-for-word from Sallust's account.[49] The same theme was later to assume an even greater prominence in quattrocento humanist histories designed to celebrate the virtues of republi-

[43] Latini, *Trésor*, 292: 'pais fait maint bien et guerre le gaste'.

[44] See Libri, *Arringhe*, 79, for the connection between being able 'permanere in gran tranquillitate' and the capacity 'aquistar honor et bon stato'. Cf. also 99, 114, 147.

[45] See Ceffi, *Dicerie*, 27, for the claim that, if your city 'possa mantenersi in buono e pacifico stato', this will conduce 'a vostro onore e grandezza'. For other formulas to the same effect see 36, 47, 61.

[46] For a survey contrasting the 'orientations' of peace and liberty in this period see N. Valeri, *La libertà e la pace: orientamenti politici del rinascimento italiano* (Turin, 1942).

[47] Sallust, *Bellum Catilinae*, VI–XIII, pp. 10–22.

[48] For a classic survey of this transition see F. Ercole, *Dal commune al principato* (Florence, 1929).

[49] This is pointed out in Rubinstein, 'Some Ideas on Municipal Progress', 172 and n.

can freedom.[50] The fear that long periods of peace may lead to ener-vation and decadence is forcefully expressed, for example, at several points in Poggio's *Historiae Florentini Populi*. A love of peace, he implies, may sometimes pose a threat to liberty.[51] If freedom and self-government are to be upheld against the encroachments of tyranny, it may sometimes be necessary to fight for liberty instead of insisting on peace at any price.

There is one point, however, on which all these writers are agreed. Even if it may sometimes be necessary to wage war on others in the name of liberty and *grandezza*, the preservation of peace within one's own city must never be jeopardised. The avoidance of internal divi-sions and discord is regarded by everyone as an indispensable con-dition of civic greatness.[52]

Once again, it is Sallust who is most often quoted to this effect. The passage invariably cited is the speech from the *Bellum Iugurthinum* in which the king of Numantia addresses Jugurtha and his other two heirs. 'I bequeath to all three of you', he is made to say, 'a kingdom that will prove strong if you conduct yourself well, but weak if you behave badly. For it is by way of concord that small communities rise to greatness; it is as a result of discord that even the greatest communities fall into collapse.'[53]

The negative aspect of this admonition was taken up by all the pre-humanist writers on city government. 'It is due to the fact that all cities nowadays are divided within themselves', Giovanni da Viterbo insists, 'that the good effect of government is no longer felt.'[54] Latini

---

[50] See the discussion of Poggio's republicanism in J. Oppel, 'Peace vs. Liberty in the Quattrocento: Poggio, Guarino, and the Scipio–Caesar Controversy', *Journal of Medieval and Renaissance Studies*, 4 (1974), 221–65.

[51] See the discussion, modelled on Sallust, at the start of Poggio's *Historiae*, v, in Poggio Bracciolini, 'Historiae Florentini Populi' in *Opera Omnia*, ed. R. Fubini, 4 vols. (Turin, 1966), ii. 81–493, at 299 and cf. the account in Oppel, 'Peace vs. Liberty', 223–4.

[52] On civic discord as a prime enemy of peace see Q. Skinner, 'Ambrogio Lorenzetti: the artist as political philosopher', *Proceedings of the British Academy*, 72 (1986), 8–9 and 33.

[53] Sallust, *Bellum Catilinae*, x. 6, p. 148: 'Equidem ego vobis regnum trado firmum, si boni eritis, sin mali, imbecillum. Nam concordia parvae res crescunt, discordia max-umae dilabuntur.' The last sentence was apparently proverbial: it is quoted as such in Seneca, *Epistulae Morales*, iii. tr. R. Gummere (London, 1925), XCIV. xlvi. 40. It is strongly echoed by a number of pre-humanist writers—e.g. by Orfino da Lodi (see Lodi, *De regimine*, 57) and by the author of *De Laude Civitatis Laudae* (see Waitz, 'De Laude', 372).

[54] Viterbo, *Liber de regimine civitatum*, 221 cols. 1–2: 'Nam cum civitates omnes hodie sunt divise . . . cesset bonus effectus regiminis.'

makes the same point in the course of advising magistrates on what to do if they find themselves in charge of a city 'at war with itself'. 'You must point out how concord brings greatness to cities and enriches their citizens, while war destroys them; and you must recall how Rome and other great cities ruined themselves by internal strife.'[55] Matteo de' Libri offers precisely the same advice in a model speech designed for captains of city militias to declaim in order to stiffen the resolve of ruling magistrates to deal with internal faction-fights. 'Think of Florence and Siena, and of how they have destroyed themselves by internal war; think of Rimini, and of many other places throughout this country, and of how internal hatred has ruined them.'[56]

More optimistically, many of these writers also take up the positive aspects of Sallust's argument. 'Cities that are ruled and maintained in a state of peace', Giovanni da Viterbo declares, 'are able to grow, to become great, and to receive the greatest possible increase.'[57] Latini underlines the same point, referring his readers directly to Sallust for the judgement that, just as discord destroys the greatest undertakings, so 'small things, through concord, are able to grow great'.[58] Likewise Matteo de' Libri, in a model speech designed for *Capitani* to deliver if civic discord impends, advises them to remind the parties involved that 'concord and unity cause everything to advance and grow great'.[59]

One of the problems that most preoccupies these writers is accordingly that of understanding how civic concord can best be preserved. The authority to whom they generally turn at this juncture is Cicero, for whom the ideal of a *concordia ordinum* had been of such overriding importance. Cicero had laid it down in a highly influential passage in Book I of the *De officiis* that the surest way 'to introduce sedition and discord into a city is to look after the interests of only

---

[55] Latini, *Trésor*, 404: 'die comment concorde essauce les viles et enrichist les borgois, et guerre les destruit; et ramentevoir Romme et les autres bonnes viles ki por la guerre dedans sont decheues et mal alees'.

[56] Libri, *Arringhe*, 147: 'Pensative de Florencia, de Sena, commo son gite per la guerra dentru . . . Pensative de Rimino, comm' è conço per l'odio dentro, e de multe terre de quella contrata.' Cf. also 193.

[57] Viterbo, *Liber de regimine civitatum*, 231 col. 2: 'civitates reguntur et tenentur pacifice, crescunt, ditantur et maximum recipiunt incrementum'.

[58] Latini, *Trésor*, 292: 'Salustes dist, par concorde croissent les petites choses et par discorde se destruisent les grandismes.' For earlier allusions to Sallust's formulation see above, n. 53.

[59] Libri, *Arringhe*, 18: 'la concordia et l'unitate acrese et avança tuti bene'.

one part of the citizens, while neglecting the rest'.[60] It follows that the key to preserving civic concord must be to give precedence to the ideal of the common good over any selfish or factional interests. Cicero had summarized this conclusion in the form of two basic precepts for the guidance of magistrates, both of which he claimed to have taken from Plato. 'First, they must look after the welfare of every citizen to such a degree that, in everything they do, they make this their highest priority, without any consideration for their own advantage. Secondly, they must look after the welfare of the whole body politic, never allowing themselves to care only for one part of the citizens while betraying the rest.'[61]

Among the writers I am considering, both these suggestions about the avoidance of discord were widely taken up. In the 'Oculus pastoralis', the model speech of the incoming *podestà* ends with the assurance that he will act 'to promote the welfare of the whole community' thereby guaranteeing it 'honour, exaltation and benefit, and a happy state'.[62] Giovanni da Viterbo quotes the entire passage from Cicero's *De officiis* in which the connections between the avoidance of discord and the promotion of the common good are explained.[63] Latini also quotes Cicero's precepts,[64] and subsequently adds in his chapter 'Of Concord' that, if this virtuous condition is to be attained, 'we must follow nature and place the common good above all other values'.[65]

This still left the question of how to ensure in practice that the common good is followed, and thus that no member of the community is ever neglected or unfairly subordinated to anyone else. Here again the writers I am considering remain in complete agreement with their Roman authorities. This can only be brought about, they

---

[60] Cicero, *De officiis*, tr. W. Miller (London, 1913), I. xxv. 85, p. 86: 'Qui autem parti civium consulunt, partem neglegunt, rem perniciosissimam in civitatem inducunt, seditionem atque discordiam.'

[61] Ibid.: 'unum, ut utilitatem civium sic tueantur, ut, quaecumque agunt, ad eam referant obliti commodorum suorum, alterum, ut totum corpus rei publicae curent, ne, dum partem aliquam tuentur, reliquas deserant'.

[62] See Franceschi, 'Oculus pastoralis', 26, on the need to act 'pro utilitate communitatis istius' in order to bring it 'ad honorem, exaltationem et comodum ac felicem statum'.

[63] See Viterbo, *Liber de regimine civitatum*, 268 col. 2.

[64] See Latini, *Trésor*, 267.

[65] Ibid. 291: 'devons nous ensivre nature et metre avant tout le commun profit'. For further references in Latini to the idea of the common good, see his concluding chapter, esp. 408, 415, 417. Cf. also the references to the 'bene comune' in Ceffi, *Dicerie*, 46, 57.

all declare, if our magistrates uphold the dictates of justice in all their public acts. The ideal of justice they define, in accordance with the principles of Roman law, as a matter of giving to each his due, *ius suum cuique*. But to ensure that everyone receives his due, they argue, is the same as ensuring that no one's interests are excluded or unfairly subjected to those of anyone else. The ideal of justice is thus seen as the bedrock: to act justly is the one and only means to promote the common good, without which there can be no hope of preserving concord and hence of attaining greatness.

Once again, Sallust provides one of the main inspirations for this argument. As he had put it with characteristic succinctness in the *Bellum Catilinae*, it was 'by acting with justice as well as with industry that the Roman republic grew to greatness'.[66] But the writers I am considering are even more indebted at this point to a similar passage from the start of Cicero's *De officiis*. Introducing the topic of justice, Cicero had begun by declaring that it constitutes the primary means 'by which the community of men and, as it were, their common unity, is preserved'.[67]

These sentiments are often transcribed almost *verbatim* by the pre-humanist writers on city government. Giovanni da Viterbo begins his treatise by laying it down that the prime duty of chief magistrates is 'to render to each person his due, in order that the city may be governed in justice and equity'.[68] The importance of this principle, as one of his model speeches later explains, stems from the fact that 'when cities are ruled by these bodies of justice, they grow to greatness, become enriched and receive the greatest possible increase.'[69] Latini likewise argues at the start of his chapter 'On the government of cities' that 'justice ought to be so well established in the heart of every *signor* that he assigns to everyone his right'.[70] The reason, he similarly explains, is that 'a city which is governed according to right

---

[66] Sallust, *Bellum Catilinae*, x. 1, p. 16: 'labore atque iustitia res publica crevit'.

[67] Cicero, *De officiis*, I. vii. 20, p. 20: 'qua societas hominum inter ipsos et vitae quasi communitatis continetur'. Cf. also the claim in Cicero, *De inventione*, tr. H. Hubbell (London, 1949), III. liii. clx. 328 to the effect that it is *iustitia* which serves to maintain the *communes utilitates*.

[68] Viterbo, *Liber de regimine civitatum* 220 col. 1: 'ius suum cuilibet reddatur, et regatur civitas in iustitia et equitate'.

[69] Ibid., 231 col. 2: 'Per haec enim frena [iustitia et equalitas] civitates reguntur ... crescunt, ditantur et maximum recipiunt incrementum.' Cf. also 234 cols. 1 and 2.

[70] Latini, *Trésor*, 392: 'Justice doit estre si establement fermee dedens le cuer au signor, k'il doinst a chascun son droit.'

and truth, such that everyone has what he ought to have, will certainly grow and multiply, both in people and in wealth, and will endure for ever in a good state of peace, to its honour and that of its friends'.[71]

By the time we come to the writers of vernacular *Dictamina* at the end of the century, we find these connections between justice, the common good, and the attainment of greatness being presented almost as a litany. 'He who loves justice', as Matteo de' Libri proclaims, 'loves a constant and perpetual will to give to each his right; and he who loves to give to each his right loves tranquillity and repose, by means of which countries rise to the highest *grandeça*.'[72] Giovanni da Vignano writes in virtually identical terms, thereby furnishing yet a further summary of the ideology I have been anatomizing. Justice forms the basis of good government; to act justly is to give to each his due; to give to each his due is the key to maintaining civic concord; and 'it is by means of all these things', Giovanni concludes, 'that countries are able to rise to *grandeça*'.[73]

With this injunction to love justice and treat it as the foundation of civic greatness,[74] we reach the heart of the ideology articulated by the early *Dictatores*. But there still remained one question of the highest practical importance. Under what system of government have we the best hope of ensuring that our leading magistrates do in fact obey the dictates of justice, such that all these other benefits flow from their rule?

It is at this point that the *Dictatores* respond with their celebration of the system of government most familiar to them: the system based on ruling councils chaired by elected magistrates. If justice is to be upheld and civic greatness attained, they all agree, government by hereditary princes or *Signori* must at all costs be avoided; some form of elective and self-governing system must always be maintained.

---

[71] Latini, *Trésor*, 403: 'La cités ki est governee selonc droit et selonc verité, si ke chascuns ait ce k'il doit avoir . . . certes, ele croist et mouteplie des gens et d'avoir et dure tousjours en bone pais a l'onour de lui et de ses amis.'

[72] Libri, *Arringhe*, 34: 'quel k'ama iustitia ama constante e perpetua voluntate de dare soa raxone a çascuno; e ki ama soa raxone a çascuno, ama tranquilitate e reposo, per le qual cose le terre montano in grand grandeça'. Cf. also 130, 160–2.

[73] Vignano, *Flore de parlare*, 296: 'per le qua' cose fare le terre montano in grandeça'.

[74] For the significance among these writers of the specific injunction 'Diligite iustitiam' see Skinner, 'Ambrogio Lorenzetti', 14–17.

Once again, the authorities most often invoked in support of this basic political commitment are the apologists of the Roman republic in its final phase. The vehement anti-Caesarism of Cicero's *De officiis* naturally made it a key text.[75] But the most frequently quoted argument against hereditary rule was yet again taken from Sallust's *Bellum Catilinae*. The danger with kingship, Sallust had declared, is that 'to kings, good men are objects of even greater suspicion than the wicked.'[76] The reason is that 'to kings, the good qualities of others are invariably seen as a threat'.[77] This explains why 'it was only when the city of Rome managed to become liberated from its kings that it was able, in such a short space of time, to rise to such greatness.'[78] Only when everyone is allowed to contend for honour, without fear of exciting envy or enmity from their rulers, can the greatest heights of civic glory be scaled.

Among the pre-humanist writers, it is Latini who reiterates this argument with the strongest emphasis. His chapter 'Of Signories' opens with the briskest possible statement of the case. 'There are three types of government, one being rule by kings, the second rule by leading men, the third rule by communes themselves. And of these, the third is far better than the rest.'[79] At the start of his chapter 'On the government of cities' he proceeds to give his grounds for this conclusion. Where kings and princes enjoy ultimate control, as in France and most other countries, they consider only their own interests, 'selling offices and assigning them to those who pay most for them, with little consideration for the good or benefit of the townsfolk'.[80] But where the citizens themselves retain control, as in Italy, 'they are able to elect, as *podestà* or *signore*, those who will act most profitably for the common good of the city and all their subjects'.[81]

[75] For Cicero's denunciation of Julius Caesar as a tyrant see *De officiis*, III. VII. 23, p. 190.

[76] Sallust, *Bellum Catilinae*, VII. 3, p. 12: 'Nam regibus boni quam mali suspectiores sunt.'

[77] Ibid. 'semperque eis [viz. regibus] aliena virtus formidulosa est'.

[78] Ibid. 'Sed civitas . . . adepta libertate quantum brevi creverit.'

[79] Latini, *Trésor*, 211: 'Seignouries sont de iii manieres, l'une est des rois, la seconde est des bons, la tierce est des communes, laquele est la trés millour entre ces autres.'

[80] See ibid. 392 for the accusation that, in France and other kingdoms, rulers 'vendent les provostes et les baillent a ciaus ki plus l'achatent (poi gardent sa bonté ne le proufit des borgois)'.

[81] Ibid. 392: 'en Ytaile . . . li communité des viles eslisent lor poesté et lor signour tel comme il quident qu'il soit plus proufitable au commun preu de la vile et de tous lor subtés'.

The pre-humanist writers assign no distinctive name to the form of government they most admire. They remain content to describe it simply as one of the types of *regimen* or *reggimento* by which a *civitas* or *commune* can lawfully be ruled.[82] Where they are any more specific, they merely add that the *regimen* in question can be described as one in which power remains in the hands of the commune itself.[83] Save for one or two remarks in Giovanni da Viterbo,[84] and later in Albertino Mussato,[85] there are no signs of the later disposition to use the term *res publica* to distinguish such elective forms of government from hereditary monarchies. Still less is there any hint of the suggestion canvassed by Cicero at one point in the *De officiis* to the effect that such regimes are the only forms of *res publicae* truly worthy of the name.[86]

There is one point, however, at which a number of these theorists make use of a concept that was later to become central to—indeed definitive of—the political vocabulary of Renaissance republicanism. As we have seen, they treat it as a distinctive virtue of elective systems that they guarantee the equality of all citizens before the law. No one's interests are excluded, no one is unfairly subordinated to anyone else. But this, they point out, is in effect to advance a thesis about political liberty. It is to say that only under elective regimes are individuals able to live a free way of life, unconstrained by any unjust dependence or servitude. As a result—following a usage already established by Cicero[87]—they begin to describe such regimes

---

[82] See, for example, Faba, *Dictamina Rhetorica*, 54; Viterbo, *Liber de regimine civitatum*, 222 col. 1; Ceffi, *Dicerie*, 45.

[83] See, for example, Latini, *Trésor*, 211, 392.

[84] See Viterbo, *Liber de regimine civitatum*, 255 col. 2; 262 col. 1; and 272 col. 1 for the use of the term *res publica* to describe self-governing cities.

[85] A. Mussato, *De Gestis Italicorum Post Mortem Henrici VII Caesaris Historia*, ed. L. Muratori in *Rerum Italicarum Scriptores* (Milan, 1727), x, cols. 569–768, at col. 722: 'Formam publicam tenendam in civitate, ne figura reipublicae adeo usque deleta sit, quin faciem effigiemque habere censeatur.'

[86] See Cicero, *De officiis*, II. VIII. 29. This passage, implying that Rome was only a true *res publica* under its traditional constitution, is, I think, crucial to understanding the process by which the term *res publica* eventually ceased to be used to refer to any type of body politic, and instead came to be used specifically to describe elective systems of government such as Cicero had in mind.

[87] See, for example, his distinction between living under tyranny and living 'in libera civitate' in Cicero, *De officiis*, II. VII. 23–4, p. 190. Cf. also II. XXII. 78–9, p. 254 on the liberty of citizens.

as 'free governments', commending them as the only means of ensuring that every citizen is permitted to live 'in a free state'.[88]

We already encounter an intimation of this development at the
start of Giovanni da Viterbo's *Liber de regimine civitatum*, where he
argues that the term *civitas* itself derives from the phrase *civium
libertas*.[89] A further hint occurs in Bonvesin della Riva's panegyric
on Milan, whose chapter in praise of the city's traditional form of
communal government is entitled 'The commendation of Milan by
reason of its liberty'.[90] A generation later, the contrast with the servitude to be expected under hereditary *Signori* is strongly drawn by
Albertino Mussato in recounting the fall of the Paduan commune.
Mussato repeatedly equates the attempt by his fellow-citizens to
uphold their *res publica* against the challenge of the Della Scala with
the attempt 'to fight in defence of the liberty of our native land'.[91]

It is in Filippo Ceffi's *Dicerie*, however, that the upholding of liberty is most emphatically connected with elective forms of government. In his model speech for citizens to use when receiving a new
podestà, Ceffi characterizes such magistrates as the preservers of
liberty.[92] In a later speech designed for a similar occasion, he advises
citizens to remind the incoming *podestà* of their expectation 'that
they will be able to live both in safety and in a state of liberty' under
his rule.[93] Most striking of all is his model speech designed for citizens to use in the event of having to capitulate to a *signore*. Here
Ceffi explicitly equates such a change of government with the forfei-
ture of liberty. What he advises the leaders of a commune to say in
such a predicament is that 'due to the harshness of war, we find our-

---

[88] It is thus an exaggeration to maintain, as for example Witt has done, that 'a
republican concept of *libertas*' only re-emerges in 'the early years of the
Quattrocento'. See Witt, 'The Rebirth of the Concept of Republican Liberty in Italy'
in *Renaissance Studies in Honor of Hans Baron*, A. Molho and J. Tedeschi (eds.)
(Florence, 1971), 175. But cf. ibid. 186–8 for an interesting discussion of some earlier
accounts.

[89] Viterbo, *Liber de regimine civitatum*, 218 col. 2: 'Civitas autem dicitur civium
libertas.' Cf. also the connection between liberty and self-government noted in 271 col.
1.

[90] Riva, *De Magnalibus Mediolani*, 166: 'De commendatione Mediolani ratione lib-
ertatis.'

[91] See, for example, Mussato, *De Gestis Italicorum*, col. 658: 'pro patria [*sic*] libertate decertant'.

[92] Ceffi, *Dicerie*, 32. Cf. also 35.

[93] Ibid. 41: 'che noi possiamo iscampare e vivere liberamente sotto la vostra seg-
noria'. Cf. also 44.

selves obliged to hand over our liberty and our system of justice, which have been in our possession for many years'.[94]

If we now turn to Machiavelli's discussion of republican liberty in the *Discorsi*, we find many continuities between his arguments and those of the earliest protagonists of republicanism. For even when advancing his most consciously novel claims, Machiavelli remains in close intellectual contact with the assumptions of the writers I have so far been examining, and above all with their Roman authorities.

One of the features of Machiavelli's analysis that most astonished his contemporaries was his defence of the 'tumults' that disfigured the political life of early republican Rome.[95] According to Machiavelli, it was actually 'due to the disunion between the Plebs and the Senate', and the turmoil to which this gave rise, that Rome 'managed to become a perfect republic'.[96] The resolution of this paradox is proferred in Book I, chapter 4. Those who condemn Rome's tumults, Machiavelli declares, 'are failing to recognise that there are two contrasting outlooks in every republic, that of the leading men and that of the ordinary citizens, and that all the laws made in favour of liberty are born of the disunity between them'.[97] Such critics, he suggests, 'thus appear to be complaining about the very things that were the primary cause of Rome's maintaining her freedom'.[98] Rome's critics are 'concentrating on the clamour and outcry

---

[94] Ibid. 61: 'per asprezza di guerra, siano condotti a donare nostra libertade e giustizia, la quale abbiamo posseduta per molti anni'. As Rubinstein has shown, the assumption that the preservation of liberty requires the maintenance of a self-governing republic became a commonplace of political rhetoric in Florence in the later 14th c. See the important discussion in N. Rubinstein, 'Florence and the despots: some aspects of Florentine diplomacy in the fourteenth century', *Transactions of the Royal Historical Society*, 5/2(1952), 21–45. It appears, however, that what was generally being claimed in such arguments was that the preservation of liberty *requires* political independence and republican self-government, not that the term 'liberty' somehow *means* 'political independence' or 'republican self-government' as Rubinstein suggests at 29–30.

[95] On contemporary reactions to Machiavelli's argument see, for example, Q. Skinner, *The Foundations of Modern Political Thought*, i, *The Renaissance* (Cambridge, 1978), 181–2.

[96] Machiavelli, *Discorsi*, I. 2, in id., *Il Principe e Discorsi*, ed. S. Bertelli (Milan, 1960), 135: it was 'per la disunione della Plebe e del Senato' that Rome 'feca una republica perfetta'.

[97] *Disc.* I. 4, p. 137: 'non considerino, come e' sono in ogni republica due umori diversi, quello del popolo et quello de' grandi; e come tutte le leggi che si fanno in favore della libertà, nascono dalla disunione loro'.

[98] Ibid.: 'coloro che dannono i tumulti intra i Nobili e la Plebe mi pare che biasimino quelle cose che furono prima causa del tenere libera Roma'.

that arose from her tumults' when they ought to be reflecting instead
'on the splendid consequences to which they gave rise'.[99] These
splendid consequences, as Machiavelli's chapter heading explains,
were that 'the disunion between the plebs and the senate in Rome
enabled that republic to become at once free and great'.[100]

This analysis has been interpreted as Machiavelli's way of voicing
dissent from the widespread admiration among his contemporaries
for the proverbial serenity of Venice.[101] As we have seen, however,
the assumption that internal discord is invariably fatal to civic greatness had been central to the whole development of Italian republicanism. Everyone had treated the preservation of concord, the
avoidance of internal strife, as indispensable to upholding the common good and thereby attaining greatness. By insisting that tumults
represent a prime *cause* of freedom and greatness, Machiavelli is
placing a question mark against this entire tradition of thought.
What he is repudiating is nothing less than the Ciceronian vision of
the *concordia ordinum*, a vision hitherto endorsed by the defenders
of self-governing republics in an almost uncritical way.

There is a further point at which Machiavelli appears to be offering a critical commentary on traditional republican thought. This is
in his formulation of the doctrine that political actions should be
judged not by their intrinsic rightness but by their effects. The notorious passage in which he puts forward this doctrine occurs in his
discussion of Romulus' founding of Rome in Book I, chapter 9. 'No
discerning person', he maintains, 'will ever criticize anyone for
taking any action, however extreme, which is undertaken with the
aim of organising a kingdom or constituting a republic. For it is right
that, although the fact of the extreme action may accuse him, its
effect should excuse him. It is those who use violence to destroy
things, not to reconstitute them, who alone deserve blame.'[102]

This way of expressing the point again suggests a criticism of conventional pieties. As we have seen, it had generally been assumed

[99] *Disc.* I. 4, p. 137, 'che considerino piú a romori ed alle grida che di tali tumulti
nascevano, che a buoni effetti che quelli partorivano'.

[100] Ibid. p. 136: 'Che la disunione della Plebe e del Senato romano fece libera e
potente quella republica.'

[101] For example in Pocock, *Machiavellian Moment*, 186. Cf. also 196–9.

[102] Machiavelli, *Discorsi*, I. 9, ed. Bertelli, pp. 153–4: 'né mai uno ingegno savio
riprenderà alcuno di alcuna azione straordinaria, che per ordinare un regno o consti-
tuire una republica usasse. Conviene bene che, accusandolo il fatto, lo effetto lo scusi
. . . per ché colui che è violento per guastare, non quello che è per racconciare, si debbe
riprendere.'

that the common good can only be secured if rulers behave with complete justice, ensuring that everyone receives his due and that no one is unfairly subordinated to anyone else. Machiavelli's strongly contrasting conclusion derives from a recognition of the fact that this is unduly optimistic, since the two ideals are potentially incompatible. When you act to promote the common good, you always run the risk 'that this will sometimes turn out to the disadvantage of one or another private individual'.[103] It follows that, if the promotion of the common good is genuinely your goal, you must be prepared to abandon the idea of justice. This is the hard lesson that Romulus is praised for having learned so well. He realized that 'when the effect is good, as it was in his case, this will always serve to excuse whatever was done'.[104] By contrast, this is the principle that Piero Soderini, the leader of the Florentine republic during Machiavelli's own lifetime, is severely criticized for having failed to grasp. Soderini never appreciated that 'one must at no point allow an evil to continue out of regard for a good when the good can easily be overwhelmed by the evil'. As a result he refused to do evil in order that good might come of it; and as a result of that decision he brought ruin on the republic as well as himself.[105]

I turn finally to consider the positive resemblances between the arguments of the *Discorsi* and the earliest traditions of Italian republicanism. The continuities are much more fundamental than has usually been recognized. For all the novelty of his analysis, Machiavelli remains content to fit his ideas into a traditional framework, a framework based on linking together the concepts of liberty, the common good, and civic greatness in a largely familiar way.

First of all, Machiavelli fully endorses the long-standing view that the highest ends to which any city can aspire are those of civic glory and greatness. He initially announces this commitment in the opening chapter of Book I. First he considers those cities which were originally founded by their own citizens 'without having any particular prince to direct them'.[106] Among these, he observes, both Athens and

---

[103] *Disc.*, II. 2, p. 280: 'quantunque e torni in danno di questo o di quello privato'.
[104] *Disc.*, I. 9, pp. 153–4: 'quando sia buono [viz., lo effetto] come quello di Romolo, sempre lo scuserà'.
[105] *Disc.*, III. 3, p. 387: 'non si debbe mai lasciare scorrere un male rispetto ad uno bene, quando quel bene facilmente possa essere da quel male oppressato'.
[106] *Disc.*, I. 1, p. 126: 'sanza altro principe particulare che gli ordinasse'.

Venice can be numbered, 'both of which managed to rise from these small beginnings to the *grandezza* they now enjoy'.[107] Next he considers the contrasting case of cities originally founded by princes. 'Due to the fact that such cities do not have free beginnings', he argues, 'it very seldom happens that they are able to rise to greatness.'[108] Not only does Machiavelli announce the theme of *grandezza* at the outset; he also hints at a link between *grandezza* and *libertà*, thereby introducing what later proves to be one of his major arguments.

Turning next to the case of ancient Rome, Machiavelli repeatedly makes it clear that for him the basic question is how the early republic managed to rise to such unparalleled heights of greatness. The question recurs throughout Book I, in the course of which Machiavelli discusses the Roman republic constitution. He constantly asks himself what features of the constitution enabled the republic 'to attain Roman *grandezza*',[109] 'to come to its ultimate *grandezza*,'[110] 'to arrive at that *grandezza* which it acquired'.[111] The same topic recurs even more prominently in Book II, the main concern of which is to analyse Rome's military policies. Here Machiavelli primarily devotes himself to examining the techniques of warfare that enabled the Romans 'to attain *grandezza*'[112] or, more imposingly, 'to help themselves on the way towards supreme *grandezza*'.[113] Finally, the same theme is no less pervasive in Book III, the principal aim of which is 'to show how much the actions of individual men contributed to making Rome great, and brought about in that city so many good effects'.[114]

Machiavelli also endorses the traditional belief in the importance of the common good. He agrees that, unless each citizen behaves with *virtù*, and in consequence places the good of his community above all private ambitions and factional allegiances, the goal of civic *grandezza* can never be attained. He states this assumption most firmly in Book II, chapter 2—the crucial passage in which he spells

[107] *Disc.*, I. 1, p. 126, 'talché ogni piccolo principio li poté fare venire a quella grandezza nella quale sono'.
[108] Ibid.: 'E per non avere queste cittadi la loro origine libera, rade volte occorre che le facciano progressi grandi.'
[109] *Disc.*, I. 6, p. 146: 'pervenire alla romana grandezza'.
[110] *Disc.*, I. 20, p. 185: 'venire a quella sua ultima grandezza'.
[111] *Disc.*, I. 6, p. 143: 'venire a quella grandezza dove ei pervenne'.
[112] See *Disc.*, II. 13, p. 312, speaking of 'i modi necessari a venire a grandezza'.
[113] *Disc.*, II. 6, p. 294: 'per facilitarsi la via a venire a una suprema grandezza'.
[114] *Disc.*, III. 1, pp. 383–4: 'dimostrare a qualunque quanto le azioni degli uomini particulari facessono grande Roma e causassino in quella città molti buoni effetti'.

out the special virtues of republican government. 'It is not the pursuit of individual good', he declares at that point, 'but rather the pursuit of the common good that brings greatness to cities.'[115] It is because of their clear recognition of this fact, Book I repeatedly affirms, that the highest praise must be accorded to those who have founded constitutions. Romulus, for example, is said to have understood the importance of the common good so well that even his fratricide can be excused, since this too 'was something that was done for the common good and not out of personal ambition'.[116] The same perception is said to have guided the leading citizens of Rome whose achievements are outlined in Book III. Fabius, Manlius, Camillus, and many others are particularly singled out for helping Rome along the pathway to greatness by acting 'entirely in favour of the public', placing 'the public welfare' and 'the public benefit' above all other values.[117]

This analysis is corroborated by Machiavelli's account of corruption. To be a corrupt citizen is to place one's own ambitions or the advantages of a party above the common good. It is Machiavelli's contention that to act in this way is invariably fatal to the cause of civic freedom and greatness. As he explains early in Book I, it is always private or factional forces 'that ruin a free way of life'.[118] The claim is underlined in the discussion of the Decemviri later in Book I. 'It is when the people cannot agree to make a law in favour of liberty, but instead form parties that turn to support some particular leader, that tyranny at once rises up.'[119] Finally, Machiavelli draws the same moral from his account of the fall of the Roman republic in Book III. 'Sulla and Marius managed to find troops willing to follow them in actions contrary to the common good, and it was by

---

[115] *Disc.*, II. 2, p. 280: 'non il bene particulare ma il bene comune è quello che fa grandi le città'.

[116] *Disc.*, I. 9, p. 154: 'quello che fece fusse per il bene comune e non per ambizione propria'.

[117] See *Disc.*, III. 23, p. 452 on Manlius acting 'tutto . . . in favore del publico'; III. 30, p. 467 on Camillus acting 'ad utile publico'; III. 47, p. 502 on Fabius acting 'per beneficio publico'.

[118] *Disc.*, I. 7, p. 147: 'forze private . . . che sono quelle che rovinano il vivere libero'.

[119] *Disc.*, I. 40, p. 227: 'E quando e' non convengano a fare una legge in favore della libertà, ma gettasi qualcuna delle parti a favorire uno, allora è che subito la tirannide surge.'

these means that Caesar was then able to place his country in subjection.'[120]

Machiavelli's constitutional proposals are also largely dependent on traditional arguments. He presents them most clearly—both in a negative and a positive form—in the programmatic passage at the start of Book II. His negative thesis states that the common good is scarcely ever promoted under princely or monarchical rule. The explanation he offers is precisely the one that the earliest protagonists of republican government had taken from Sallust: kings are always liable to be suspicious of just those men of eminent talent who are most capable of serving their country well. In expressing this doubt, moreover, Machiavelli writes in a manner strikingly reminiscent of Sallust's own account. Even under the rule of a *virtuoso* tyrant, he declares, 'no benefit to the body politic can possibly result'. For 'no one exercising a tyranny can ever confer honours on any citizens under his rule who are truly good and capable, since he will never wish to have cause to fear them'.[121] This means that 'it is usually the case, whenever there is a princely form of rule, that the prince's behaviour is harmful to the city, while the behaviour of the city is harmful to the prince'.[122]

Machiavelli's positive thesis states that the only way to ensure the promotion of the common good must therefore be to maintain a republican form of government. The inference is resoundingly drawn in the same crucial passage at the start of Book II. 'There can be no doubt that it is only in republics that this ideal of the common good is properly considered. For it is only in republics that everything which needs to be done to attain this objective is followed out.'[123]

The vocabulary Machiavelli employs at this point would not of course have been familiar to the pre-humanist writers on city government. Following their Roman authorities, they had generally used the terms *res publica* and *repubblica* to denote the broad idea of the body politic, and thus to speak of any lawfully constituted regime.

[120] *Disc.*, III. 25, p. 456: 'Silla a Mario peterono trovare soldati che contro al bene publico gli seguitassono; per questo Cesare potette occupare la patria.'

[121] See *Disc.*, II. 2, p. 280, claiming that even under 'uno tiranno virtuoso', 'non ne risulterebbe alcuna utilità a quella republica . . . perché e' non può onorare nessuno di quegli cittadini che siano valenti e buoni che egli tiranneggia, non volendo avere ad avere sospetto di loro.'

[122] Ibid.: 'quando vi è uno principe, dove il più delle volte quello che fa per lui offende la città, e quello che fa per la città offende lui'.

[123] Ibid.: 'E sanza dubbio questo bene comune non è osservato se non nelle republiche: perché tutto quello che fa a proposito suo si esequisce.'

Nevertheless, the claim Machiavelli uses the term *repubblica* to express is one that all of them would have endorsed. As we have seen, they had all taken it for granted that, if the common good is to be upheld, it is indispensable to maintain an elective system of government as opposed to any form of princely or monarchical rule.

Finally, Machiavelli proceeds to draw from this line of reasoning the inference that the earliest apologists of the communes had already drawn. He insists that it is only under such elective constitutions that the goal of civic greatness can ever be achieved. He presents this final conclusion in two stages, and at each point he again invokes and develops a number of traditional arguments.

He begins by connecting the capacity to achieve civic greatness with the enjoyment of 'a free way of life'. The key statement of the case again appears at the start of Book II. 'It is easy to understand how an affection for living a free way of life springs up in peoples. For one sees by experience that cities have never increased either in power or in wealth unless they have been established in liberty.'[124] This point is then underlined—as in a number of pre-humanist writings on city government—by means of a strong allusion to Sallust's argument in the *Bellum Catilinae*. As we have seen, Sallust had observed that 'it was only when the city of Rome managed to become liberated from its kings that it was able, in such a short space of time, to rise to such greatness'. Machiavelli expresses the same sentiment in a remarkably similar style. 'Above all it is most marvellous to consider the greatness to which Rome rose after she had liberated herself from her kings.'[125]

Having connected liberty with greatness, Machiavelli completes his argument by adding that it is only possible to live 'in a free state' under a self-governing republic. It is true that he is not completely consistent in drawing the corollary that servitude will prove inevitable under monarchical forms of government.[126] But in general

---

[124] Ibid.: 'E facil cosa è conoscere donde nasca ne' popoli questa affezione del vivere libero: perché si vede per esperienza le cittadi non avere mai ampliato né di dominio né di ricchezza se non mentre sono state in libertà.'

[125] Ibid.: 'Ma sopra tutto maravigliosissima è a considerare a quanta grandezza venne Roma poiché la si liberò da' suoi Re.'

[126] He remarks at the outset that he will concentrate on those cities which 'have been far removed from all external servitude, and have at once been able to govern themselves by their own will'. See *Disc.*, I. 2, p. 129, speaking of cities 'lontano da ogni servitù esterna, ma si sono subito governate per loro arbitrio'. At that point he assumes that such self-governing arrangements can take the form 'either of republics or of principalities'. See ibid.: 'governate . . . o come republiche o come

he makes a sharp distinction between the freedom of republics and the slavery imposed not merely by tyrants[127] but even by the best kings and princes.[128] He first insists on the contrast at the beginning of Book I. Describing the early history of Rome, he concedes that 'Romulus and the other kings enacted many good laws of a kind compatible with a free way of life.' 'Nevertheless,' he goes on, 'their aim was to establish a kingdom and not a republic, with the consequence that, when the city became free, it still lacked many things that needed to be established in favour of liberty.'[129] The implication that one can only hope to live in genuine liberty under a republic is later spelled out at a considerable number of points. The moment, for example, when the Romans first 'elected two consuls in place of their king' is described as 'the beginning of their free way of life'.[130] Likewise, the period when the various peoples of Italy 'were all of them free' is described as a time 'when one never hears tell of there being any kings'.[131]

The essence of Machiavelli's republicanism can thus be summarized in the form of two connected propositions: first, that no city can ever attain greatness unless it upholds a free way of life; secondly, that no city can ever uphold a free way of life unless it maintains a republican constitution. With this statement of the case, Machiavelli not only presents a wholehearted defence of traditional republican values; he also presents that defence in a wholeheartedly traditional way.

principato'. In the course of his subsequent analysis, moreover, he reverts at several points to the suggestion that monarchical regimes may sometimes be compatible with liberty, and thus with the maintenance of what he calls a genuinely 'civil' or 'political' way of life. See, for example, I. 25, p. 193 and III. 1, p. 380.

[127] Freedom and tyranny are of course consistently contrasted. For general statements see *Disc.*, III. 7, p. 412 and III. 8, p. 416. For the case of Athens see I. 2, pp. 133–4. For the case of the later Tarquins in Rome see I. 17, pp. 177–8 and III. 2, p. 384.

[128] For the fullest statement of the argument that it is only possible to live in freedom under a self-governing regime and that such regimes are to be contrasted with principalities, see *Disc.*, I. 16, 173–5.

[129] *Disc.*, I. 2, 134: 'Perché Romolo e tutti gli altri Re fecero molte e buone leggi, conformi ancora al vivere libero; ma perché il fine loro fu fondare un regno e non una republica, quando quella città rimase libera vi mancavano molte cose che era necessario ordinare in favore della libertà.'

[130] See *Disc.*, I. 25, p. 192 for the claim that it was when the Romans 'in cambio d'uno re creati duoi consoli' that they established 'loro vivere libero'.

[131] See *Disc.*, II. 2, p. 279 for the claim that the time when the people of Italy 'erano tutti popoli liberi' was a time when 'né si ragiona mai che vu fusse alcuno re'. The same chapter goes on (283) to explain the loss of a love of liberty in modern Italy in terms of the fact that there are fewer republics than in ancient times.

4.   Was there a Renaissance in Music?

JESSIE ANN OWENS

FEW musicologists have challenged the notion that a 'Renaissance' occurred in music.[1] Most use the term to denote a music historical period from about 1430 to 1600, although there is considerable disagreement about the precise temporal boundaries.[2] I suspect that its use persists in part because there are obvious benefits to such period designations. 'Renaissance' can serve, for example, as a kind of short-hand designation in college music history survey courses or in the academic marketplace, as part of a job description, or as a way of organizing paper sessions at scholarly meetings. But surely the main reason why it continues to be used is the sense that there was something new (at whatever point might be chosen as the beginning boundary), some break from the past. In this essay, I would like to reflect both on the perception of change among writers of the fifteenth and sixteenth century and on the history of the use of the term

A longer version of this article appeared under the title 'Music Historiography and the Definition of "Renaissance" ', *Music Library Association Notes*, 47 (1990) 305–21. The present version, in keeping with its position in this volume, attempts to make a somewhat stronger case for a revisionist view of the term Renaissance. During the course of my work on this topic I received helpful suggestions from a number of colleagues and from fellow participants at the Courtauld conference; I extend special thanks to Lewis Lockwood and David Fallows.

[1] One exception is Reinhard Strohm, who in the preface to his *Music in Medieval Bruges*, rev. edn. (Oxford, 1990), p. v, states: 'I have not found it necessary to express my respect for Flemish music of the fifteenth century by using the keyword "Renaissance". It is open to discussion to what extent the term can be stretched without becoming purely decorative—perhaps that is already the case when it is applied to music at all.'

[2] Lewis Lockwood, 'Renaissance', *The New Grove Dictionary of Music and Musicians* (London, 1980), offers an account of the Renaissance as a period, using the temporal boundaries 1430–1600, that represents the prevailing understanding of the period. Most scholars place the beginning date anywhere from *c.*1400 to 1450 or even later; a few argue for 1300.

'Renaissance' as a period designation in musicology. My aim is to raise questions about its validity and usefulness.

The use of 'Renaissance' to describe a period in music history can be traced, at least indirectly, to Jacob Burckhardt.[3] In discussing music, Burckhardt did not write with his customary authority and in fact he devoted only a few pages to music. Most of his remarks concerned the social status of music, the use of instruments, performance by noble amateurs, and so on. He noted the predominance of Flemish rather than Italian composers. Echoing sentiments that had reached a fever pitch in nineteenth-century Germany, he praised Palestrina, 'whose genius still works powerfully among us'.[4]

Burckhardt's ideas about the Renaissance were transmitted to music history through the work of his friend and admirer, August Wilhelm Ambros, whose *Geschichte der Musik* marked the beginning of modern musical scholarship.[5] Ambros entitled the third volume, published in 1868, *Geschichte der Musik im Zeitalter der Renaissance bis zu Palestrina*.[6] Perhaps not surprisingly, Ambros was not entirely consistent in his use of the word 'Renaissance'; Naegele argued that he gave it at least three different meanings.[7] It referred to the true spirit of music: 'Our contemporary music is true Renaissance art'.[8] Renaissance also meant a rebirth or a revival of interest in antiquity. Ambros used it to refer to the movement associated with the Camerata in Florence at the end of the sixteenth century to rediscover ancient techniques for expressing the text—what we would now call the beginnings of baroque music. Finally, he used

---

[3] Jacob Burckhardt, *The Civilization of the Renaissance in Italy*, tr. S. G. C. Middlemore (New York, 1954), 289–92.

[4] For an idea of the massive bibliography on this subject, see *Palestrina und die Kirchenmusik im 19. Jahrhundert*, i, *Palestrina und die Idee der klassischen Vokalpolyphonie im 19. Jahrhundert*, ed. Winfried Kirsch (Regensburg, 1989). James Haar offers an insightful account of the understanding of the Renaissance during the 19th c.:'Music of the Renaissance as Viewed by the Romantics', in Anne du Shapiro (ed.), *Music and Context: Essays for John M. Ward* (Cambridge, Mass., 1985).

[5] A. W. Ambros, *Geschichte der Musik*, 4 vols. (Breslau, 1862–78, 1882). The fourth volume appeared posthumously, a fifth consists of examples to accompany vol. 3. The fundamental account of Ambros and his work continues to be Philipp Otto Naegele, 'August Wilhelm Ambros: His Historical and Critical Thought', Ph.D. dissertation (Princeton University, 1954). I follow Naegele's view of Ambros's indebtedness to Burckhardt; for a different view, see Haar, 'Music of the Renaissance', 127.

[6] James Haar reaches just the opposite conclusion: 'the one-and-a-half volumes devoted to music of the fifteenth and sixteenth centuries are not subtitled "The Renaissance" '. Haar's view of the relationship between Ambros and Burckhardt contrasts sharply with that of Naegele, whose views I have followed in this essay.

[7] Ambros, *Geschichte der Musik*, ii. 91–153.   [8] Ibid. ii. 149.

Renaissance to mean music from around 1450 to 1550 or 1600.[9] In this last sense, the term gained widespread acceptance.

How did it happen that Ambros designated as 'Renaissance' a period beginning in the mid-fifteenth century, when historians of literature and the fine arts set the boundaries much earlier, as early as 1300? There are several closely related answers that are linked by a common problem, namely, the loss of a musical past.

Music as an art form exists both in the ephemeral state of a performance and in a fixed, though inevitably schematic form in musical notation. It lives in the present as long as it continues to be performed or as long as the notation can be read. Once it ceases to be performed or can no longer be understood in its notated form, it disappears.

We can observe this loss of a musical past in the writings of music theorists from the fifteenth and sixteenth centuries. A number of writers provide rudimentary sketches of music history by listing composers in various categories (see Appendix 1). Many of them simply divide composers into two groups: earlier and later, living and dead, or *antichi* and *moderni*. Others divide the past into periods. Few of the writers have any sense of a past that extends further back in time than a few generations. For most of them, the past remains within the bounds of human memory.[10] The absence of any chronological sweep is striking, particularly in comparison to Vasari's view of the artistic developments from Cimabue onward to his own day.

Most of these writers valued music of the present more highly than that of the past. Several noted how different music was in this respect from the other arts. The sixteenth-century German writer Othmar Luscinius, for example, remarked: 'And how strange that we find in matters of music a situation entirely different from that of the general state of the arts and letters: in the latter whatever comes closest to venerable antiquity receives most praise; in music, he who does

---

[9] The 'Renaissance' volume covers: 'The Time of the Netherlanders' (from the second half of the 15th c. to the end of the 16th c., including Ockeghem, Josquin, Lasso); 'Music in Germany and England' (from the end of the 15th c. to the end of the 16th c., including Adam von Fulda, Fayrfax, Byrd); 'Italian Music of the Fifteenth Century' (a misleading heading actually appropriate only to the first section; subsequent sections deal with the Venetian School in the 16th c. and early 17th c., and the central and southern Italian precursors of Palestrina).

[10] It is interesting to compare these views of the musical past with those that consider the political or literary past. See Robert Black, 'Ancients and Moderns in the Renaissance: Rhetoric and History in Accolti's *Dialogue on the Preeminence of Men of his Own Time,*' *Journal of the History of Ideas,* 43 (1982).

not excel the past becomes the laughing stock of all.'[11] The Swiss humanist Heinrich Glarean, in complaining about composers who would not pay proper respect to earlier composers, revealed the existence in his day of a striking preference for music that was literally hot off the press: 'In fact, there are those in our time who despise the ancients and will not examine a song unless it has just recently come from a writer, still glowing hot from the anvil, as it were.'[12] With this intense interest in the new, compositions could become 'old' very quickly. Antonfrancesco Doni, for example, had one of the interlocutors in his *Dialogo della musica* (1544) dismiss the music of Arcadelt—a composer active in Florence in the 1530s—as 'troppo vecchio', although it could scarcely have been more than a decade old.[13]

Many of the writers identified a particular composer as a hero responsible for bringing music to its present state of perfection and correcting the abuses of the past. Each generation had its own hero, often called by terms such as the father of music or the prince of music.[14] In many cases, analogies were drawn with contemporary masters from the fine arts or literature or with past greats of music. From the middle of the fifteenth century until the end of the sixteenth, at least five composers were singled out. For LeFranc and Tinctoris, it was John Dunstable, *fons et origo*. For Folengo, Glarean, Coclico, Bartoli, and Calvisius, it was Josquin, whom Bartoli called the Michelangelo of music. Zarlino thought that Willaert was the new Pythagoras. Megnier thought that Lasso deserved the crown. Monteverdi called Cipriano de Rore the founder of the *seconda pratica*, the new way of thinking about the relationship between text and music.

Many of the writers criticized older music, though it is not clear how much of it they actually knew; only a few specifically acknowl-

[11] Othmar Luscinius, *Musurgia seu praxis musicae* (Strasbourg, 1536), 97–8, tr. Edward Lowinsky, in Bonnie J. Blackburn (ed.), *Music in the Culture of the Renaissance and Other Essays* (Chicago, 1988), 58.

[12] Heinrich Glarean, *Dodecachordon* (Basel, 1547), tr. Clement A. Miller, Musicological Studies and Documents, 6 (American Institute of Musicology [n.p.], 1965), 151.

[13] Antonfrancesco Doni, *Dialogo della musica* (Venice, 1544), fo. 9ᵛ. Concerning Arcadelt, see Iain Fenlon and James Haar, *The Italian Madrigal in the Early Sixteenth Century* (Cambridge, 1988), 69. Brian Vickers kindly pointed out to me similar shifts in taste evident in Elizabethan drama.

[14] Paula Higgins, in a forthcoming study, has assembled a number of additional references to the composer or master teacher as father.

edged having seen old compositions. Sometimes writers simply said that newer music is better without condemning older music. A far more common stance, however, was to criticize older music while praising that of the present. Tinctoris flatly condemned older music: 'There does not exist a single piece of music, not composed within the last forty years, that is regarded by the learned as worth hearing.' He admitted to having had 'in his hands certain old songs, called apocrypha, of unknown origin, so ineptly, so stupidly composed that they rather offended than pleased the ear'.[15]

Most of the writers, while acknowledging the classical and biblical origins of music, believed that music as they knew it was not very old. Sebald Heyden, writing in 1540, set the origins just beyond human memory, but no older than one hundred years: 'There are many indications that the invention of musical figures as presently constituted is not so old, but rather occurred a little before the memory of men of our time. In the first place, almost no records of songs for several voices are found anywhere which are proven to be more than one hundred years old.'[16] His knowledge of fifteenth-century music came from reading Tinctoris's *Proportionale* rather than from a familiarity with the music itself. Glarean, whose *Dodecachordon* was published in 1547 but completed probably by 1539, had a view similar to Heyden's; he believed that polyphony was not much older than seventy years, dating to about 1470:

But first it must be said that we wanted to provide three kinds of examples, reflecting the three ages of music. Indeed, the first (although we present very few of them) are old and simple, belonging to the infancy of this art; I believe the first inventors of this art composed in this way 70 years ago, nor (as far as we can determine) is this art much older.[17]

There are several explanations for this curious—and incorrect—belief that polyphony was a recent invention. One is that writers apparently had little access to older music. In 1581 Vincenzo Galilei stated that the polyphony of his day ('the way of singing many

---

[15] Johannes Tinctoris, *Liber de arte contrapuncti*, modern edn., *Johannis Tinctoris Opera Theoretica*, ed. Albert Seay, Corpus scriptorum de musica, 22 (American Institute of Musicology [n.p.], 1975), prologus, tr. Oliver Strunk, in *Source Readings in Music History from Classical Antiquity through the Romantic Era* (New York, 1950), 198.

[16] Sebald Heyden, *De arte canendi* (Nuremberg, 1540), fo. A2^r, tr. Clement A. Miller (American Institute of Musicology [n.p.], 1972), 18.

[17] Glarean, *Dodecachordon*, 240; the translation is based on Miller's, 248. Concerning the dating, see Miller's introd., 9.

melodies together') had been practised for no longer than 150 years, but he admitted that if his readers wanted 'an authoritative example of this modern practice that is so old, I don't know if they will be able to find one'.[18] Galilei was writing in Florence, closely involved with intellectuals and patrons of music, presumably accorded ready access to private libraries. Not only was he unaware that polyphonic music even existed in the thirteenth and fourteenth centuries, but he could not even cite an example of music from the middle of the fifteenth century. The oldest music he knew came from the Petrucci prints at the beginning of the sixteenth century. Even when writers had access to earlier music, the evidence suggests they did not always know what they had. Thomas Morley, writing in 1597, took Glarean as his authority concerning the beginnings of polyphony: 'so that reckoning downeward, from Glareanus his time, which was about 50 yeares agoe, we shal find that the greatest antiquity of our pricksong, is not above 130 yeares olde' (i.e. about 1470).[19] Yet he included excerpts of two pieces that were actually much earlier, evidently without realizing how old they were.[20] There are exceptions, to be sure. John Baldwin included several fifteenth-century pieces in the commonplace book he compiled at the end of the sixteenth century.[21] Zarlino cited theoretical evidence for polyphony as early as the ninth century and he referred to two parchment manuscripts in his possession that contained songs for two and three voices. The cover of one of the manuscripts bore the date 1397, and Zarlino suggested that the contents were even older.[22]

Another factor that may have contributed to this curiously limited view of the past is the nature of musical notation. Between about 1250 and 1500 the notation of rhythm underwent profound changes. Change was taking place so quickly that writers often presented both current and earlier practices when discussing notation. For example, Jacques de Liège, writing about the notational crisis that took place in music around 1320, compared the ancient and modern ways of

---

[18] Vincenzo Galilei, *Dialogo della musica antica et della moderna* (Florence, 1581), 80.

[19] Thomas Morley, *A Plaine and Easie Introduction to Practicall Musicke* (London, 1597), annotations to p. 9.

[20] I am indebted to David Fallows and Andrew Wathey for bringing these pieces to my attention.

[21] London, British Library, R.M. 24.d.2, facsimile edition, ed. Jessie Ann Owens (New York, 1987). My thanks to David Fallows for reminding me of this counter-example.

[22] Gioseffo Zarlino, *Sopplimenti musicali* (Venice, 1588), 17–18.

notating semibreves; by 'ancient' he meant the practices of Franco of Cologne and Petrus de Cruce some 75 years earlier.[23] At the beginning of the sixteenth century, Pietro Aaron explained the practices of the *moderni* regarding mode, tempus, and prolation, then discussed the practices of the *antichi*, since some of their music might still be found; 'ancient' is taken to mean roughly seventy-five years earlier, that is, composers of the mid-fifteenth century.[24] A third instance occurs in the writings of Lodovico Zacconi from the end of the sixteenth century. Before launching into a lengthy and detailed account of a notational system that was, in effect, no longer relevant, he made a telling statement about memory:

And even if nothing leaves one's mind on purpose, those subjects learned through memorization that are either infrequently recalled or actually replaced by newer things turn into shadow, dream or smoke. Among the topics under discussion that can easily be forgotten, we can mention the lessons and songs using mode, tempus and prolation. Having put these topics aside and not recalled them often, many people who previously understood them can no longer remember them.[25]

Zacconi admitted that modern singers could no longer sing 'ancient' music (i.e. the music of Josquin). The only reason he saw for learning the notation used in Josquin's music was the pure pleasure of knowing it—an intellectual satisfaction rather than a practical benefit. But he also realized that if this knowledge was not taught, the music would disappear completely. It is surely significant that all three writers presented the current practice and the one immediately preceding it, but not the practices of the more distant past.

It seems abundantly clear that musicians in the fifteenth and sixteenth century had a peculiarly restricted view of the past. Composers and musicians, unlike artists, could not see their past on a church wall. Nor, if we believe Zacconi, would they necessarily have been able to read it, had they found it on a library shelf. With few exceptions, the music they heard was new music; there was no 'early music' movement.[26] As an art form dependent on

---

[23] See Michael Long, 'Musical Tastes in Fourteenth-Century Italy: Notational Styles, Scholarly Traditions, and Historical Circumstances', Ph.D. dissertation (Princeton, NJ, 1981), 48–53.

[24] Pietro Aaron, *Thoscanello de la musica* (Venice, 1523), bk. 1, ch. 38.

[25] Lodovico Zacconi, *Prattica di musica* (Venice, 1592), fo. 85r.

[26] A possible exception to this statement is the new interest evident during the middle and end of the 16th c. in 'old' music, i.e. music of the early 16th c.; the titles of a number of printed anthologies boast of having both old and new music.

performance, music had a relatively short life: once a piece stopped being performed it was lost. Music had an immediate past, but no distant past beyond the span of human memory. There could be no Vasari for music historiography.

The conditions that created this distinctive view of the musical past continued to play a decisive role in music historiography of the eighteenth and nineteenth centuries and particularly in the emerging understanding of the Renaissance as a music-historical period. The development of music history as a discipline, from its beginnings at the end of the eighteenth century, coincides with the gradual recovery of lost repertories, and with them of a musical past.[27] The first great historians of music—Burney, Hawkins, Gerbert, Forkel, whose histories were all published in the last quarter of the eighteenth century—knew very little music composed before the time of Josquin; what they knew of earlier centuries came primarily from reading music theory.[28] The musical past, in other words, was as lost to them as it had been to Tinctoris, Glarean, and Zacconi, probably for the same reasons: a lack of access to the sources and the difficulty of deciphering the unfamiliar notations. Burney provided a telling account of his attempt to acquire transcriptions of the music of Guillaume de Machaut:

Neither the Abbe Lebeuf, nor the Count de Caylus [Burney's two sources of information about Machaut], have produced specimens of Machau's musical compositions; indeed, the Count frankly confesses, that, though he had studied them with the utmost attention, and consulted the most learned musicians, he has been utterly unable to satisfy his curiosity concerning their intrinsic worth. A correspondent at Paris had promised me transcripts of some of these pieces, which however are not yet arrived.[29]

Burney's description of the notation reveals its strangeness to him: 'In the music, which is written with great care and neatness, notes in a lozenge form, with tails to them, frequently occur; these, whether

[27] For an excellent account, see Frank L. Harrison, 'The European Tradition: The Origins of Music History', in Frank L. Harrison, Mantle Hood and Claude Palisca, *Musicology* (Englewood Cliffs, NJ, 1963).

[28] Charles Burney, *A General History of Music from the Earliest Ages to the Present* (London, 1776–89); citations from 2nd edn. with notes by Frank Mercer (New York, 1935); John Hawkins, *A General History of the Science and Practice of Music* (London, 1776); Martin Gerbert, *De cantu et musica sacra a prima ecclesiae aetate usque ad praesens tempus* (St Blaise, 1774); J. N. Forkel, *Allgemeine Geschichte der Musik* (Leipzig, 1788–1801).

[29] Burney, *A General History*, i. 615–16.

the heads were full or open, were at first called Minims; but when still a quicker note was thought necessary, the white or open notes only had that title . . .'[30]

The earliest composer to achieve a distinct musical identity was Josquin des Prez (*c*.1440–1521). Burney and Hawkins, although they could not be more different from one another in taste and temperament, both acquired a passion for his music, which they learned by transcribing it into score from sixteenth-century prints. They learned about his life from Glarean's biography, published in 1547, and from other published accounts.[31]

Why Josquin and not Machaut or Dufay, major figures from the fourteenth and fifteenth centuries? The timing of the arrival of a print culture—for music, it was 1500—meant that Josquin had a historiographical fate far different from that of either Dufay or Machaut.[32] The music, of Josquin was widely available in sixteenth-century printed editions, while that of Dufay and Machaut was preserved only in a relatively small number of manuscripts. Many of the important manuscripts containing music of the thirteenth to the fifteenth centuries were rediscovered only in the nineteenth century. The music of Josquin was also relatively simple stylistically, certainly easier to transcribe than that of the earlier composers. It was only in the nineteenth century that scholars began to rediscover how to transcribe earlier, more complicated polyphony.[33]

The discovery of sources and the new-found ability to decipher them led to a dramatic increase in the publication of old music in modern editions.[34] This detective work of finding old sources, deciphering the notation, and publishing the music enabled each generation of scholars to push further back in time the frontier of knowledge about early music. By the 1830s Kiesewetter knew enough

[30] Ibid. i. 614–15.

[31] Don Harrán, 'Burney and Ambros as Editors of Josquin's Music', *Josquin des Prez. Proceedings of the International Josquin Festival-Conference*, ed. E. E. Lowinsky (London, 1976), 147.

[32] On Dufay, see David Fallows, *Dufay* (London, 1982; 2nd edn., 1987), 257–9, 271; on Machaut, see Hans Lenneberg, *Witnesses and Scholars: Studies in Musical Biography* (New York, 1988), 31.

[33] See e.g. the foreword to Johannes Wolf, *Geschichte der Mensural-Notation von 1250–1460* (Leipzig, 1904) or 'Notation: Polyphony *c*.1260–1500', in *The New Grove Dictionary of Music*.

[34] See the discussion in Haar, 'Music of the Renaissance', 132, and Rudolf Bockholdt, 'Französische und niederländische Musik des 14. und 15. Jahrhunderts', in *Musikalische Edition im Wandel des historischen Bewußtseins*, ed. Thrasybulos G. Georgiades (Kassel, 1971), 149–74.

about Dufay to establish him as the head of what he called the 'First Netherlands Epoch'; he knew enough fourteenth-century music to realize that there was also a 'Vor-Dufayische Epoch', but there was not as yet an understanding of who the principal figures were or what the music was like.[35] Three decades later, when Ambros— Kiesewetter's nephew—wrote his history of music, the Squarcialupi codex, an important source of Italian fourteenth- and early fifteenth-century polyphony, had been discovered but its music had not yet been transcribed. For Ambros, fourteenth-century Italian music could be dismissed: 'The Florentine reformers of the fine arts and architecture in 1400 would . . . surely have stepped forward straightway as musical reformers as well, had the music of the Italians not lain in its swaddling clothes until after 1500, and had it then not been entirely dependent and conditioned by a highly developed Netherlandish art.'[36]

It was not until 1902 and 1903, with the publication of important studies by Friedrich Ludwig and Johannes Wolf, that scholars began to understand the brilliant flowering of music that took place in Florence and northern Italy, and in France as well, during the fourteenth century.[37] In 1904, Wolf christened the period 'Ars nova'; later scholars would debate the validity of considering the French and Italian developments under the separate names of 'French Ars nova' and the 'Italian Trecento'.

The timing of these discoveries had a significant impact on our understanding of 'Renaissance'. Had Ambros been aware of fourteenth-century music, particularly Italian music, had he known more about Francesco Landini, I think it probable that he would have constructed a far different hypothesis about the Renaissance in music.

More than forty years later, Hugo Riemann began his five-volume *Handbuch der Musikgeschichte*.[38] Following Ambros, he called the second volume, published in 1905, *Die Musik des Mittelalters* (*bis*

---

[35] R. G. Kiesewetter, *Geschichte der europäisch-abendländischen oder unserer heutigen Musik* (Leipzig, 1834).

[36] The translation is by Naegele, 'August Wilhelm Ambros', ii. 142.

[37] Johannes Wolf, *Florenz in der Musikgeschichte des 14. Jahrhunderts*, Habilitationsschrift (Berlin, 1902); extracts in *Sammelbände der internationalen Musikgesellschaft* iii (1901–2). Friedrich Ludwig, 'Die mehrstimmige Musik des 14. Jahrhunderts', *Sammelbände der internationalen Musikgesellschaft*, iv (1902–3). Concerning the history of editing Trecento music, see Marie Louise Martinez-Göllner, 'Musik des Trecento', in *Musikalische Edition*, ed. T. G. Georgiades (Kassel, 1971), 134–48.

[38] Hugo Riemann, *Handbuch der Musikgeschichte* (Leipzig, 1904–13).

1450) and the third volume, published in 1907, *Das Zeitalter der Renaissance bis 1600*. Between 1905 and 1907 he changed his mind about the temporal boundary between the Middle Ages and the Renaissance. The new scholarship on the Italian Trecento had convinced him that the Renaissance should be moved back to 1300, and he regretted that the second volume had already been published using the date 1450.[39]

Our present understanding of the Renaissance appears to have as one of its cornerstones an accident of historiography: Ambros's attempt to apply Burckhardt's notion at a time when there was no adequate understanding of music before 1450. I suspect that the second cornerstone is the literal acceptance of Tinctoris's view of a dramatic change in musical style. When we put Tinctoris's remarks into the wider context of writing about the past, however, it becomes clear that many writers perceived shifts in style. None had a sufficient knowledge of the past to serve as evidence for the construction of a music historical period.

In terms of the music itself, I can find little justification for using 'Renaissance' to denote a period beginning in 1430 or 1450. The evidence suggests instead that we should think of a single period extending from about 1250 or 1300 to 1550 or 1600, a period that is unified by its use of a particular notational system (the mensural system) and by its musical language (the language of counterpoint, music organized as individual lines woven together). Since this large span of time encompasses many different styles and sounds, 'Renaissance' is an equally inappropriate label for the period as a whole.

I think it would be prudent to restrict our use of 'renaissance' (with a small 'r') to specific instances of interest in the revival or rebirth of classical music and learning. One instance was the revival of interest in classical music theory during the fifteenth and sixteenth centuries, traced by Claude Palisca in *Humanism in Italian*

---

[39] Heinrich Besseler, 'Das Renaissanceproblem in der Musik', *Archiv für Musikwissenschaft* 23 (1966), 3–5. It is not clear why Riemann's proposal for an early beginning of the Renaissance did not prevail. It was used by a few scholars (Schering, Wiora, Engel), but largely ignored—not even debated—by others. In recent years it has been affirmed once again by Besseler and by Kurt von Fischer. See Besseler, 'Das Renaissanceproblem in der Musik'; Kurt von Fischer, 'Sprache und Musik im italienischen Trecent: Zur Frage einer Frührenaissance', in *Musik und Text in der Mehrstimmigkeit des 14. und 15. Jahrhunderts*, ed. Ursula Günther and Ludwig Finscher (Kassel, 1984), 37–54.

Renaissance Musical Thought.[40] A second instance was the attempt to revive, recreate, and imitate actual Greek musical practices that occurred at the end of the sixteenth century. Either of these movements might well bear the label 'renaissance' in the classic sense of rebirth.

Appendix 1   Periodization in Theoretical Writing

Johannes Tinctoris, *Proportionale musices* (*c.*1473–4), prologus:

novae artis fons et origo: Dunstaple
contemporanei: Dufay, Binchois
moderni: Okeghem, Busnois, Regis, Caron

Pietro Aaron, *Thoscanello de la musica* (Venice, 1523), Bk. I, ch. 38:

antichi: Busnois, Ocheghen, Duffai, Giovani di monte
——— , *Toscanello in musica* (Venice, 1529; cited from 1539 edn.), fo. I^r:
antichi: Orto, Alessando agricola, Pierazzon de larue, Iapart, Compere, Isach, Obrech [all pub. in *Odhecaton A*]
moderni: Iosquino, Giovanni motone, Antonio di fevin, Richafort, Constanzo festa, Longueval, Verdeloth, Piero de larue[!], Lheritihier

Giovanni Maria Lanfranco, *Scintille di musica* (Brescia, 1533), dedication:

antichi: Iosquino, Pierson della Rue, Agricola, Giovan Monton, Riccaforte
viventi: Adriano Villaert, Costanzo Festa, Iachetto, Hesdin

Sebald Heyden, *De arte canendi* (Nuremberg, 1540; after Tinctoris), fo. A2^v:

primo: Dunstapli
deinde: Dufay, Binchoi
donec: Ocgekhem, Busnoe, Caronte

Heinrich Glarean, *Dodecachordon* (Basel, 1547), 240:

prime . . . velut huius artis infantiae: 70 years ago
altera pubescentis: 40 years ago
tertia huius perfectae iam artis: 25 years ago

Adrian Petit Coclico, *Compendium musices* (Nuremberg, 1552; repet. Sebasiani in 1563):

theorici: Tubal Hebraeus, Lamech, Anphion, Orpheus, Boetius, Guido Arenensis, Ockghem, Iacobus Obrecht, Alexander

[40] Claude Palisca, *Humanism in Italian Renaissance Musical Thought* (New Haven, Conn., 1985).

mathematici: Io. Geyslin, Io. Tinctoris, Franchinus, Dufay, Busnoe, Buchoi, Caronte

musici praestantissimi: Iosquinus de Pres, Petrus de Larue, Brumel, Henricus Isaac, Ludovicus Senfel, Adrain VVillarth, Le brun, Concilium, Morales, Lafage, Lerithier, Nicolaus Gombert, Criquilon, Champion, and Iaquet, Pipelare, Nicolaus Paien, Courtois, Meyster Ian, Lupi, Lupus, Clemens non Papa, Petrus Massenus, Iacobus de Buis

poetici: students of previous group

Hermann Finck, *Practica musica* (Wittenberg, 1556):

novi inventores . . . *qui propius ad nostra tempora accedunt*: Iohan: Greisling, Franchinus, Iohan Tinctoris, Dufai, Busnoe, Buchoi, Caronte

c.1480 . . . *praestantiores*: Henricus Finck, Iosquinus de Pratis, Okekem, Obrecht, Petrus de larue, Brumelius, Henricus Isaac, qui partim ante Iosquinum, partim cum illo fuerunt, et deinceps Thomas Stoltzer, Steffanus Mahu, Benedictus Ducis

Nostro verò tempore: Nicolaus Gombert, Thomas Crecquilon, Iacobus Clemens non Papa, Dominicus Phinot, Cornelius Canis, Lupus Hellinc, Arnolt de Prug, Verdilot, Adrian Vuilhart, Gossen Iunckers, Petrus de Machicaurt, Iohan Castileti, Petrus Massenus, Matheus Lemeistre, Archadelt, Iacobus Vaet, Sebastian Hollander, Eustachius Barbion, Iohan Crespel, Iosquin Baston

Gallus Dressler, *Praecepta musicae poeticae* (1564):

primus genus: Josquinus
secundus: Heinricus Isaac, Senfel
tertius: Clemens, Gombertus, Crequillus
quartus: Orlandus

Cosimo Bartoli, *Ragionamenti accademici* (Venice, 1567):

[*first group*]: Ocghem (fu quasi il primo che in questi tempi, ritrovasse la Musica quasi che spenta del tutto); Iosquino (discepolo di Ocghem); dopo Josquino: Giovan Monton, Brumel, Isac, Andrea de Silva, Giovanni Agricola, Marchetto da Mantova

[*second group*]: Adriano [Willaert], Costanzio Festa, Verdelotto, Archadel, Giachetto da Mantova, Gombert, Crechiglione, Christiano Olanda, Clemens non Papa, Scobeto, Morales, Cipriano Rore, Francesco Corteccia, Matio rampollini

Lodovico Guicciardini, *Descrittione* . . . *di tutti i paesi bassi* (Antwerp, 1567):

tutti morti: Giovanni del Tintore di Nivelle, Iusquino di Pres, Obrecht Ockegem, Riccafort, Adriano VVillaert, Giovanni Monton, Verdelot,

Gomberto, Lupus lupi, Cortois Crecquillon, Clemente non Papa, and
Cornelio Canis
vivono: Cipriano de Rore [d. 1565], Gian le Coick, Filippo di Monti,
Orlando di Lassus, Manchicourt, Barbi, Iusquino Baston, Christiano
Hollando, Giaches di VVaet, Bonmarche, Severino Cornetto, Piero du
Hot, Gherardo di Tornout, Huberto VVaelrant, Giachetto di Berckem

Pietro Gaetano, *Oratio de origine et dignitate musices* (between 1565 and
1574), fo. 19^r–20^v:
prima aetas: beyond human memory
altera deinceps (drawn from the writings of Tinctoris): Duffai, Demomarto,
Busnois, Heloi, Barburgan, Binthois
tertiam aetas: Ocheghen, Josquin de pres, Brumel, Fevim, Monton, Petrus de
larue, Andreas de sylva
quarta aetas: Adrianus uillaert, Nicolaus Gomberth, Carpentras, Janechin,
Lheritier meus Praeceptor, Constantius festa, Morales, Jachet, Verdelot,
et alii. Huic [Willaert] deinceps mortuo, Ciprianus Rore, Josephusque
Zarlinus eius discipuli in magisterium alter post alterum successere
quinta aetas: contemporaries

Lodovico Zacconi, *Prattica di musica* (Venice, 1592), fo. 7^r:
antichi: (a) filosofi: Pitagora, Platone, Macrobio, Anfione, Diodoro, Boetio,
S. Agostino, e molti altri; (b) compositori: Iusquino, Gio, Mottone
l'Ochghen, Brumello, Henrico Isaac, Lodovico Senfelio, e molti altri
vecchi: Adriano Vuilarth, Morales, Ciprian Rore, il Zerlino, il Palestina e
altri, i quali furono dopoi, and appresso l'età nostra
moderni: gl'auttori sono ancora vivi, ò se pur sono morti, sono mancati giovani, e inanzi l'età senile

Giulio Cesare Monteverdi, 'Dichiaratione della lettera stampata nel quinto
libro de' suoi madrigali', in Claudio Monteverdi, *Scherzi musicali a tre
voci* (Venice, 1607):
prima pratica: Occheghem, Josquin de pres, Pietro della Rue, Iovan Motton,
Clemens non Papa, Gombert, Messer Adriano, Zerlino
seconda pratica: Cipriano Rore, Ingegneri, Marenzo, Giaches Wert,
Luzzasco, Giaccopo Peri, Giulio Caccini

Johannes Nucius, *Musices poeticae sive de compositione cantus praceptiones*
(Neisse, 1613)
primum[:] circa annum Christi 1400. aut certe paulo post. Dunxstapli Anglus
a quo primum figuralem musicam inventam tradunt
[second]: Dupfai Binchoy per quos musicam celebriorem redditam scribunt

[third]: Iohannes Okhenhaim vel Okhenkem, Busuoe, Charonte, Iosquinus, Isaac, Crequillon, Gomberth, Clemens non Papa, Senflius, Verdeloth, Lerithier, Stolzer, Lemlin, Iacchet, Pamminger, Heigell, Dominicus Finot, Iohannes Cortois, Benedictus Ducis, Claudin, Carpentras

5. *Renovatio* or *Conciliatio?* How Renaissances Happened in Venice

PATRICIA FORTINI BROWN

PARADIGMS, once fixed, are notoriously hard to put aside. A recent book on the city-state in five cultures from the Bronze Age to the modern period offers a case in point. Seeking to broaden the canon by taking a comparative and global approach, the book also inadvertently highlights the problem facing students of European history in the Renaissance period. The section on Italy features a three-part bibliography with the following headings: (*a*) Italian city-states generally; (*b*) Florence; and (*c*) other city-states. These categories tidily sum up the historiographical problem. Cities as disparate as Ferrara, Genoa, Milan, Orvieto, Padua, Perugia, Pistoia, Rome, Siena, and Venice are relegated to a miscellany, effectively serving as foils to Florence, the ultimate paradigm, not only of the Renaissance city-state, but also of 'Renaissance' as a cultural phenomenon.[1] Indeed, despite efforts to widen the canon, Florentine studies still tend to hold the field and to dominate the literature.

For all that, the comparative approach provides a useful model for transcending paradigms. And yet, with the current tendency toward specialization, reinforced by the profoundly localized character of Italian historiography, it is probably too much to ask any single scholar to do the whole job and get the facts right. A more focused initiative on city-states that expanded the dialogue beyond the usual chronological boundaries, but kept within the Western tradition, was made by a group of scholars at Brown University with a conference whose papers were recently published under the title *City States in Classical Antiquity and Medieval Italy: Athens and Rome, Florence*

[1] Robert Griffeth and Carol G. Thomas (eds.), *The City-State in Five Cultures* (Santa Barbara, 1981), 214–16.

and Venice.[2] Proposing a four-part paradigm, they aimed 'to undertake a parallel reading of the history and analysis of the development, structures and conflicts—social, economic, and political—of
both sets of cities, using insights gained from one to illuminate the
other'.[3]

The result was illuminating in many ways, for it pointed up incon-
gruities as well as parallels. Sensitive areas emerged; at least two
seem worth noting. The first was linguistic. Despite a shared vocabulary and imagery, it is apparent that the participants often used the
same terms to talk about different things. Even the modern hybrid
city-state required definition and circumscription.[4] Interpretation
becomes even more problematic when we confront the verbal and
visual *topoi* of past cultures—often reassuringly familiar and just as
often alien to one another as well as to us in meaning and purpose.

The second source of potential misunderstanding lay in the nature
of available evidence. One of the motivating factors for the conference had been the possibility of drawing analogies from the written
testimony of the medieval period in order to throw light on problems in the ancient world, where the documentary material is much
less abundant and more fragmentary. Aside from the problem of
making valid arguments by analogy, it becomes clear that one cannot always ask the same questions of different kinds of evidence. The
lack of congruence in types of historical documentation is, of course,
just as relevant for the Renaissance proper as for the pendulating
play between antiquity and the Middle Ages. The Florentine *ricor-
danze*, for example, were constructed with different aims from the
Venetian civic chronicle. Even though each form of historical writing was compiled for family use, we will often be as frustrated in our
attempt to find out about the origins of the city in the first instance
as we will be in trying to learn more about the origin of the family
in the second.

So it is a risky business to allow any single centre to define,
absolutely, the paradigm. Moreover, as Enrico Castelnuovo observes,
the definition of a centre depends on one's viewpoint. Using Vasari

---

[2] Anthony Molho, Kurt Raaflaub and Julia Emlen (eds.), *City States in Classical
Antiquity and Medieval Italy: Athens, Rome, Florence, and Venice* (Stuttgart, 1991;
Ann Arbor, 1992).
[3] Ibid. 11; see also 19–30, Wilfred Nippel, 'Introductory Remarks: Max Weber's
"The City" Revisited'.
[4] Ibid. 33–51, Nicole Loraux, 'Reflections of the Greek City on Unity and Division';
53–69, Timothy J. Cornell, 'Rome: The History of an Anachronism'.

as a case in point, he notes that centres can even be made peripheral retroactively.[5] Often misunderstanding artistic intentions outside Florence and Rome, Vasari's praise for art and artists in northern Italy and elsewhere that did not fit into his approved canon of central Italian art was often faint indeed.[6]

Moving closer to our own time we come to Burckhardt, another creator of paradigms, with *The Civilization of the Renaissance in Italy*. While he gave conscientious attention to courts and cities throughout Italy, he also created a new binary model with his oppositional pairing of Florence and Venice in a chapter entitled 'The Republics'.[7] But it is a duality that might have seemed strange to the principals involved, for they had their own *paragone*. While all cities in this period competed with one another in displays of wealth and power, they characteristically pressed their claims in civic panegyric not by comparing themselves with one another directly, but rather with the great civilizations of antiquity.

Indeed, for the Venetian diarist Marin Sanudo and for his fellow citizens, the standard of comparison was clearly not Florence. He avowed:

One can therefore compare the Venetians to the Romans (who raised such stately edifices) on account of the buildings, both private and public, being erected at the present time. Indeed it can be said, as another writer has done, that our republic has followed the Romans in being as powerful in military strength as in virtue and learning. He writes, moreover, 'Greece was the seat of learning and powerful in arms; now the Venetians are the learned ones, now the lion is strongly armed'.[8]

While Sanudo is notable for his attention to circumstance and detail, similar claims had been made by chroniclers for cities north

[5] Enrico Castelnuovo, 'Introduction to Part I: Center and Periphery: Dissemination and Assimilation of Style', in *World Art. Themes of Unity in Diversity* (Acts of the XXVIth International Congress of the History of Art), ed. Irving Lavin (University Park, Penn., 1989), 43–7, at 47; cf. 49–58, Jan Bialostocki, 'Some Values of Artistic Periphery'.

[6] e.g. see Patricia Fortini Brown, *Venetian Narrative Painting in the Age of Carpaccio* (New Haven, Conn., 1988), 235–6.

[7] Still viable, as attested by the recently begun series of Villa I Tatti Papers cited in n. 60 below. In a welcome change of direction, the most recent edition pairs Florence and Milan.

[8] Marin Sanudo, *De origine, situ et magistratibus urbis venetae ovvero La Città di Venetia (1493–1530)*, ed. A. C. Aricò (Milan, 1980), 34, tr. from David Chambers and Brian Pullan with Jennifer Fletcher (eds.), *Venice: A Documentary History, 1450–1630* (Oxford, 1992), 16–17.

and south of the Alps since late antiquity, when Byzantine writers
had proclaimed Constantinople as the New Rome and called themselves Romans.[9] The maturing of the Italian commune was accompanied by numerous claims of rebirth of, succession to, parity with,
and even superiority over the cities of the ancient world: most
notably Rome and Athens, but also Constantinople and Jerusalem.
Sanudo's Florentine counterpart, Goro Dati, was thus only following a centuries-old tradition when he claimed that 'the Florentines,
who founded and remade Florence, formed the city like Rome as
much as they could, although it would be small, but giving it as
much resemblance as possible . . ..'[10]

Were Sanudo and Dati simply claiming the same thing? Not really:
for all the obvious parallels, Dati clearly had the edge over Sanudo
in one particular sense. He could claim with archaeological certainty
a physically-grounded Roman foundation for his city, and here
again, as in so many things, Venice was different. The often-noted
fact that Venice may well be the only major city in Italy that had no
Roman past of its own not only allows us to provide an alternative
model to the Florentine experience; it demands it.[11] This brings us
to the main concern of this essay. In it, we will take up Sanudo's
challenge and look at the recurring phenomenon of civic *renovatio*
in the formation of a Venetian historical consciousness and in the
assertion of a Venetian civic identity: in short, how renaissances happened in Venice.[12]

[9] William Hammer, 'The Concept of the New or Second Rome in the Middle
Ages', *Speculum*, 19 (1944), 50–62, at 51, who observes that in the Middle Ages the
terms *Roma Nova* and *Roma secunda* were typically applied to cities that sought to
rival Rome: Constantinople, Aachen, Trier, Milan, Rheims, Tournai and Pavia. Cf.
Robert Lee Wolff, 'The Three Romes: The Migration of an Ideology and the Making
of an Autocrat', *Daedalus*, 88 (1959), 291–311, at 293.

[10] Goro Dati, *Istoria di Firenze di . . ., dall'anno MCCCLXXX all'anno MCCCCV*
(Florence, 1735), 107, cited by Enrico Guidoni, 'Roma e l'urbanistica del Trecento',
in Federico Zeri (ed.), *Storia dell'arte italiana*, v, *Dal Medioevo al Quattrocento* (Turin,
1983), 347.

[11] Cf. G. Marzemin, *Le origini romane di Venezia* (Venice, 1937); Wladimiro
Dorigo, *Venezia origini. Fondamenti, ipotesi, metodi*, 3 vols. (Milan, 1983); and now
Alberto Francesconi, 'Una città sommersa tutta da scoprire', *Marco Polo*, 89 (1991),
12–13. See the response of Juergen Schulz, 'Urbanism in Medieval Venice', in Molho,
Raaflaub and Emlen (eds.), *City-States in Classical Antiquity and Medieval Italy*,
419–20 n. 2.

[12] The theme is treated from a different perspective in Patricia Fortini Brown, 'The
Self-Definition of the Venetian Republic', in Molho, Raaflaub and Emlen (eds.), *City
States in Classical Antiquity and Medieval Italy*, 511–48. It also forms part of my book-
in-progress, tentatively entitled *Venice and Antiquity: The Venetian Sense of the Past*
(New Haven, Conn., forthcoming).

The small 'r' is intentional, for examples of Venetian responses to antique civic paradigms (implicit or otherwise) appear already in the thirteenth century, well before the period that is usually called the Renaissance.[13] Beginning with the early Christian *renovatio* of the Basilica of San Marco, convincingly described by Otto Demus, we will move on through its further elaboration in the trecento and into the fifteenth century and the Renaissance proper. Here the propensity towards renewal takes on a more pronounced multifaceted character, with coexisting allusions in art and architecture to the past civilizations of Rome, Byzantium, and Jerusalem. While all these tendencies continue throughout the sixteenth century, in this essay we will consider the phenomenon from its earliest symptoms up to the period around 1509, the watershed year of the War of the League of Cambrai.

Venetian archaeological self-fashioning had begun as early as the ninth century with the construction of the first Church of San Marco as the palatine chapel of the doge on the model of Justinian's Church of the Holy Apostles in Constantinople. When San Marco was rebuilt in the eleventh century on the same plan, the architects would have been working from a model that was by then five hundred years old [FIG. 5.1]. It would be misleading to attribute both echo and re-echo to the same motivations, for Venice was still closely tied to the Byzantine Empire in the ninth century, while two hundred years later she had already emancipated herself politically and economically. It is thus quite possible that the first replication was primarily intended to claim political legitimacy (by invoking an imperial palatine model for the state church) and the second to imply ecclesiastical authority (by claiming pre-eminence in conserving and continuing the ancient Christian past).[14]

[13] For two fine analyses of the current state of the field on the issue of *Renaissance*, see Denys Hay, 'Historians and the Renaissance during the Last Twenty-Five Years', in id., *The Renaissance: Essays in Interpretation* (London, 1982), 7; and Gerhart B. Ladner, 'Terms and Ideas of Renewal', in Robert Benson and Giles Constable with Carol D. Lanham (eds.), *Renaissance and Renewal in the Twelfth Century* (Cambridge, Mass., 1982), 1–33.

[14] Otto Demus, 'A Renascence of Early Christian Art in Thirteenth-Century Venice', in *Late Classical and Mediaeval Studies in Honor of Albert Mathias Friend, Jr.* (Princeton, 1955), 348–61; Id., 'Oriente e Occidente nell'arte veneta del Duecento', in *La civiltà veneziana del secolo di Marco Polo* (Florence, 1955); id., *The Church of San Marco in Venice: History, Architecture, Sculpture*, Dumbarton Oaks Studies, vi (Washington, DC, 1960). See also Ernst Kitzinger, 'The Arts as Aspects of a Renaissance: Rome and Italy', in Benson, Constable and Lanham (eds.), *Renaissance and Renewal*, 637–70.

Fig. 5.1 San Marco and the Ducal Palace, Venice, from the south-west

The earliest surviving Venetian chronicle also dates to the eleventh century. Written by John the Deacon, it addresses the delicate question of Venice's obscure beginnings with a model of two Venices. For John, the predecessor of the present city was not Constantinople, but Aquileia, capitol of the first Venice, 'in which the Holy evangelist Mark, illuminated by divine grace, preached the gospel of our lord Jesus Christ'. The second Venice was founded by inhabitants of the first, who took refuge on the islands of the lagoon at the time of the Lombard invasions in the sixth century. John the Deacon thus established a genealogy for the upstart community, which could now trace its ecclesiastical authority directly back to St Mark the Evangelist.[15]

Two outside observers interpreted the message (whether gained from written or visual sources) in terms of rebirth and filiation. St Peter Damian proclaimed Venice both 'a reborn Aquileia' by virtue of

[15] Giovanni Diacono, *Cronaca Veneziana*, *Cronache veneziane antichissime*, ed. Giovanni Monticolo (Rome, 1890), 59–60, 13. See also Giovanni Lorenzoni, 'Origini di Venezia', *Arte Medievale* 1 (1983), 39–48; Antonio Carile and Giorgio Fedalto, *Le origini di Venezia* (Bologna, 1978), and *Storia della cultura veneta*, i, *Dalle origini al Trecento* (Vicenza, 1976).

her possession of St Mark's relics, and a daughter of Rome by reason of affinity between those relics and St Peter, the prince of the Apostles. Pope Gregory VII expanded on the theme by praising Venice's liberty, which she had received *ab antiqua* from her Roman roots.[16] If the Byzantine character of San Marco was recognized as such, it does not seem to have been a hindrance to either writer in reaching back further into the Western past and defining the republic of Venice as a rightful successor to Rome as an apostolic city true and proper.[17]

Was the Venetian revival of a late antique model in San Marco unique in the eleventh century? The answer is a qualified yes and a qualified no. The wholesale appropriation of a Byzantine prototype was unusual at the time, but the retrospective tendency was not. It can be viewed as part of a broader movement of heightened civic awareness of antique authority in the emerging free communes.[18] In a number of cases, the proper placement of even the most fragmentary architectural *spolia* seems to have endowed a contemporary building with a resonance of the political authority of ancient Rome. Pisa Cathedral is a case in point. Embedded in the wall of its south transept and apse are a number of blocks with Roman inscriptions, deliberately positioned so that the letters would be visible, albeit, in several cases, upside down [FIG. 5.2]. Recent studies show that Pisa imported hundreds of such marbles from Ostia and Rome in the eleventh and twelfth centuries, even though there were abundant remains on the site. Displayed as trophies in the fabric of the Cathedral, they established a privileged link between Pisa and Rome. The perfectly-formed majuscule lettering, no matter how fragmentary, implied that Pisa was not only the daughter, but also the successor, to Rome.[19]

---

[16] Gina Fasoli, 'Nascità di un mito', in *Studi storici in onore di Gioacchino Volpe* (Florence, 1958), i. 445–79, at 460, citing Petri Damiani, *Opera Omnia* (Paris, 1743), 36–7; and Gregory VII in *Monumenta Germaniae Historica*, Epist. sel., ii. 175, 341.

[17] Cited in Fasoli, 'Nascità di un mito', 447–79, at 460–1.

[18] From a rich literature, see Lelia Cracco-Ruggini and Giorgio Cracco, 'Changing Fortunes of the Italian City from Late Antiquity to Early Middle Ages', *Rivista di filologia e istruzione classica*, 105/4 (1977), 448–75 at 463–75; Jacques Le Goff, 'L'immaginario urbano nell'Italia medievale (secoli V–XV)', in *Storia d'Italia. Annali 5. Il paesaggio*, ed. Cesare De Seta (Turin, 1982), 5–43; and Chiara Frugoni, 'L'antichità: dai *Mirabilia* alla propaganda politica', in Salvatore Settis (ed.), *Memoria dell'antico nell'arte italiana*, ii, *L'uso dei classici* (Turin, 1984), 5–72.

[19] Gustina Scaglia, 'Romanitas pisana tra XI e XII secolo. Le iscrizioni romane del Duomo e la statua del console Rodolfo', *Studi Medievali*, 13 (1972), 791–843; and Michael Greenhalgh, ' "Ipsa ruina docet": l'uso dell'antico nel Medioevo', in Settis (ed.), *Memoria dell'antico*, i. 134–8.

Fig. 5.2 Pisa Cathedral, the exterior wall of the apse

It was also during the eleventh century that the Florentines began construction of their Baptistery. Its marble revetted Romanesque architecture looked so Roman to later viewers that Giovanni Villani, writing in the early fourteenth century, was not alone in affirming that it had been built in antiquity as a temple dedicated to Mars.[20]

The Venetian initiative, however, has a distinctly different flavour. With allusions more ecclesiastical than temporal, the deliberate archaism of San Marco's construction was only a prologue to the purposefully retrospective paleo-Christian character of its thirteenth-century decoration campaign. As Otto Demus argues so persuasively, a number of sculptural reliefs both inside and outside the church were carved in imitation of fifth- or sixth-century models, probably ill-gotten gains of the Fourth Crusade, taken from Constantinople after 1204 when the Venetians and the French had joined forces to sack the city [FIG. 5.3]. The victory had marked Venice's debut as an imperial power and remained vivid in civic memory. The oppor-tunistic fabrication of 'historical artifacts' was accompanied by the mosaic decoration of the atrium with scenes modelled directly on the Cotton *Genesis*, an early Christian manuscript. For Demus, this was yet another example of a *renovatio* that was intended to give the city a legitimate Christian history grounded in the 'age of the apostles'.[21]

In two recent studies, Juergen Schulz builds on Demus's idea of an early Christian *renovatio* at San Marco and extends it to embrace the architectural elaboration of the entire complex around the Piazza San Marco in a Roman *imperial*, as well as Christian, revival. Schulz suggests that the scheme, completed in the 1260s, was inspired by the late Roman *fora* of Constantinople, with their colonnades, temples, rows of shops, and monumental columns [FIGS. 5.4 and 5.5]. In his view it was a tangible expression of Venice's own rise to empire.[22]

[20] Mario Salmi, 'La "Renovatio Romae" e Firenze', *Rinascimento*, 1 (1950), 5–24, esp. 7. See also Nicolai Rubinstein, 'The Beginnings of Political Thought in Florence: A Study in Mediaeval Historiography', *Journal of the Warburg and Courtauld Institutes*, 5 (1942), 198–227; and Charles T. Davis, 'Il Buon Tempo Antico', in Nicolai Rubinstein (ed.), *Florentine Studies: Politics and Society in Renaissance Florence* (London, 1968), 45–69.

[21] Kurt Weitzmann, 'The Genesis Mosaics of San Marco and the Cotton Genesis Miniatures', in Otto Demus, *The Mosaics of San Marco in Venice* (Chicago, 1984), ii. 105–42.

[22] Juergen Schulz, 'Urbanism in Medieval Venice', 419–66, at 437–40; id., 'La piazza medievale di San Marco', *Annali di architettura*, 4–5 (1992–3), 134–56. I am most grateful to Professor Schulz for allowing me to read this piece in typescript before publication.

FIG. 5.3 San Marco, west façade, Porta Sant'Alipio with a lintel relief, carved in a 5th–6th century proto-Byzantine style

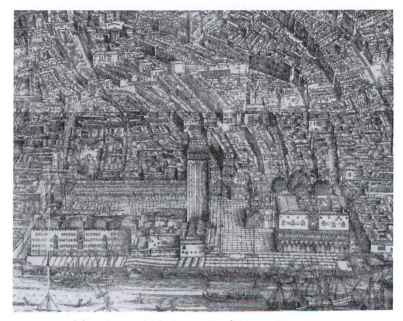

FIG. 5.4 Detail from Jacopo de' Barbari, *View of Venice*, 1500

Schulz's arguments remind us of another category of objects: those recently-acquired pieces that were not copied or faked, but deliberately left untouched. These were simply stuck on to the fabric of the church or placed near it as trophies and include, for example, the triumphal bronze quadriga installed above the main entrance, the so-called pillars of Acri and the Byzantine marble reliefs and the four porphyry swordsmen set into the wall of the Treasury. Unabashedly booty, these pieces were all the more visible, and symbolically resonant, for being left intact and arranged in a seemingly random manner.[23] As David Lowenthal points out, artifacts such as these have a particularly ambivalent status, being simultaneously past and present with a commingling (and sometimes confusion) of ancient and modern roles. By their very nature they are incomplete—parts of a once

[23] See Demus, *The Church of San Marco*, 29, 112–14; and Edward Muir, 'Images of Power: Art and Pageantry in Renaissance Venice', *American Historical Review*, 84 (1979), 16–52.

Fig. 5.5 *Constantinople*, a detail, in Cristoforo Buondelmonte, *Liber Insularum Archipelagi*

larger whole.[24] Signifying both a presence (in themselves) and an absence (of their original whole), they testified not simply to Venice's early Christian past, but also to her triumphant present: a rising republic whose doge was—for a time—Lord of a Quarter and Half a Quarter of the Byzantine Empire. Pietro Ziani (d. 1228), the first Doge to assume that title, could thus be proclaimed the equal of Roman emperors on his tomb:

[24] David Lowenthal, *The Past is a Foreign Country* (Cambridge, 1985), 74–87, 248. See also Salvatore Settis, 'Continuità, distanza, conoscenza. Tre usi dell'antico', in id. (ed.), *Memoria dell'antico nell'arte italiana*, iii, *Dalla tradizione all'archeologia* (Turin, 1986), 375–486, at 382 and 466–72. Settis observes: 'È dunque l'uso delle rovine, dei frammenti, si carica inevitabilmente di una tensione verso l'intero: che sarà, anche verso il recupero del significato originario.'

Rich, honest, patient and in all things sage,
None could be his equal amongst the high-born and wise,
Not even Caesar and Vespasian were they still alive.[25]

How, then, does one interpret the other 'foreign' elements—French Gothic, German, Saracen—that are worked into the Venetian equation at San Marco? Finding many Islamic motifs in San Marco and the Ducal Palace, along with other buildings in Venice built in the thirteenth and fourteenth centuries, Deborah Howard asks whether these appropriations were simply responses to the aesthetic taste of a trading nation with important activity in the Middle East, or whether they could have held specific symbolic meanings for Venetians. In the latter case they may well have signified the Christian rather than the Islamic East.[26] Indeed, without excluding references to Byzantium, Staale Sinding-Larsen looks at the same area around San Marco and sees in it an image of Jerusalem. Allowing that many churches in the Middle Ages were compared to the Holy Sepulchre, he cites the anonymous chronicler of the twelfth-century *Chronicon altinate*, who proclaimed that San Marco had been built 'according to the example that he had seen at the temple of our Lord in Jerusalem'.[27]

Clearly, original intentions and meanings of the same building may change over time, and corporate patrons probably mean multiple intentions by definition. Sinding-Larsen goes further than this, however, and sees deliberate ambiguity. He concludes: 'The method of adapting suggestions that avoid declarations that are too explicit appears characteristic for Venice in its ideological attitude: this is an attitude of total diplomacy.' But is it diplomacy or a sort of all-encompassing conciliation? In any case, as Sinding-Larsen observes, the sum and substance of all these imported elements is something new in the new setting: not really Byzantine (or Islamic), but Venetian.[28]

[25] 'Dives, probus, patiens et in cunctis planus | Nulus sibi similis nobilis vel sanus | Nec si Caesar viveret et Vespasianus.' Cited by Schulz, 'The Medieval Piazza di San Marco'.

[26] Deborah Howard, 'Venice and Islam in the Middle Ages: Some Observations on the Question of Architectural Influence', *Architectural History*, 34 (1991), 59–74.

[27] Cited by Staale Sinding-Larsen, 'St. Peter's Chair in Venice', in Moshe Barasch and Lucy Freeman Sandler (eds.), *Art the Ape of Nature: Studies in Honor of H. W. Janson* (New York, 1981), 35–50, esp. 42–3.

[28] Staale Sinding-Larsen, 'Venezia e le componenti artistiche bizantine e cristiano-orientali nel secolo XIII. Prospettive di ricerche', in Michelangelo Muraro (ed.), *Componenti storico-artistiche e culturali a Venezia nei secoli XIII e XIV* (Venice, 1981), 37–43.

Venice's fabrication of a dignified past found its most eloquent literary expression in the third quarter of the century in Martino da Canal's *Estoires de Venise*. Introducing two politically resonant episodes in the legend of St Mark—the *praedestinatio* and the *apparitio*—he offered proof to Venetians that their city had had a fore-ordained and divinely-sanctioned destiny from the time of Christ. The new events were now inserted into the full narrative sequence of Mark's life that was restated in mosaic form in the Basilica.[29]

Canal incorporated other emendations into his *Estoires* that gave the city an even more primitive foundation in the pre-Christian *and* pre-Roman past. Avowing that the inhabitants of the first Venice were of noble Trojan ancestry—always free men who had never paid tribute to anyone—with a famous founding father in the person of Antenor, he also gave the establishment of the second Venice a more precise, and earlier, chronology. Instead of the Lombards, it was now the 'impious pagan named Attila, most savage, with a great army', who had driven the Christian descendants of the original Trojan settlers to take refuge in wood huts on the uninhabited islands of the lagoon. By pre-empting the Lombards with Attila, *Flagellum Dei*, the chronicler could now distinguish the Venetians as specifically *Christian* refugees, fleeing unambiguously pagan hordes.[30]

In 1292 the chronicler known to us only as Marco went further than Canal and claimed that the first Trojan colonists had arrived in the Venetian lagoon (and not just Aquileia) immediately after the fall of Troy, while Rome would be founded only 454 years later. 'And on account of this', he contended, 'it is well known that the first construction of Rialto preceded the construction of the city of Rome'.[31]

The century ended with yet another attempt to imply antique origins for San Marco. These were the years immediately after the closure of the Great Council in 1297, a time of heightened civic self-consciousness, and the case is instructive, for like Marco and

---

[29] Martino da Canal, *Les Estoires de Venise: Cronaca veneziana in lingua francese dalle origini al 1275*, ed. Alberto Limentani (Florence, 1972), 218–19 and 340–1. See also Brown, 'Self-Definition of the Venetian Republic', 518–23; and ead., *Venetian Narrative Painting*, 33–7.

[30] Canal, *Les Estoires*, 6–7. See also Carile, 'La formazione', 64–5; and Brown, 'Self-Representation of the Venetian Republic', 513–15.

[31] Cited in Antonio Carile, 'Aspetti della cronachistica veneziana nei secoli XIII e XIV', in A. Pertusi (ed.), *La storiografia veneziana fino al secolo XVI* (Florence, 1970), 80. Cf. Barbara Marx, 'Venezia—altera Roma? ipotesi sull'umanesimo italiano', *Quaderni del Centro Tedesco di Studi Veneziani*, 10 (1978), 3–4.

Martino da Canal's chronicles, it suggests a desire to drive down the civic roots more deeply, beyond the early Byzantine stratum, in this case right into Roman soil. It involved the completion of a set of costly bronze *cancelli* for the exterior portals of the west façade. Two pairs had been installed already in the first half of the thirteenth century in the main entrances to the church, one set in the central portal and the other inside the atrium, closing it off from the south entrance in the ante-vestibule (now the Cappella Zen). These were legitimate antiques, datable to the sixth century. Probably booty from the Fourth Crusade, they feature a grillwork pattern of *opus clatratum* in a paleo-Byzantine style and were apparently adapted for reuse on the Basilica by Venetian masters. In the new sets of bronze doors that were then made to fill the lateral portals of the façade, the sculptor followed the general form of *opus clatratum*, but he made it more robust, solid, and regular. Clearly working under the influence of *earlier* classical models, he reinterpreted the Byzantine motif *all'antica*—in the Roman manner.[32]

The new doors featured two other important innovations. First, in keeping with the growing self-consciousness of artists of this period, the sculptor was no longer anonymous, with the door to the left of the central portal bearing the inscription: 'MCCC—MAGISTER BERTVCIVS AVRIFEX VENETVS ME FECIT'. Second, on the corresponding door to the right of the main entrance, each cross-bar now featured three large, very Roman looking, female heads flanked by small figures of pagan divinities each holding a cornucopia [FIG. 5.6]. These were—in Demus's words—'copies as close to forgeries as possible', cast from moulds made from classical originals.[33]

Originality was clearly not the point, and the borrowing was not accidental. But why, then, would Bertuccio have signed his name so proudly to a counterfeit? Because, it seems to me, that may be precisely the point. Bertuccio's pride in his craftsmanship would have been matched by Venetian pride in a costly new set of bronze doors. No one was fooled, nor were they meant to be. The newness of the doors was just as important as their antique look. With this

---

[32] Renato Polacco, 'Porte e cancelli bronzei medioevali in S. Marco a Venezia', *Venezia Arti*, 3 (1989), 14–23; id., *San Marco: La basilica d'Oro* (Milan, 1991), 144–8. Also A. Prosdocimi, 'Le porte antiche dell'atrio di San Marco a Venezia', *Atti dell'Accademia Nazionale dei Lincei*, Rendiconti. Cl. Scienze morali, storiche, filologiche, 8/2 (1947), 529–39.

[33] Demus, *Church of San Marco*, 140, 180–1. Cf. Prosdocimi, 'Le porte antiche', 532–4.

Fig. 5.6 San Marco, west façade, a detail of the second bronze door from the right

deliberately ambiguous double-play, the Venetian sense of the past seems to move into a new phase. Bertuccio's doors take the thirteenth-century *renovatio* one step further. While they allude to an authentic pre-Byzantine, Roman past within the Venetian present, they proclaim that this present, as well, is something new and unique in itself and perhaps superior to Rome.

The formative period for the invention of a civic history culminates in the term of Doge Andrea Dandolo (1343–54). Through a number of artistic and literary initiatives, he attempted to further ground the republic in a legitimated historical past.[34] With his incorporation into the *Chronica Extensa* of a newly-discovered and undoubtedly spurious document dating Venice's foundation at Rialto

---

[34] See C. Ravegnani, 'Andrea Dandolo', in *Dizionario Biografico degli Italiani*, xxxii (Rome, 1986), 432–40, with bibliog.

on the day of the Annunciation in 421, he gave the city an even more impressive Christian pedigree.[35]

One of Dandolo's principal campaigns of art patronage involved the remaking of the Pala d'Oro, probably the single most precious object in the Basilica. The project involved the resetting of all the Byzantine enamels and jewels in a new, intricately-worked Gothic gold frame.[36] Latin inscriptions added to the object that purported to 'document' its prior history were confirmed with textual entries in the *Chronica Extensa*.[37] Dandolo thus created an artifact that, if fashioned after the fact, was not just a work of art but a historical document true and proper.[38] And yet, in the remodelling of the Pala d'Oro with a Gothic frame as well as the additional inscriptions, there is evidence of a paradigm shift. The textual additions imply that what gave the most authority at this point was not simply a Byzantine or early Christian style *per se*, but the authentication of the written word.

Nonetheless, archaizing tendencies continued to resurface in projects related to San Marco. In the new marble iconostasis made at the end of the fourteenth century, the Dalle Massegne brothers once again took the retrospective archaeological approach. In its form and iconography the screen suggests an intentional reference to the iconostasis of Old St Peter's in Rome, built under Gregory III in the

---

[35] Andreae Danduli, *Venetiarum Chronica per extensum descripta*, ed. Ester Pastorello, in *Rerum Italicarum Scriptores*, NS, 12/1 (Bologna, 1938–58), 53. Cf. V. Lazzarini, 'Il preteso documento della fondazione di Venezia e la cronaca del medico Jacopo Dondi', in *Atti dell'Istituto Veneto di scienze, lettere ed arti*, 75/2 (1915–16), 96–116; and E. Franceschini, 'La Cronachetta di Maestro Jacopo Dondi', in *Atti dell'Istituto Veneto di scienze, lettere ed arti*, 99/2 (1939–40), 969–84.

[36] See W. F. Volbach, 'Gli smalti della Pala d'Oro', and Hans R. Hahnloser, 'Le oreficerie della Pala d'Oro', in H. R. Hahnloser (ed.), *La Pala d'oro* (Florence, 1965), 3–71, 79–111. Cf. J. Deer, 'Die Pala d'Oro in neuer Sicht', *Byzantinische Zeitschrift*, 62 (1969), 308–44; Rodolfo Gallo, *Il Tesoro di S. Marco e la sua storia* (Venice and Rome, 1967), 157–66; and Margaret Fraser, 'The Pala d'Oro and the Cult of St. Mark in Venice', in *XVI Internationaler Byzantinistenkongress. Akten*, ii. pt. 5, Wien, 4–9 Oct. 1981, in *Jahrbuch der Österreichischen Byzantinistik*, 32/5 (1982), 273–9.

[37] Danduli, *Chronica*, 225, 284.

[38] Patricia Fortini Brown, 'Committenza e arte di stato', in *Storia di Venezia*, iii, *Formazione dello stato patrizio*, ed. G. Arnaldi, A. Tenenti and G. Cracco, Istituto della Enciclopedia Italiana/Fondazione Giorgio Cini (Rome: forthcoming). Cf. Debra Pincus, 'Andrea Dandolo (1343–1354) and Visual History: The San Marco Projects', in C. M. Rosenberg (ed.), *Art and Politics in Late Medieval and Early Renaissance Italy: 1250–1500* (Notre Dame, 1990), 191–206.

eighth century.[39] Venice was again reaffirming a venerable past that was linked directly to Christian Rome.

Expansion into the Terraferma brought Venice a material Roman past of her own with the appropriation of cities of ancient foundation like Padua, Verona, and Brescia. Already in the last decade of the fourteenth century, the medallist Marco Sesto had designed a pseudo-antique medal in the best tradition of Venetian counterfeiting with a portrait of the emperor Galba. A female figure standing on a wheel of Fortune and holding the vexillum of St Mark is portrayed on the reverse, accompanied by the inscription 'PAX TIBI VENETIA'. David Rosand proposes quite plausibly that she is a personification of Venetia as the ancient Dea Roma.[40] Venetian panegyrists also responded to Leonardo Bruni's new model for encomiastic literature, with a specifically Venetian laudatory agenda.[41]

In 1421, on the occasion of the millenary Jubilee of Venice's foundation, the notary Lorenzo de Monacis dedicated his *Oratio elegantissima . . . in laude et edificatione alme civitatis Venetiarum* to Doge Tommaso Mocenigo.[42] While the piece fits into a long-standing *laus civitatis* tradition,[43] it contains three elements of particular significance for the Venetian concept of *renovatio*. First, it sets up a spiritual antithesis between Rome and Venice. In contrast to Rome's servile beginnings and corrupting taste for power and luxury as it rose to empire, Venice had been free from its very origins and because of the sober virtue of her citizens was entrusted by divine will with the mission of preserving and defending liberty. Second, the providential character of Venice's birth had continued, with the city

---

[39] Wolfgang Wolters, *La scultura gotica veneziana (1300/1460)* (Venice, 1976), 62–7, 146, 213–14, 223; and Polacco, *San Marco*, 173. For Venetian state patronage in the Trecento, see Brown, 'Committenza'.

[40] David Rosand, 'Venetia Figurata: The Iconography of a Myth', in id. (ed.), *Interpretazioni veneziane: Studi di storia dell'arte in onore di Michelangelo Muraro* (Venice, 1984), 180 (177–96), who defines four major themes of personification that develop and coexist during the period *c.*1350–1600: Justice, Roma, the Virgin, and Venus.

[41] See Alison Brown, 'City and Citizen: Changing Perceptions in the Fifteenth and Sixteenth Centuries', in Molho, Raaflaub and Emlen (eds.), *City-States*, 93–111, at 96.

[42] Mario Poppi, 'Un'orazione del cronista Lorenzo de Monacis per il millenario di Venezia (1421)', *Atti dell'Istituto Veneto di Scienze, Lettere ed Arti*, Classe di scienze morali, lettere ed arti, 131 (1972–3): 464–97, with a transcription of the text; Marx, 'Venezia—altera Roma?', 3–18.

[43] See the fundamental study, Antonio Medin, *La Storia della Repubblica di Venezia nella Poesia* (Milan, 1904).

enjoying the constant intervention of God throughout her history. Third, that history was still in process, with the best seemingly yet to come as demonstrated by a peculiarly Venetian variant of a Three Ages model of historical periodization: *Infantia*, a golden age lasting about two hundred years from the city's foundation to the Lombard invasions when men lived simply, without ambition, luxury, or treachery; *Adolescentia*, another two-hundred-year period, but this one of growth and struggle, during which the nascent republic was ennobled by the patriarchate and new episcopal sees; and *Juventus*, inaugurated with the transfer of the ducal seat to Rialto and the election of the first doge—events that marked the birth of the Republic of the present-day, 'that having begun at Rialto has been growing for six hundred years and more'.[44]

During the decades after de Monacis wrote the *Oratio*, Venice's identity as capital of an expanding territory called for an even more dignified presence to the outside world. While San Marco was never neglected, the masterworks of state patronage during the quattrocento involved secular buildings. Interestingly enough, aside from the completion and embellishment of the Ducal Palace with a new west wing facing the Piazzetta and the construction of the doge's apartments after a fire, the biggest projects concerned portals and entryways: the Porta della Carta (1438–42/3), the Arco Foscari (1438–early 1480s), the Arsenale portal (1457–60), the Scala dei Giganti (*c.*1485–93), and the Torre dell'Orologio (1496–9).[45]

Given Venice's expansionist *politique*, the emphasis on portals and arches reflects a (probably unknowing) congruence with Alberti's view of the triumphal arch: 'the greatest ornament to the forum or crossroad would be to have an arch at the mouth of each road. For the arch is a gate that is continually open. Its invention I ascribe to those who enlarged the empire.'[46] Tellingly, Venice—the city

[44] Poppi, 'Un 'orazione', 488–91: 'que iam annis sexcentis et ultra in Rivoalto feliciter inchoata in augmento' (488). The golden age imagery of the first period derives from a 6th-c. account of Cassiodorus, *Variarum libri XII*, XII, no. 24. Cf. August Buck, ' "Laus Venetiae" und Politik im 16. Jahrhundert', *Archiv für Kulturgeschichte*, 57 (1975), 186–94.

[45] For an overview see Deborah Howard, *The Architectural History of Venice* (London, 1980), 79–85, 102–12. See also Umberto Franzoi, Terisio Pignatti, and Wolfgang Wolters, *Il Palazzo Ducale di Venezia* (Treviso, 1990).

[46] Leon Battista Alberti, *On the Art of Building in Ten Books*, tr. Joseph Rykwert, Neil Leach and Robert Tavernor (Cambridge, Mass., 1988), 265 (bk. viii, ch. 6); cf. Debra Pincus, *The Arco Foscari: The Building of a Triumphal Gateway in Fifteenth Century Venice* (New York, 1976), 156–7.

without walls—needed no gateways, but built them anyway in the heart of the city.

Over the course of some fifty years, the entry to the Ducal Palace would be developed as a true and proper *Via triumphalis*, with the Porta della Carta leading through a covered passageway to the Arco Foscari—a Roman triumphal arch in the midst of the Palace complex—and culminating in the Scala dei Giganti, a staging area for ducal coronations [FIG. 5.7]. The evolution of the project traces another sort of triumph, as well, in which Roman antique forms and motifs progressively overwhelm the traditional flamboyant Gothic idiom to create a new Venetian Renaissance architecture.[47] The ambitious Doge Francesco Foscari had his own medal struck with

FIG. 5.7 Arco Foscari and Scala dei Giganti, Ducal Palace, Venice

[47] The stylistic evolution is traced meticulously by Pincus, *Arco Foscari*, with an overview on 34–75. See also John McAndrew, *Venetian Architecture of the Early Renaissance* (Cambridge, Mass., 1980).

a figure of Justice on the reverse and framed with the inscription 'VENETIA MAGNA'.[48]

Foreigners had no difficulty in saluting the republic as a new Rome. Giovanni da Spilimbergo, a grammarian and humanist in the recently-annexed Friuli, hailed it as a Second Rome. Filippo Morandi, a recent arrival from Rimini, proclaimed Doge Francesco Foscari as 'dux augustus' in his *Carmen* of 1440–1 and praised Venetian patricians as ideal descendants of the Romans. Porcellio Romano dedicated his *Commentari* to the same doge in 1453 and circumspectly identified the Venetian *pregadi* with the Roman senate in its claims to dignity, 'yet not to empire or dominion'. Towards the end of the century Francesco Arrigoni of Brescia could write that the refugees of Trojan ancestry who had settled the lagoon had succeeded in saving the *genus antiquum Latii* from the barbarians, thus protecting for posterity the authentic Roman heritage.[49]

Venetian writers, however, took a more measured tone. Aware that Venice's imperialist activities were already too closely identified with imperial Rome by critics throughout Italy, they continued to stress Venice's uniqueness from any other city, and, indeed, its moral superiority to Rome.[50]

In Marcantonio Sabellico's *Rerum venetarum ab urbe condita libri XXXIII*, commissioned by the government in 1483, written in aulic Latin on the model of Livy, and published in 1487, a particularly hyperbolic strain of humanist historiography came to fruition in Venice. Sabellico allowed that Venetians may have to concede to the Romans in splendour and grandeur, but not in sanctity of laws, in equity of justice, and in goodness (*bontà*).[51] In a short guide to the city appearing fifteen years later, he stressed not only Venice's complete uniqueness of site and condition and its moral and spiritual superiority, but also its enduring permanence. A 'stable, perpetual and durable empire' that had by then lasted a thousand years, here

---

[48] Rosand, 'Venetia figurata', 180.

[49] All cited by Marx, 'Venezia—altera Roma?', 6–15.

[50] Ibid. 13–14.

[51] From the Italian translation, *Dell'historia venetiana* (Venice, 1668), Proemio, p. 1. See also Gaetano Cozzi, 'Cultura politica e religione nella "pubblica storiografia" veneziana del "500" ', *Bollettino dell'Istituto di storia della società e dello stato veneziano*, 1963–4, at 5–6: 215–94, at 219–22; id., 'Marin Sanudo il Giovane: dalla cronaca alla storia', in Agostino Pertusi (ed.), *La storiografia veneziana fino al secolo XVI: Aspetti e problemi* (Florence, 1970), 333–58, at 338–42.

too it surpassed Rome.[52] The same claims were reiterated by Sanudo in his own *De situ urbis*, written in the same period.[53]

The Venetian patrician, Bernardo Giustiniani, wrote a history of the origin of Venice at the same time that Sabellico was producing his thirty-three books. Despite the fact that his work was better ordered, more literary and more critical in its use of sources than Sabellico's, it found less favour with the Signoria, who may have counted its high-minded objectivity against it.[54] The measured tones of Giustiniani's preface promised little competition to the pompous rhetoric of Sabellico: 'There are many more curious about history who happen to see the city of the Venetians or to hear something about it, and who are wont greatly to wonder at what so novel and unusual a reason for living might have induced men born on the earth, accustomed to meadowlands, to establish a city amidst the swamps.'[55]

Giustiniani drew on all the main works of the Venetian *cronachistica* tradition, but he did so selectively. Significantly, he picked up the providential theme of Lorenzo de Monacis and linked the rise of Venice directly to the decline of Rome:

[Venice] was preserved by divine command so that those who excelled in piety or religion, either expelled from home by factions, or tired by lengthy tribulations, might have a refuge to which they could flee with their wives and children, and so that finally, after long misfortunes, they might seek a port of safety for themselves and their holy relics.[56]

For Giustiniani, even Christian Rome of his own day, for all its sacred treasures, was no more impressive than Venice. He had told the Venetian cardinals in 1483, 'that Venice was their true parent and the Church only a step-mother'.[57] Allowing that the republic's power and prosperity had brought her fear and envy from the outside, he insisted that her greatest foe was in the Muslim East. After the fall of Constantinople in 1453, whose ruin had been God's warning to his countrymen, Venice was now the 'sea-wall of Christianity'

---

[52] Marcantonio Sabellico, *Del Sito di Venezia* (1502), ed. G. Meneghetti (Venice, 1957), 10.

[53] Sanudo, *De situ urbis*, 16–17.   [54] Cozzi, 'Cultura politica', 221.

[55] Cited in Patricia Labalme, *Bernardo Giustiniani. A Venetian of the Quattrocento* (Rome, 1969), 258.

[56] Ibid. 265.

[57] Ibid. 296, citing Giustiniani's 'Responsio ad sacrum collegium' (28 May 1483), *Orationes*.

against the Turks. Her own destruction would mark the end of the Christian republic.[58]

If not the new Rome, was Venice to be seen, then, as the new Constantinople or even the new Jerusalem? Along with the increased Greek presence in the city and the continuous pressure from the Turks during the latter half of the fifteenth century, signs of a Byzantine revival in art and architecture have been observed by scholars. Along with Giovanni Bellini's icon-like Madonnas,[59] these signs included, most notably, a group of churches designed by Mauro Codussi and his circle. Deriving from a Byzantine quincunx centralized plan with nine bays and five domes, their basic form is viewed by James Ackerman as a reaction to the Gothic tradition and an alternative to an early Renaissance classical style.[60] Significantly, the revivals were confined to the plan and did not carry through to interior elevations, which generally featured an early Renaissance style in the manner of Brunelleschi and Alberti. The nature and meaning of this revival is complex. Ackerman suggests that the impulse was born in conservative patrician circles with ecclesiastical connections and populist tendencies and an anti-pagan or even anti-humanist agenda. Manfredo Tafuri, however, characterizes the patrons of San Salvador, the last of the group (begun 1506/7) and a church with profound civic meanings, as members of a different circle within the patrician élite, who had links to Florentine humanism and were involved in philological and antiquarian studies [FIG. 5.8]. In the final elaboration of the church, he argues, they 'forced the neo-Byzantine program to speak a humanistic language'.[61]

During precisely the same period and within the neo-Byzantine revival, Lionello Puppi sees the recurrence of a Venice–Jerusalem metaphor. It took a number of forms, both experiential and iconographical. Along with the revival of the cults of a number of oriental saints and of Saint Theodore in particular, the accounts of pilgrims passing through the city *en route* to the Holy Land testify to an awareness of the urban space of Venice as part of a continuous sacred itinerary that culminated in Jerusalem [FIGS. 5.9 and

---

[58] Ibid. 272, 304.

[59] Rona Goffen, 'Icon and Vision: Giovanni Bellini's Half-Length Madonnas', *Art Bulletin*, 57 (1975), 487–518.

[60] James Ackerman, 'Observations on Renaissance Church Planning in Venice and Florence, 1470–1570', in *Florence and Venice: Comparisons and Relations*, Villa I Tatti Papers, ii (Florence 1979–80), ii. 287–307.

[61] Manfredo Tafuri, *Venice and the Renaissance* (Cambridge, Mass., 1989), 33.

Fig. 5.8 San Salvador, Venice, view of the nave vault

5.10].[62] Pious travellers like the German friar Felix Faber appreciated
the noble Christian origins of the city and recognized the absolute

[62] Lionello Puppi, *Verso Gerusalemme: Immagini e temi di urbanistica e di architettura simboliche* (Rome, 1982), 62–76; id., 'Venezia come Gerusalemme nella cultura
figurativa del Rinascimento', in A. Buck and B. Guthmueller (eds.), *La città italiana
del Rinascimento fra Utopia e Realtà* (Venice, 1984), 117–36.

FIG. 5.9 Erhard Reeuwich, *View of Venice*, detail of woodcut

uniqueness of its urban form as proof of its divinely-inspired destiny. Faber found the sight of the church of San Marco 'so surprising that, according to common opinion, it seems to be made by angels rather than by men.'[63] Venetians themselves referred to their city as *la terra sancta nostra* and *la sancta città*. Bringing the Holy Land into the meeting halls of the *scuole* in great cycles of painted histories set in the Orient, they also posited biblical scenes in settings that had been refashioned from the urban fabric of Venice itself [FIG. 5.11].[64]

What are we to make of the extraordinary ability of Venice's ruling élite to bring about these chameleon-like transformations or renaissances? In a brilliant study, Tafuri offers a cogent recapitulation of

[63] Felice Fabri, *Venezia nel MCDLXXXVIII*, tr. Vincenzo Lazzari (Venice, 1881), 66.

[64] See Puppi, 'Venezia come Gerusalemme', 117–36; and Brown, *Venetian Narrative Painting*, *passim*. See also David Rosand, *Painting in Cinquecento Venice: Titian, Veronese, Tintoretto* (New Haven, Conn., 1982), 124–30. The staging of Biblical scenes in contemporary settings was, of course, quite common in the art of the period and was not unique to Venice.

FIG. 5.10 Erhard Reeuwich, *View of Jerusalem*, detail of woodcut

FIG. 5.11 Carpaccio, *Presentation of the Virgin*, Brera, Milan

the Venetian *renovatio* in his observation that 'the new was called upon to develop what had been present at the moment of its genesis; there was no appeal to return to a perfection that had been destroyed by a repeated "fall" '.[65] It may be objected that this argument for continuity is little different from the medieval attitude described by Panofsky and others wherein there is no perception of a disjunction with antiquity. But such an interpretation does not capture the nuances of the Venetian ideal of *renovatio* rather than *restitutio*. It is not without significance that commissions for replacing or remaking works of state art in Venice—paintings, mosaics, buildings—invariably used the language of renewal—*ristaurare, instaurare, riconzare*—rather than of restitution.[66] Tafuri's citation of an entry in the *Diarii* of Marin Sanudo sums up the Venetian view better than any second-hand interpretation:

Today the 25th, Friday, was the day of the Annunciation of the Madonna, on which day, in 421, there began the city of Rivoalto [Rialto: the present Venice] and the first stone was laid, on that day was formed the world, was crucified Our Lord Jesus Christ, according to Saint Augustine; it was in 1507 on this day that the first stone was laid for the new reconstruction of the church of San Salvador on this ground.

The renewal of the church was thus set into a timeless continuity that was rooted in the city's own perfect beginnings.[67]

Insisting throughout the centuries on its absolute uniqueness, Venice—that is, her patrician élite—did not aspire to be another Rome, another Constantinople, or another earthly Jerusalem. They knew that their city was more, and it is here that the *topos* of the celestial Jerusalem comes into play. For to them, Venice had been founded—and remained—'outside human custom'.[68]

It can thus be claimed that the Venetian *renovatio* is different from the Roman, the Florentine, or any other. In fact, we seem to be witnessing a two-part process, which involves both *renovatio* in terms of refurbishment of what already exists and *conciliatio* in terms of appropriation of the alien in a unifying process. What might appear

[65] Tafuri, *Venice and the Renaissance*, 15, but see also the full discussion on 1–50. Cf. the thoughtful review of Tafuri by Cesare Vasoli in *Studi Veneziani*, 13 (1987), 362–77; and Gino Benzoni, 'Venezia, ossia il mito modulato', *Studi Veneziani*, NS, 19 (1990), 15–33.

[66] Brown, *Venetian Narrative Painting*, 84–5.

[67] Sanudo, *I Diarii*, vol. liii, col. 72 (tr. from Tafuri, *Venice and the Renaissance*, 22).

[68] Puppi, *Verso Gerusalemme*, 62–76; 'Venezia come Gerusalemme', 117–36.

to be a wilful eclecticism has an ideological basis rooted in—and analogous to—the patrician consensus. Indeed, it is willed—not wilful. One searches for a more telling term than *renovatio* for a process wherein so many disparate elements—antique, Gothic, Tuscan Renaissance, Islamic, Byzantine—are brought together in a new artistic synthesis that is all-encompassing in its capacity to appropriate, chameleon-like in its ability to transform, utopian in its transcendence of time and place, and uniquely Venetian.

PART II

Groups and Individuals:
The Social Context of Revival

6.   Creating Memory: Monumental Painting and Cultural Definition

WILLIAM HOOD

THE aspect of Florentine culture that I discuss in this essay is the use of monumental painting for corporate self-representation in the first half of the fifteenth century.[1] The relationship between medium and message was synergetic, and it provides a helpful perspective on cultural definition *in* the Renaissance, whatever one thinks of the usefulness of 'self-representation' as a category for cultural definition *of* the Renaissance. In this paper I shall limit myself to some remarks on how reform movements in the religious orders, usually called 'observances', represented their institutional ambitions through the mural paintings in their cloisters. A broader and lengthier treatment, however, would show that self-definition contributed to the meaning of other works of art commissioned by religious orders in the period, and of secular projects as well.

All the major religious orders underwent long periods of intense self-scrutiny and adopted various programmes of revitalization in the last decades of the fourteenth and the first half of the fifteenth

[1] Since the summer of 1990, when I gave an earlier and much shorter version of this paper, this material has appeared in a far more extended argument, with a full apparatus, in my *Fra Angelico at San Marco* (New Haven, Conn., 1993). I offer here a synthesis of points made in ch. 6, 'Ritual Sites: Florentine Painted Cloisters and the Representation of History', 123–46; for full documentation and illustrations, I refer the reader to that publication. Likewise, my summary remarks about the various 'observant' reforms of the religious orders are derived from ch. 1 of *Fra Angelico*, 'The Myth of Original Perfection and the Ideals of the Dominican Observance', 15–28. I am grateful to Alison Brown and Patricia Rubin for inviting me to speak at the London conference; and if it hadn't been for Alison Brown's firm but gentle urging, the overview provided in this essay would never have come into being. Finally, I wish to acknowledge my gratitude to Carl Brandon Strehlke for having pointed out two errors of omission in my discussion of painted cloisters (review, *Burlington Magazine*, vol. 135, no. 1086 (1993), 634–6).

century. Obviously this was an international movement, but its consequences for Florentine society are of particular interest for a number of reasons. First, Florentine merchants, and Cosimo de' Medici
in particular, took propagandistic advantage of the mendicant observances' primary characteristic, which was a return to institutional
poverty.[2] This meant that observant Franciscan and Dominican communities voluntarily forswore amassing endowments of capital that
would guarantee income. For patrons, therefore, gifts to mendicant
observant houses needed to be outright donations of goods that did
not generate income, in other words, far smaller gifts of what might
be called 'interest' rather than 'principal'. Thus it was that buildings
and paintings, books and liturgical ornaments, all of them visible and
even ostentatious donations to observant houses, became stratagems
of clan rivalry in fifteenth-century Florence. Second, but only partly
in consequence of their popularity with merchant patrons, reform
establishments like San Marco attracted some of the most talented
of young people who sought a life in religious vows. Men like
Giovanni Dominici, Antonino Pierozzi, Giuliano Lapaccini, and
Santi Schiattesi, all observant Dominicans, were distinguished leaders and intellectuals far outside the immediate boundaries of their
local religious communities. Rich merchants and bankers underwrote
the economic consequences of reform, young men and women
entered reformed novitiates in increasing numbers, and lay people of
all social ranks swelled the lists of confraternities and other organizations headquartered at religious houses associated with church
renewal. Finally, not the least reason for the observances' visibility
in Florentine public affairs is the fact that Florence was the primary
seat of the papal court for much of this period, and every pope from
Martin V to Nicholas V was a vigorous supporter of the reform
efforts in all the orders.

For these reasons the observant process figures so prominently in
historical literature that it is easy to assume that the reformers were
as well received in their own day as they seem to be in ours. That,
however, would be a mistake. Religious institutions are inherently
conservative, and people who were conservative by temperament
constituted the majority of membership in these orders. Conservative
people dislike change, even change that they themselves admit is for

---

[2] See, in particular, N. Rubinstein, 'Lay Patronage and Observant Reform', in
T. Verdon and J. Henderson (eds.), *Christianity and the Renaissance* (Syracuse, NY,
1990), 64–82.

the better. Every observant movement was under constant pressure and even threat from the more strident voices in the large majority that remained loyal to the traditional and mitigated—'conventual'—interpretation of the order's rule and customs. Even so, neither observants nor conventuals wanted to hazard an internal rupture over what were essentially matters of discipline not doctrine. All wanted to remain united as Camaldolese or Olivetans, as Dominicans or Franciscans, regardless of how urgent the need for change seemed to be.[3]

Maintaining institutional unity meant accommodating the demands of reform-minded members while guaranteeing the stability of those who did not share the zeal for radical change. Because the observant leaders enjoyed a good deal of prestige and even power outside their own orders, it is easy to forget that figures like Saint Bernardino of Siena and Saint Antonino of Florence were by no means typical of Tuscan Franciscans and Dominicans of their own day. The conventuals of every order always outnumbered the observants, and the conventuals were quick to temper the observants' enthusiasm when that seemed on the brink of imprudence.

It was therefore important that the observants assure the conventuals that they were not trying to form an order within an order, to betray the ideal of unity by revolt. Observances thus characterized themselves through the strategies of what one might call revisionist history. They selectively edited their order's foundation myths, reinterpreted ancient customs and revitalized the popularity of early legends and lore. In other words, the observants in each order went out of their way to heighten, even to exaggerate, the unique ethos that they shared with the conventual majority. Obviously, one consequence of this programme was that the Franciscan observants gradually became more distinctly 'Franciscan' than the conventuals, the Dominican observants more 'Dominican', and so on. Thus a significant consequence of the observant movement as a whole was to emphasize how each order was different from all the others.

So it was that Florentine observant foundations in the second quarter of the fifteenth century found themselves in an odd political position. In spite of their equivocal status within their individual

[3] The Friars Minor failed in this regard when independent groups rose up in an order already fractured in the 13th c. and 14th c. by similar disagreements over basic principles.

orders, there was no lack of strong local support from both secular and curial authorities. Aided by the financial and political generosity of powerful Florentines and endorsed by the papal court in residence at Santa Maria Novella, observant communities established themselves with entirely new or extensively refurbished churches and conventual buildings. Among other things, this meant that new cloisters increasingly dotted the map of the city. At least a dozen observant foundations were established in Florence between about 1420 and about 1450. A number of these commissioned large-scale fresco ensembles to be painted on the walls of their recently-constructed or remodelled cloisters. In exactly the same years, of course, Florentine artists and their patrons were pushing the possibilities of a representational style in painting to new and, I think it can be said, unprecedented limits. This is the confluence of events that makes painted cloisters such interesting sites for studying the use of mural paintings as vehicles for cultural self-definition in quattrocento Florence.

The long Florentine residencies of Popes Martin V (1419–20) and Eugenius IV (1434–43) made Santa Maria Novella, the conventual Dominican establishment where the papal court was housed, the centre of ecclesiastical politics in the period. Indeed, the last sessions of the Council of Florence were celebrated there. It was likely that in these years, from about 1422 to about 1439, the great entrance cloister at Santa Maria Novella was embellished with an enormous and complex programme of frescos. These were painted in *terraverde* monochrome with accents of black, white, and burnt sienna—which is why it is called the Chiostro Verde—by a mostly anonymous team of artists who seem to have been associated with Lorenzo Ghiberti. The exception implied by 'mostly' is Paolo Uccello, whose two contributions to the programme, on the east wall, have been much discussed both iconographically and chronologically. By happy accident, the programme of the Chiostro Verde provides an ideal foil for the exactly contemporary projects in the cloisters of Florentine reform communities. In concert with the fourteenth-century frescos in the chapter house opening onto the Chiostro Verde, this scheme is a celebration of the Dominican order and of Santa Maria Novella itself, 'triumphalistic' if ever there was such.

The frescos of the Chiostro Verde are almost certainly an extension, or even result, of the cycle painted by Andrea Bonaiuto in the chapter room in the 1360s. On three walls of the chapter room's main chamber are allegories based on the careers of Saints Dominic,

Peter Martyr and Thomas Aquinas, each of whom is depicted as a kind of avatar of one of the great Passion feasts represented in the vault above: the Resurrection (Saint Dominic); the Ascension (Saint Peter Martyr); and Pentecost (Saint Thomas Aquinas). In its turn, the programme in the vault devolves from the main, altar, wall, where Andrea painted the Way to Calvary, the Crucifixion, and the Noli Me Tangere. Reading backwards, as it were, it becomes all but certain that these paschal subjects continued and conceptually expanded the programme, now lost, which decorated the chancel-like subspace set into the altar wall. As the main liturgical function of the chapter room was the annual celebration of the feast of Corpus Christi, those vanished scenes are likely to have represented that part of the Passion narrative before the Crucifixion, probably the Entry into Jerusalem, Christ Washing the Apostles' Feet, the Communion of the Apostles (perhaps in place of the Institution of the Eucharist), and the Agony in the Garden. Taken as a whole, then, the propagandistic message of the chapter room at Santa Maria Novella was the legitimacy and even necessity of the Dominican order's ministry in spreading the apostolic, gospel message through preaching (Saint Dominic), teaching (Saint Thomas Aquinas), and witnessing by a martyr's death (Saint Peter Martyr).

Although their execution postdates Andrea Bonaiuto's frescos by as much as seventy years, the subjects in the Chiostro Verde suggest that they completed a developed but abandoned project contemporary, and in absolute conceptual harmony, with the programme in the chapter room. Just as the Passion cycle in the chapter room presents the essence of God's self-revelation *post legem,* so the scenes in the cloister, all derived from early chapters of Genesis, illustrate the revelation *ante legem.* This is accomplished on the three cloister walls corresponding to the chapter room walls dedicated to each of the three Dominican saints. On the first, flanking the church at the cloister's east side, are shown scenes from the Creation to the Flood. On the two other walls is an extended cycle of the lives of Abraham and Jacob. Obviously, none of these episodes is derived from Dominican history; indeed, the only non-biblical narrative in the entire suite are the scenes from the life of Saint Peter Martyr on the interior of the entrance wall into the chapter room. As there is no 'history' here, there can be no revision of it. What there is instead are the exceedingly complex, and exceedingly self-promoting, assertions that the Dominican order is the legitimate and authentic extension of the apostolic church itself and that Santa Maria Novella is the jewel in the Dominican crown, a kind of Saint Peter's of the Order of Preachers.

While this is not the place even to outline how singular the Chiostro Verde is in the context of late-trecento and early-quattrocento cloister decoration in Tuscany, one should remark that cloisters decorated with fully-developed programmes of any kind are exceedingly rare. In at least this one respect, therefore, the cloister at Santa Maria Novella belongs to that remarkable group of no fewer than at least seven Florentine monastic cloisters that were embellished with iconographically-unified ensembles in the second quarter of the fifteenth century. In addition to the Chiostro Verde at Santa Maria Novella, these cloisters belonged to the communities at: Santa Maria del Carmine, painted *c.*1422–8; Santa Maria degli Angeli, of *c.*1432–3; the Florentine Badia, whose Chiostro degli Aranci was frescoed *c.*1436; San Marco, painted by Fra Angelico in the 1440s; San Miniato, which may be dated to the late 1440s; and Sant' Apollonia, whose only partially preserved paintings were made by Andrea del Castagno at the same time, that is, the late 1440s.

As already suggested, the Chiostro Verde is entirely unlike these other cloisters for the specific reason that it belonged to a conventual house and the others to reformed or observant houses. That is one reason why the Chiostro Verde is such a handy foil for the others. A second reason is the theme of its programme. The other painted cloisters in this group may be distinguished from the Chiostro Verde, which is also the earliest, by their almost total inversion of the institutional values and claims to be found there. Where the scenes at Santa Maria Novella are drawn from biblical texts, the scenes at the other sites are based on monastic texts. Where the programme at Santa Maria Novella relates the Dominican order to the entire history of salvation, the programmes in the other cloisters promote the special, even unique, values of the religious life. Where the themes at Santa Maria Novella are universal, in that they could be understood on some level by almost anybody, those in the other cloisters would be discernible only to those initiates familiar with the specialized literature on which they are based. This means, of course, that the programmes in these cloisters were addressed, first, to members of that particular order and, second, to those whom the resident community introduced to the themes and legends painted in the semi-public space of the cloisters. Where the paintings at Santa

Maria Novella proclaim the usefulness of the Dominican order to the church at large, the other cloisters focus almost entirely on the usefulness of religion in achieving the personal holiness of those who lived under that particular order's rule, customs, and discipline.

Probably contemporary with the execution, though not the planning, of the frescos in the Chiostro Verde were the paintings by Masaccio and Fra Filippo Lippi in the cloister at Santa Maria del Carmine. As one of the paintings records the dedication of the church in 1422 and Masaccio died in 1428, we may be sure that the Carmine cloister was decorated at about the same time that work began in the Chiostro Verde. Moreover, the fragmented remains of Lippi's contribution and Vasari's full description of the now-lost scene by Masaccio make it clear that the Carmine cloister, like the Chiostro Verde, was painted in *terraverde* monochrome. But there the comparison ends. What is known of the Carmine programme sets it apart from the Chiostro Verde in two important ways. First, in the Chiostro Verde the cloister walls were treated as symbolically neutral planes for receiving paintings. By contrast, at the Carmine the frescos were situated according to an architectural hierarchy that was determined by the function of various spaces: important entrances, the chapter room wall, and so on. Second, the programme at the Carmine, in so far as it can be reconstructed, was solely focused on the Carmelite order and on the establishment of the Carmelites in Florence. Lippi's assignment was to paint an allegory of Carmel's antiquity and its distinguished descent from the early desert Fathers. He did this by adapting a rare subject, known as the Thebaid, that depicted hermits and other ascetics in a kind of monastic wilderness. In Lippi's treatment, however, the hermits are not the anonymous holy men usually encountered in Thebaid scenes, like the ones at Cercina or the Campo Santo in Pisa, for example. Rather, in every case they wear the Carmelite habit of a brown tunic with a white—or in some cases black-and-white striped—cloak.

However rare the Thebaid may be as a subject of painting in the quattrocento, it seems to have been an important consideration for those members of Florentine reform or observant houses who were responsible for planning cloister programmes for their monasteries or friaries. The closely related ensembles at Santa Maria degli Angeli, the Florentine Badia and San Miniato demonstrate that importance. Paolo Uccello's cloister paintings for Santa Maria degli Angeli have disappeared without a trace. This is particularly lamentable because

they were almost certainly the precedents for the cognate programmes in the Chiostro degli Aranci at the Badia, which may be
securely dated to about 1436, and in the upper cloister at San
Miniato, another project of Uccello's and datable to the late 1440s.
Most obviously, these paintings shared the monochrome palette of
the Thebaid subject; and one should remark that monochrome
colour schemes in cloisters are scarce, even though the natural earth
pigments that give them their hues are extremely resistant to fading
in sunlight. But early trecento cloisters in Siena, the only other time
and place where the practice seems to have been fairly common,
were painted in fully chromatic palettes, as was Fra Angelico's work
at San Marco in the 1440s.

Beyond those interesting but inconclusive formal considerations, I
think it likely that the Thebaid at the Carmine may partly have suggested the ancient monastic text of Gregory the Great's life of Saint
Benedict to the planner(s) of the cloister at Santa Maria degli Angeli.
It was entrusted, as already mentioned, to Paolo Uccello, but its
ideator may well have been Ambrogio Traversari, who was prior of
the Angeli in the early 1430s and who was particularly fond of
Gregory's *Dialogues*, where his life of Saint Benedict may be found.
Like the Thebaid, the *legenda Benedicti* recalls the earliest phases of
monastic life, still current, of course, in the various branches of
Benedictine monasticism, which in quattrocento Florence meant not
only the original group founded at Subiaco by Saint Benedict himself
(the monks at the Badia), but also those of the later monastic reforms
like the Camaldolese (Santa Maria degli Angeli), the Vallombrosans
(Santa Trinita), the Olivetans (San Miniato), and the Silvestrines
(San Marco, until they transferred to San Giorgio alla Costa in 1436).
These texts, then, root the monastic congregations (and, so they
claimed, the Carmelites) in historical Christian antiquity, a distinction that none of the rival orders of canons or friars, especially the
Franciscans and Dominicans, could claim for itself. One way to
interpret the popularity of the Thebaid and *legenda Benedicti* in
Florentine cloisters, then, is as monastic one-upmanship.

Whatever the planners' motives, the *legenda Benedicti* with some
interpolations of the Thebaid is the foundation for each of the three
monastic programmes under discussion. So far as can be known
from the verbal descriptions of Uccello's now-lost paintings at the
Angeli, the scenes there simply illustrated Saint Benedict's life,
although the monochrome palette of the Thebaid was employed. At

the Chiostro degli Aranci—a charming, fascinating, and even weird anomaly of Florentine painting—the *legenda Benedicti* provided the illustrational parts of the extensive programme there. But in the dado running below the scenes the painter represented various monastic fathers, like those in the Thebaid, with texts reminding the viewer of the antiquity and holiness of monastic life. At San Miniato, which postdates the other two monastic cloisters by at least a decade, the *legenda Benedicti* and the Thebaid are thematically interwoven, Benedictine monasticism represented, as it were, as the most distinguished outgrowth of the earlier forms of monasticism that grew up in the Egyptian desert near Thebes (hence, 'Thebaid').

Drawing on Saint Gregory's *Dialogues* as a source for subject-matter in monumental painting was an exercise in Christian humanism, and this is one of several reasons why the originator of the idea may have been Ambrogio Traversari himself. Certainly it is the case that each of these Florentine monasteries figured significantly and even centrally in the reform of monasticism that exactly paralleled the observant movements in the newer orders of friars and canons. In other words, it would be missing the point entirely to interpret the sudden appearance of the life of Saint Benedict on the walls of Benedictine cloisters as a kind of antiquarianism. Far from it. This was an instance in which antique revival was entirely in the service of urgent problems in the immediate present. There is nothing romantic or nostalgic about the programmes at the Angeli, the Badia, or San Miniato. All of them were attempts to address what was perceived as a major crisis at the very core of the Western church, namely, the regeneration of religious life with all its original fervour and austerity.

Finally, we turn to the elegant, sparse decoration of the cloister at San Marco. Because it is beautifully preserved, because it has been easy of access to the general public for a long time, and because it was painted by Fra Angelico, this is the best-known painted cloister in the canon of Florentine Renaissance art. But it is also the most anomalous.

At San Marco there is not the slightest reference to a narrative text. This distinguishes its programme entirely from the biblical narratives at Santa Maria Novella, the dedication scene at the Carmine and the various interpretations of the *legenda Benedicti* in the cloisters of the three monasteries. Moreover, the sheer quantity of decoration at San Marco is extraordinarily spare. Fra Angelico painted only one large scene, showing a kneeling Saint Dominic embracing the Crucifix, and the remaining paintings are five overdoor lunettes. Finally, the colour scheme of San Marco's cloister sets it entirely apart from the others. Not only did Fra Angelico eschew the practice of *terraverde* monochrome, but he used a fully chromatic palette. The large scene showing Saint Dominic and the Crucifix, in particular, owes much of its visual force to the careful, one might even say obsessive, attention that the artist paid to every nuance of colour across the large planes of heads, hands, and feet.

Like those in the cloisters in the reform houses, but unlike the Chiostro Verde, the frescos at San Marco are carefully framed by architecture, and in its turn that framing is entirely symbolic and hierarchical. The five overdoors, for example, marked and articulated the entrances to the important spaces opening off the cloister. Thus, Saint Peter Martyr enjoins silence to those about to enter the church through the door over which the saint is figured; Saint Dominic scourging himself indicates the entrance to the chapter room, where the daily Chapter of Faults resulted in ritual scourging; Christ as the Man of Sorrows, and thus a symbol of the eucharist, fills the lunette over the entrance into the refectory; Christ being received as a pilgrim by two friars marks the entry to the guesthouse; and the lunette showing Saint Thomas Aquinas with an open book against his chest probably indicates where the library was installed before Cosimo de' Medici built the present library to house the collection of Niccolò Niccoli.

The imposing vertical field showing the life-size figures of Saint Dominic and the crucified Christ forms a pendant to the entrance into the cloister from the piazza outside. They are directly on the north–south axis parallel to the church, and the size and shape of Fra Angelico's fresco exactly corresponds to the doorway that Michelozzo designed as the public entrance into the cloister. Like the scenes from the life of Saint Benedict or the Thebaid, the emphasis here is on the founder's asceticism, self-denial and personal holiness, a pointed contrast to the interpretation of Saint Dominic visible in the chapter room at Santa Maria Novella. Unlike the Benedictines or even the Carmelites, however, the Dominicans had no ancient myth to use as a vehicle for celebrating their particular route to holiness. Thus, they drew not on the life of Saint Dominic, but on a hitherto obscure text that the Dominican observance had brought back into currency. This was a manual of instruction in prayer for Dominican novices known as *De modo orandi*. The method of praying indicated by the title was none other than Saint Dominic's own, and it was made available by thirteenth-century friars in the Bologna convent who purported to have witnessed with their own eyes the founder in various forms of prayer. Of particular interest is the fact that the original text implies that all manuscript copies were intended to be illustrated with miniatures showing Saint Dominic in each of the nine prayer 'modes' described in the text. This is the source for the big fresco in the San Marco cloister. Once again, one notices its decidedly penitential character and its new emphasis on the order's asceticism and spirituality, rather than on its fame and accomplishments in the church at large. In this way, the programme at San Marco is entirely consistent with the other Florentine cloisters under discussion, again with the notable exception of the Chiostro Verde. Although San Marco was officially a daughter house of Santa Maria Novella, its decoration was designed to demonstrate institutional values that were directly opposed to those celebrated at the order's main Florentine establishment.

Three aspects of these Florentine cloisters throw light on my topic, which is the use of monumental paintings as instruments of cultural definition. First, almost the entire group of paintings was carried out in a narrow time-span of about twenty-five to thirty years. Inasmuch as the programmes themselves would make even one of the cloisters remarkable for the period, one can only conclude that the narrow chronological spectrum and the fact that this practice occurred only in Florence indicate that each programme was designed with the others in mind. In other words, I think we may assume that these institutions were highly conscious of the visibility and utility of these cloisters as sites for advertising their corporate identities. Second, in every case the subjects and their distribution were chosen to broadcast the community's claims to the legitimacy and authenticity of its reform efforts *in the symbolic language of its order's unique ethos*. Third, of course, the new paintings were accessible to a viewing audience much wider than the resident friars, monks, or nuns, who presumably knew these messages intimately and had no need for their display, as it were, on the walls of their cloisters. As public access to these cloisters, at least by men, seems to have been common, and as we know that important clerics and laymen frequented these monastic houses, one might suppose that they, rather than the religious themselves, were the primary audience at which these paintings were aimed.

The painted cloisters of fifteenth-century Florence demonstrate a novel purpose for the venerable practice of conventual decoration. Of the frescos in duecento and trecento Florentine cloisters, only the ones at Santo Spirito were clearly designed with iconographical unity and programmatic distribution in mind. Even for religious houses of enormous prestige outside Tuscany, like San Domenico in Bologna or San Francesco in Assisi or San Paolo fuori le mura in Rome, there is no evidence that medieval cloisters anywhere were normally thought of as places for the public display of monumental images that related the lore of the order to which the cloister belonged. On the contrary, the almost invariable rule of cloister decoration everywhere, and before about 1420 in Florence as well, was that both the subjects and locations of paintings were determined by the families who owned patronal rights to burials in those cloisters.

In each of these Florentine cloisters, the paintings concern the genesis and genius of the order itself. Although biblical and hagiographical subjects occur frequently, they appear for allegorical and metaphorical, rather than narrative, purposes only. The religious content, strictly construed, was subordinated to historical and political claims of the orders in whose service the themes were depicted. The function of cloister decoration in early quattrocento Florence was entirely different to the function of monumental paintings in Florentine churches—sometimes the same sites as the painted cloisters—in the same period.

The purpose of these strategies of visual self-representation, whether they occurred in mendicant or monastic contexts, was to create memory. By that, I mean that religious communities used images in their public spaces to visualize singular interpretations of their own histories, interpretations that verified their claims to a unique institutional authenticity because of their strict allegiance to the reform ideals of one or another order. This type of monumental painting therefore communicated political and historical, as well as theological and moral, messages to an audience rarely if ever addressed through the painted decoration of monastic complexes, namely, the informed—and empowered—laity. These monumental paintings were part of a campaign in public relations, and the purpose of the decoration was to embed the order's interests in the memories of those whose support it needed to muster. This propaganda crusade was successful partly because the interests of the two groups, lay and religious, intersected in the new images painted in

Florentine cloisters. Like monks and friars, educated Florentines paid serious attention to serious religious matters. And they also paid serious attention to painting.

It happened that in the same decades when the papal court made Florence into a surrogate Rome, the city's artists were greatly expanding the repertory of painting's tasks as a metaphorical language. For this reason both art and religion must figure prominently in any attempt to characterize culture in Renaissance Florence. Indeed, the scarcity of papers about Renaissance religion in this anthology may indicate a certain discomfort with juxtaposing the two terms, 'Renaissance', so resonant of originality, and 'religion', sounding a conservative, even regressive, tone. However that might be a problem for other areas of Renaissance studies, it is not a problem for the history of art. The observant reforms were arenas of radically new approaches to the old problems of shaping consciousness while saving souls, and to that end the visual arts were enlisted as never before.

7. Individuals and Families as Patrons of Culture in Quattrocento Florence

F. W. KENT

ACCORDING to the late Felix Gilbert, a number of recent English-speaking historians of Renaissance Florence have written 'books on Florence without the Renaissance'. 'One must wish', Gilbert added, 'it will not be entirely forgotten that what originally brought scholars into the Florentine archives was the quest for an explanation and understanding of the unique achievements of Florence's culture'.[1] While a number of the archival scholars to whom Gilbert refers in fact had other, rich and perfectly legitimate concerns, his implied reproach still has the power to discomfort those of us raised, so to speak, on Jacob Burckhardt. And there have been other critics who have found wanting the synthesizing abilities, not to say cultural sensibilities, of the archive-obsessed. Barbara Diefendorf, referring specifically to historians of the family, has asked 'if it is possible to establish a relationship and not just a mere juxtaposition between family culture and Renaissance culture.'[2] It is 'a sad state of affairs', Edwin Muir has said in reviewing David Herlihy's and Christiane Klapisch's *Les Toscans et leurs familles*, that 'only a few lines have been thrown across the chasm that separates Renaissance social and cultural history'.[3]

Even granting that Muir is right in asserting that 'in the long run Renaissance historians must explain how Florence produced so many

---

[1] F. Gilbert, 'The Other Florence', *The New York Review of Books*, 9 Oct. 1986, 43–4. I should like to thank the editors for their comments upon earlier versions of this paper and Carolyn James for her advice throughout.

[2] B. B. Diefendorf, 'Family Culture, Renaissance Culture', *Renaissance Quarterly*, 40 (1987), 661–81, esp. 662.

[3] E. Muir, 'New Light on Old Numbers: The Political and Cultural Implications of *Les Toscans et leurs familles*', *Journal of Interdisciplinary History*, 11 (1981) 477–85, esp. 485.

innovative, creative individuals within the space of a few generations',[4] one must still insist on how tall an order that is. Burckhardt
himself was not able to write, to his own satisfaction, the history of
Italian architecture and art which was to complement *The
Civilization of the Renaissance in Italy*. His attempt to do so he dismissed in a letter of April 1863 as 'inadequate both in principle and
in execution . . . [I've] put it back in my desk, probably forever'.[5]
As conscientious a university teacher and extramural lecturer as
Burckhardt was for the rest of his long life, certainly he did not lack
the leisure to complete his work. 'The philosophical vein is entirely
wanting in me', he was wont to say in his letters,[6] and perhaps in
that admission the reason for his failing to write a grand synthesis
of Renaissance Italian cultural history should be sought.

In this last respect, if in no other, many Renaissance historians in
the late twentieth century are thoroughgoing Burckhardtians. Yet
from a number of different starting points, theoretical and disciplinary, more has been done and is being done to talk about Florentine
society and Florentine culture in the same breath than has been
allowed. Some years before Gilbert himself praised Richard
Goldthwaite's *The Building of Renaissance Florence*, published in
1980, as being in the great tradition, this economic historian, with
daring and learning, had already applied his insights into the
Florentine economy and society to the study of quattrocento palace
architecture.[7] Even more controversial—yet still almost impossible
for an art historian, or any other sort of historian, to ignore—are
Richard Trexler's contributions to the study of Renaissance ritual.[8]
A social historian such as Diane Owen Hughes has written percep-
tively of Italian family portraiture;[9] her art-historical colleague at the

    [4] E. Muir, 'New Light on Old Numbers: The Political and Cultural Implications of
Les Toscans et leurs familles', *Journal of Interdisciplinary History*, 11 (1981) 477–85,
esp. 485.
    [5] *The Letters of Jacob Burckhardt*, selected, ed., and tr. by A. Dru (New York,
1955), 129.
    [6] Ibid. 235 and *passim*. But on this theme, see E. H. Gombrich, *In Search of Cultural
History* (Oxford, 1969), esp. 14–25.
    [7] F. Gilbert, 'The Medici Megalopolis', *The New York Review of Books*, 21 Jan.
1982, 62–6. R. A. Goldthwaite, 'The Florentine Palace as Domestic Architecture',
American Historical Review, 77 (1972), 977–1012.
    [8] See, among his many studies, esp. R. Trexler, *Public Life in Renaissance Florence*
(New York, 1980).
    [9] D. O. Hughes, 'Representing the Family: Portraits and Purposes in Early Modern
Italy', *Journal of Interdisciplinary History*, 17 (1986), 7–38.

University of Michigan, Patricia Simons, tackles the same theme, and with an intimate knowledge of the historical literature touching it.[10] Interesting suggestions concerning Michelangelo's working methods and artistic ambience spring from the art historian William Wallace's reading of recent work on Tuscan social networks[11]—and so one might go on. At bottom, however, I do not much like this talk of art historians 'borrowing' from historians, and vice versa, of daring individuals throwing very thin ropes over yawning disciplinary chasms. For there is still very much alive a tradition of Renaissance scholarship, decisively shaped and handed on by Aby Warburg, which allows—indeed demands—that historians of political institutions and theory (say, Nicolai Rubinstein and Quentin Skinner) should discuss Lorenzetti's frescos in the town hall at Siena,[12] a tradition that makes it difficult (almost pointless) to debate whether Amanda Lillie, when discussing Tuscan quattrocento villas and their patrons, is an art historian or a social historian,[13] a tradition that gave us Michael Baxandall's *Painting and Experience*, a *tour de force* of the Warburgian approach,[14] and Alison Brown's biography of the Medicean bureaucrat Messer Bartolomeo Scala, in which the politics of Renaissance literary culture clearly emerge.[15]

All of this conceded, there is little to be smug about. A distinguished American press thought it quite appropriate to bring out, quite recently, an English translation of Martin Wackernagel's *The World of the Florentine Renaissance Artist*, first published in Leipzig in 1938, and still very useful.[16] There would be a massive job of cross-disciplinary synthesis to be done if one wanted to write a Wackernagel to satisfy the 1990s. Furthermore, one would have to

---

[10] P. Simons, 'Portraiture and Patronage in Quattrocento Florence with special reference to the Tornaquinci and their Chapel in S. Maria Novella', unpub. Ph.D. thesis (University of Melbourne, 1985).

[11] W. E. Wallace, 'Michelangelo at Work: Bernardino Basso, friend, scoundrel and capomaestro', *I Tatti Studies*, 3 (1989), 235–77, to cite only one among many studies.

[12] N. Rubinstein, 'Political Ideas in Sienese Art: The Frescoes by Ambrogio Lorenzetti and Taddeo di Bartolo in the Palazzo Pubblico', *Journal of the Warburg and Courtauld Institutes*, 21 (1958), 179–207; Q. Skinner, 'Ambrogio Lorenzetti: The Artist as Political Philosopher', *Proceedings of the British Academy*, 72 (1986), 1–56.

[13] A. Lillie, 'Florentine Villas in the Fifteenth Century: A Study of the Strozzi and Sassetti Country Properties', unpub. Ph.D. thesis (University of London, 1986).

[14] M. Baxandall, *Painting and Experience in Fifteenth Century Italy* (Oxford, 1972).

[15] A. Brown, *Bartolomeo Scala (1430–1497): Chancellor of Florence* (Princeton, 1979), Italian tr. L. Rossi and F. Salvetti Cossi (Florence, 1990).

[16] M. Wackernagel, *The World of the Florentine Renaissance Artist*, tr. A Luchs (Princeton, 1981).

define Renaissance culture, or rather cultures, in writing such a book, to talk about what differentiated one artistic style from another and even to dare to enquire why stylistic change occurred—and to do these things without having recourse to the world view which informed the work of Alfred von Martin, Arnold Hauser, and Frederick Antal, whose sense of Renaissance society was so very different from that of almost all more recent historians.[17] The temptation is there, given the imposing dimensions of this task, to define Renaissance culture too quickly and too tautologically, as, for example, the late David Herlihy has done in suggesting that, because demographic factors gave women considerable domestic authority in Tuscany, they therefore assumed an important cultural role which reinforced 'certain typical traits of this civilization: its aesthetic sensibility, its subtlety, and its admiration for refined expression and elegant *topoi*'.[18] Tautology and crucial issues of definition aside, the formulation is anyway absolutely contradicted by most scholars (not to mention by the contemporary who described Botticelli's painting as having an 'aria virile'!),[19] although one historian has pointed out that clerical critics of quattrocento Florentine society regarded it as increasingly 'effeminate'.[20] The culture and very appearance of the refined and elegant Florentine *Cité des dames* discerned by David Herlihy has struck most modern observers, however, as very masculine (some would say, of its art, homoerotic), especially in comparison with 'feminine' Venice.[21] 'The Florence of the early Renaissance . . . was not a tenderly feminine city', Christiane Klapisch has written,[22] to which Michael Rocke, in a fine recent dissertation, would add that it was a society where homoerotic values and behaviour touched not just a 'subculture' but a remarkably large percentage of

[17] A. von Martin, *Sociology of the Renaissance* (London, 1944); F. Antal, *Florentine Painting and its Social Background* (London, 1948); A. Hauser, *The Social History of Art*, 2 vols. (London, 1951).

[18] D. Herlihy and C. Klapisch-Zuber, *Les Toscans et leurs familles* (Paris, 1978), 606, in a chapter written by David Herlihy (see p. 9). Elsewhere Herlihy has emphasized this theme—for example in id., *The Family in Renaissance Italy* (St Louis, Mo., 1974)—only to soften it more recently: 'Did Women Have a Renaissance? A Reconsideration', *Medievalia et Humanistica*, NS, 13 (1985), 1–22.

[19] Quoted and discussed by Baxandall, *Painting and Experience*, 26, 78, 110.

[20] Trexler, *Public Life*, 367–99.

[21] M. Plant, 'Madonna in Venice', *Art and Text*, 30 (1988), 20–9, esp. 25; M. McCarthy, *The Stones of Florence* (Harmondsworth, 1972).

[22] C. Klapisch-Zuber, *Women, Family and Ritual in Renaissance Italy*, tr. L. Cochrane (Chicago, 1985), 118.

the male population, especially the young.[23] Klapisch, and other historians of Florentine society, would point out that the agnatic family and patriarchal political structures of the Florentines that predisposed them to prize what one contemporary vividly called 'la vena mascolina'[24]—sons, in short—led them to describe the assistance requested of a grand Medici male patron as 'virile help' (*maschio aiuto*), that of a gentlewoman as 'the soft and compassionate way'.[25]

Now if, as I suspect, Florence indeed was 'not a tenderly feminine city', such an observation might in the long run help us to understand, if not precisely to define, Renaissance culture; but it would do so only after one had sorted out, painstakingly and with close attention to the social and cultural language and values of quattrocento people, essential questions of definition. The social historian cannot simply assert the existence, let alone the importance, of such a connection, just as the historian of ideas should not conduct what Anthony Grafton has recently described as a 'kind of smash-and-grab raid on social and economic history'.[26] As in recent admirable research, each scholar must carefully build bridges, not throw grappling irons, between society and culture, each should work with art-historical objects, and with contemporary writing about them, as well as with tax records, private letters, and family diaries. One should go on studying—loosely to adapt some advice given long ago by E. H. Gombrich[27]—particular people or groups of persons paying for, using, indeed creating Renaissance art; particular paintings, chapels, or palaces—or, it might be, works of literature; and

[23] M. J. Rocke, 'Male Homosexuality and its Regulation in Late Medieval Florence', see p. 20 n. 32 above.

[24] Piero Borromei, letter to Carlo Guasconi, 20 July 1462; Archivio di Stato, Firenze (henceforth ASF), Conventi Soppressi, 78, 313, fo. 244r. See too F. W. Kent, *Household and Lineage in Renaissance Florence* (Princeton, 1977).

[25] The first phrase is Matteo Franco's, writing to Piero di Lorenzo de' Medici, 23 Mar. 1493; S. Mantovani, 'Due Lettere Inedite di Matteo Franco (1447–1494)', in B. Maracchi Biagiarelli and D. E. Rhodes (eds.), *Studi offerti a Roberto Ridolfi* (Florence, 1973), 369–75, esp. 369. Bernardo Rucellai advised Luisa Strozzi on 14 Oct. 1482 to pursue a petition not with Lorenzo de' Medici but rather by 'qualche altro modo dolce e compassionevole con Niccolò per mezo di vostra sorella': Biblioteca Comunale, Forlì, Autografi Piancastelli, 1902. As here, I shall only quote in the original language when the text is unpublished.

[26] A. Grafton, 'Humanists and Sewers: A Comment and a Coda', *Renaissance Quarterly*, 42 (1989), 812–16, esp. 815.

[27] E. H. Gombrich, *Norm and Form* (London, 1966), 29; and *In Search of Cultural History*.

the complex human and intellectual contexts of which each was a part.

Years ago Gombrich also pointed out that the Florentine Renaissance flourished 'in a social context of which we know too little'.[28] A generation later, one would be better advised to say that it flourished in a social context about which we know a good deal, without always being able to agree on what it is that we know, or how to use that knowledge other than for very specialized purposes. What follows is one person's understanding of that social context (an interpretation with which many will disagree), and his suggestions as to some lines that might be drawn between society and culture.

Burckhardt's Renaissance Italy, in his celebrated phrase, 'began to swarm with individuality' as its men and women were freed from 'countless bonds'. If the Swiss scholar was disarmingly vague about what these quintessentially medieval bonds were, one surely glimpses them in his famous statement that medieval man was 'conscious of himself only as a member of a race, people, party, family or corporation'.[29] Psychological freedom was really what Burckhardt seems to have been most interested in, but his influential followers among historians today—for example, Richard Goldthwaite and Marvin Becker—have supplied a more precise institutional context for the birth of this 'individualism': the decline of medieval solidarities and corporations such as clans, guilds, and neighbourhoods, and the emergence, from clan-like structures, of small independent nuclear-conjugal families with a sense of economic individualism and social isolation.[30] While this, or similar social explanations of Renaissance cultural individualism, have long had their critics—a century ago, Edward Armstrong wrote that while he more or less agreed that 'the Florentine Renaissance was the emancipation of the individual from the environment of circumstances . . .', still 'much needless nonsense

[28] E. H. Gombrich, *Symbolic Images* (London, 1972), 30.

[29] J. Burckhardt, *The Civilization of the Renaissance in Italy*, tr. by S. G. C. Middlemore (London, 1950), 81, 171. See too A. Brown, 'Jacob Burckhardt's Renaissance', *History Today*, 38 (1988), 20–6.

[30] Among his many essays, see M. B. Becker, 'An Essay on the Quest for Identity in the Early Italian Renaissance', in J. G. Rowe and W. H. Stockdale (eds.), *Florilegium Historiale: Essays Presented to W. K. Ferguson* (Toronto, 1971), 294–312; R. A. Goldthwaite, *Private Wealth in Renaissance Florence* (Princeton, 1968); and 'The Florentine Palace'.

has been talked and written on the subject'[31]—they still amount to a powerful interpretation in the hands of a Goldthwaite, and one which is perennially attractive to the general reader of history.

To other historians, fifteenth-century Florence looks very different indeed. Smallish households were the statistical norm in all classes, to be sure, but many, if not most, people lived part of their lives in families of several generations and with a complex structure, above all in fraternal families or households headed by a grandfather. Sprawling households of several generations, and tiny nuclear families, rather than representing different eras—the medieval and early modern respectively, were stages in the so-called domestic developmental cycle. Among the well-to-do and politically established citizens at least—and almost certainly among many rural communities—individual households were conscious of belonging, usually through the male line, to larger 'houses', called variously *case*, *lignaggi*, *consorterie*, and so on. The majority of households of a *casa* usually lived close to one another—there is ample evidence that most kinsfolk were 'sociable' together—and shared certain everyday and ritual responsibilities. Communal legislation acknowledged that agnatic kinsmen often acted together, and at times rewarded and at others punished them for doing so, for the state feared the potential and actual power of over-mighty and united lineages. The 'family', then, meant several things to a Renaissance Florentine, who normally was hardly an isolated individual, whether he or she liked it or not.[32]

Indeed beyond these patrilineal families, there were still other familial bonds, those formed by marriage and called *parentadi*. *Parenti*, relations by marriage, seem to have been important to all classes, not least to the urban *popolo* who, it seems, often lacked wider patrilineal ties. Recent research has shown that for women especially these familial bonds created by marriage, and through the maternal lines, mattered a good deal.[33] 'All Cornishmen are cozens', it was said in the seventeenth century, a statement a number of

[31] E. Armstrong, *Lorenzo de' Medici and Florence in the Fifteenth Century* (New York, 1896), 280.

[32] The literature is immense; for a recent historiographical and bibliographical survey, see F. W. Kent, 'La famiglia patrizia fiorentina nel Quattrocento. Nuovi orientamenti nella storiografia recente', in D. Lamberini (ed.), *Palazzo Strozzi: Metà Millennio 1489–1989*, Atti del Convegno di Studi, Firenze, 3–6 Iuglio (Rome, 1991), 70–91.

[33] Ibid. 85–91.

Florentine patricians came near to paraphrasing. He would not mention in his commonplace book, Giovanni Rucellai wrote in 1476, every *parentado* established by the coming and going in marriage of girls in and out of the whole Rucellai lineage 'because they are so numerous, involving half the city'; still, he lists scores of maternal cousins, connections of his paternal grandfather's line alone.[34]

At a more sophisticated intellectual level than Rucellai's, one finds articulated the notion that the city, for 'citizens' at least, was—or ought to be—a series of family blocs linked by marriage and held together by friendship, *'amicitia,* the sole support of a city', according to Matteo Palmieri, a conception borrowed from Cicero above all and already well known to Brunetto Latini's generation a century and a half before.[35] So, strikingly, the Medicean client Filippo Arnolfi wrote to Piero di Cosimo de' Medici in 1465 of a united city as being 'one friendship'.[36] For one can argue that the Mediceans, with a view to creating this 'one friendship', first exiled or otherwise excluded from civic life the men and families they regarded as incorrigible or simply too threatening, and then sought gradually to centralize under their own management the numerous bonds of friendship, fraternity, and dependence—the patron–client relationships as some would say—which criss-crossed Florentine society. These various social relationships, often created by kinship in its several senses, were in effect frequently indistinguishable from bonds of neighbourhood and affection, or from those of godparenthood and of the fraternal sociability born of the experience of sharing communal office together, and of belonging to the same lay religious confraternities.[37] Perhaps the first physical setting of this multi-stranded

---

[34] Quoted by C. Klapisch-Zuber, *La Famiglia e le Donne nel Rinascimento a Firenze* (Rome, 1988), 54.

[35] Matteo Palmieri, *Vita Civile*, ed. G. Belloni (Florence, 1982), 161–2; Skinner, 'Ambrogio Lorenzetti'.

[36] ASF, Archivio Mediceo avanti il Principato, XVII, 459, 12 Sept. 1465: 'la union vostra [between Piero de' Medici and Luca Pitti] esser capo della amicizia di chotesta città'.

[37] On these themes, and for bibliography, see D. Kent, *The Rise of the Medici: Faction in Florence 1426–34* (Oxford, 1978); id., 'The Dynamic of Power in Cosimo de' Medici's Florence', in F. W. Kent and P. Simons (eds.), *Patronage, Art, and Society in Renaissance Italy* (Oxford, 1987), 63–77; F. W. Kent and P. Simons, 'Renaissance Patronage: An Introductory Essay', in id., *Patronage, Art, and Society*, 1–21; R. F. E. Weissman, *Ritual Brotherhood in Renaissance Florence* (New York, 1982); A. Molho, 'Cosimo de' Medici: *Pater Patriae* or *Padrino*?', *Stanford Italian Review*, 1 (1979), 5–33; id., 'Il patronato a Firenze nella storiografia anglofona', *Ricerche storiche*, 15 (1985), 5–16; id., 'Patronage and the State in Early Modern Europe', in A. Maczak and

social existence was the local neighbourhood, often dominated by one's kin, with its street corners and benches, or the parish—of which we need to know more—and the administrative district or *gonfalone*, whose members met in a prominent local church.[38] In the quattrocento, most people went on being buried in these neighbourhood churches, Sharon Strocchia has shown, for all that confraternal loyalties sometimes worked against parochial bonds, as did, later, the Savonarolan devotion to San Marco.[39] Beyond these intimately experienced neighbourhoods, and more than their sum, lay the city at large, an ideal setting for the 'public politics of republican discussion and patronal jobbery, the ebb and flow of whose talk, gossip, and "fixing" passed through the piazzas, the loggias, the street-corners, or *canti*, and the taverns, sweeping around and in and out of the [patrician] palaces'.[40]

From the point of view of an anti-Medicean contemporary, of course, Florence was—as the soon-to-be-exiled Agnolo Acciaiuoli graphically put it, also in 1465—a 'paradise inhabited by devils',[41] and indeed the city was still prone to serious outbreaks of factionalism and violence, even if less catastrophically so than in earlier centuries. Arnolfi's very description of the city as 'one friendship' was made precisely at the time the city was about to split into several 'friendships', that is to say factions, a tragedy he was seeking to avert by urging Piero de' Medici to negotiate with his erstwhile *amici* such as Luca Pitti, who had now become his rivals.[42] Families and neighbourhoods could be the building blocks, friendships the adhesive, needed for civic integration, but dynastic and other loyalties could be the very forces that split the city, above all when one great family such as the Medici was seen to be acquiring an unprecedented

E. Muller-Luckner (eds.), *Klientelsysteme im Europa der Frühen Neuzeit* (Munich, 1988), 233–42.

[38] D. V. Kent and F. W. Kent, *Neighbours and Neighbourhood in Renaissance Florence* (Locust Valley, NY, 1982); N. Eckstein, 'The District of the Green Dragon: Neighbourhood Life and Social Change in Renaissance Florence', unpub. Ph.D. thesis (Monash University, 1991), forthcoming as a book to be published by Olschki.

[39] S. T. Strocchia, 'Burials in Renaissance Florence', unpub. Ph.D. diss. (University of California at Berkeley, 1981), 105–7, 160–1, 360; L. Polizzotto, 'Dell'arte del ben morire: The Piagnone Way of Death 1494–1545', *I Tatti Studies*, 3 (1989), 27–87, esp. 56–8.

[40] F. W. Kent, 'Palaces, Politics and Society in Fifteenth-Century Florence', *I Tatti Studies*, 2 (1987), 41–70, esp. 59.

[41] Ibid. 63.

[42] Cited in n. 36. On these events, see N. Rubinstein, *The Government of Florence under the Medici (1434 to 1494)* (Oxford, 1966), pt. II.

position within the republic. This was also a city characterized by other profound divisions, among them those of gender, of income, and of social class, as Herlihy and Klapisch, Strocchia, Samuel Cohn, Anthony Molho, and others have pointed out.[43] For all these divisions, there is some evidence that poor and politically disenfranchised men and women were included in, indeed could be in a position to influence, the complicated social networks and various institutions sketched above. This is precisely why the *popolo*, who (the police records tell us) drank and fought with patricians in the taverns, characteristically split along factional as much as along class lines at times of political crisis for their social betters.[44]

In sum, if there were forces working towards social and civic integration in quattrocento Florence, these encountered great and divisive odds and by no means always prevailed, which is in no way to say that the city was divided into neat socio-economic classes, as von Martin and many of his generation argued. Burckhardt's view, however, that in Italian society 'the main current ... went steadily towards the fusion of classes in the modern sense of the phrase', seems as remote from the complicated social reality perceived by most late-twentieth-century scholars as does his assertion that Renaissance Italians had no sense of themselves as members of a people, party, family, or corporation.[45]

And what of good old-fashioned Renaissance individualism in this complex society of friends (and enemies), neighbours, religious *confrères*, godparents, and kinsmen? One may take it for granted that, as the heirs of the intellectual traditions of twelfth- and thirteenth-century Europeans, many educated quattrocento Florentines were concerned with 'self-discovery' and with the worth of human relations explored through the inspiration of classical texts, if Colin Morris's extraordinarily broad definition of medieval individualism is to be invoked. Burckhardt's individualism, too, included these qualities, to which he added a strong dash of the fierce egoism and

[43] Herlihy and Klapisch-Zuber, *Les Toscans*; Molho, 'Cosimo de' Medici'; Klapisch-Zuber, *La Famiglia*; id., *Women, Family and Ritual*; S. K. Cohn, *The Laboring Classes in Renaissance Florence* (New York, 1980); S. Strocchia, 'Remembering the Family: Women, Kin and Commemorative Masses in Renaissance Florence', *Renaissance Quarterly*, 42 (1989), 635–54.

[44] F. W. Kent, 'La famiglia patrizia', 88–9; F. W. Kent and P. Simons, 'Renaissance Patronage', 8–11; D. V. Kent and F. W. Kent, 'Two Vignettes of Florentine Society in the Fifteenth Century', *Rinascimento*, 23 (1983), 237–60.

[45] Burckhardt, *Civilization*, 81, 217.

'self-centredness' one finds in the *OED* definition. There is no necessary contradiction between a person's being 'individualistic', even in the sense of egoistic, and belonging to a Florentine society of the sort sketched above; just as, *mutatis mutandis*, what Caroline Bynum calls the twelfth-century 'discovery of self' was inseparable from 'a new sense of becoming part of a group'.[46] Renaissance art patrons frequently expressed their strong sense of self by using personal insignia, but almost invariably alongside the heraldic paraphernalia of their agnatic lineages.[47] Similarly, many Tuscan diarists wrote their family commonplace books, their *ricordi*, which among a number of other things revealed, as Burckhardt noted with his usual acuteness, an impulse towards autobiographical individualism, to inform their descendants of their own and their ancestors' doings.[48] Goldthwaite is right in saying that the Florentines were economic individualists, in the sense that individuals or households formed their society's basic economic units, even if he underestimates the extent to which these separate households co-operated economically with those of their kin.[49] However, it does not follow that individualistic economic behaviour shaped all other activities and feelings in its own 'private' image. Why, indeed, cannot that proposition be turned on its head, by our suggesting that the many and overlapping social ties of which Florentines could avail themselves, persuaded

[46] C. Morris, *The Discovery of the Individual 1050–1200* (London, 1972); C. Walker Bynum, 'Did the Twelfth Century Discover the Individual?', in id., *Jesus as Mother* (Berkeley, 1984), 82–109. See, too, C. Morris, 'Individualism in Twelfth Century Religion. Some Further Reflections', *Journal of Ecclesiastical History*, 31 (1980), 195–206. See too R. F. E. Weissman, 'Reconstructing Renaissance Sociology: The "Chicago School" and the Study of Renaissance Society', in *Persons in Groups*, ed. R. C. Trexler (New York, 1985), 39–46, and id., 'The Importance of Being Ambiguous: Social Relations, Individualism and Identity in Renaissance Florence', *Urban Life in the Renaissance*, ed. S. Zimmerman and R. F. E. Weissman (Newark, 1989), 269–80.

[47] F. W. Kent, *Household and Lineage*, 288–92. In general, see N. Z. Davis, 'Boundaries and the Sense of Self in Sixteenth-Century France', in T. C. Heller, M. Sosna and D. E. Wellbery (eds.), *Reconstructing Individualism . . .* (Stanford, Calif., 1986), 53–63.

[48] Burckhardt, *Civilization*, 203. For a recent survey, see F. Pezzarossa, 'La Memorialistica tra Medioevo e Rinascimento', *Lettere Italiane*, 31 (1979), 96–138; G.-M. Anselmi, F. Pezzarossa, and L. Avellini, *La Memoria dei Mercatores* (Bologna, 1980), and now W. J. Connell, '*Libri di famiglia* and the Family History of Florentine Patricians', *Italian Culture*, 8 (1990), 279–92.

[49] Goldthwaite, *Private Wealth*; id., 'Organizzazione economica e struttura famigliare', in *I ceti dirigenti nella Toscana tardo comunale* (Florence, 1983; no ed.), 1–13. See too F. W. Kent, 'La famiglia patrizia', 77–8.

some of them, at least, to feel at once safe and free enough to
fly their several economic kites? Be that as it may, if we can accept
that Renaissance Florentines were 'individualists' who nevertheless
belonged to several and overlapping social networks, what implications might this proposition have for their activities as patrons, and
users, of Renaissance culture, even for how we might—implicitly at
least—begin to define that culture or cultures?

A vivid and economical way of proceeding is to sketch a collective
portrait of a grand Florentine patron of Renaissance architecture and
the related arts, active, say, between Brunelleschi's time and the
young Giuliano da Sangallo's—a portrait drawn from the volumi-
nous literature and given refinement by some unpublished archival
details—and to try to place this patron's activities in the social landscape depicted above. This is, of course, not to say that the actions
of this man—for in Florence, though not in courtly Italy, a man
without exception this grand patron is—are only, or merely, explic-
able in terms of such a depiction; nor to say that he is, in trendy disguise, traditional 'Renaissance man' revivified. One should also add
that his portrait must remain a partial one, until it becomes a group
portrait which includes the artists and artisans whom he employed
and with whom in a real sense he collaborated. Such men might well
have been his friends, neighbours, tenants, or clients (in several
senses of that last word), talented individuals, to be sure, whose lives
and artistic careers will be better understood when we re-examine
them in the light of the recent literature on Florentine politics and
society, a task one cannot undertake here.[50] Nor is there time to discuss the numerous Florentine men (and some women) who, as active
if 'minor' patrons of devotional pictures, altarpieces, church vest-
ments, and tapestries, were indeed more typical in their very modest
normalcy than their grander cousin, whom we shall call Giovanni X.

Giovanni X is a *pater familias* of mature years, from a well-off,
politically-established but not necessarily ancient lineage. Having
served his apprenticeship as a young man by making small or minor
domestic and ecclesiastical commissions, such as the purchase of marriage furniture, the first important act of his patronal life may well be
the building of a new palace—Giovanni is probably a banker with
access to fluid capital—almost always on the site of ancestral houses,

[50] For example, Eckstein, 'District of the Green Dragon', has much to say on the
painters' community of Drago Verde.

some or all of which he may incorporate into the new fabric, in a parish or district long frequented by his wider family. (His poorer paternal cousins probably make do with merely renovating their neighbouring houses, while Giovanni fills his with paintings, sculpture, and furnishings—whether or not in the spirit of a collector is open to debate!) As he grows older, Giovanni endows in his neighbourhood church a burial chapel, decorated with frescos possibly depicting himself and his immediate (very occasionally, more distant) family, and perhaps with a classicizing sarcophagus. He usually goes on contributing to the upkeep and decoration of tombs or chapels owned collectively there by his patrilineal kin, and acknowledges matrilineal ties by paying for memorial masses in this or other churches. Giovanni X's reasoning about this typical patronal behaviour, this close association of the dead and the living, presumably resembles that of a 'real' Florentine, Lorenzo di Neri Vettori, in his will of 1479. 'And because after this life we need somewhere else to live', Vettori declared, he elected to be buried 'in San Iacopo sopr'Arno our parish and *popolo*'—the church nearest to his ancestral houses—in his own sepulchre, or 'at the foot of the stairs of the main chapel, which chapel belongs to us Vettori'. Lorenzo wanted 'a simple marble slab without carvings and leaf patterns', inscribed only with the Vettori arms and his own name.[51] Too simple, this, for Giovanni X, who would have approved rather of a comment made by another contemporary, Piero del Tovaglia: 'If I spend 2,000 florins on my house, my dwelling on earth, then five hundred devoted to my residence in the next life seems to me money well spent.'[52] Indeed at this time, while (by the way) at least flirting with the idea of having sculpted a marble bust of himself, a grand patron such as Giovanni almost certainly also patronizes the main church of his quarter, or

---

[51] ASF, Notarile Antecosimiano, G 593 (testamenti 1459–1510), fos. 327ʳ–28ᵛ, 23 Aug. 1479: 'E perchè abbiamo bisogno d'altra habitazione dopo la presente vita, benchè insensibili, pure per essere riposti in uno luogo diterminato io voglio, e chosì dispongo e lascio, che se a mia vita io non facessi fare una sepoltura overo avello in Santo Iacopo Soprarno, nostra parrocchia e popolo, a piè delle scale della cappella maggiore nel mezzo, la quale cappella è di noi Vettori [it should be done by his heirs]. . . . La spesa di detto avello e sepoltura voglio che sia a ssufficienza e non a ponpa; solamente voglio che sia una lapida di marmo semplice, sanza intagli e fogliami, solamente con l'arme e col nome mio, e degli attententi [*sic*] e propinqui se vorrino quivi esser riposti quando verrà il termine loro'.

[52] In a letter of 8 May 1471 to Lodovico Gonzago, pub. B. L. Brown, 'The Patronage and Building History of the Tribuna of SS. Annunziata in Florence . . .', *Mitteilungen des Kunsthistorischen Institutes in Florenz*, 25 (1981), 59–146, esp. 126.

some other celebrated religious foundation in his city, as his paternal ancestors and other living *consorti* may have done. He may contribute to the upkeep or building of chapels of the lineage there, and offer a pulpit or even some capital work such as a cloister, library, or refectory. He dreams of completing the famous church's façade, something he fails to do unless he is indeed Giovanni di Paolo Rucellai.[53]

To escape the infernal dust of all this urban building, and following an ancient instinct, Giovanni X and his family go frequently to their rural estates set among other lands which belong to his wider paternal family and connections. There, and also sometimes further away from Florence, he remodels (or more unusually rebuilds) his villa, with its beautiful garden and prosperous farms, sparing some money for the decoration and endowment of a local church or oratory. He and his paternal kin may well collectively support a rural chapel, or hospital for poor pilgrims, on or near their ancestral lands, just as, back in Florence, they may remain joint owners of a medieval tower, or of a loggia built by their ancestors. In certain other respects, too, Giovanni X's patronal activities are collective. He may very well help support the ritual and artistic activities of his religious confraternity, and sit as an *operaio*, member of the works' committee, for various guild and ecclesiastical institutions; and he may be frequently asked by other patrons and by artists for his advice or arbitration on matters artistic and patronal. As a member of his parish and district, he almost certainly contributes to the upkeep and decoration of the local church where his district has its formal meetings. If Giovanni is a rich parishioner of the church of San Lorenzo, his and his colleagues' activities there amount almost to ecclesiastical patronage by a political faction, that of the Medici. (Competition with his peers, however, a desire to emulate his social superiors, these were impulses to commission works of art quite as powerful as, and sometimes at odds with, a sense of piety or of collective identification with others.) While Giovanni X may have been among the minority of patrons who clearly had a particular sense of artistic taste to express, he was most unlikely to have been an *amateur* architectural draughtsman, sculptor, or painter, although such figures do half emerge, tantalizingly and rarely, from the documents.[54]

---

[53] F. W. Kent, A. Perosa, B. Preyer, P. Sanpaolesi, and R. Salvini, *Giovanni Rucellai ed il suo Zibaldone*, ii, *A Florentine Patrician and his Palace: Studies* (London, 1981), 62–5.

[54] U. Middeldorf, 'On the Dilettante Sculptor', *Apollo*, 107 (1978), 310–22.

Who is Giovanni X? He is Filippo Strozzi, Giovanni Rucellai, Francesco Sassetti, Giovanni Tornabuoni, Cosimo de' Medici, Tommaso Spinelli, Piero Mellini, *et al.*, patrons who hardly need introduction,[55] or a figure such as Francesco Nori or Tommaso Soderini whose patronage is known to specialists.[56] To be sure, not all of these men's activities conformed precisely to Giovanni X's too-perfect career. Sassetti, for example, built a villa rather than a town *palazzo*.[57] Another banking colleague of the Medici, Nori, was also unusual in merely adapting a rather old-fashioned palace in Florence, while apparently putting greater energies into a villa which Vespasiano da Bisticci described around 1480 as replete with 'fountains and fishponds with the greatest abundance of water everywhere, hanging gardens, chapels rebuilt as new, all of it walled, perforce, and indeed very magnificent'.[58] Separate from Giovanni X and his 'circle' there was, it is true, another group of rich and powerful Florentines (Neri Capponi for one), who chose not to become really conspicuous patrons at all, doing little more than improving their ancestral property and churches. Then there was a man such as Girolamo Rucellai, who was a consistent if minor patron of San Girolamo at Fiesole, where he was buried, a church with no ancestral or local family connections. Girolamo's personal devotion to his

[55] It is not possible to give full bibliographies here. Recent works include: on Strozzi, Lamberini (ed.), *Palazzo Strozzi*; on Rucellai, F. W. Kent *et al.*, *Florentine Patrician*; on Sassetti, Lillie, 'Florentine Villas'; on Tornabuoni, Simons, 'Portraiture and Patronage'; on Cosimo de' Medici, G. Cherubini and G. Fanelli (eds.), *Il Palazzo Medici Riccardi di Firenze* (Florence, 1990); on Tommaso Spinelli, H. Saalman, 'Tommaso Spinelli, Michelozzo, Manetti and Rossellino', *Journal of the Society of Architectural Historians*, 25 (1966), 151–64 and C. R. Mack, 'Building a Florentine Palace: The Palazzo Spinelli', *Mitteilungen des Kunsthistorischen Institutes in Florenz*, 26 (1982), 261–84; on Piero Mellini, P. Morselli, 'Corpus of Tuscan Pulpits 1400–1550', unpub. Ph.D. diss. (University of Pittsburgh, 1979), 98–114, and D. Carl, 'Die Kapelle Guidalotti-Mellini im Kreuzgang von S. Croce. Ein Beitrag zur Baugeschichte', *Mitteilungen des Kunsthistorischen Institutes in Florenz*, 25 (1981), 203–30.

[56] On Nori, see B. Preyer, 'The "chasa overo palagio" of Alberto di Zanobi: a Florentine Palace of about 1400 and its Later Remodeling', *Art Bulletin*, 65 (1983), 387–401, F. W. Kent, 'Quattrocento Florentine Taste in Palaces: Two Notes', *Australian Journal of Art*, 6 (1987), 17–24, and S. R. McKillop, 'L'ampliamento dello stemma mediceo e il suo contesto politico', *Archivio storico italiano*, 150 (1992), 641–713. On Soderini, see Eckstein, 'The District of the Green Dragon'.

[57] Lillie, 'Florentine Villas'.

[58] G. M. Cagni, *Vespasiano da Bisticci e il suo Epistolario* (Rome, 1969), 180. Vespasiano also mentions Nori's villa in a letter of 1471: F. W. Kent, *Bartolommeo Cederni and his Friends: Letters to an Obscure Florentine* (Florence, 1991), 105. On his palace, see Preyer, 'The "chasa overo palagio" '.

name saint may explain his unusual behaviour.[59] Most seeming variations from Giovanni X's model career are, however, more apparent
than real. If in mid-century the prominent Medicean politician
Messer Giovanni Canigiani (1404–77) moved from his own parish of
Santa Felicita to another where he acquired two fine houses, his
adopted neighbourhood in Via de' Bardi nearby, and in the same
ancestral quarter of Santo Spirito, was hardly alien territory, since it
was already the home of his relations-in-law and of several other of
his Canigiani kin. Giovanni was, moreover, to be buried in his ancestral Santa Felicita, whose beautiful sacristy he began to build at some
expense during the 1470s.[60] The banker Castello Quaratesi (born
c.1396) started his career as a patron in the 1450s with his very ambitious project to rebuild the church and convent of San Francesco al
Monte, which dominated his ancestral quarter of Santo Spirito, yet
he is traditionally said also to have wanted to finish the façade of
Santa Croce, in another quarter. His passion for things Franciscan
may explain his plans for a church outside his own area of the
Oltrarno; however, he was to be buried in his parish church of San
Niccolò in Santo Spirito, which was also heavily endowed by his
numerous Quaratesi kin, whom he remembered in his will of 1465.[61]
If, as Alison Luchs has interestingly pointed out, many chapel
owners at the Cistercian church of Cestello departed from family
tradition by their activities there in the latter half of the quattrocento, most were not buried in the Cistercian foundation, which they

[59] F. W. Kent, *Household and Lineage*, 262–3.

[60] For his career, see *Dizionario Biografico degli Italiani*, 18 (1975), 93–4. This man's architectural patronage merits closer study. My brief account is drawn from ASF, Catasto, 905 (i), fos. 417ʳ–19ʳ; 992, fos. 90ʳ–92ᵛ; and from his will of 15 Mar. 1473/74 (ASF, Notarile Antecosimiano, B 726 (testamenti 1455–95), inserto 2, fos. 152ʳ–56ʳ) with its reference to the 'sacristiam et cappellam per dictum testatorem inchoatam in dicta ecclesia S. Felicitatis ad finem perduci et perfici et etiam sacris cel-ebrari amore Dei et ob remedium anime sue' (now published in part by F. Fiorelli Malesci, *La Chiesa di Santa Felicita a Firenze* (Florence, 1986), 328–9). For this project Canigiani bequeathed some 600 florins, only 150 of which had been spent by his heirs by 15 Feb. 1480/1 (ASF, Catasto, 992, fo. 92ʳ); the project was perhaps still incom-plete in 1498 (ASF, Decima Repubblicana, 2, fos. 139ʳ–42ᵛ). Saalman has discussed his palaces in 'Tommaso Spinelli', 161–2, 164.

[61] Quaratesi, too, deserves more attention. The above I draw from his tax report of 1458 (ASF, Catasto, 785, fos. 77ʳ–80ʳ) and his will of 25 April 1465 (ASF, Notarile Antecosimiano, B 726, fos. 23ʳ–28ᵛ). See too F. Moisè, *Santa Croce di Firenze* (Florence, 1845), 90–1, 492, and I. Moretti, *La Chiesa di San Niccolò Oltrarno* (Florence, 1972/3).

supported for a variety of often personal reasons ably rehearsed by Luchs.[62]

One may also begin to account for the patronal behaviour of some more socially obscure patrons—people without firm local roots and long family traditions, such as those possessed by Giovanni X and his look-alikes—if one knows well their social networks, their friends or *amici*, who for such people seem often to have replaced family as a model for patronal and other behaviour. Iacopo Bongianni (*c*.1443–*c*.1506), a merchant of Santa Croce artisan origins, lived by 1480 in the Scala district of Santo Spirito. When, however, he decided to become an ecclesiastical patron, he chose substantially to endow and rebuild the monastic church of Santa Chiara in yet another, and distant, part of Santo Spirito. Although Iacopo was to be buried in Santa Chiara—his father, by the way, had remained faithful in death to Santa Croce—neither his coat-of-arms, nor anybody else's, was to be displayed there. One way of explaining Bongianni's unusual mixture of extravagant but anonymous piety, in a district other than his ancestral one—there are, of course, other possible explanations—is to remember that he had a life-long association, as employee and client, with Giovanni Rucellai and his elder son, Pandolfo. The latter, a banker turned Dominican in Savonarola's San Marco, was famous for his piety. Pandolfo was also an ecclesiastical patron, though not on the scale of his celebrated father, who commissioned Alberti to design most of his projects. It was these two men, the sources make clear, who in effect became family to Bongianni and his brother Francesco—Iacopo himself was childless—inspiring him (we might conjecture) to build and decorate in order to express the explicit Savonarolan devotion he manifests in the 1490s: witness his prayerful portrait in the *Adoration of the Shepherds* by Lorenzo di Credi which he commissioned in that decade for Santa Chiara, where, by the way, several of his kinswomen were nuns.[63]

[62] A. Luchs, *Cestello: A Cistercian Church of the Florentine Renaissance* (New York, 1977), 47–8, 50.

[63] For archival references and recent bibliography on Bongianni, see R. Ristori, 'Un mercante savonaroliano: Pandolfo Rucellai', in *Magia, Astrologia e Religione: Convegno polacco-italiano* (Florence, 1972; no ed.), 30–47; F. W. Kent *et al.*, *Florentine Patrician*, 74, 88, 90; F. W. Kent, 'Lorenzo di Credi, his patron Iacopo Bongianni and Savonarola', *Burlington Magazine*, 125 (1983), 539–41; id., 'A Proposal by Savonarola for the Self-Reform of Florentine Women (March 1496)', *Memorie Domenicane*, NS, 14 (1983), 335–41. For his father's wish to be buried in S. Croce, see ASF, Notarile Antecosimiano, F 365 (anni 1478–81), unfoliated draft dated 28 Aug. 1480.

The behaviour of a very insignificant artistic patron indeed, one Bartolommeo Cederni (1416–82), also reveals the influence of more powerful and famous friends. Cederni, so far as we know, commissioned a total of two paintings, both by the popular Neri di Bicci; one was for the church of San Romolo, in the Piazza de' Signori, the other for the Badia Fiorentina, where he lies buried behind an old-fashioned wall plaque in the cloister. Why did Cederni, a bank employee without family or connections, have himself buried in the Badia (to which, most unusually, he also bequeathed his father's chapel in San Romolo) when he lived all his life in the same modest house in yet another parish, San Apollinare? Cederni's personal devotion to the Benedictines at the Badia provides one reason, but it can hardly be distinguished from his life-long association with other, greater, patrons of the church, the influential Pandolfini family, whose intimate correspondent and factotum—conceivably distant relative—the obscure Cederni was.[64] The ecclesiastical architectural patronage of two other 'new men' in the late fifteenth century, Ser Giovanni Guidi and Antonio di Bernardo Miniati (at the convents of San Gallo and of Le Murate respectively), is largely accounted for by their devoted bureaucratic service and personal allegiance to Lorenzo de' Medici, himself a notable patron of both foundations.[65]

Indeed, such bonds of more specifically political friendship (not to say the whole changing political culture) may also help explain an interesting patronal phenomenon to be observed from mid-quattrocento century onwards, the emergence of what one would be almost tempted to call a heightened 'individualism' among several patrons, if one could only detach that word from its Burckhardtian roots. So Messer Bongianni Gianfigliazzi (born c.1418) takes over the main chapel in his ancestral church of Santa Trinita early in 1464, for its construction diverting from his clan chapel in the same church funds bequeathed him by his brother for pious purposes. The new

[64] F. W. Kent, *Bartolommeo Cederni, passim*; id., 'The Cederni Altar-Piece by Neri di Bicci in Parma', *Mitteilungen des Kunsthistorischen Institutes in Florenz*, 33 (1989), 378–9.
[65] F. W. Kent, 'New Light on Lorenzo de' Medici's convent at Porta San Gallo', *Burlington Magazine*, 124 (1982), 292–4; id., 'Lorenzo de' Medici, Madonna Scolastica Rondinelli e la politica di mecenatismo architettonico nel convento delle Murate a Firenze (1471–1472)', forthcoming in the proceedings of the conference on *Arte, Committenza ed Economia a Roma e nelle Corti del Rinascimento (1420–1530)*, Rome, 24–7 Oct. 1990.

chapel, brilliantly painted by the patrician artist Alesso Baldovinetti, was to be the burial place, Gianfigliazzi's will of the same year insists, only of himself and his wife and their descendants, and, should she wish, of his sister-in-law. The chapel should display 'the arms of the house of the Gianfigliazzi and the device of the said testator, with the name, patronymic and surname of the said testator, builder and constructor of this chapel . . .'.[66] Somewhat later, in 1485, Piero Mellini stipulated that in his newly-built sepulchre in his family's ancestral church of Santa Croce there should be interred only his son, Domenico, and his direct descendants in the male line, 'and everyone of the stock, progeny and family of the said Domenico . . . *not* [my emphasis] others of the house or kinsfolk or family of Mellini'.[67] Of the several similar declarations I have found by serendipity, none was more forthright than that made by Leonardo di Zanobi Bartolini, who in 1495 said of his chapel in Cestello that it 'belongs to the above Leonardo himself and not to others of the Bartolini house'.[68] Now one cannot simply say of these people that they were Renaissance individualists cutting themselves off from their families and traditional 'medieval' institutions. Gianfigliazzi was given the main chapel of Santa Trinita by a parish committee of his neighbours, including another Gianfigliazzi, and he enjoyed cordial relations with his wider family, portraits of several of whom appeared in the frescos.[69] Piero Mellini explicitly says that his Mellini kin, as well as his son, may make use of his other burial places in Santa Croce. His being so exclusive about the new tomb may reflect the fact that he did not want to share it with two other families, with different surnames, to whom (it now emerges) he was technically related.[70]

[66] ASF, Notarile Antecosimiano, V 293, inserto 4, fos. 55ʳ–58ʳ: 'ponendovi l'arme della chasa de' Gianfiglazzi e'l segnio [del bancho, cancelled] d'esso testatore, chol nome, prenome e chognome d'esso testatore, constructore e edificatore d'essa chappella, se parrà a detti suoi heredi e executori' (fo. 55ᵛ); the Latin version of the will is dated 14 July 1464 (ibid., fos. 46ʳ–49ʳ). The act of donation by the monks and *operai* is in ASF, Notarile Antecosimiano, C 405, inserto 1463, no. 31, 16 Feb. 1463/4. On the chapel's decoration, see R. W. Kennedy, *Alesso Baldovinetti* (New Haven, Conn., 1938), 136–7, 167, 172, 177.

[67] Transcribed by Morselli, 'Corpus of Tuscan Pulpits', 108 (codicil dated 19 May 1485); and see 98–114 for Piero's other patronage at S. Croce; also Carl, 'Die Kapelle Guidalotti-Mellini', 203–30.

[68] Luchs, *Cestello*, 263, and see 50.   [69] For references, see n. 66.

[70] Morselli, 'Corpus of Tuscan Pulpits', 108, gives the relevant passage from a codicil. ASF, Tratte, 1075, fo. 15ᵛ (a document of *c*.1485 listing those families with different surnames nevertheless subject to the *divieto* laws) lists the Barducci and

No doubt a number of explanations of these men's behaviour could be offered by specialists of various persuasions, for example by liturgical scholars. What a historian of society sees is a singling out of self from the gathered kin, a calling attention to one's own particular achievements, which then, so to speak, define a distinctive group of descendants—without destroying a sense of belonging to the wider paternal kin group. Gianfigliazzi's chapel, the document of donation says, was 'for the perpetual memory of the said Bongianni',[71] which was perhaps also Piero Mellini's motive for commissioning his portrait bust by Benedetto da Maiano in 1474.[72] A little earlier, in 1463, the della Robbia sculptural workshop apparently produced the first of its family coats-of-arms to bear an inscription identifying the particular patron, in this case Roberto Lioni.[73] This seems to reflect a growing sense of exclusiveness, rather than individualism, which may be connected with the growth of private chapels for worship within patrician palaces.

In these decades the Minerbetti, Nerli, Scala, Nori, and others all followed the chapel-building example of Cosimo de'Medici in his Via Larga palace.[74] Almost every name mentioned above, whether that of Gianfigliazzi, Lioni, or Francesco Nori, is that of a patrician politician very closely bound to the Medici—and often to each other[75]—by friendly and partisan ties; Bartolomeo Scala was a Medicean bureaucrat par excellence.[76] Even more carefully and calculatingly than his ancestors had done, Lorenzo de' Medici seems to

Ottavanti as *consorti* of the Mellini. Piero Mellini in his several wills certainly bequeaths his estate to his distant Mellini kin, should his direct descendants fail: ASF, Notarile Antecosimiano, G 619 (anni 1456–96), fos. 160ʳ–163ʳ, 165ʳ–167ʳ, 222ʳ–225ᵛ, 390ʳ–391ᵛ.

[71] 'Remaneat et sit de memorie [*sic*] dicti Bongiannis in perpetuum' ASF, Notarile Antecosimiano C 405, inserto 1463, no. 31, 16 Feb. 1463/4.

[72] Morselli, 'Corpus of Tuscan Pulpits', 101.

[73] A. Marquand, *Robbia Heraldry* (Princeton, 1912), pp. xvi, 13–14.

[74] L. Pellecchia, 'The Patron's Role in the Production of Architecture: Bartolomeo Scala and the Scala Palace', *Renaissance Quarterly*, 42 (1989), 258–91, esp. 272–3, which reports work in progress on this theme by Philip Mattox.

[75] To cite just one example concerning three palace builders who were neighbours and Mediceans. Tommaso Spinelli describes Piero Mellini in his will of 4 Dec. 1468 as 'eius fidelissimum amicum' (ASF, Notarile Antecosimiano, P 357 (testamenti 1460–80), fo. 74ʳ). Mellini bought the houses he refashioned into a palace from Francesco Nori (ASF, Catasto, 1005, ii, fo. 589ʳ), who was his nephew. The Medicean links of these and the other men mentioned can be explored in Rubinstein, *Government*, especially the appendices, and in the bibliography cited in this paper.

[76] Brown, *Bartolomeo Scala, passim*.

have singled out such individuals, or small groups of related individuals, to be his friends—and this in a polity with increasingly fewer
positions of real authority which, it was argued, should be distrib-
uted with discrimination, since there were some lineages with 'more
branches and more abundant worthy men' than others, as a law of
1484 put it.[77] Agnatic kinsmen who had traditionally expected to
share honour and office within the family group now found themselves explicitly competing against each other, and wrote letters to
Lorenzo—where once they might have sought his help through a relative's mediation, or applied direct to some other magnate—asking
for Medicean grace to descend upon the writer even at the expense
of his own cousins and *consorti*.[78] Lorenzo increasingly singled out
men from their kin—the better to manage them, one may suppose—
and his favourites seem duly to have acknowledged their special status in the distinctive tombs and busts and coats-of-arms they
commissioned. Not least because of his Medicean connections, a
man such as Bongianni Gianfigliazzi enjoyed a special position in his
family, neighbourhood, and in Laurentian Florence at large, as the
Abbot of Vallombrosa acknowledged in a letter to the young
Lorenzo de' Medici of October 1467. When Lorenzo apparently complained—on Gianfigliazzi's behalf—of some offensive action by a
monk towards Gianfigliazzi, the Abbot replied that 'we could not be
more displeased had it happened to anybody else in Florence, your
own house excepted, first because of who Bongianni is, then for the
sake of neighbourhood and for what he is doing for the church, viz.
the main chapel'. In this chapel in Santa Trinita, we might add,
Lorenzo de' Medici himself, according to Vasari, was depicted
among the Gianfigliazzi.[79]

Despite the tendency of such Medicean men to exhibit a sense of
exclusiveness, they seem likely only to have formed a minority, when
one considers that in the 1480s great lineages such as the Biliotti were

---

[77] Quoted by Rubinstein, *Government*, 212. This paragraph anticipates work of
mine in progress.

[78] See F. W. Kent, *Household and Lineage*, 184, 205–6, 225–6, 295–6.

[79] ASF, Mediceo avanti il Principato, XX, 342, Franciscus [Altoviti], abbot, 4 Oct.
1467, to Lorenzo de' Medici: 'Don Sancti . . . non poteva offendere persona in Firenze,
dalla casa vostra in fuori, che più ci fusse dispiaciuto, prima per l'uomo che è
Bongianni, per la vicinanza e per quello fa nella chiesa, cioè la capella maggiore'.
Altoviti's invoking 'neighbourhood' may refer to his own family's living near to
Santa Trinita, as well as to the close proximity of the Gianfigliazzi houses to the
church.

still founding chapels of the whole *consorteria*.[80] Thus, they were hardly cracking, let alone breaking, the mould in which Giovanni X's patronage, and that of his generation, was set, whose dimensions and shape had been formed by Florentine society in the mid-quattrocento, and by Cosimo de' Medici's patronal example. They left it to their leader, Cosimo's grandson Lorenzo de' Medici, to begin to do that from the 1470s onwards: Lorenzo, with his ambitious quasi-princely urbanistic projects (set in his ancestral quarter, it must be admitted), his brand new, stylistically innovative, villa at Poggio a Caiano, on land he acquired on the Pistoian road that had no traditional Medicean association, his meta-patronage, not to say his interference in other people's building projects, his right royal collection of antique gems and *objets d'art*, his own artistic creativity, and his carefully orchestrated cult of himself as the Maecenas of a new golden age. While dynastic and aristocratic (so to speak, traditional Florentine) impulses still drove Lorenzo, yet he increasingly expressed them in new ways, and to new ends, in a society which itself was changing, not least because of the impact of his and his family's political and cultural policies. In the aftermath of 1992, the five hundredth anniversary of Lorenzo's death which has seen so much scholarly discussion of him and his place in Florentine and Italian politics and society, historians will no doubt be in a better position to talk with both precision and breadth about what late-fifteenth-century Florentine culture was like, and about how this brilliant individual and his family drew on its traditional values while contributing to their redefinition.

---

[80] ASF, Conventi Soppressi, 122, 128, fo. 71ᵛ, 11 Dec. 1483. Eleven Biliotti signed an agreement concerning a new chapel in S. Spirito to replace their old one.

8. The Humanist Villa Revisited

AMANDA LILLIE

THE accepted view of the early Renaissance villa—that is the one embraced by Georgina Masson, André Chastel, Ludwig Heydenreich and James Ackerman, and to a lesser extent by David Coffin and Cristoph Frommel—is an idealized one, 'a fantasy impervious to reality', as Ackerman has described it in his recent book on *The Villa*.[1] The fantasy has an impeccable ancient pedigree, for it can be traced back to Greece of the eighth century BC in the *Works and Days* of Hesiod, and it flourished in the Rome of Caesar and Augustus with the agricultural treatises of Varro and Columella, not to mention the pastoral verse of Horace and Vergil.

The fantasy was revived in written form again after 1300 in the letters of Petrarch describing his life at Vaucluse and Arquà, and in a more pragmatic form in the agricultural treatise of the Bolognese Pietro de' Crescenzi.[2] Eulogistic descriptions of the Florentine countryside and its villas also begin at this time with Villani's account of the *contado*,[3] and Boccaccio's setting for the *Decameron*. The pastoral ideal and ideology was not only expressed in the form of odes, epistles, treatises, and stories; for it had also been given concrete form in the great landed estates and villas of the Roman Empire,

---

[1] G. Masson, *Italian Villas and Palaces* (London, 1966), 9, 11, 176–9; A. Chastel, *Art et humanisme à Florence au temps de Laurent le Magnifique* (Paris, 1961), 148–51; L. Heydenreich, 'La villa: genesi e sviluppi fino al Palladio', *Bollettino del Centro Internazionale di Studi di Architettura 'Andrea Palladio'*, 9 (1969), 11–22; J. S. Ackerman, *The Villa: Form and Ideology of Country Houses* (London, 1990), 9–34, 63–87; D. Coffin, *The Villa in the Life of Renaissance Rome* (Princeton, 1979); C. Frommel, *Die Farnesina und Peruzzis Architektonisches Frühwerk* (Berlin, 1961), 85–119.

[2] See, for example, Petrarch's letters, *Le Familiari*, ed. V. Rossi, 4 vols. (Florence, 1933–42), Bks. VI. 3; VIII. 3; XI. 12; XII. 8; XIII. 8; XVI. 6; XVII. 5; tr. M. Bishop, with a further selection from the *Epistolae variae* and the *Epistolae rerum senilium* (Bloomington, Ill., 1966); P. de' Crescenzi, *Trattato della Agricultura*, 3 vols. (Milan, 1805).

[3] G. Villani, *Cronica*, ed. G. Aquilecchia (Turin, 1979), xi. 94; 212–13.

which were themselves celebrated in the letters of Pliny the Younger and in the murals of Pompeii and Bosco Reale, for example.

This rural vision has proved to be perennially seductive for the urban middle class and aristocracy, as it also continues to attract generations of scholars. The astonishing consistency and longevity of the idea is irresistible for Ackerman, who traces the continuous strand through history from the Villa of the Mysteries to Fallingwater.[4] In particular, the perceived unity of theory and practice has proved to be intellectually compelling, as Heydenreich found in 1969:

> Between 1450 and 1500 there emerged in Italy, outside the towns, a new type of secular architecture: the villa as country house . . . in this process of development the literary conception of the country house as retreat or *locus amoenus* is unified with the practical function of the building . . .. The confluence of the literary and architectural impulses render the villa the most characteristic example of a distinctly humanist architecture, where the aesthetic components play an equivalent role to the ethical ones.[5]

Most of the writers concerned with Renaissance villas are more interested in the sixteenth century when this confluence of literature and architecture had indeed taken place; but in their search for the first signs of this phenomenon, they seize upon the five Medici villas near Florence and pronounce the emergence of a new building type. The new type may be said to have fully emerged with Lorenzo de' Medici's villa of Poggio a Caiano, begun by 1485 (Fig. 8.1);[6] but before this, the development of a new, classicizing rural building type was slow and erratic. Above all, in investigating the emergence of the *all'antica* villa, the method of superimposing literary conceptions onto the buildings has not proved helpful for an understanding of architectural form and development, and our view of the Florentine villa in the fifteenth century has barely changed since Patzak's *Palast und Villa in Toscana* of 1908–13.[7]

---

[4] Ackerman, *The Villa*.

[5] I have translated from Heydenreich, 'La villa', 11–12.

[6] P. Foster, *A Study of Lorenzo de' Medici's Villa at Poggio a Caiano*, 2 vols. (New York, 1978); F. W. Kent, 'Lorenzo de' Medici's Acquisition of Poggio a Caiano in 1474; and an Early Reference to his Architectural Expertise', *Journal of the Warburg and Courtauld Institutes*, 42 (1979), 250–7.

[7] B. Patzak, *Die Renaissance und Barockvilla in Italien*, 3 vols. (Leipzig, 1908–13), i–ii, *Palast und Villa in Toscana*. The most helpful recent studies with further bibliography are M. Gori-Sassoli, 'Michelozzo e l'architettura di villa nel primo rinascimento', *Storia dell'Arte*, 23 (1975), 5–51; G. Gobbi, *La villa Fiorentina: Elementi storici*

FIG. 8.1 Medici villa at Poggio a Caiano, from 1485

The architectural form of the Medici villa of Careggi should be a warning to scholars who imagine that the humanist interests of those who met at the villa might be directly expressed in the architecture (FIG. 8.2). Unlike their inherited estates in the Mugello, Careggi was a new acquisition for the Medici, bought by Cosimo's father Giovanni di Bicci in 1417. The purchase document shows that it was already an impressive complex: a *palatium* with a courtyard, loggia, well, and cellars, with its own chapel, stables, dovecote, tower, and walled garden, as well as two houses for tenant farmers.[8] Patzak concluded that the main reconstruction campaign took place after Cosimo's return from exile (*c.*1435) and before 1440, since a document records that about 1,300 florins had been spent on building at Careggi up until 1440. Building and decoration were probably complete by 1459 when Galeazzo Maria Sforza visited the villa and praised its beauty in a letter to his father.[9]

e critici per una lettura (Florence, 1980); and L. Giordano, ' "Ditissima Tellus". Ville quattrocentesche tra Po e Ticino', *Bollettino della Società Pavese di Storia Patria*, 40 (1988), 145–295.

[8] M. Ferrara and F. Quinterio, *Michelozzo di Bartolomeo* (Florence, 1984), 251–2.
[9] Patzak, *Palast und Villa*, 75–7, 166 n. 89.

Fɪɢ. 8.2 Medici villa at Careggi, east façade

The most important *all'antica* features of the house are the twin loggias with composite capitals which face each other across the courtyard. However, these loggias are linked on the east side by very different, apparently outmoded, octagonal piers bearing water-leaf capitals (Fɪɢ. 8.3). The curving east wall, whose irregular shape was determined by the presence of the public road that ran past the house, almost certainly belongs to the old house bought in 1417; and the octagonal piers supporting a corridor built along the inside of that wall may survive from the old house, if they are not part of an early Medici building campaign.[10] According to Vasari, it was

[10] Saalman has argued that the deliberate juxtaposition of contrasting forms, one apparently old-fashioned or gothic, the other modern or classicizing, was a characteristic formula of Michelozzo's, in 'The Palazzo Comunale in Montepulciano: An Unknown Work by Michelozzo', *Zeitschrift für Kunstgeschichte*, 28 (1965), 9. Patzak, *Palast und Villa*, 78, believed that the octagonal piers with water-leaf capitals were part of the medieval house. The problem is not easily solved since octagonal piers with water-leaf capitals were popular for about fifty years from the 1390s until the 1440s; see A. Rensi, 'L'Ospedale di San Matteo a Firenze: Un cantiere della fine del trecento', *Rivista d'Arte*, 39 (1987), 84, 112–15. Dated examples can be found in the portico of the Hospital of San Matteo, documented as between 1391 and early 1392, ibid. 89; the Palazzo Da Uzzano, *c.*1411–21, in B. Preyer, 'The "chasa overo palagio" of Alberto di Zanobi: A Florentine Palace of about 1400 and its Later Remodelling', *Art Bulletin*,

FIG. 8.3 Medici villa at Careggi, courtyard

65 (1983), 387 n. 4; the Spedale of S. Antonio at Lastra a Signa, 1416–21, in G. Tampone (ed.), *Studi e ricerche sul nucleo antico di Lastra a Signa* (Florence, 1980), 116–32.

Michelozzo who designed the renovations at Careggi, and all subsequent scholars have attributed to him the regularization of the courtyard with two identical porticoes, and the barrel-vaulted passages giving free access between the garden and the courtyard.[11]

The pragmatic solution adopted by combining castellated and classicizing forms is sometimes contrasted with the Medici palace being built *ex novo* in the late 1440s and 1450s, just when the courtyard at Careggi may have been rebuilt. Were old-fashioned or piecemeal solutions acceptable in the country because they were less publicly visible, whereas a town palace was a better investment in status? We should remember that Careggi was already an imposing structure when the Medici bought it, and owners were loathe to demolish when they could renovate and convert older structures. After all, the Medici palace in town was built on the site of relatively insignificant buildings while the old family house (the *casa vecchia*) was left intact for the heirs of Cosimo's brother two doors up the road.[12]

The Medici palace in town was not itself a new building type. Brenda Preyer has shown how the three-storeyed rectangular block with ground-floor rustication and a central courtyard with loggias, was already established by 1421 when the Palazzo Da Uzzano was completed.[13] At the Palazzo Medici the type was regularized and refined in an *all'antica* language.[14] As the Palazzo Medici retains the essential structural features of the Florentine palace type, so, it could be argued, Careggi conforms to the characteristic fortified type of country house. Surely one of the main reasons that an *all'antica* villa type was slow to evolve, was the sheer difficulty of accommodating classical elements within the castellated framework. Urban builders

[11] G. Vasari, *Le vite de' più eccellenti pittori, scultori ed architettori*, ed. G. Milanesi (Florence, 1906, repr. 1981), ii. 442.

[12] The two largest buildings demolished to make way for the Palazzo Medici were one house profitably let for 24 florins a year and the Albergo di S. Caterina, along with nineteen or twenty smaller dwellings; see I. Hyman, *Fifteenth Century Florentine Studies: The Palazzo Medici; and a Ledger for the Church of San Lorenzo*, Ph.D. thesis (New York, 1968), 57–89. See also D. Carl, 'La Casa Vecchia dei Medici e il suo giardino', in G. Cherubini and G. Fanelli (eds.), *Il Palazzo Medici Riccardi di Firenze* (Florence, 1990), 38–43.

[13] W. Bombe, *Nachlass-Inventare des Angelo da Uzzano und des Lodovico di Gino Capponi* (Leipzig, 1928, repr. Hildesheim, 1972); Preyer, 'The "chasa overo palagio"', 387 n. 94.

[14] For a recent analysis of the design of Palazzo Medici in relation to the traditional Florentine palace type, see B. Preyer, 'L'architettura del palazzo medico' in Cherubini and Fanelli (eds.), *Il Palazzo Medici Riccardi*, 58–65.

could retain the powerful and defensive image they desired by using massive rustication and prominent cornices, which were classically reinterpreted but fundamentally a continuation of fourteenth-century developments; whereas a far more radical transformation had to take place in the country.

The other reasons for the slow adoption of classical forms in the country are well known. There was a lack of models, since so little remained of ancient villas above ground and none had been excavated.[15] Vitruvius's description of the Roman house was terse and ambiguous, and there was no illustrated edition before Fra Giocondo's of 1511.[16] Furthermore, it is likely that during the early Renaissance a pastoral landscape was more important than a specific architectural setting. A bucolic environment had been the essential feature in antiquity and it was not until the late republic and early Empire that a specific, grand architectural style became associated with the rural ideal.[17] As in antiquity, the Renaissance was also slow to express the pastoral ideal in an architectural form.

On the other hand, the positive desire to maintain an idiom that was associated with ancestral power, with the longevity of the lineage and its old rural origins, encouraged landowners to retain castellated forms. The Medici villas of Trebbio, Cafaggiolo and Careggi all belong to the type of castellated villa favoured throughout the fourteenth century and still popular for most of the fifteenth. The term 'castellated villa' may seem to be a misnomer, for castles and villas are usually seen in contradistinction as two quite separate architectural types, the medieval form preceding the Renaissance form. However, the stylistic transition was not straightforward, for castellated features not only survived, often in combination with classical features, but they were even deliberately revived in the late fifteenth and sixteenth centuries.[18] Like the chivalric values with which they were associated, towers and castellation persisted.

---

[15] J. S. Ackerman, 'Sources of the Renaissance Villa' in id., *The Villa*, 29–30, 63. The villa of Settefinestre is the only example that has come to light so far of an ancient villa, large parts of whose walls survived, and were recorded in a late 15th-c. drawing; see P. Ruschi, 'La villa romana di Settefinestre in un disegno del XV secolo', *Prospettiva*, 22 (1980), 72–5.

[16] See L. Pellecchia, 'Architects Read Vitruvius: Renaissance Interpretations of the Atrium of the Ancient House', *Journal of the Society of Architectural Historians*, 51 (1992), 377–416.

[17] Ackerman, *The Villa*, 12, 20, 39, 41, 51–7, 60–1.

[18] Important examples are the Villa Salviati, see L. Zangheri, *Ville della Provincia di Firenze. La città* (Milan, 1989), 296–8; the Medici Villa of Petraia, see ibid. 78–95,

Furthermore, it is clear from fifteenth-century documents and literature that the two architectural forms functioned in the same way.
Fortified structures were estate centres, family residences and delight-
ful rural retreats, just as unfortified houses were. In addition there
were many practical reasons for the preference for fortification. A
defensive structure could still be useful, as a deterrent, as well as in
case of attack by roving brigands, mercenary armies, or conspiring
political rivals.[19] Towers had important agricultural uses and, even
in the landowner's house, they functioned as granaries and pigeon
lofts, damp-proof and thief-proof.[20]

Careggi can also very usefully illustrate the pitfalls encountered by
architectural historians in their determination to categorize country
houses and define distinct types. Frommel suggested four categories:
the villa castle, the villa palace, the villa farm and the suburban
villa.[21] As we have seen, Careggi might be said to belong to all four
types since it is castellated, suburban, had productive farms, and was
described by contemporaries as a *palagio*. It is a misconception that
functions can necessarily be separated or restricted. The two most
famous quotations about Careggi illustrate two of its very different
functions: Vespasiano da Bisticci describes Cosimo rising on a
February morning to spend two hours pruning in his vineyard before
going in to read St Gregory's *Moralia*;[22] and Cosimo supposedly
wrote to Ficino, 'yesterday I came to the villa of Careggi, not to cultivate my fields, but my soul. Come to us, Marsilio, as soon as possible. Bring with you our Plato's *De summo bono*.'[23] In both cases

and F. Chiostri, *La Petraja, villa e giardino* (Florence, 1972); and the Ginori villa of
Baroncoli, see L. Ginori-Lisci, *Baroncoli, la dimora rurale di Carlo il Vecchio de' Ginori*
(Florence, 1950), and D. Lamberini, *Calenzano e la Val di Marina*, 2 vols. (Florence,
1987), i. 259–65.

[19] A. Lillie, 'Florentine Villas in the Fifteenth Century: A Study of the Strozzi and
Sassetti Country Properties', Ph.D. thesis (London, 1986), 172–3. On town palaces
used for defensive purposes, see F. W. Kent, 'Palaces, Politics and Society in Fifteenth-
Century Florence', *I Tatti Studies*, 2 (1987), 63–5.

[20] Lillie, 'Florentine Villas', 161–4.

[21] C. Frommel, 'La Villa Madama e la tipologia della villa romana nel rinascimento', *Bollettino del Centro Internazionale di Studi di Architettura 'Andrea Palladio'*,
9 (1969), 47. Heydenreich's categories are similar: the *villa-castello*, the *villa suburbana*, and the '*villa* in the true sense of the word', in Heydenreich, 'La villa', 12.

[22] Vespasiano da Bisticci, *Vite di uomini illustri del secolo XV*, ed. P. d'Ancona and
E. Aeschlimann (Milan, 1951), 419. The 'Morali' must refer to St Gregory's commentary on the Book of Job, the *Expositio in Librum Iob, sive Moralium Libri XXV*.

[23] Cited by Ackerman, *The Villa*, 73; tr. from M. Ficino, *Opera omnia* (Basel, 1576),
repr. ed. M. Sancipriano, 2 vols. (Turin, 1962), 608. For a recent view of this passage,
see A. Field, *The Origins of the Platonic Academy of Florence* (Princeton, 1988), 3–4.

farming and intellectual pursuits are treated as complementary and compatible activities typically associated with villa life.

After 1450 there is concrete evidence of a search for a new type of villa, and Giovanni di Cosimo's Villa Medici at Fiesole is the first example of this new form of country house, built between 1453 and 1457 (FIG. 8.4).[24] Unlike the earlier Medici villas which were all adapted from older structures, this was built *ex novo*. It had no tower or castellated features, and unlike the other villas its shape was symmetrical and compact. Although it is difficult to establish precisely the original plan (FIG. 8.5), it is likely that wide loggias facing towards gardens on the east and west were yoked by a central *sala* on the ground floor.[25] It has been remarked that this design is like a

FIG. 8.4 Medici villa at Fiesole (1453–7), from the south-east

[24] For the construction date of the villa, see Ferrara and Quinterio, *Michelozzo*, 253; A. Brown, *Bartolomeo Scala, 1430–1497* (Princeton, 1979), 17; Ackerman, *The Villa*, 289 n. 18; A. Lillie, 'Giovanni di Cosimo and the Villa Medici at Fiesole', in A. Beyer and B. Boucher (eds.), *Piero de' Medici 'il Gottoso' (1416–1469)* (Berlin, 1993), 196.

[25] Frommel, *Die Farnesina*, 87–8; C. Bargellini and P. de la Ruffinière du Prey, 'Sources for a reconstruction of the Villa Medici, Fiesole', *Burlington Magazine*, 111 (1969), 597–605; G. Galletti, 'Villa Medici a Fiesole' in G. Morolli, A. Acidini Luchinat, L. Marchetti (eds.), *L'Architettura di Lorenzo il Magnifico* (Florence, 1992), 79–81.

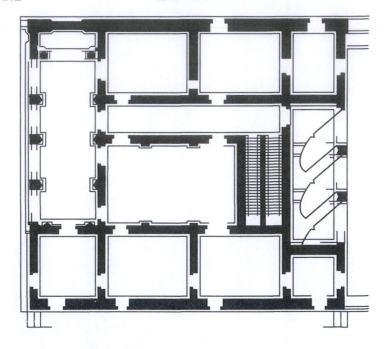

Fig. 8.5 Medici villa at Fiesole, plan

Florentine town house turned inside out. Instead of a forbidding exterior with loggias facing inwards onto a central courtyard, the void occupying the centre of the house has become an interior *sala*, and the exterior walls have been opened up by loggias.[26]

A common misconception, that the villa at Fiesole was an isolated house and garden with no working farms attached, is partly dispelled by Giovanni di Cosimo's purchase of a large farm at Fiesole in late 1457 or early 1458. Woodland was cleared to create new vineyards and Giovanni converted the holding into three small farms with new farm houses. Apart from wine, the farms produced wheat and limited quantities of beans, barley, spelt, wood, and small livestock.[27]

---

[26] Patzak, *Palast und Villa*, 92; Frommel, *Die Farnesina*, 88.

[27] ASF, Catasto 924 (1469), fo. 308ᵛ, 'Uno podere posto parte nel popolo di San Chimenti e parte nel popolo di S. Michele a Muscholi cho' loro vochaboli e chonfini, che già furono 2 poderi chon due chase che ll'una era rovinata e nell'antra [altra] abitava el lavoratore, di che per potere trovare meglio l'[h]anno fatto 3 poderetti chon

He bought another vineyard nearby, and this modest policy of expansion was continued by his brother Piero after Giovanni's death with the purchase of more vineyards and olive groves in 1465,[28] and by Lorenzo the Magnificent, who acquired four *pietra serena* quarries nearby and a barber's shop on the *piazza* at Fiesole.[29] Certainly, in comparison with the other Medici estates in the Mugello, at Careggi and elsewhere, Fiesole was never a large agricultural enterprise, and on that steep slope it can never have been intended to be. Yet the reductionist view of Fiesole as a 'pleasure house', untainted by motives such as profit and utility,[30] bears little resemblance to what we know of fifteenth-century villa ideology, where *utilitas* was so often linked to the notion of beauty, and where no landowner lost an opportunity to make a profit. From the wealth of archival sources dealing with rural property and rural pursuits, it is evident that country houses without farmland were very rare.[31] The anti-utilitarian approach also rings false in terms of humanist villa ideology itself, for *oeconomia* and *utilitas* were essential components in the ancient view of rural life and rural architecture, both being revived in Alberti's treatises *Villa, I Libri della Famiglia* and to a lesser extent in his *De re aedificatoria*.[32]

tre lavoratori; [h]anno la presta di Ł.30 e 3 paia di buoi F[iorini].75; e per adattarli a 3 possessioni v'è murato e speso di molti denari a sboschare e porre vingnia . . . Lavorali Nencino di Piero e figliuoli e 2 poderuzzi, e l'antro [l'altro] lavora Marcho e Lucha d'Andrea. Rendono l'anno in parte e chon detto podere sono 3 pezzi di terra di valuta di F.55 tra sodi e boschi; in tutto rendono in parte: grano staia 80 | fave staia 12 | orzo staia 8 | vino barili 10 | spelda staia 12 | lengnie chataste 3.

El detto podere chomperò Giovanni mio fratello dal 1457 in quà da Archancielo di Messer Bartolomeo da Monte Ghonzi, gonfalone Vaio, charta per mano di . . . [blank]. El detto podere dà detto Archangelo nel 1457 dalla sua scritta 247 . . . Fiorini 785.14.4. Tra tuti e 3 detto poderi vi si truova su 80 chapi di beschie [bestie] minute di stima e valuta di F.18 . . . F.40.'

[28] ASF, Catasto 924 (1469), I, fo. 308ᵛ.

[29] ASF, Decima repubblicana 28 (1498), fo. 455ʳ; *Libro d'inventario dei beni di Lorenzo il Magnifico*, ed. M. Spallanzani and G. Gaeta Bertelà (Florence, 1992), 179.

[30] Ackerman, *The Villa*, 78, 'Michelozzo's simple arcaded cube was the first modern villa designed without thought or possibility of material gain'.

[31] For example, in a survey of thirty-eight 15th-c. estates belonging to the Strozzi and Sassetti clans, only one land-owner's house (that belonging to the painter Zanobi Strozzi near the Badia Fiesolana) was not attached to farm-land; see Lillie, 'Florentine Villas'.

[32] The archaeological evidence for Roman Italy is summarized by Percival, 'even in the fashionable areas the most luxurious villas tended more often than not to include a section devoted to farming . . . the villa was only very exceptionally other than a business enterprise', in J. Percival, *The Roman Villa* (London, 1988), 53. Alberti's short treatise entitled *Villa*, in *Opere volgari*, ed. C. Grayson (Bari, 1960), i. 359–63,

However, authors such as Ackerman and Frommel are right to stress the novel aspects of Fiesole, for the usual motives for acquiring a villa site were lacking. There were no ancestral Medici lands here; this was no rural power base; the agricultural profits would always be modest; and there was no pre-existing villa on the site, whose reputation might have attracted Giovanni, as his nephew Lorenzo was later attracted to Palla Strozzi's site at Poggio a Caiano. It was not on a main road and access was steep and difficult for visitors. The spectacular view was this villa's *raison d'être*, and for that reason too the house was closely integrated with its surroundings. The integration of house and land is evident in the outward facing loggias, open to the gardens and the view, in the creation of terraces so that people could step out of the house into a sort of open-air drawing room (FIG. 8.6), and in the way the levels of the house and garden, supported on their retaining walls, follow the contours of the hillsides (FIG. 8.7).[33] This was a brilliant design solution that provides a fine illustration of how architecture may be inspired by and perfectly adapted to its site.

Another misconception derives from Vasari's statement that this villa contained not only 'camere, sale ed altre stanze ordinarie', but also rooms for special purposes, 'alcune per libri, e alcune altre per la musica'.[34] However, the two surviving inventories of 1482 and 1492 make it clear that living quarters were relatively restricted: only one large *sala* on the ground floor with three *camere* and an *anticamera*, and upstairs three more *camere* and one *anticamera*, apart from the kitchen and two servants' rooms. There is no mention of music rooms, nor are any instruments listed in either inventory.[35] As for books, just one *scrittoio* is mentioned in the 1482 inventory,

456–8, influenced by the writings of Hesiod and Cato, is entirely concerned with farming, and with the honest labour associated with country life. In this context leisure is suspect: 'E dicono che la fame e il bisogno abita vicino all'ozio'. In *I Libri della famiglia* (*Opere volgari*, i. 1–341), the third book entitled 'Economicus', includes a discussion of rural life (188–209) recommending thrift and self-sufficiency in order to achieve maximum productivity and a healthy, tranquil, cheerful life.

[33] Frommel, *Die Farnesina*, 88; Ackerman, *The Villa*, 73–7, notes that 'this may have been the first formal garden in the Renaissance to be conceived as an extension of the architecture', although he adds that it was designed 'to stand off from rather than to merge into its natural environment'; Galletti, 'Villa Medici', 80, suggests that the terraced site may have been inspired by the hanging gardens of Babylon.

[34] Vasari, *Le vite*, ii. 442–3.

[35] ASF, MAP, CIV, 4: 'Inventario della chasa di Fiesole fatto questo di 15 di dicenbre 1482'; *Libro d'inventario dei beni di Lorenzo il Magnifico*, 168–78.

FIG. 8.6 Medici villa at Fiesole, east loggia and upper terrace

attached, together with a lavatory, to what had been Giovanni de' Medici's own *camera*.[36] The sense of a commodious and grand establishment conveyed by Vasari's text is therefore largely dispelled by the inventories. On the other hand, Vasari's reference to a large number of storage and service rooms conveniently built into the sub-structure of the house is upheld, for the area devoted to services and agriculture was almost as great as that of the residential apart-ments.[37] Ironically, for those who wish to make a strict division between humanist villas and farm houses, it was the menial and

[36] ASF, MAP, CIV, 4; although no books were listed in the 1482 inventory, paint-ings were included and the *scrittoio* contained 'una tavoletta di San Girolamo' and 'una Vergine Maria in chamera'.

[37] Vasari, *Le vite*, ii. 442–3, emphasizes the successful combination of splendour and utility at Fiesole, when he describes Fiesole as 'un altro magnifico ed onorato palazzo, fondato dalla parte di sotto nella scoscesa del poggio con grandissima spesa, ma non senza grande utile: avendo in quella parte da basso fatto volte, cantine, stalle, tinaie ed altre belle e comode abitazioni.' The 1492 inventory, *Libro d'inventario dei beni di Lorenzo il Magnifico*, 168–70, lists the following rooms in the lower levels: 'salotto a uso di vendemia . . . camera che è in sul salotto detto, chiamata la camera della citerna . . . l'altra camera detta la camera de' famigli in su detto salotto . . . l'agiamento e andito di detta camera . . . chamera detta la camera da colare . . . cella overo volta di sopra a detto salotto . . . l'altra volta allato a questa, detta quella della state . . . stanza dell'olio a rinchontro di detta.'

FIG. 8.7 Medici villa at Fiesole, south façade and lower terrace

agricultural functions of the household, rather than intellectual pursuits, that were incorporated into the design and specially catered for in an ingenious and modern way.

A study of other villas that date from the elusive thirty years between the construction of the Villa Medici at Fiesole in the 1450s and Poggio a Caiano in the 1480s suggests that this was a period of experiment before the emergence of a new building type that conformed to the *all'antica* style. Significantly, the example of Fiesole with its compact, symmetrical plan and its hospitable loggias, was not immediately taken up, perhaps because of the novelty of its design and its difficult site. On the other hand an example from the 1460s illustrates a very different solution to the problem.

Francesco Sassetti's villa at La Pietra is a town palace transposed into the countryside (FIG. 8.8). Unlike many villas, it is three-storeyed, and its massive, regular block with a central courtyard, three grand *sale*, and seven complete residential apartments, is only slightly smaller than the Palazzo Medici in town. The sequence of spaces on entering the house at La Pietra is a common feature in urban domestic architecture, leading on a central axis through a

FIG. 8.8 Sassetti villa at La Pietra (*c.*1462–*c.*1470), south façade

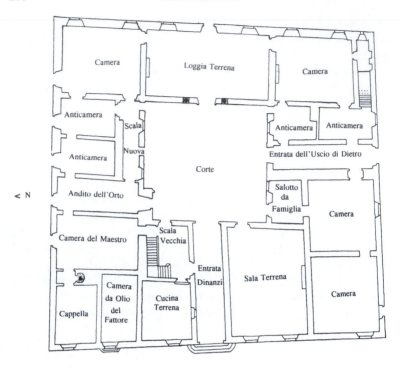

Fig. 8.9 Sassetti villa at La Pietra, reconstructed ground-plan

vaulted hallway into a courtyard with a loggia at the far end. Its plan takes that of the Palazzo Medici as a starting point (Fig. 8.9), but the three hallways [*androni*] (Fig. 8.10) and the loggia converging in the central courtyard divide the ground floor into four distinct apartments, achieving a more systematic and coherent organization of interior space than the Palazzo Medici. The cohesion of the Sassetti villa design was also due to the adoption of a single plan consistently employed for all three storeys of the house, a principle that had been adopted for Pius II's palace at Pienza, another building that exploited the advantages of the urban palace type in a semi-rural setting.[38]

There were obvious practical reasons for Sassetti's choice of this sort of house. The site was suburban, exactly one mile from the city walls. And it satisfied Sassetti's need for a big family palace that

[38] Lillie, 'Florentine Villas', 406–8.

FIG. 8.10 Sassetti villa at La Pietra, hallway

could be built immediately after his return from Geneva, instead of laboriously having to acquire a large site in town. The house was certainly under construction in 1462 and was inhabited by the early 1470s.[39]

Furthermore, there may have been a literary or intellectual motive, for Vitruvius recommends that villa builders dissatisfied with modest farm-houses should follow his design for town houses:

Si quid delicatius in villis faciundum fuerit, ex symmetriis quae in urbanis supra scripta sunt constituta, ita struantur, uti sine inpeditione rusticae utilitatis aedificentur.

If a touch of elegance is required in a farm-house, it should be built in a symmetrical manner, which things are described above for town-houses, yet without interfering with the needs of agriculture.[40]

Sassetti owned a manuscript of Vitruvius,[41] and it is likely that the Vitruvian solution for a grander villa was deliberately adopted here. In a similar vein Alberti in his *De re aedificatoria* praises suburban villas that combine the dignity of the town house with the delights and pleasures of the country house.[42]

This, therefore, is a building that fulfils a number of criteria for a humanist villa. Its owner collected Latin manuscripts, employing the humanist scholar Bartolomeo Fonzio as his librarian,[43] as he later consulted Fonzio over the iconography and classical inscriptions for his burial chapel in Santa Trinita.[44] The villa itself was praised in letters and poems by three humanists: Ficino, Fonzio and Ugolino Verino.[45] Its design apparently derives from a specific antique

---

[39] Lillie, 'Florentine Villas', 373–4.

[40] Vitruvius, *De Architectura*, 2 vols. (Cambridge, Mass., 1970), tr. F. Granger, vol. ii, bk. VI, cap. vi, 42–3. I am grateful to Charles Robertson who drew my attention to this passage.

[41] Biblioteca Laurenziana, 30, 10; A. de la Mare, 'The Library of Francesco Sassetti (1421–90)', in C. H. Clough (ed.), *Cultural Aspects of the Italian Renaissance: Essays in Honour of Paul Oskar Kristeller* (Manchester, 1976), 163, 178; C. H. Krinsky, '78 Vitruvius Manuscripts', *Journal of the Warburg and Courtauld Institutes*, 30 (1967), 37. Sassetti's Vitruvius is an early 15th-c. French manuscript bound in one volume with Cato's *De Agri Cultura* and Varro's *Rerum rusticarum libri III*.

[42] L. B. Alberti, *L'Architettura* [*De re aedificatoria*], ed. G. Orlandi and P. Portoghesi, 2 vols. (Milan, 1966), vol. ii, bk. IX, ch. ii, 790–1.

[43] De la Mare, 'The Library of Francesco Sassetti', 165.

[44] F. Saxl, 'The Classical Inscription in Renaissance Art and Politics', *Journal of the Warburg and Courtauld Institutes*, 4 (1941), 26.

[45] A. Lillie, 'Francesco Sassetti and his Villa at La Pietra', in E. Chaney and N. Ritchie (eds.), *Oxford, China and Italy: Writings in Honour of Sir Harold Acton on his Eightieth Birthday* (London, 1984), 83–93.

FIG. 8.11 Sassetti villa at La Pietra, detail of *sgraffito* decoration in the courtyard

literary source—Vitruvius; and it contains many classicizing elements from the palmettes (FIG. 8.11) and the *putti* carrying festoons
incised on the courtyard façade to its miniature domed oratory. Yet
these generically *all'antica* features are motifs taken, not directly
from antique sources, but from the most accessible up-to-date
source, that is, from buildings recently constructed in town.[46] What
then does the term 'humanist villa' tell us about the appearance of a
building which fits better into an architectural history of the urban
palace than it does into an architectural history of the villa?

There are four possible definitions of the term 'humanist villa'.

1. It may refer to a house belonging to a humanist scholar, in
which case the term describes the inhabitant rather than the appearance of the building. In practice, humanist scholars were more likely
to celebrate the buildings of wealthy patrons or build grand schemes

[46] Lillie, 'Florentine Villas', 406–25.

in their imaginations than on the ground.[47] (Examples are Ficino's farm at Careggi; Poggio Bracciolini's villa at Terranuova; Michele Verino's villa at Lecore; Giannozzo Manetti's villa of Vacciano; Vespasiano da Bisticci's villa 'il Monte' at Antella.)

2. The term may refer to the site of humanist discourse, a place where humanists met to discuss ideas and texts. In this case the term describes the function of the building. (Examples are the Medici villa of Careggi, the Paradiso degli Alberti at Pian di Ripoli, the Pandolfini villa at Signa, the Acciaiuoli villa at Montegufoni.)

3. The term may refer to the subject of humanist discourse, a place that humanists wrote about in classicizing terms, often evoking ancient descriptions of villa life. In this case the term describes the building's literary role and how it was perceived. (Examples are the Sassetti villa at La Pietra, the Medici villas of Careggi, Fiesole, Poggio a Caiano.)

4. The term may refer to a house whose architectural form was guided by notions of what ancient villas looked like; or which was designed to be a tangible expression of the humanist pursuits of the inhabitants. In this case the term describes the appearance of the building. (Examples are the Villa Medici at Fiesole, the Medici villa of Poggio a Caiano.)

These definitions frequently overlap and any or all of them may apply to one building. For example, the Villa Medici at Fiesole can justifiably be described as a humanist villa in every sense.

The fundamental question is whether a building type can be defined by function alone, or whether that particular function must be associated with particular architectural forms in order to become a type. In the case of the humanist villa, there is a discrepancy between function and form in the early history of the type. The Villa Medici at Fiesole is the one important exception, but apart from this, as a term describing architectural form, it should be used with great caution before the late fifteenth century and the construction of Poggio a Caiano.

Although very few villas associated with Florentine humanism

---

[47] Bartolomeo Scala is a prime example of a scholar who found the funds to build a *villa suburbana* in the ancient manner, see A. Brown, *Bartolomeo Scala*, and L. Pellecchia, 'The Patron's Role in the Production of Architecture: Bartolomeo Scala and the Scala Palace', *Renaissance Quarterly*, 42 (1989), 258–91. For the financial status of Florentine humanists see L. Martines, *The Social World of the Florentine Humanists 1390–1460* (London, 1963), ch. 3 and apps. I–II.

have been studied, the concrete evidence available supports this view. It is striking how dissimilar the houses are, and how pragmatic their owners. For example, the loggia of the Pandolfini villa at Ponte a Signa retained its water-leaf capitals;[48] whereas Giovanni Rucellai's Villa Lo Specchio at Quaracchi (FIG. 8.12), and the Tornabuoni villa at Chiasso Macerelli,[49] both shared clannish capitals with shields that were probably once painted with the family coats of arms, rather than employing any semblance of a classical order. Thus, even wealthy bankers and merchants involved in the new intellectual movement chose other options when it came to expressing their cultural affiliations. A topiary hedge in the form of Cicero at Quaracchi,[50] frescos depicting the Liberal Arts and Venus with the three Graces at Chiasso Macerelli,[51] were effective embellishments that did not require demolition, nor the inconvenience and expense of construction. Likewise, in a clan like the Strozzi, those most closely concerned with humanism—Palla di Nofri Strozzi (patron of Chrysoloras), Matteo di Simone Strozzi, and Piero di Benedetto Strozzi (humanist scribe and rector at the Pieve di Ripoli)—did not, as far as we know from the surviving buildings, employ classicizing architectural forms in their country houses.[52] Ultimately financial restraints and practical considerations presided.

There is an important distinction to be made between the physical construction of *all'antica* architecture and a pervasive ideology or literary framework that describes buildings in an *all'antica* language and superimposes an ideal ancient model on an imperfect, tangible present. The problem stems from a simplified view of ancient and Renaissance pastoral literature that accepts the notion of *otium* at face value, and then proceeds to apply it literally to the most functional of art forms. Rather than assuming that literary texts can

---

[48] Tampone, *Lastra a Signa*, 91–115. Known as the Villa del Ponte a Signa or the Casa di Gangalandi, this is the house to which Agnolo Pandolfini retired from political life, living 'like another Lucullus'; see Bisticci, *Vite*, 470–1.

[49] Zangheri, *Ville della Provincia di Firenze*, 24–31.

[50] A. Perosa (ed.), *Giovanni Rucellai ed il suo Zibaldone*. Part I, *Il Zibaldone quaresimale* (London, 1960), 22; F. W. Kent, 'The Making of a Renaissance Patron of the Arts', in A. Perosa (ed.), *Giovanni Rucellai ed il suo Zibaldone*. Part II, *A Florentine Patrician and his Palace* (London, 1981), 81.

[51] R. Lightbown, *Sandro Botticelli*, 2 vols. (Berkeley, Calif., 1978), i. 94–7; ii. 60–3.

[52] Lillie, 'Florentine Villas', 60, 64–5, 110, 293, 488–91, 492–3; Piero Strozzi was, in any case, too poor, A. de la Mare, 'Messer Piero Strozzi, a Florentine Priest and Scribe', in A. S. Osley (ed.), *Calligraphy and Paleography: Essays presented to Alfred Fairbank on his 70th Birthday* (London, 1965), 55–68.

FIG. 8.12 Giovanni Rucellai's Villa Lo Specchio at Quaracchi, courtyard

explain buildings, it may be more helpful to turn the argument around and discover whether buildings and their physical environment can shed light on the construction of Renaissance literary models. After all, buildings are the most substantial form of concrete evidence available and they have too rarely been brought into play when considering the nature of invention and imitation in the literary construction of Renaissance pastoral.

9. Burckhardt Revisited from Social History

SAMUEL K. COHN

SINCE publication of Jacob Burckhardt's *Civilization of the Renaissance*, social historians have extended the boundaries of his 'civilization' to encompass social groups and interests that at best he subsumed with vague phrases such as 'the faith of the people'.[1] New avenues of research, perhaps most importantly the history of the family, have recently used but have qualified Burckhardt's Renaissance, some fitting new findings into the old paradigm,[2] others rejecting it altogether.[3] The social historian might, however, go beyond a simple affirmation or negation of Burckhardt (which a psychohistorian would argue is the same thing[4]) to penetrate the categories of his generalizations, showing inconsistencies in the match between, say, individualism and modernity.

Take the development of agriculture. First, a marked transformation in the countryside did correspond *grosso modo* with the Renaissance of the late trecento and early quattrocento at least in the

---

[1] J. Burckhardt, *The Civilization of the Renaissance in Italy*, tr. S. G. C. Middlemore (London, 1878; first pub. 1860).

[2] See for instance Richard Goldthwaite, *Private Wealth in Renaissance Florence: A Study of Four Families* (Princeton, 1968); id., 'The Florentine Palace as Domestic Architecture', *American Historical Review*, 77 (1972), 977–1012; id., *The Building of Renaissance Florence: An Economic and Social History* (Baltimore, 1980); id., 'The Medici Bank and the World of Capitalism', *Past & Present*, 114 (1987), 3–31; id., 'The Empire of Things: Consumer Demand in Renaissance Italy', in F. W. Kent and Patricia Simons (eds.), *Patronage, Art and Society in Renaissance Italy* (Oxford, 1987), 153–75.

[3] F. W. Kent, *Household and Lineage in Renaissance Florence: The Family Life of the Capponi, Ginori and Rucellai* (Princeton, 1977); and implicitly in David Herlihy, 'Family Solidarity in Medieval Italian History', in D. Herlihy, Robert Lopez, and Vsevolod Slessarev (eds.), *Economy, Society and Government in Medieval Italy* (Kent, Oh., 1969), 173–84; and D. Herlihy and Christiane Klapisch-Zuber, *Les Toscans et leurs familles: Une étude du catasto florentin de 1427* (Paris, 1978), 525–51.

[4] See e.g. Rudolph Binion, *Soundings: Psychohistorical and Psycholiterary* (New York, 1982).

contado of Florence[5] (for Siena, it happened earlier[6]). It was a transformation that we might argue in Whig fashion pointed in the direction of modernity—increased urban investment, increased productivity, and an intensification of market relations. From the perspective of the peasant producer, however, an organization of production spread that ran directly counter to Burckhardt's other pillar of Renaissance 'civilization'—individualism. In the place of small individual proprietors, the *mezzadria* system or sharecropping developed. Through extended family structures, the new dependent rural labourers, the *mezzadri*, while shielded from the vagaries of bad harvests, market fluctuations, and taxation, lost their earlier independence as individual peasant proprietors and, in terms of Florentine fiscality, had even lost their adulthood, becoming the tax-exempt children of absentee urban landlords.[7]

Similarly, I have argued in *The Labouring Classes in Renaissance Florence* that the development of a more centralized and sovereign state in quattrocento Florence created new social networks for artisans and *sottoposti* in the wool industry that pointed in the very opposite direction from Burckhardt's individualism. In contrast to the social interactions of the late fourteenth century from which city-wide forces of insurrection could arise, the communities of labourers and artisans of fifteenth-century Florence turned inward around their neighbourhood parishes; relations of propinquity and kinship as opposed to free-ranging individual choice or political ideology dominated their social interactions.[8]

Burckhardt's élitist notion of civilization may now appear naïve to many social historians, and the inconsistencies between state development, individualism, and modernity may seem all too easy to pry apart. I would argue, however, that in one sense his approach to the

---

[5] D. Herlihy, *Medieval and Renaissance Pistoia: The Social History of an Italian Town, 1200–1430* (New Haven, Conn., 1967), 121–47; id., 'Santa Maria Impruneta: A Rural Commune in the Late Middle Ages', in N. Rubinstein (ed.), *Florentine Studies* (London, 1968), 242–76; Herlihy and Klapisch-Zuber, *Les Toscans*, 268–86.

[6] Philip Jones, 'From Manor to Mezzadria', in *Florentine Studies*, 193–241; I. Imberciadori, *Mezzadria classica toscana con documentazione inedita del sec. 9 al sec. 14* (Florence, 1951); Giuliano Pinto, *La Toscana nel tardo medio evo: Ambiente, economia rurale, società* (Florence, 1982); G. Pinto and Paolo Pirillo (eds.), *Il contratto di mezzadria nella Toscana medievale*, 2 vols. (Florence, 1987); Stephan Epstein, *Alle origini della fattoria toscana: L'ospedale della Scala di Siena e le sue terre (metà '200–metà '400)* (Florence, 1986).

[7] Herlihy and Klapisch-Zuber, *Les Toscans*, 277–8.

[8] S. K. Cohn, *The Laboring Classes in Renaissance Florence* (New York, 1980).

Renaissance remains more sophisticated than the one taken currently by most social, economic, and political historians of the Renaissance. Instead of concentrating on a single city or city-state, his investigations ranged up and down the Italian peninsula and on occasion was truly comparative, such as his first chapter on the state, where the culture of republics were compared to that of the Signorie.

This essay will extend its boundaries beyond the now conventional context of a single city-state and will employ a comparative framework, but will not sing Burckhardtian praises. Instead, I seek to expose a fundamental contradiction not only within Burckhardt's classical definition but also in what has continued as one canonical view underlying art and the literary, intellectual, political, and even economic history of the Renaissance.[9] This contradiction does not lie just between one development, such as the growth of the state, and another, such as individualism, but lies at the very heart of that notion so central to Renaissance historiography: individualism. My study of just under 3,400 last wills and testaments comprising over 40,000 separate, itemized bequests from six cities in central Italy—Florence, Siena, Pisa, Arezzo, Perugia and Assisi—outlines an argument about fame and glory in the Renaissance, not along the usual lines taken from humanist propagandists and the lives of their patrician or princely patrons, but for populations that included urban workers and reached into villages well off the beaten track.[10] In each of these cities testaments can be found for peasants, artisans, and even disenfranchised labourers in the wood industry. Their final

---

[9] See for instance Erwin Panofsky, *Tomb Sculpture: Four Lectures on Its Changing Aspects from Ancient Egypt to Bernini*, ed. H. W. Janson (New York, 1964), 67–96; Peter Burke, *Culture and Society in Renaissance Italy, 1420–1540* (New York, 1972), 29, 251, 288; Ingo Herkoltz, '*Sepulcro' e 'Monumenta*' del Medioevo (Rome, 1985); P. O. Kristeller, 'The Immortality of the Soul', in Michael Mooney (ed.), *Renaissance Thought and Its Sources* (New York, 1979), 181–96; Stephen J. Greenblatt, *Renaissance Self-Fashioning from More to Shakespeare* (Chicago, 1980), 1–9; H. Baron, 'Franciscan Poverty and Civic Wealth in Humanist Thought', *Speculum*, 13 (1938), 1–37; Marvin Becker, 'Individualism in the Early Italian Renaissance: Burden and Blessing', *Studies in the Renaissance*, 19 (1972), 273–97; id., 'Aspects of Lay Piety in Early Renaissance Florence', in Heiko Oberman and Charles Trinkhaus (eds.), *The Pursuit of Holiness in Late Medieval and Renaissance Religion: Papers from the University of Michigan Conference* (Leiden, 1974), 177–200; and the work of Richard Goldthwaite (see n. 2).

[10] *The Cult of Remembrance and the Black Death: Six Renaissance Cities in Central Italy* (Baltimore, 1992).

choices over the distribution of property give testimony to sentiments central to Burckhardt's Renaissance.

From the supposed capital of Renaissance culture, Florence, to the market town, Assisi, which St Francis had catapulted into the history of world religions, the second strike of pestilence, in 1363, and the years immediately following in each of these city-states marked a critical turning-point in the history of mentalities. From fragmenting their charitable bequests into small sums sprinkled over a wide range of causes, testators began to stockpile their pious gifts, focusing on less than a handful of charities and demanding later dividends that would deliver spiritual returns as well as concrete remembrance in the terrestrial sphere. As with Petrarch's experience of 1348 and his reliving of that trauma when it returned to Milan in 1361, the attitudes towards that 'scourge against mankind' changed radically with its recurrence, for patricians as well as peasants, throughout the regions of central Italy investigated by this book. More than in 'the revival of antiquity' or the acting out of antique models of behaviour,[11] the cause of the new sensibilities toward the self and 'earthly glory' can be located in matters closer to hand and more accessible to wide swaths of the population—the immediate psychological effects of the late trecento and the double experience of plague.

This history of mentality, however, can be stripped of a Whiggish teleology always pointing to the so-called modern man. Individual fame, the cult of remembrance, and earthly glory, instead of being synonymous with 'individualism', can be shown to have been deeply embedded in the development of an ideology and social structure that was antithetical to Burckhardt's 'civilization'—a throw-back to what for him, as well as for prominent social and economic historians after him,[12] was akin to the Middle Ages and feudalism.[13] Rather than concentrating on these developments over time, in this essay I wish to focus on differences over geography. While the general transition in piety marked the histories of each of these city-states,

---

[11] Federico Chabod, 'The Concept of the Renaissance', *Machiavelli and the Renaissance* (New York, 1958), 149–200.

[12] See for instance Alfred von Martin, *Sociology of the Renaissance* (New York, 1944; German edn., Stuttgart, 1932): and more recently the work thus far cited of Richard Goldthwaite (see n. 2).

[13] For a similar critique of the literature, see my *Death and Property in Siena, 1205–1808* (Baltimore, 1988), 97–158; and Diane Hughes, 'Representing the Family: Portraits and Purposes in Early Modern Italy', *Journal of Interdisciplinary History*, 17 (1986), 7–38.

despite the wide differences in population, wealth, economy, law, government, and political culture, the testamentary practices found in them, these city-states were certainly not mirror images of one another, especially in the period of the most dramatic spread of the mendicant movement's preaching, and culture, in the years from the 1270s to 1363.

Since Hans Baron's monumental work[14] (and for art history as far back as Vasari's *Lives*[15]), Florence has been seen as the centre-piece of a new Renaissance mentality, which from Florence—and because of Florence—emanated throughout large parts of the Italian penin-sula.[16] More recently, historians armed with anthropological studies have railed against this 'Florentine exceptionalism' and have empha-sized the city's almost timeless and spaceless 'mediterranean' char-acteristics.[17] My study of thousands of individual choices over property (both pious and non-pious) suggests that neither model is suitable. Instead of Florentine 'exceptionalism' or a Mediterranean-world culture, the six cities divide sharply into two groups.

[14] H. Baron, *The Crisis of the Early Italian Renaissance: Civic Humanism and Republican Liberty in an Age of Classicism and Tyranny*, 2 vols. (Princeton, 1955); other works roughly contemporaneous with Baron's heralded a similar interpretation, see e.g. E. Garin, *L'Umanesimo italiano* (Bari, 1952), tr. *Italian Humanism* (New York, 1965); id. (ed.), *Portraits from the Quattrocento*, tr. Victor and Elizabeth Velen (New York, 1972); Myron Gilmore, *The World of Italian Humanism, 1453–1517* (New York, 1952).

[15] G. Vasari, *Le vite de' più eccellenti pittori, scultori e architettori: nelle redazioni del 1550 e 1568*, edited by Rosanna Bettarini and Paola Barocchi (Florence, 1966–   ).

[16] One can certainly cite earlier examples in which Florence featured prominently as the highest expression or spearhead of a new Renaissance culture: Heinrich Leo, *Entwicklung der Verfassung der lombardischen Städte bis zu der ankunft Kaiser Friedrich I* (Hamburg, 1824); or even, 'Leonardo Bruni, *Oratio de Laudibus Florentinae Urbis*', in H. Baron (ed.), *From Petrarch to Leonardo Bruni: Studies in Humanistic and Political Literature* (Chicago, 1968), 219–63.

[17] See for instance Julius Kirshner, *Pursuing Honor while Avoiding Sin: The Monte delle doti of Florence* in *Quaderni di 'Studi Senesi'*, no. 71 (Milan, 1978); Richard Trexler, *Public Life in Renaissance Florence* (New York, 1980); Thomas Kuehn, ' "Cum Consensu mundualdi": Legal Guardianship of Women in Quattrocento Florence', *Viator*, 13 (1982), 309–33; Anthony Molho, 'Visions of the Florentine Family in the Renaissance', *Journal of Modern History*, 50/2 (1978), 304–11; Elaine G. Rosenthal, 'The Position of Women in Renaissance Florence: Neither Autonomy nor Subjection', in Peter Denley and Caroline Elam (eds.), *Florence and Italy: Renaissance Studies in Honour of Nicolai Rubinstein* (London, 1988), 369–81; Ronald Weissman, *Ritual Brotherhood in Renaissance Florence*; and more emphatically, id., 'Taking Patronage Seriously: Mediterranean Values and Renaissance Society', in *Patronage, Art and Society in Renaissance Italy*, 25–45; P. Gavitt, *Charity and Children in Renaissance Florence* (Ann Arbor, 1990), 79, 84, 279; and most objectionably, Peter Burke, *Historical Anthropology of Early Modern Italy* (Cambridge, 1987).

By the 1270s, testators in all these places began to fragment their patrimonies, and especially their pious offerings, into numerous but tiny monetary sums. In planning for the afterlife, they practised what itinerant preachers of the mendicant orders preached. Despite lives of commercial success, accumulation and usury, hard-headed artisans, shopkeepers, and merchants, when making their final arrangements for their estates and souls, strove to avoid earthly hubris and 'vain' attempts to ensure earthly memory. The grip of this mendicant mentality, however, did not hold with equal tenacity from place to place. While in three of the cities (Assisi, Pisa, and Siena) the mechanisms for ensuring earthly remembrance after death hardly surface in the testaments until the recurrence of plague in 1363, in the other three (Arezzo, Florence, and Perugia) the ideals of earthly fame never vanished and became more pronounced through the trecento.[18]

Not only can these differences between the two groups of cities be measured by the extent to which testators fragmented and monetized their bequests; these ideals resonate through their differences in burial practices, fideicommission clauses and other restrictions on the future flow of property, as well as in testamentary commissions for art, from monumental burial chapels to ten-lire altarpieces.

Charitable legacies abound early on in the testaments from Arezzo, Florence, and Perugia, that called for earthly forms of fame and remembrance. Thus an Aretine notary[19] and son of a notary, whose will dates from 1338, concentrated his last thoughts on the preservation of prized possessions and the connections between worldly things and earthly posterity. Unlike the long itemized lists of pious bequests of paltry sums to a myriad of ecclesiastical institutions with few strings attached, characteristic of wills in Assisi, Siena, and Pisa, the biggest portion of this testament turned on only two bequests: one set aside property to finance the construction of his burial chapel and the future flow of its *ius patronatus*; the other carefully divided his private library of 156 titles bound in sixty-six volumes between the Dominican and Franciscan houses of Arezzo. He then specified in systematic detail the friars' library privileges and

[18] Cohn, *The Cult of Remembrance*, ch. 3.

[19] Although this testator is not identified in his testament as a notary and in fact carries the title of 'Dominus', Ubaldo Pasqui, 'La biblioteca di Ser Simone figlio di ser Benvenuto di Bonaventura della Tenca', *Archivio storico italiano*, 5/4 (1889), 250–5, claims that 'Ser' Simone was born around 1280, was a notary and either a judge or a lawyer and taught at the university (Studio aretino) as a Maestro.

the rules for preserving his collection *ad infinitum*—down to the locks and cages to secure these properties' physical preservation.[20] This gift, reminiscent of Petrarch's concern with Boccaccio dispersing his library,[21] cannot find a parallel in a large sample of Sienese testaments until 1512.[22]

Letters and libraries did not, however, constitute the main avenue through which these testators sought to leave earthly imprints of their names and reputations. Aretines, Perugians, and Florentines, in marked contrast to those from the other three cities, patronized works of art from their earliest surviving testaments. While only one in a hundred from Siena before 1426 left instructions to build chapels or monumental graves, nearly one in ten from Arezzo left substantial properties for the purposes of memorializing their bones and those of their future progeny.[23] In Siena, not until the latter half of the fifteenth century did testators attempt to regulate through their wills the succession of chaplains elected to skim off the *usufructus* of their landed properties, to sponsor the singing of perpetual masses in commemoration of their own and their predecessors' souls.[24] In contrast, those from the second set of towns, like the Aretine notary, early on assumed the *ius patronatus* as a familial good and passed it down through the male line. Nor did this attention to leaving lasting memorials to accompany one's bones fall simply within the purview of the well-to-do. Those who could not afford chapels in Arezzo, Perugia, and Florence often individuated their earthly remains with commissions for sculpted arms, tombstones, or paintings to be placed over their graves.[25] Requests for such markers are

---

[20] *Archivio di Stato*, Florence (hereafter, *ASF*), *Diplomatico* (hereafter, *Dipl.*), Domenicani di Arezzo, 1338.viii.12. According to Ubaldi, 'La biblioteca', 251, Simoneus's desires for the perpetual preservation of his library were thwarted, his library dispersed in the campaigns of 1381 and 1384, when marauding bands of French and Italian soldiers 'barbarously' sacked churches, monasteries and private residences, 'robbing books and furnishings of every sort'. Helen Wieruszowski, 'Arezzo as a center of Learning and Letters in the Thirteenth Century', *Traditio*, 9 (1953), 321–91, esp. 382–3; and in *Atti e Memorie della Academia Petrarca di Lettere, Arti e Scienze*, NS, 34 (1968–9), 2–82, has pointed to this library as 'another important contribution to the new (humanist) movement in Arezzo', but neither she nor anyone else has commented on the testator's passion, and the measures he demanded, to preserve his library after his death, or on other aspects of the testator's zeal for earthly immortality.

[21] Petrarch, *Lettere senili*, ed. Giuseppe Fracassetti (Florence, 1869), I, 5, 40–8.

[22] Cohn, *Death and Property in Siena*, 90–1.

[23] Cohn, *The Cult of Remembrance*, ch. 4.

[24] Cohn, *Death and Property*, 102–13.

[25] Cohn, *The Cult of Remembrance*, ch. 6.

extraordinarily rare in Assisi and Pisa until the quattrocento and do
not appear in Sienese testaments until the end of that century.[26]

Testamentary patronage of other less costly works of art also present sharp differences between the two groups of cities. In a sample
of 446 testaments leaving 3,088 pious bequests before 1426, the
Sienese commissioned only six paintings. In Arezzo, by contrast, the
desire to leave such a concrete mark for one's earthly fame in sacred
places peppered the early trecento documents and increased in frequency after the recurrence of plague. These commissions, moreover,
descended the social ladder to the ranks of peasants and wage-
workers.[27]

On occasion, they evoked explicitly the desire for individual
immortalization through their execution and maintenance. In the
year of the Black Death, for instance, the son of a blacksmith living
in the Casentine town of Bibbiena, located in the bishopric of
Arezzo,[28] devoted a large section of his modest will to commissioning a painting, from which he desired remembrance. First, he
demanded that the painter place above the sacred figures the inscription: 'this painting has been ordered by Pasquino the son of
Montagne, the donor.' Then, next to the figure of Mary the artist
was to paint 'a figure in the likeness of this person Pasquino' and on
the other side, his deceased father genuflecting. Above each of them
a second inscription was to make it clear: 'Here is Montagne, the
Blacksmith; here is Pasquino [the son].'[29]

In the same year a *condottiere* employed by Florence but living in
Arezzo left all of his armour to the Aretine Misericordia—all, that
is, except his helmet, which he insisted be kept everlastingly above
his tomb to be constructed in the Aretine church of the Servites. In
his second charitable bequest, the soldier's ardour for earthly memory outstripped the self-indulgence of the blacksmith's son. In commissioning an altarpiece for the village parish of his birthplace, the

---

[26] Cohn, *Death and Property*, 61.   [27] Cohn, *The Cult of Remembrance*, ch. 7.

[28] In the Valdarno casentinese, 32 km north of the city; see Emanuele Repetti,
Dizionario storico della Toscana (Florence, 1833), i. 310–13.

[29] ASF, Dipl., Olivetani di Arezzo, 1348: 'conventus s. Bernardi de Aretii pingi
faciant fratres predicti conventus figuram s. Mariae Virginis cum filio in bracchiis in
eorum maiore ecclesie et ab uno latere figuram s. Iohannis Evangeliste, et ab alio latere figuram s. Marie Magdalene, figuram s. Antoni cum litteris . . . si cum hac ipsius
fieri fecit Pasquinus f[ilius] q[uondam] Montagne eius donator. Et ab una figura
Virginis Marie pingatur unam ymaginem persone ipsius Pasquini et ab alia parte
ymaginem Montagne olim patris sui genibusflexis et dicatur a capite cuius eorum "hic
est Montagne Mareschalchus, hic est Pasquinus Montagne".'

soldier did not even bother with religious figures, but instead demanded that his own figure alone appear above the altar: thus casting himself as the saintly one for future parishioners to venerate. In addition to this earthly hubris over sacred matters, the image cut by the laconic terms of this testament portrays a man straight from the pages of Burckhardt's *Civilization*. He left behind a progeny of five illegitimate children to whom he bequeathed unequal sums of money.[30] Still others left small sums for church repairs but demanded that their munificence be remembered by ordering their names to be inscribed in the beams of their parish churches.[31]

Explicit proclamations of fame and memory come as well from Perugia. In one instance, a notary's widow ordered in an annunciation that she, the testator, be painted 'in her very likeness (*ad similtudinem*)'. This, she insisted, was to preserve 'her true memory (*sue memorie in veritate*)'.[32] Another woman from a tiny Perugian village ordered her parish to have, above her grave, where her father was previously buried, a painting of St George with her father depicted quite literally tooting his horn with one hand and with the other flying a flag inscribed with the family name and arms.[33]

Furthermore, Perugians like Aretines were not content to ponder the extraterrestrial on their deathbeds, nor while negotiating their last decisions over property in good health, but they made plans that would later shape and determine the future behaviour of their heirs and other offspring. For instance, in 1393 the last demands of a Perugian nobleman reached into the future affairs of his heirs. He left his cousin as universal heir but required him to build a bridge leading to their ancestral house. The testator further ordered the bridge to be divided equally with another man and his wife and then to remain 'perpetually' the communal property of 'all those from his house (*debeat comunis dictarum domorum*)'.[34]

---

[30] *Archivio di Capitolare (Arezzo)*, Notarile, no. 57 (Pace Pucci), fos. 143ʳ–151ʳ (1348.ix.21). 'Item reliquit . . . ecclesie sancti Antonii de Tragetto 25 florini de auris . . . in pictura et pro pictura facienda in ipse ecclesie de persona dicti testatoris . . .'

[31] For instance the Aretine Pierozius, son of the notary Federigi, in his 1374 will gave 10 florins to repair the roof of the church of Saints Cosma and Damiano. For this charity, he demanded that his name be inscribed in one of the beams (*et ponatur inscribatur in ligno tetti nominem dicti testatoris*). *Archivio dei Laici* (hereafter, *Arch. dei Laici*), reg. 726, ff. 60ʳ–61ʳ (1374.vi.2).

[32] *Archivio di Stato, Perugia* (hereafter, *ASPr*), *Pergamene*, Monte Morcino, no. 228 (1389.iii.4).

[33] *ASPr*, *Notarile, Protocolli*, no. 22, fo. 110ʳ⁻ᵛ (1401.vi.26).

[34] Ibid., no. 7, fo. 84ʳ⁻ᵛ (1393.v.26).

More than in any other town, Perugians sought ways of circumventing the passage of their properties to those they wished to exclude from the future enjoyment and possession of their patrimonies. At the same time, they pondered the plight of future heirs even beyond their immediate children and other living members of their households. The most extraordinary provision made in these documents, in any city, for the future security of offspring and descendants came from a Perugian nobleman in 1383. The 'magnificent *miles*, dominus Franciscus, son of the late d. Ugolini', left his sons as his universal heirs. If they should die without sons, the dowry of his daughter was to be doubled to 2,000 florins. If all his sons and their male children should die without heirs, then his granddaughter's dowry was to be also supplemented by 1,000 florins. In these cases, his residuary estate (which included landed possessions and houses in nine villages) should provide the funds to build a monastery on the hill called Castellare in the village of Cordigliano. It was to be completed within one year following his death and placed under the rule of the Olivetani. All the monks were to reside perpetually in this monastery and live well with the rights and from the fruits and resources of the legacy. If the Olivetani declined his legacy, he would substitute the Sienese hospital of Santa Maria della Scala to build a hospital on this same hill within one year. In return, the knight Lord Francescus required of the monastery or hospital that if any of the progeny of his house, male or female, legitimate or illegitimate (*spureus*), should prove 'deficient in some faculty' and 'unable to survive on his own', then the institution was obliged to accept this descendant into their community and to provide food and clothing so long as he remained inscribed and obedient to the superiors of this place.[35]

The Florentine testaments fit a similar pattern in both quantitative and qualitative terms; art commissions and efforts at individual and familial immortalization appear as early as the first years of the trecento.[36] Some of these would be remarkable for any period in the wills from those cities where the grip of mendicant piety held most firmly. For instance, in 1312 Ricchuccius, a parishioner of Santa Maria Novella, sought to preserve his memory by attaching it to art. At five lire a year he financed oil to be burnt continually in the Dominican church under the crucifix 'made by the distinguished

[35] ASPr, Perg., Mt. Morcino, no. 202 (1383.xi.5).
[36] Cohn, *The Cult of Remembrance*, ch. 7.

painter named Giottum Bondonis' and 'in the presence of a lantern made of bones', which, he reminded the friars, he had earlier purchased for them. He further insisted that the Prior of Santa Maria Novella and the Guardian of the Franciscans at Santa Croce, when preaching, praise the earthly deeds of this testator and those of his beloved uncle, Ricchus, recalling to their assembled congregations that both had served as captains of the *laudese* confraternity of Santa Maria Novella. These churchmen were further 'to restore to memory' the time when the testator had been the executor of his former uncle's testament, and through his uncle's largess had 'brought honour to these friaries and to the entire province through his administration'.[37]

As the example of the blacksmith's son's commission suggests, obsessions with leaving lasting marks on earthly posterity were not confined to the testaments of the rich and prominent. In 1343 a Florentine who doubled as a tavernkeeper and gravedigger gave a field in the rural suburb of Novoli, west of Florence, to the hospital of Santa Maria della Scala, but required the brothers of the hospital to construct a 'walled' statue of the Madonna and Child on the road in front of his field. The Madonna, constructed with bricks, mortar, and stones, was to stand at least six *brachiorum* (or 15 feet) above the ground.[38]

Nor were these testamentary commissions always so monumental. Florentines, Aretines, and Perugians often ordered the beds they bequeathed to hospitals to be painted with coats of arms and other family regalia. In one case, a blacksmith left 14 lire for the difficult task of adorning his bed, to be given to the poor lying in the hospital of Borgo San Lorenzo, 'with an image in the likeness of the majesty of God'.[39] Other trecento testaments from these towns demanded art that could cost a pittance: wax images of the Madonna or family coats of arms to be painted on candle-stick holders to stand in sacred places in perpetuity.[40]

In the face of mendicant sermons condemning the earthly hubris grounded in temporal properties and family pride, these devotional acts attest to testators' zeal to extend their earthly traces and to immortalize their names, at least in Arezzo, Florence, and Perugia. In Siena attempts to preserve the memory of lineages by plastering

[37] *ASF, Dipl.*, S. M. Novella (1312.vi.15).
[38] *ASF, Dipl.*, S. Maria Nuova (1343.iv.25).
[39] Ibid. (1323.ix.21).   [40] Cohn, *The Cult of Remembrance*, ch. 6.

holy places with family coats of arms date only from the end of the quattrocento and never penetrated the testaments of artisans. In Florence, the practice, as the biting irony of one of Franco Sacchetti's stories suggests and later to be repeated gleefully by Giorgio Vasari,[41] appears early on, reaching even members of the labouring classes.[42] The 1368 testament of a wool carder, who did not even possess a family name, required the *hospitiliarius* of Santa Maria Nuova to paint his 'arms' on a torch, which he gave to the hospital and which was to be kept burning on the hospital's altar every Sunday *in perpetuum*.[43]

Attitudes towards property found in testamentary clauses governing the flow of non-pious bequests also show the same grouping and division among the six city-states. Early on, Aretines, Florentines, and Perugians used their wills to govern from the grave the succession of their properties and the future behaviour of heirs. Mazes of contingency clauses to circumvent possible future demographic eventualities or an heir's failure to fulfil conditions imposed by the testator fill the final sections of these wills. These clauses often went beyond the formula preventing heirs from alienating real property. Some insisted that sons and daughters remain obedient to their mothers, brothers, or uncles or else forfeit rights to the patrimony; others blocked the future flow of property, such as gifts to married daughters, with the conditions that their husbands never touch the properties. Others demanded renovations down to architectural details. Such were the demands that can be found in the testament of one Aretine merchant. In his final itemized act, instead of beseeching his heirs to have masses sung for his soul or to distribute charitable sums, he ordered them to tear down one of his stables and to construct in its place a wrap-around veranda to a house of residence in the countryside.[44] Still others drew up complex architectural plans to divide precisely the rooms among heirs, to determine not only property rights, but even their heirs' future movements—rights of

[41] Vasari, *Vite*, 'Vita di Giotto', testo II, 120–1.

[42] F. Sacchetti, *Il Trecentonovelle*, ed. Antonio Lanza (Florence, 1984), no. lxiii, 122–3, 'A Giotto, gran dipintore, è dato uno palvese a dipingere da un uomo di picciolo affare. Egli, facendosene scherne, lo dipinge per forma che colui rimane confuso.' Sacchetti concludes with the following moral about those who do not know their place: 'Cosi costui, non misurandosi, fu misurato; ché ogni tristo vuol fare arma e far casati; e cotali che li loro padri seranno stati trovati agli ospedali.'

[43] ASF, *Dipl.*, Osp. di S. M. Nuova, 1368.viii.24.

[44] ASF, *Not. antecos.*, no. 9981, 38^v–42^v, 1416.viii.5.

passage, the use of corridors, stairways, wells, and courtyards. After one such blueprint governing the future movements of heirs, an Aretine villager from Fronzola[45] sought further to ward off future squabbles between his widow and sons by demanding that they build a partition wall to divide what had formerly been a communal courtyard.[46]

Thus far, our comparative analysis may have shown little more than that the Burckhardtian notions of fame and memory cut beneath those social levels provided by his sources and that these sentiments were stronger in some places than in others. Like the Aretine *condottiere* who left behind five illegitimate children and his helmet to glorify his grave, what could be more Burckhardtian than the individual testator asserting his individuality by attempting from the grave to govern future events in the secular realm? The roots of these geographical differences, I argue, expose relationships that contradict the very terms of Burckhardt's Renaissance as well as the views of more recent historians.

Should we look for long-term, distant origins: did Roman versus Etruscan traditions or, even further back, tribal configurations of prehistoric Italy underlie these patterns found for the late duecento and early trecento? Or, closer to our findings, did the invasions and three-centuries'-long dominance of the Lombards, create a social fabric for understanding these long-term structures of mentality? Instead, Marc Bloch's criticisms of 'the idol of origins' appear well advised. First, the differences among the cities do not appear to have been of such ancient origins. From the earliest testaments until 1275 the differences in the choices and patterns of bequests were minimal. Second, the geographical groupings of cities and their territories do not correspond with any of these earlier settlement patterns; they do not conveniently divide along a north–south, an east–west, a Tuscan–Umbrian, or a Lombard versus Byzantine line. It was not even a matter of propinquity; the two city-states in closest proximity—Perugia and Assisi—show as radical a difference in the pre-plague patterns of piety as any two towns in this analysis. Third,

---

[45] Fronzola, Frongola, Frònzola, Fonzano: about 2 km south of Poppi in the Valdarno casentinese; Repetti, *Dizionario storico*, ii. 347.

[46] *Arch. dei Laici*, reg. 726, 51ʳ–52ʳ, 1374.v.23; these points are elaborated on at length in Cohn, *The Cult of Remembrance*, ch. 5, 'Property'.

had the fifth-century invasions been the decisive force, then the area
of the Duchy of Perugia, which retained Byzantine rule and Roman
law, should have shown distinctive characteristics in the later Middle
Ages.

Nor do these two triads of city-states divide according to population size or wealth. The political histories of these places also fail to
lend much help. True, Florence and Perugia were traditional Guelf
strongholds, but Arezzo and Pisa (where testamentary giving represented opposite sides of the spectrum) were the bastions of
Ghibelline power in central Italy. Nor can we point to the form of
government; the two city-states which placed the reins of control
under the *signoria* with a single noble family were again at opposite
ends—Pisa and Arezzo. Moreover, the importance of anti-magnate
laws and the extent to which nobles were able to share in the political power of the mercantile élites during the trecento explains little.
Two of the city-states where testators attempted more forcefully to
preserve earthly memory and to manipulate future events from the
grave were also ones again on opposite ends of the spectrum. While
the Florentine Ordinances of Justice of 1293 became emblematic of
the anti-magnate legislation sweeping through northern and central
Italy in the late duecento and early trecento, the feudal lords from
the rural Casentino (Pietramala) took control over Arezzo at the
beginning of the trecento. In addition, these patterns over space do
not correspond with religious characteristics, such as Dominican
popularity versus Franciscan. While suggestive when Dominican
Florence[47] is compared with Franciscan Assisi, the correspondence
ceases to hold when the other cities come into the analysis. In
Arezzo, the Franciscan influence looms large in the literary and artistic evidence as well as in the statistics of pious bequests. In this early
city of humanist learning, the Dominicans did not even rank second
among the mendicant orders.[48]

---

[47] In addition to the statistics on pious giving presented here, see Frederick Antal,
*Florentine Painting and Its Social Background: The Bourgeois Republic before Cosimo
de'Medici's Advent to Power: XIV and early XV Centuries* (London, 1947), 74; and
Daniel Lesnick, *Preaching in Medieval Florence: The Social World of Franciscan and
Dominican Spirituality* (Atlanta, 1989).

[48] See Cohn, *The Cult of Remembrance*, ch. 2.

Nor does the presence of universities help us along. Four of these cities—Perugia,[49] Siena,[50] Arezzo,[51] and to a lesser extent Pisa[52]— possessed venerable universities before the Black Death, but they do not correspond to those cities that championed a zeal for remembrance early on. The link between early centres of humanist learning and the cult of remembrance might be offered as the key for explaining the patterns of piety in Florence and Arezzo,[53] but then how is Pisa, on the other side of the spectrum in testamentary giving, to be explained—a centre of learning equal to or even more important than these cities in the late duecento?[54] Finally, despite Paul Grendler's recent and excellent overview on schooling in the Renaissance, we still know little about differences in the systems and organizations of education from city-state to city-state, especially before the quattrocento.[55] The one systematic comparative study with which I am familiar draws a distinction between the emphasis on merchant and mathematic learning in Florence as against a more literary emphasis found for Arezzo.[56] But these two cities, as we have

[49] See Giuseppe Ermini, 'Fattori di successo dello studio perugino delle origini', *Storia e arte in Umbria nell'età comunale: Atti del VI Convegno di Studi Umbri, Gubbio 26–30 maggio 1968*, pt. 2 (Perugia, 1971), 289–309; and id., *Storia dell'Università di Perugia*, 4 vols. (Florence, 1971–5).

[50] Peter Denley, 'Academic Rivalry and Interchange: the Universities of Siena and Florence', in Denley and Elam (eds.), *Florence and Italy*, 193–208: 'The thirteenth century saw the beginnings of two Tuscan *studi*, that of Arezzo, which dates almost from the beginning of the century, and that of Siena, whose origins can be traced back to documents of the 1240s, but which formally opened in 1275' (194).

[51] Wieruszowski, 'Arezzo as a center for learning and letters in the thirteenth century', *Traditio*, 9 (1953), 321–91; and Robert Black, *Benedetto Accolti and the Florentine Renaissance* (Cambridge, 1985), 17 ff.; Corrado Lazzeri, *Guglielmino Ubertini: Vescovo di Arezzo (1248–1289) e i suoi tempi* (Florence, 1920), 103–13; the 1255 statutes of the Aretine studium are the oldest of any university.

[52] Angelo Fabroni, *Historia Academiae Pisanae*, 3 vols. (Pisa, 1791–5).

[53] See most recently, R. Black, 'Humanism and Education in Renaissance Arezzo', *I Tatti Studies*, 3 (1989), 171–237.

[54] See Ignazio Baldelli, 'La letteratura volgare in Toscana dalle Origini ai primi decenni del secolo XIII', in *Letteratura italiana: Storia e geografia I: L'età Medievale* (Turin, 1987), 69–70: 'Parallelamente al fiorire del volgare scritto, rilevante la presenza della cultura latina a Pisa . . . I maggiori centri di produzione dei più antichi testi volgari sono anche fra i maggiori centri di letteratura, a tutti i livelli, in latino. . . . Nell'area toscana, la coincidenza fra presenza culturale latina e attività in volgare scritto è patente a Pisa. . . . La prima città in cui si coglie la novità della scrittura monumentale non isolata, ma anzi come prassi difusa, è Pisa, la prima città in Italia e in Europa.' See also Armando Petrucci, *La scrittura: Ideologia e rappresentazione* (Turin, 1986), 3–15.

[55] Paul Grendler, *Schooling in Renaissance Italy: Literacy and Learning 1300–1600* (Baltimore, 1989).

[56] Black, 'Humanism and Education'.

found, were similar in their early patterns of piety and in the emphasis placed on the self and lineage.

The one structural characteristic that does correlate closely with these differences over space is the importance of the male line in property descent and its corollary, the disadvantageous property status of women. Where concern with the souls and memory of ancestors and the devolution of property through the patrilines were strong, mendicant values proved less hegemonic. Here, at the heart of Burckhardt's classic formulation of Renaissance individualism, lies a crucial contradiction. Those societies where testators were most obsessed with earthly glory and the preservation of memory, whether achieved through clauses blocking the alienation of property or through the construction of burial complexes advertising the profane symbols of family pride, were also the ones where testators were governed most by the constraints of their ancestors. These testators' attempts to govern from the grave the future behaviour of religious beneficiaries and heirs might well be interpreted as evidence for the assertion of 'individualism'—what Stephen Greenblatt calls 'the attempt to fashion other selves'.[57] At the same time, however, these assertions of individualism acted on the societal level creating a barrage of new restrictions on the free and individual disposition of property not only for heirs but for subsequent generations of testators. In addition, testators' efforts to memorialize their corporeal remains and to establish ancestral graves reverberated through the individual burial choices of future generations of testators. By the end of the trecento, especially women in Arezzo, Florence, and Perugia rarely made independent choices any longer over their corporeal remains; they were either buried in the tombs of their husbands' lineages or, if unmarried, in those of their fathers.[58]

Furthermore, in those societies where the ideals of earthly memory were more in evidence early on, women certainly exercised less individual choice in their discretionary power over property than where mendicant values dampened any zeal for earthly self-preservation. Far from exemplifying the status of women, Florence, where the cult of remembrance was as strong as anywhere studied in this book, was the worst place to have been born a woman, at least in terms of power over property. Fewer Florentine women determined

[57] Greenblatt, *Renaissance Self-Fashioning*, 3.
[58] Cohn, *The Cult of Remembrance*, ch. 4.

the individual fate of their properties through the instrument of the will, and when they did, the constraints of law—the *mundualdus*—and marriage weighed more heavily on them than elsewhere. By contrast, in Pisa, where lineage was weak and the cult of remembrance less pervasive, women redacted wills early on almost as often as men. Moreover, they commonly imposed their choices over property, both dotal and non-dotal, while their husbands lived. Unlike women in Florence—where such practice was rare and when it did occur was no less than an instrument by which the husband assumed all the earlier total control over his wife's patrimony—Pisan women customarily gave their husbands only a standard 15 lire. Finally, husbands' property settlements for their future widows were more favourable in the three cities Assisi, Pisa, and Siena, where the mendicant patterns of self-abnegation were most entrenched. To assume the *usufructus* of the husbands' property in Arezzo, Florence, and Perugia, widows customarily had to relinquish their claims to their dowries, while for the other three towns, the dowry remained inviolable.

More importantly, the comparative framework brings another dimension to the very character of Renaissance individualism, fame, and earthly glory. The split of the towns into two groups was not random but followed at least one underlying principle: those city-states where testators tried to hold on to earthly goods past the grave, to remain alive through legalistic contingency clauses, and to proclaim their earthly fame through commissioning works of art, were places which in Burckhardt's eyes, seen from another angle, would have appeared the most medieval and feudal. They were the ones where testators invoked most often and emphatically the ideology of lineage, and which channelled property down the male line by fidecommission clauses encumbering future generations of heirs.[59] As the examples above suggest, testators in Arezzo, Florence, and Perugia strove for earthly remembrance, fame, and glory, but not as individuals cut from the moorings of their *domus* or clan. Rather the fame and memory these individuals expressed was that of the lineage. Their memory was inextricably bound with that of their ancestors, and family lineage provided the very channels by which this new 'this-worldly' reputation was to be perpetuated. Renaissance fame, in other words, ran down the veins of male bloodlines. In

[59] Ibid., ch. 5.

conclusion, individual choice over property for men and especially women from patrician as well as peasant families was stronger in those societies—Pisa, Siena, and Assisi—where mendicant preachers had been more successful in encouraging testators to believe that family and other earthly goods were transitory matters 'held on loan', as Saint Catherine[60] railed, and 'impediments to the soul', as Francesco Petrarch proclaimed in his Augustinian-inspired last will and testament.[61]

[60] *I, Catherine: Selected Writing of St. Catherine of Siena*, ed. and tr. Kenelm Foster and Mary J. Ronayne (London, 1980), letter to monna Giovanna of Siena, 132–3.
[61] *Petrarch's Testament*, ed. Theodore Mommsen (Ithaca, NY, 1957).

PART III

Rereading the Renaissance Body

10.   The Republic's Two Bodies: Body Metaphors in Italian Renaissance Political Thought

JOHN M. NAJEMY

AT the centre of a whole series of Renaissance cultural myths—including some political ones—lies a particular and famous image of the human body: stately, proportioned, elegant, prominently visible but always decorous, a dream of idealized beauty that, by some curious irony, is often classified under the rubric of naturalistic representation. The Renaissance celebrated the harmony, order, and dignity of the human body in terms that owed much to the ancient Greek analogy of man and the universe as well as to Biblical notions of the similitude of God and man.[1] 'What harmony of limbs, what shapeliness of features, what figure, what face could be or even be thought of as more beautiful than the human?' wrote Giannozzo Manetti in book I ('On the Distinguished Attributes of the Human Body') of his *On the Dignity and Excellence of Man*. 'When those ancient and most wise men became aware of this,' Manetti added, 'they dared to portray the gods in the likeness of man . . .', and 'when they studied all of the . . . mechanisms of the human body diligently and accurately, [they] thought such a fabrication was formed

I wish to thank the members of the Brown University Renaissance Colloquium and the organizers of the Eric Cochrane Memorial Lecture series at the University of Chicago for the opportunity to read earlier versions of this essay and for the many helpful comments I received on both occasions. Special thanks to Robert Bartlett, Elissa Weaver, Alison Brown, and Quentin Skinner for their thoughtful criticisms and suggestions.

[1] Two general introductions to these themes are Leonard Barkan, *Nature's Work of Art: The Human Body as Image of the World* (New Haven, Conn., 1975) and David George Hale, *The Body Politic: A Political Metaphor in Renaissance English Literature* (Paris, 1971), ch. 2, pp. 18–47.

and made in the image of the universe, so they considered that man was called a microcosm by the Greeks. . . .' Marsilio Ficino argued that the body is indeed fit to receive the soul as its guest 'on account of its erect posture . . . the marvellous beauty of all the various members . . . and especially . . . the most harmonious complexion, or total composition which is shown by the delicate, soft, firm and brilliant suppleness of the flesh which could only exist with the most precise balance of the elements. . . . Since the balance [*moderatio*] of our body is so great and so sublime that it seems to imitate the harmony of the heavens, it is no wonder that a celestial soul for a time inhabits this building so similar to heaven.'[2]

Given the prominence of such idealized images of the body in Renaissance humanism and high culture, it should come as no surprise that body metaphors and analogies in Renaissance political thought were usually intended to endow the intangible but asserted constructs of political association with the celebrated attributes of the human body: balance, order, harmony, unity, and integrity. As Elaine Scarry has written: 'When some central idea or ideology or cultural construct' is 'manifestly fictitious' and lacks 'ordinary forms of substantiation', 'the sheer material factualness of the human body will be borrowed to lend that cultural construct the aura of "realness" and "certainty".'[3] Any collection or aggregation of persons or things whose unity has to be affirmed against the, initially at least, more compelling evidence of diversity and fragmentation is fair game for the metaphor. We speak, for example, of a 'body of law', a 'body of knowledge', or a 'body of work' (indeed of a 'corpus of writings') precisely when we wish to urge or argue the wholeness or completeness of an aggregation whose unity might be doubted and in any case must be constructed or construed. The assumption behind this perhaps unconscious strategy is that the body offers an undeniable image of unity, of order, and of correspondence among the parts that either needs no verification, is its own verification, or can indeed be verified by 'ordinary forms of substantiation'—whatever those may be. How especially tempting it must have been to make use of the metaphor in this way during a period that held such a generally reassuring view of the human body.

---

[2] Tr. Charles Trinkaus, *In Our Image and Likeness: Humanity and Divinity in Italian Humanist Thought*, 2 vols. (Chicago, 1970), i. 233; ii. 474–5.

[3] Elaine Scarry, *The Body in Pain: The Making and Unmaking of the World* (New York, 1985), 14.

In this essay I propose to sample how the metaphor, its strategies and assumptions, worked—and sometimes did not work—in the efforts of some Italian Renaissance writers to lend an 'aura of "realness" and "certainty" ' to the cultural constructs of political association. We need to begin with the word 'body' itself. As our own language does, Latin and Italian recognized a variety of meanings for *corpus* and *corpo*. In one of his letters, Seneca arranged these meanings into three categories of bodies: continuous bodies, such as a man; composite bodies, such as a ship or a house; and bodies made up of things that remain distinct and separate, such as an army, a people, or a senate.[4] The jurist Sextus Pomponius slightly rewrote this passage, and his version was later included in Justinian's *Digest* as follows:

There are three kinds of *corpora*. The first is held together by a single spirit and is called *unitum*, such as a man, a tree, or a stone. The second consists of things joined together, that is, of many things cohering among themselves, which is called *connexum*, like a building, a ship, or a box. And the third consists of separated things, such as many whole bodies, but which are covered by one name, like a people, a legion, or a flock.[5]

Seneca's and Pomponius' three categories can be restated as follows: first, the single thing that is intuitively a unity; second, physically conjoined things that constitute a constructed, functional unity; and third, physically separate and distinct things that are construed as a nominal unity. There will be a lot more to say about the first category, with its fuzzy definition of the body in the simplest sense as something 'held together [*continetur*] by a single spirit', but for the moment let us notice that the human body—man (*homo*)—is only one example among others of this sort of body. The second and third categories involve composites, respectively physical and nominal, of many bodies of the first category. The *Corpus Iuris Civilis* itself is a body in the sense of the second category: a conjoining of originally distinct and separate texts into a connected, functional whole.

The third category brings us to politics: to the process of naming,

---

[4] Seneca, *Epistulae Morales*, ed. and tr. Richard M. Gummere (Cambridge, Mass., 1925; repr. 1962), vol. iii, epistle CII, pp. 170–1: 'Quaedam continua corpora esse, ut hominem; quaedam esse composita, ut navem, domum, omnia denique, quorum diversae partes iunctura in unum coactae sunt; quaedam ex distantibus, quorum adhuc membra separata sunt, tamquam exercitus, populus, senatus. Illi enim, per quos ista corpora efficiuntur, iure aut officio cohaerent, natura diducti et singuli sunt.'

[5] Justinian, *Digest*, 41. 3. 30. On this text, see Pierre Michaud-Quantin, *Universitas: Expressions du mouvement communautaire dans le moyen-âge latin* (Paris, 1970), 60–1.

and hence of creating, a single body out of a multiplicity of separate and distinct bodies. We can illustrate this with two common examples of bodies in this sense. The merchant companies of medieval and Renaissance Italy were associations of investing partners, each of whom contributed a stipulated share of the company's total capital. Although the partners and their shares were distinct and differentiated from one another, the shares being neither equal nor common property, a company represented itself to the outside world as a legal entity that was one and the same, as if it were a single person, and the total of the shares of capital owned by a company's partners was called its *corpo*. A second example is that of guilds and federations among guilds, which were sometimes, but not always or even regularly, referred to as bodies. A guild was a fictive, juridical person, and the generic term in medieval legal language for associations that were persons in the eyes of the law was *universitas*, a word that made it possible to talk about associations like guilds, communes, and republics without invoking the metaphor of the body. But *universitas* was abstract, slippery, and, in Scarry's words, 'manifestly fictitious': it was a *nomen intellectuale*, as the canonist Sinibaldo dei Fieschi (later Pope Innocent IV) put it. And when legal theorists asked what exactly a *universitas* was, they sometimes had recourse to the notion of the body, perhaps because they read in the *Digest* (3. 4. 1) that *universitates* were associations permitted to 'have a body [*corpus habere*]'. In the twelfth century the jurist Johannes Bassianus defined *universitas* by applying the third of the three types of bodies as explained by Seneca and Pomponius: 'A *universitas* is a collection of many bodies separated from each other but with one name specifically designated to refer to them.'

In the words of the thirteenth-century canonist Hostiensis, to create unity out of multiplicity was to 'make a body [*facere corpus*]'.[6] For analogous reasons perhaps, political associations also occasionally called themselves bodies. In the 1290s the guilds of Padua agreed to a military union that they described as 'unum corpus et una societas, fraternitas sive liga'—one body and one company, brotherhood or league. And a couple of years later they created a political federation which was, as they said, 'uno corpore et una unione unite'— united by one body and one union.[7] Although it seems likely that the

---

[6] Michaud-Quantin, *Universitas*, 63.

[7] Melchiorre Roberti, *Le Corporazioni padovane d'arti e mestieri*, in *Memorie del reale istituto veneto di scienze, lettere ed arti*, 26/8 (1902), 55.

notary who wrote this phrase must have been familiar with that classification of bodies that found its way from Seneca through Pomponius into the *Digest*, we may notice that he applies the language of the body in the first sense (that which is *unitum*) to what should have been a body in the third sense, and, indeed, doubly so: after all, a federation of guilds was, if anything, a collection of distinct bodies that were themselves collections of distinct bodies. Our notary's purpose in using this particular phrase is not so much legal or logical precision as rhetorical persuasion. His emphasis is on the oneness, wholeness, and solidarity of the guild federation, and he invokes the body (as opposed to the more complex notion of a collection of bodies) in order to provide a familiar and incontestable image of unity and integrity.

If indeed some basic strategy is at work in political metaphors of the body, it would seem to be grounded in the need to establish a principle not only of unity and integrity, but also of order and correspondence among the parts. And it is here, in the dilemma of parts and whole, that the metaphor begins to reveal its own problematic agenda. The very assertion of the unity of a composite body, whether of conjoined or of physically separate elements, inescapably calls attention to the fact that such bodies are made up of parts that at some time or place had not been one and, for certain purposes or from other viewpoints, might still not be. Such composites are called bodies precisely in order to deflect this possibility. But if we return for a moment to Seneca's and Pomponius' definition of the body in the first sense—that which is maintained in its unity by a single spirit—we see that even the image of the body simple, of which as we said the human body is one example, is implicitly caught up in the language of parts and whole. A body that has to be maintained or contained (literally, held together) as a unity is at some level subject to the same potential disaggregation that threatens composite bodies. The metaphor is, in a word, dialectical: it simultaneously affirms, even as it seeks to exclude, the possibility of fragmentation and disunity.

Metaphors of the body thus prove to be a problematic, sometimes inappropriate, and ultimately a structurally conflicted way of talking about political associations. But, to turn the problem around, the conflict in the metaphor (and the different images of politics to which it gives rise) opens up a dimension of ambivalence about the body itself. The metaphor may *intend* to provide a secure source of

attributes by which we can grasp the 'realness and certainty' of the
cultural constructs of political association, but what happens if the
images of the human body prove to be no less, and no less ambigu-
ously, cultural constructs in need of 'realness and certainty'? From
what I can see in the texts, there seems to be a lot more mystery,
uncertainty, and worry in the Renaissance image of the body than
we might at first suspect, for a period whose modern reputation rests
in great measure on its alleged discovery and promulgation of a
canonical image of the human body.

In his little essay on 'The Body Politic', written in 1899, Frederic
Maitland doubted that we could ever devise a true science of the
body politic: 'To me', he wrote, 'it seems that if we start with the
comparison suggested by such phrases as "body politic" or "social
organism" we are not within sight of that sort of knowledge that
every old woman in a village has and has long had of the human
body.' The root of the difficulty with any scientific notion of the
body politic, he asserted, was that 'we have no means of forming
the idea of the *normal* life of a body politic. . . . We do not know,
if I may so put it, that Siamese twins are abnormal.' But Maitland
nonetheless considered that the ancient 'comparison of a state or
nation to a living body' was a valuable tool for the political theorist:

But for this comparison, the vocabulary of the historian and of the political
theorist would be exceedingly meager, and I need not say that a rich, flexible, delicate vocabulary is necessary if there is to be accurate thinking and
precise description. For the presentation—nay, for the perception—of unfamiliar truth we have need of all the metaphors that we can command, and
any source of new and apt metaphors is a source of new knowledge. The
language of any and every science must be in the eyes of the etymologist a
mass of metaphors and of very mixed metaphors.[8]

Maitland's appreciation of the centrality of metaphors in any scientific discourse probably wins a nod of approval from most of us. But
there is also in Maitland's words a certain residue of positivism: the
perception of truths, the conviction that a science of the body natural has always been the empirical and experiential property of

---

[8] Frederic W. Maitland, *Selected Essays*, ed. H. D. Hazeltine, G. Lapsley and P. H.
Winfield (1936; repr. Freeport, NY, 1968), 243–4, 250. The emphasis is Maitland's.
Randall McGowen offers illuminating observations on metaphors of the body in early
modern political and social thought in 'The Body and Punishment in Eighteenth-
Century England', *Journal of Modern History*, 59 (1987), 651–79.

'every old woman in a village' and, most of all, the notion of commanding metaphors, making them work for us to produce accurate
thinking, precise description, and new knowledge. Body metaphors
in political discourse may be and do some or all of the things that
Maitland proposes, but are we quite sure that we have, as he puts it,
an idea of the 'normal life' of even the body natural?

Let me illustrate this level of worry with a quick look at a passage from Augustine's *City of God* that may help to set the terms of
the problem. In his chapter on 'the good things with which the
Creator has filled even this condemned life', Augustine devotes a
page or two to the human body. In it, he says, we see 'how great
the goodness of God appears. . . . Are not the sense organs and
other members so arranged in it, and the appearance, shape and
stature of the whole body so adapted, that it shows clearly that it
was designed to serve a rational soul?' The notion of the body's
adaptation to the requirements of the rational soul is offered on
grounds of utility, service, instrumentality, and control. But
Augustine then encounters a moment of doubt: 'the harmony of all
the parts', he says, 'is so well proportioned and their balance so
beautiful as to make it uncertain whether in designing the body the
consideration of utility counted for more, or that of beauty.' This
question is then reinforced by the observation that 'in any case, we
see nothing created in the body for the sake of utility that does not
also have the effect of beauty'. We could understand a lot more
about all this, Augustine says, if we knew what really goes on inside
our bodies and not just what appears on the surface or from its functions, but he then makes clear that the kind of knowledge he would
like is not to be had from medical science or dissections of bodies. It
is a matter rather of 'the numerical proportions by which all things
are united and joined to each other. . . . If these numbers could be
known, the beauty of proportions in the inner organs too, which
make no display of beauty, would produce such delight that it would
be preferred to every visible form that pleases the eyes . . .' Augustine
is now distancing himself from the utilitarian image of the body,
and he concludes:

If therefore there is no member—at least among those which are visible,
about which no one is in doubt—which is intended for some service but is
not also beautiful, while there are some that have beauty alone and no use
[Augustine mentions the nipples and beards of men's bodies], I find it easy
to deduce that in creating the body a noble mien was put before practical

need. For need is bound to pass away, and the time will come when we shall enjoy nothing but one another's beauty, without any lust.[9]

Now we may not read the opposition between beauty and utility as a particularly anxious one, but the tension is there, fed by our ignorance of what lies beneath the surface of our own bodies and by the possibility that, in time, the beauty of the body will displace its utility and that, having once been masters of bodies designed to serve us, we may become the passive admirers of their self-justifying perfection. Augustine is in effect asking here whether bodies might not have purposes of their own, or, perhaps, as he would put it, whether the Creator did not have plans for the human body that escape the realm of service to the rational soul. And the question here might be: where in all of this do we find any 'idea of the normal life' of the human body?

The fundamental tension underlying this uncertainty and worry turns on issues of ownership and control, on whether and how far the body is or can be instrumentalized and tamed to the purposes of its master, or whether it has agendas of its own and things in store for us that we can barely imagine. In a broad sense, the body itself was—as it always is—a political issue, both object and actor in struggles for power and control. And perhaps for this reason the body natural was inevitably drawn into representations of those wider struggles for power and control that we call politics. In other words, it may be the very fact of conflict between different images of the body that made it, on a subconscious level, so apt a metaphor for human collectivities, even as its intended purpose was to deny or deflect conflict.

The generation or two of Italian political theorists following the translation and popularization of Aristotle's *Politics* predictably made frequent use of metaphors and analogies of the body. The Florentine Dominican Remigio de' Girolami appealed to the body in order to assert the priority and superior claims of the political whole—in this case, the commune—against those of its parts. Quoting Aristotle, Remigio argued that any part of the body ceases to be that part if it is separated from the whole, essentially because

[9] Augustine, *City of God*, XXII, 24, tr. William M. Green (Cambridge, Mass., 1972), vii, 330–5. On Augustine and the body, see Peter Brown, *The Body and Society: Men, Women, and Sexual Renunciation in Early Christianity* (New York, 1988), 387–427.

it can no longer perform the functions ordained for it by the whole body. Thus, just as the body confers identity and function on its parts, the political whole similarly does so for its citizen-parts. But this principle of unity and order among the parts is also a vision of power that could sometimes turn violent. 'Thus,' according to Remigio, 'just as for the health of the whole body we sometimes set aside the welfare of individual members, which are even occasionally amputated, similarly for the peace of the city it is necessary to ignore the interests of individual citizens.'[10] Remigio's image of the body, as of the commune, simultaneously orders the parts into functional harmony and threatens them with mayhem. The same combination of consensus and violence will reappear in civic humanist representations of the body natural and the body politic.

It is Marsilius of Padua who reveals to us most clearly the conflict in the metaphor, although perhaps without intending to. The *Defensor Pacis* begins with the assumption that

the state [*civitas*] is like an animate nature or animal. For just as an animal well disposed in accordance with nature is composed of certain proportioned parts ordered to one another and communicating their functions mutually and for the whole, so too the state is constituted of certain such parts when it is well disposed and established in accordance with reason.

This body, we may say, is a republic of equal parts co-operating for the health of the whole. Analogously, says Marsilius, the tranquillity of the state is that 'good disposition . . . whereby each of its parts will be able perfectly to perform the operations belonging to it', whereas 'intranquillity will be the diseased disposition, . . . like the illness of an animal, whereby all or some of its parts are impeded from performing the operations belonging to them'.[11] On the strength of this analogy, Marsilius proceeds to a constitutional theory in which the differentiation and functional autonomy of the parts of the state are the marks of the 'perfect' and most highly evolved community. With the notions of illness and health, Marsilius, who was after all trained in medicine was indeed offering an idea of the 'normal life' of both the body natural and the body politic. But Marsilius also had other ways of using the body metaphor. When he

[10] Remigio de Girolami, *De Bono Pacis*, in Maria Consiglia de Matteis, *La 'Teologia politica comunale' di' Remigio de' Girolami* (Bologna, 1977), 56, 61–2.

[11] *The Defensor Pacis of Marsilius of Padua*, I. ii. 3, ed. C. W. Previté-Orton (Cambridge, 1928), p. 8. Tr. Alan Gewirth, *Marsilius of Padua: The Defender of Peace* (New York, 1967), 9.

needs an image of command as opposed to co-operation, of authority as against equality, Marsilius invents a different body in which, as he says in chapter 15, 'there is formed first in time and in nature a certain organic part of the animal itself'—'the heart, or something analogous to the heart'. 'This first-formed part of the animal is nobler and more perfect in its qualities and dispositions than the other parts of the animal.' Here the heart actually creates and gives form and identity to the other parts of the body:

For in generating it, nature established in it a power and instrument by which the other parts of the animal are formed from suitable matter, and are separated, differentiated, ordered with respect to one another, conserved in their dispositions, and preserved from harm. . . . Lapses from their nature because of illness or other impediments are repaired by the power of this part.

'In an analogous manner', Marsilius continues, 'the soul of the *universitas civium* produces a first part called the *principatus* [government] and gives it the power [*virtus*] to establish or institute the other parts of the state.'[12] This very different body is a generative and natural hierarchy in which the parts are subordinated to the power and nobility of the chief part, and, as such, far removed from that earlier body of equal members 'communicating their functions mutually and for the whole'. Marsilius even has a third constitutional vision of the body that emerges in his arguments against the papal plenitude of power in Discourse II. In order to counter the papal claim of a right to immediate and direct authority over every member of the 'mystical body of the church', Marsilius asks whether a body would not be a 'deformed monster' if 'the finger or the hand were joined directly to the head'. In such a monstrosity, the individual members would not have their proper position, power, movement or action:

But this does not happen when the finger is joined to the hand, the hand to the arm, the arm to the shoulder, the shoulder to the neck, and the neck to the head, all by proper joints. For then the body is given its appropriate form, and the head can give to the other members, one through the other, their proper individual powers in accordance with their nature and order, and thus they can perform their proper functions.[13]

---

[12] *Defensor Pacis*, i. xv. 5–6: Previté-Orton, 69–70; Gewirth, pp. 63–4.
[13] *Defensor Pacis*, ii. xxiv. 11–12: Previté-Orton, 374–5; Gewirth, 326.

This body seems to be a constitutional monarchy in which the head (not the heart) rules, not directly, but through stages or levels of delegated, transmitted authority that respect a certain limited independence of the members.

As different from one another as these three images of the body may be, they are all variations on the same idea, namely, that the body *does* have a 'normal life' in which the parts either make themselves or are made to work for the health and well-being of the whole. They are all self-contained or self-sufficient organisms, with no connection or interaction with other bodies or with their environment. All three highlight functional relationships among the parts of a whole that is, in Mary Douglas's terms, a 'bounded system', and it is because of this isolation, this demarcation of boundaries, and this circumscribing of the body that such images can serve as models in a theoretical description of the self-sufficient and sovereign state, whether a republic, a principality, or a constitutional monarchy. As Douglas says in *Purity and Danger*, 'The body is a model which can stand for any bounded system. Its boundaries can represent any boundaries which are threatened or precarious. The body is a complex structure. The functions of its different parts and their relation afford a source of symbols for other complex structures.'[14] Marsilius's 'bounded' bodies are indeed systems of order, health, containment, and control, even as they can suggest in turn quite distinct constitutional images of the body politic.

But there is in Marsilius another and completely different picture of the body which reveals just how threatened and precarious those 'bounded' bodies could be. As any doctor is, I imagine, Marsilius was fundamentally ambivalent about nature: it was his ally and friend, the source of the impulse to live well and sufficiently, and at the same time a source of danger and an obstacle to be overcome. With Aristotle, Marsilius could sometimes assert that the state was a product of the 'natural impulse' to associate and to form civil communities. But Marsilius's state was also a *defender* of peace, which of itself tells us that peace needed defending—as we then learn from the book's opening pages—against all the strife and discord that was 'destroying' the Italian state. From this angle, political association was less a product of nature than of art, of the purposeful invention and preservation of 'arts and rules' that could serve as a remedy for

---

[14] Mary Douglas, *Purity and Danger* (London, 1966), 115.

noxious strife and discord. And when Marsilius asks what the ultimate and underlying source of political discord might be, he finds his
answer *in the body*, which, having first been a principle of unity and
order, is now the opposite: 'Man is born composed of contrary elements, because of whose contrary actions and passions some of his
substance is continually being destroyed [or corrupted: *corrumpitur*].' This body is not a bounded or self-sufficient system isolated from its environment: Marsilius adds that man 'is born "bare
and unprotected" from excess of the surrounding air and other elements, capable of suffering and of destruction', and it was in order
to avoid these 'harms' that 'men had to assemble together' to find
and implement the arts and rules of civil life.[15] 'It was necessary for
man to go beyond natural causes to form through reason some
means whereby to effect and preserve his actions and passions in
body and soul.' This body faces dangers from within and without,
and it is particularly vulnerable at the boundaries:

Of human actions and passions, some come from natural causes apart from
knowledge. Such are those which are effected by the *contrariety* of the elements composing our bodies, through their *intermixture*. In this class can
properly be placed the actions of the nutritive faculty. Under this head also
come actions effected by the elements *surrounding* our body through the
alteration of their qualities; of this kind also are the alterations effected by
things *entering* human bodies, such as food, drink, medicines, poisons, and
other similar things.[16] [my emphasis]

[15] *Defensor Pacis*, I. iv. 3; Previté-Orton, 13: 'quod quia homo nascitur compositus
ex contrariis elementis, propter quorum contrarias actiones et passiones quasi continue corrumpitur aliquid ex sua substantia; rursumque quoniam nudus nascitur et
inermis ab excessu continentis aeris et aliorum elementorum, passibilis et corruptibilis,
quemadmodum dictum est in scientia naturarum; indiguit artibus diversorum generum
et specierum ad declinandum nocumenta praedicta.' Tr. in Gewirth, 13.
[16] *Defensor Pacis*, I. v. 3–4; Previté-Orton, 16: 'Et quoniam ea quibus haec tem-
peramenta complentur, non accipimus a natura omniquaque perfecte, necessarium fuit
homini ultra causas naturales per rationem aliqua formare, quibus compleatur effici-
entia et conservatio suarum actionum et passionum secundum corpus et animam. Et
haec sunt operum et operatorum genera, provenientium a virtutibus et artibus tam
practicis quam speculativis.
    Actionum autem humanarum et suarum passionum quaedam proveniunt a causis
naturalibus praeter cognitionem, quales fiunt per elementorum contrarietatem nostra
componentium corpora propter ipsorum permixtionem. In quo genere reponi possunt
convenienter actiones particulae nutritivae. Quod etiam capitulum ingrediuntur
actiones, quas faciunt elementa nostrum corpus continentia per alterationem suarum
qualitatum; de quorum genere sunt etiam alterationes quae fiunt ab ingredientibus
humana corpora, veluti sunt cibi, potus, medicinae, venena, et reliqua similia hiis.' Tr.
in Gewirth, 16.

Marsilius's next few paragraphs are about the offices and parts of the state instituted as remedies for these multiple dangers emerging from and faced by the body natural: for example, agriculture, 'so that what is lost from the substance of our body may thereby be restored'; or that 'general class of mechanics, which Aristotle . . . calls the "arts" ', 'in order to moderate the actions and passions of our body caused by the impressions of the elements which externally surround us'.[17]

Let us call this Marsilius's, or the republic's, second body: a body of contraries, of unpredictable actions and passions, a theatre of danger, and a potential threat to the rational soul that presumes to control it. Its boundaries are fuzzy, shifting, and vulnerable. It is inseparable from other matter, caught up in processes of exchange, gaining and losing substance, part of some larger cycle of decay, death, and renewal that transcends the pretensions of a self that would rein it in and make it and its parts conform to a set of constitutional rules and procedures.

This second body is the enemy of rational politics and of all those closed boundaries and demarcations of self and other, function and service, rights and responsibilities, ruling and being ruled that are essential to the tranquillity of the well-ordered republic. Moreover, this body unleashes and untames the metaphor of the body politic, for, if the republic is indeed, as Marsilius and so many others insist, 'like an animate nature or animal,' might it not also be 'composed of contrary elements,' and thus subject to the same excesses of destructive actions and passions and the same impressions of the surrounding elements that afflict the body natural? Marsilius's two bodies reveal just how conflicted the metaphor could be, and the question we must ask is this: how could any discourse of the body politic reconcile, contain, or defuse the conflict in the metaphor? I would like to suggest—tentatively—that the problem does have a history in the Renaissance and that, in its broad lines, it involved two stages or moments. First, political humanism declared war on Marsilius's second body and achieved a temporary victory whose banner was the decorous body of Renaissance fame. But underneath, the old fears were at work undermining the victory, until Machiavelli decided to give the untamed body its due and, in a gesture of respect for its resilience, reformulated the body politic in its image.

---

[17] *Defensor Pacis*, I. v. 5–6: Previté-Orton, 16–17; Gewirth, 16–17.

If humanism's war against the untamed body did not begin with Petrarch, he was at least among its earliest generals. 'You ought to love your citizens as you do your children', he wrote to Francesco da Carrara in his long essay/letter on how a ruler ought to govern his state, 'or rather (if I may put it this way) as a member of your own body or as a part of your soul. For the republic is one body and you are its head.'[18] But when Petrarch wrote of his own body, of the changes in old age that made it increasingly incompetent to perform 'foul deeds'—an incompetence that he welcomed and aided—that love of one's body that he urged on Francesco da Carrara gave way to a relationship of antagonism and belligerency:

> I feel that I have triumphed over my body, that old enemy which waged many a cruel war on me, and I seem to be driving a laureled chariot up the sacred way to the Capitol of my soul, dragging at chariot-tail my conquered passions, the insidious foes of virtue firmly bound, and pleasure in chains.[19]

Here Petrarch politicizes and militarizes the opposition between body and self and imagines his victory over the body as a triumph over the enemies of the Roman Empire.

The strategies of civic humanism were less openly martial, more political and even economic. Civic humanism was notoriously fearful of the second body, of its erotic power, of its independence and unpredictability, and it never tired of preaching the need for vigilant control and discipline. Two well-known instances of this civic subjugation of the body are Leonardo Bruni's indignant rejection of Boccaccio's account of Dante's love-life and his insistence in confining Dante's sexuality to the conjugal bed; and Gregorio Dati's vow 'to keep Friday as a day of total chastity—with Friday I include the following night—when I must abstain from the enjoyment of all carnal pleasures.' Dati asked God to give him the grace to keep his promise, but he felt the need to add that for every time he broke it he would give 20 *soldi* to the poor and say twenty Our Fathers and Hail Marys.[20]

---

[18] Petrarch, *Rerum Senilium*, xiv. 1, tr. B. G. Kohl, *How a Ruler Ought to Govern His State*, in B. G. Kohl and R. G. Witt (eds.), *The Earthly Republic: Italian Humanists on Government and Society* (Philadelphia, 1978), 46.

[19] Petrarch, *Rerum Senilium*, viii. 2, tr. Morris Bishop, *Letters from Petrarch* (Bloomington, 1966), 254.

[20] Bruni's *Vita di Dante* is in Hans Baron, *Leonardo Bruni Aretino: Humanistisch-Philosophische Schriften* (Leipzig, 1928); tr. Alan F. Nagel, *The Three Crowns of Florence* (New York, 1972), 57–73. The Nagel tr. is repr. in G. Griffiths, J. Hankins, D. Thompson (eds.), *The Humanism of Leonardo Bruni: Selected Texts* (Binghamton,

But it is Matteo Palmieri who gives us the clearest elaboration of the political uses of the metaphor of the disciplined body. In *Della vita civile* Palmieri repeatedly appropriates the image of the tamed and well-ordered body as a figure for the republic. Quoting Cicero, who said that he was paraphrasing Plato, Palmieri exhorted good citizens to have care for 'the whole body of the republic [*tutto il corpo della republica*], in such a way that, as they defend one part of it, the others are not abandoned.'[21] The health of a republic consists in 'unione civile', and just as

a healthy, powerful, and well-disposed body tolerates many disorders over time, because skilful nature holds firm against the burdens placed on it, but then, overcome by excess and unable to resist, falls into illness which the body purges, and if it is not soon corrected brings about its death, in the same way powerful cities can tolerate disorganized governments for a time, but they must purge themselves before long; and if they are badly reformed they will suffer a relapse, and, when the disorder is too strong, they will come to ruin and die.[22]

Palmieri's 'body of the republic' is thus made up of parts whose unity constitutes the health of the whole. This unity is compatible with the functional diversity of the parts. When Palmieri explains that the four 'principal members' of civic virtue—prudence, justice, strength, and modesty—are all conjoined and mutually implicated so that they seem to 'proceed from one and the same body', he quickly adds that each of these virtues has its own and distinct offices (or duties), 'not unlike human members, which, all connected and conjoined to the same body, perform different operations, and although each has its own particular *ufici*, it often needs the help and consent [*consentimento*] of

NY, 1987), 85–95. Gregorio Dati recorded his vow in his *Libro Segreto*, ed. Carlo Gargiolli (Bologna, 1869), 70. Portions of this diary are tr. in English in Gene Brucker (ed.), *Two Memoirs of Renaissance Florence: The Diaries of Buonaccorso Pitti and Gregorio Dati*, tr. Julia Martines (New York, 1967); for the vow, see 124.

[21] Matteo Palmieri, *Vita Civile*, ed. Gino Belloni (Florence, 1982), 132: 'l'altro che insieme tutto il corpo della republica conservino, in modo che l'una parte difendendo non s'abandonino l'altre.' Palmieri was here translating *De Officiis*, I. xxv. 85.

[22] Palmieri, *Vita Civile*, 133: 'Et come uno sano, potente et bene disposto corpo a tempo sopporta molti disordini, perché la valente natura regge agl'incarichi datigli, poi pure, vincta dal troppo, non potendo resistere, cade in infermità ch'el purga, et se per l'avenire non si corregge, ricade a morte, cosí le potenti città a tempo sopportono i disordinati governi, ma in brieve tempo è necessario si purghino; et se sono male riformate ricaggiono, et quando il disordine è troppo valido, ruinano in perdita morte.'

the others.'[23] If the republic was a kind of body, this passage describes the human body as an ideal miniature republic, complete with office-holding, processes of consent, and a diversity of functions that preserves the common good.

But Palmieri never loses sight of the dangers that this body poses to itself. In approaching the theme of modesty, he counsels that in all they do men must follow the 'order of nature', which 'shows how wisely it formed the human body' when it

placed openly and in clear view all those parts of the body destined for honourable functions in which there is no offensive display. Those other parts necessary to the body, in whose appearance and functions there is ugliness and baseness, it hid in secrecy and located in a more remote region, so that they would not be visible and thus disrupt the beauty of the other members. Indeed, in order to conceal them even more completely, it added pubic hair at the age at which discretion and judgement begin to experience and recognize that there is some shame in those parts of the body. If therefore each person considers this diligent composition of nature and if he wishes to live honourably, he must use as secretly as possible those parts of the body that nature has concealed and remove them entirely from the presence of men, as nature warns us.[24]

This passage is almost entirely borrowed from Cicero's *De Officiis*.[25] But the explicit mention of pubic hair is Palmieri's own contribution

---

[23] Palmieri, *Vita Civile*, 64: 'Queste quatro, tutte insieme sono coniuncte et in moltissime parti implicate come procedenti da un medesimo corpo: et nientedimeno ciascuna di per sé ha ufici particulari et proprii, non altrimenti che le membra humane, le quali tutte coniuncte et insieme collegate al medesimo corpo varie operationi exercitono et, benché ciascuno abbia i suoi ufici particulari et proprii, non di meno speso ha bisogno dello aiuto o vero consentimento degli altri.'

[24] Ibid. 82: 'Per questo doviano fermare nell'animo in qualunche cosa seguire l'ordine vero di nostra natura, la quale molto consideratamente dimonstra avere formato il corpo humano, però che tutte le membra date per alcuna honesta operatione, in elle quali non era alcuna brutta dimonstratione, aperte in luogo manifesto conlocò. Altre parti necessarie al corpo, in nello aspecto et operationi delle quali era alcuna viltà brutta, in segreto nascose et posele in luogo più rimoto, acciò che non apparissino a disordinare la belleza dell'altre membra et, per più celatamente occultalle, v'agiunse i peli in quella età che la discretione et iudicio comincia a gustare et conoscere essere in quelle alcuna vergogna. Considerando dunque ciascuno questa diligente compositione della natura, se disidera honesto vivere, debbe quanto più segreto può operare le parti che la natura ha celato, et in tutto le debbe rimuovere dal comspetto degl'huomini, come la natura admonisce.'

[25] Cicero, *De Officiis*, I. xxxv, tr. Walter Miller (New York, 1928), 128–9: 'Principio corporis nostri magnam natura ipsa videtur habuisse rationem, quae formam nostram reliquamque figuram, in qua esset species honesta, eam posuit in promptu, quae partes autem corporis ad naturae necessitatem datae aspectum essent deformem habiturae atque foedum, eas contexit atque abdidit. Hanc naturae tam

to a thought left more decorously indirect by Cicero: a small but significant addition that suggests just how intense and precise Palmieri's fear of the body could be. In these remarkable lines Palmieri makes nature itself responsible for a fundamental division within the body between the lofty and the base, between the high-minded and what Bakhtin called the bodily lower stratum. The decorum and virtues of Palmieri's republican body are constructed on foundations that are hidden from view because they are shameful, offensive, and potentially productive of disorder—all the while being absolutely necessary. The threat that these lower parts pose is so great that they should not even be talked about. Palmieri advises that 'good men must be as silent as they can about those parts and their functions; and if it should indeed be necessary to speak of them, one must not call them by their own names; rather, as far as we can, we should make them sound more honourable so that their ugliness is referred to as little as possible.'[26]

Fear of the body surfaces again in Palmieri's discussion of gestures and comportment. All movements of the body should conform to 'naturale uso'. But Palmieri warns that 'the smallest gestures can reveal the greatest vices and give away true indications of what our minds are feeling'. The hands especially can 'signify our intentions, so that they not only show, but almost speak and powerfully express all our thoughts . . .' The body, in short, can sometimes say too much, and thus 'every movement must be linked to an orderly modesty.'[27] Palmieri is clearly worried about the body's potential for disruption and for a kind of betrayal: it seems almost to have a will of its own, a capacity, if given half a chance, to escape the control of its own ruling and visible parts and to reveal things best kept silent and hidden. It should therefore be no surprise that, when Palmieri returns to the 'corpo della republica' and argues, as a good civic humanist, that this body politic is best ruled by the 'moltitudine civile' rather than by a small number of expert men, he quickly notes that from this civic multitude the 'ultima plebe della città' must of

diligentem fabricam imitata est hominum verecundia. Quae enim natura occultavit, eadem omnes, qui sana mente sunt, removent ab oculis ipsique necessitati dant operam ut quam occultissime pareant; quarumque partium corporis usus sunt necessarii, eas neque partes neque earum usus suis nominibus appellant; quodque facere turpe non est, modo occulte, id dicere obscenum est. Itaque nec actio rerum illarum aperta petulantia vacat nec orationis obscenitas.' I thank Quentin Skinner for pointing out just how closely Palmieri was following Cicero in this passage.

[26] Palmieri, *Vita Civile*, 83.   [27] Ibid. 95–6.

course be excluded.[28] The lower stratum of the body politic, like that of the body natural, must be contained, unspoken, and suppressed. The decorous bodies of Renaissance civic humanism are bodies turned against themselves.

Whereas Palmieri was, to extend Petrarch's metaphor, a dutiful soldier in the civic humanist war on the body, Leon Battista Alberti adopted the stance of a bemused critic who understood some of the dangers and contradictions of this struggle. Alberti did as much as anyone to invent and propagate the Renaissance canon of the decorous and proportioned body, which, as Joan [Kelly] Gadol wrote, 'was a structure of ratios . . . a systematic rather than an aggregate whole, a unity in which the parts can never add up to the whole but are rather assigned their relative places and functions by the "rule" of the whole', and in which 'each part . . . manifest[s] a law of the whole.'[29] But in *Della famiglia* Alberti goes behind the aesthetics of the Renaissance body to its politics. The family too, like the republic, could be thought of as a body. In the speech within a speech in which the dying Lorenzo evokes the wisdom of his father Benedetto, Alberti has Benedetto say that the elders of the family should be common fathers to all the young; indeed they should be like the mind and soul of the 'entire body of the family [*tutto il corpo della famiglia*].'[30]

In book III it is Giannozzo who shows in what ways the rule of the family body is exemplified in the management of his own body. Beginning his lesson on the 'holy virtue of *masserizia* [thrift and good management]', he tells his humanist cousin Lionardo that 'it is right that the things of which we are truly and carefully thrifty had better be really our own'. Trying to imagine what those things might be, Lionardo, typically, misunderstands and says: 'I hear people say *my* wife, *my* children, *my* house—those maybe?' Giannozzo points out

---

[28] Palmieri, *Vita Civile*, 190–1: 'Virgilio dice che il vulgo sempre si volge al peggio. Da questo nasce la inferma stabilità, il poco durare et la infinita multitudine degli ordini, i quali spesso nelle città si truovono tanto diversi che più tosto confusione che ordine possono meritamente essere chiamati. La cagione certo procede da i principali governatori, i quali alle attitudini proprie o alle private di coloro da chi sono richiesti più tosto che a tutto il corpo della republica inconsideratamente si dirizono. Per questo adviene che la moltitudine civile, tracto però di quella sempre l'ultima plebe della città, rendono il iudicio migliore che non fanno i piccoli numeri degl'intendenti . . .'

[29] Joan Kelly Gadol, *Leon Battista Alberti: Universal Man of the Early Renaissance* (Chicago, 1969), 90.

[30] Alberti, *I Libri della famiglia*, ed. R. Romano and A. Tenenti (Turin, 1969), 23.

that fortune can always take such things away from us and that they thus 'belong rather to her than to us'. No, he says, the only things that 'a man can truly call his own' are his spirit, his body, and time. Giannozzo's approach to the body is thus framed by that most basic of political ideas, the distinction between what is mine and what is not mine. Giannozzo's body is his private possession and a subdued other. 'Nature', he says, 'has subjected it to the status of an instrument, a kind of cart for moving the spirit about, and nature has commanded that it should never obey any spirit but its own. . . . Nature hates to have the body escape the guardianship of its spirit, and man, above all, naturally loves liberty. He loves to live on his own, loves to belong to himself.'[31] Giannozzo seems untroubled by the apparent contradiction between the body's subjection to the spirit that owns it and the liberty that this ruling spirit of each person naturally yearns for *vis-à-vis* others. Later Giannozzo says; 'to make the spirit noble, tranquil, and happy, all the desires and longings of the body are suppressed. . . .'[32] And still later: 'I use my body in honourable, useful, and noble activities. . . . I keep myself neat, clean, and *civile*.' However we translate this last word (and I am tempted to give it a Freudian reading, as in *Civilization and its Discontents*), it lets us know that politics is never very far away from the 'thrifty management' of the body. Giannozzo finishes this sentence with a more direct link between the well-managed body and the dutiful citizen: 'I take care above all to use my hands, my tongue, and every member, as I do my intelligence and all that is mine, for the honour and fame of my country, our family, and myself.'[33] And his insistence on regular exercise as the one and only means by which he preserves his body in health reinforces the image of military training and the importance of keeping his body busy and subdued with constant activity.[34]

[31] Ibid. 204–5: 'L'altro vedi ch'egli è il corpo. Questo la natura l'ha subietto come strumento, come uno carriuolo sul quale si muova l'anima, e comandògli la natura mai patisse ubidire ad altri che all'anima propria. . . . Fugge la natura avere il corpo non in balìa dell'anima, e sopra tutti l'uomo naturalmente ama libertà, ama vivere a sé stessi, ama essere suo.' Tr. mainly from Renée Neu Watkins, *The Family in Renaissance Florence* (Columbia, SC, 1969).

[32] Ibid. 206: 'per rendere l'anima virtuosa, quieta e felice, s'abandona tutti gli appetiti e desiderii del corpo.'

[33] Ibid. 212: 'Io l'adopero in cose oneste, utili e nobili quanto posso. . . . Tengomi netto, pulito, civile, e sopratutto cerco d'adoperare così le mani, la lingua e ogni membro, come l'ingegno e ogni mia cosa, in onore e fama della patria mia, della famiglia nostra e di me stessi.' [34] Ibid. 213.

When we connect Giannozzo's advice about the body with the long exchange in Book II between Lionardo and Battista concerning the power and danger of erotic love, and with the discussion of politics and political duty that comes almost immediately after Giannozzo's lesson on the things that are 'truly ours', we begin to see Alberti's critique of the politics of the body at the centre of civic humanism. In Book II it is Battista who acknowledges 'love's awesome power' and what he calls 'some greater force, what it is I know not, which sometimes drives . . . piety out of the paternal breast.'[35] And, of course, it is Lionardo the civic humanist who is quick to condemn erotic love as madness and to insist that friendship is that useful affection that allows men to attend to public duties and is 'necessary to families, to principalities, and to republics.'[36] The suppression of the instinctual is, in short, the beginning of civic life. But for Lionardo this remains a theoretical proposition to be argued from history and literary examples.

Giannozzo, who, although no humanist and actually quite contemptuous of politics, certainly wishes to be a good, if quiet, citizen and a successful paterfamilias, lives and exemplifies this suppression which begins with the taming of his own body, purposefully circumscribed and bounded with as little contact as possible with anything outside it. Giannozzo the citizen stands in relationship to the larger political world in much the same way that his body exists in relationship to him: privatized, subdued, and dutiful. Yet Giannozzo is aware that the big world of politics—that world in which he declines to participate but would do nothing to change—is built on violence against bodies. In the middle of his diatribe against politics, he denounces magistrates as 'butchers and slaughterers' of the human body, who 'must go every evening and twist a man's arms and legs . . . and still resort to further horrible tortures. Yet, cruel man, you desire to govern?'[37] Ultimately, Giannozzo's strategy is that of the spider, which constructs a little world out of its own body, with 'all the threads spread out in rays, each of which . . . has its source, its roots or birthplace, as we might say, at the centre':

[35] Alberti, *I Libri della famiglia*, 110 ('ammirabile . . . possanza'), and 104–11 *passim*.
[36] Ibid. 119, and 111–19 *passim*.
[37] Ibid. 220: 'colui al quale ogni sera sia necessario torcere le braccia e le membra agli uomini . . . e pur convenirli usare molte altre orribili crudeltà, essere beccaio e squarciatore delle membra umane. . . . Tu adunque, uomo crudelissimo, chiederai li stati?'

The most industrious creature himself then sits at that spot and has his residence there. He remains in that place once his work is spun and arranged, but keeps so alert and watchful that if there is a touch on the finest and most distant thread he feels it instantly, instantly appears, and instantly takes care of the situation. Let the father of a family do likewise.[38]

The spider's body is at once its work of art and its prison. But new power relations have now emerged around Giannozzo's image of the body. What he had first represented as a 'strumento' obeying the orders of nature and of his spirit has become an expansive force that occupies, or colonizes, the space around it. The circumscription has pushed out beyond the original boundaries, which are no longer purely defensive, for this web also catches prey. Now if, as Giannozzo so confidently advises, the father of a family is to 'do likewise', where, we must ask, is the father's family situated *vis-à-vis* this suddenly threatening if still fearful body: among the prey? or is the family the web itself? victims or servile emanations of the paternal body? There is no need to choose, for in either case Alberti has let Giannozzo speak an analogy whose implications take the politics of the well-managed body straight into the realm of prohibited thoughts, and that is why Giannozzo does not—because he cannot—spell out its disturbing logic. But it is no coincidence that the spider speech is immediately followed by Giannozzo's long explanation of how he trained his wife to assume her dutiful and submissive role in the household, a role whose first rule was that she should 'never want another man to share this bed but me.'[39]

Alberti's critique of the politics of the tamed body includes both his recognition that this body was based on fear and anxiety and the remarkable warning that this repressed body could turn outward and become proprietary, aggressive, and even predatory.

As he did with so many of the pieties of humanism, Machiavelli rejected the tamed, bounded, and decorous body of what by his time had become authoritative tradition. He saw its contradictions and unstable tensions, its potential for self-contestation and disruption, its foundations of fear and anxiety. In certain moments Machiavelli seems bent on ridiculing and destroying this body: as, for example, in the 1509 letter to Luigi Guicciardini in which the story of his visit to a Veronese prostitute becomes the occasion for the description of

[38] Ibid. 263.   [39] Ibid. 270.

an anti-canonical grotesque body;[40] or, as in his observation in the
Discorsi (I. 17) that Rome kept itself strong and healthy by 'extin-
guishing' its corrupt monarchy and thus decapitating itself:

Considering how corrupt those kings were, if two or three more generations
had followed and their corruption had begun to spread into the members,
Rome would have been impossible to reform when those members had
themselves become corrupt. But by eliminating the head when the body was
still healthy, they were easily able to live a happy and well-ordered life.[41]

The image of a healthy, happy, headless body politic is an obvious
example of rhetorical violence aimed at the humanist canon of the
body.

But beyond his grotesque and mutilated bodies—which have to be
seen, I think, as an essentially humorous contestation of the com-
placencies of the canon—Machiavelli brought the republic's second
body back into focus. Leaving behind the circumscribed and privatized body, he insisted that 'mixed bodies', as he says in the opening
chapter of the third book of the *Discorsi*, are always caught up in
cycles—in a 'process of time'—by which whatever goodness they
possess is always on its way to corruption, which will kill the body
if it cannot return to its original principles or beginnings. Human
bodies, he says, live similar cycles of growth and corruption, 'for, as
the doctors of medicine say . . . every day something is added [to
these bodies] which at some point will need to be cured.'[42] From one
day to the next, one's body is never the same, and bodies can never
be isolated as self-contained systems. Machiavelli's body politic is
similarly untamed, aggressive, and predatory. When he claims (in
Discorsi, II. 2) that the worst servitude of all is subjection to a republic, he explains that this is so because 'the goal of a republic is
to enervate and weaken all other bodies in order to augment its

---

[40] Machiavelli, *Tutte le opere*, ed. M. Martelli (Florence, 1971), 1112.

[41] Ibid. 101: 'perché, considerando a quanta corruzione erano venuti quelli re, se
fossero seguitati così due o tre successioni, e che quella corruzione, che era in loro, si
fosse cominciata ad istendere per le membra, come le membra fossero state corrotte,
era impossibile mai più riformarla. Ma perdendo il capo quando il busto era intero,
poterono facilmente ridursi a vivere liberi ed ordinati.'

[42] Ibid. 195: 'E perché io parlo de' corpi misti, come sono le republiche e le sètte,
dico che quelle alterazioni sono a salute, che le riducano inverso i principii loro. . . .
E perché nel processo del tempo quella bontà si corrompe, se non interviene cosa che
la riduca al segno, ammazza di necessità quel corpo. E questi dottori di medicina
dicono, parlando de' corpi degli uomini, "quod quotidie aggregatur aliquid, quod
quandoque indiget curatione".'

own.'[43] It is almost as if Machiavelli had read the disturbing over-
tones of Giannozzo's spider-speech: bodies, even those that pretend
to be well-ordered and decorously paternal, exist by preying upon or
even devouring other bodies. And in the chapter (*Discorsi*, II. 5)
devoted to the disasters that sometimes obliterate civilizations—from
changes of religion and language to plagues and floods—Machiavelli
pauses for a moment to say that it seems quite reasonable to suppose
that such natural catastrophes actually do occur for this purpose:

> because just as nature often acts on its own when too much superfluous
> material accumulates in a body and brings about a purging which restores
> the health of that body, similarly nature intervenes in this mixed body of
> humankind [*in questo corpo misto della umana generazione*] whenever terri-
> tories are so full of inhabitants that they can neither live there nor go else-
> where.[44]

Bodies human and bodies politic, for Machiavelli, are always
involved in processes that subvert efforts at closure, demarcation,
and what Bakhtin called the 'border of a closed individuality'.
Machiavelli's bodies are mixed, corruptible, generative, vulnerable,
and predatory: always—again to borrow a phrase from Bakhtin—
'in the act of becoming . . . never finished, never completed'.[45]
Deconstructing the Renaissance canon of the human body was one
of the avenues by which Machiavelli tore apart the conventional
assumptions of his humanist predecessors about politics and political bodies. The 'grotesque image of the body', he seems to be saying, gets us a lot closer, even if uncomfortably so, to the way states
and republics actually work: to the pain of their birth, to the conflictual nature of their relationship with other political bodies, to the

---

[43] Ibid. 150: 'E di tutte le servitù dure, quella è durissima che ti sottomette a una
republica: l'una, perché la è più durabile, e manco si può sperare d'uscirne; l'altra,
perché il fine della republica è enervare ed indebolire, per accrescere il corpo suo, tutti
gli altri corpi.'

[44] Ibid. 155: 'E che queste inondazioni, peste e fami venghino, non credo sia da
dubitarne; sì perché ne sono piene tutte le istorie, sì perché si vede questo effetto della
oblivione delle cose, sì perché e' pare ragionevole ch'e' sia: perché la natura, come ne'
corpi semplici, quando e' vi è ragunato assai materia superflua, muove per se medes-
ima molte volte, e fa una purgazione, la quale è salute di quel corpo; così interviene
in questo corpo misto della umana generazione, che, quando tutte le provincie sono
ripiene di abitatori, in modo che non possono vivervi, né possono andare altrove, per
essere occupati e ripieni tutti i luoghi; e quando la astuzia e la malignità umana è
venuta dove la può venire, conviene di necessità che il mondo si purghi per uno de'
tre modi . . .'

[45] Mikhail Bakhtin, *Rabelais and His World* (Cambridge, Mass., 1968), 320, 317,
and generally chapter 5, 'The Grotesque Image of the Body and Its Sources', 303–67.

contrariety of elements within themselves, to the threats and dangers posed by the surrounding elements and by rival bodies, and to the process by which the violence spawned by conflicts within and without generates new bodies in an endless cycle of becoming and renewal. Machiavelli's 'mixed body of humankind' is, like Bakhtin's grotesque body, the body of the world, from which one can never isolate a mere part and say: this is my body.

What begins to emerge from even this brief sampling of texts is the radical instability of notions, and thus of metaphors, of the body. Despite its reputation for having discovered (or rediscovered) the canonical image of a body whose order, proportions, and harmony reproduced those of the entire universe and could thus serve as a model, measure, or rule for the right ordering of political communities, the Renaissance actually entertained a bewildering variety of images of the body natural. It is perhaps not so surprising that the humanists responded to this pervasive ignorance and uncertainty about the body with ennobling myths about the body's perfect proportions and enduring dignity. Uncertainty about the body was in all likelihood just as productive of anxiety for people in the Renaissance as it is for us, and the myth of the body's harmony, order, and dignity (and of the actual or desired reflection of the same in worlds outside the body) was summoned to deflect the uncomfortable awareness of just how little was in fact known about the body. More difficult is the question of how to explain the particular constellation and variety of images of the body that clustered beneath the humanist myth-making in the spaces opened by that uncertainty (and, sometimes, as we have seen, even in the same text). Why did Renaissance writers who wished to make use of the metaphor of the body politic so often (and against their declared purposes) destabilize the metaphor and, in the process, any notion of the normal life of the body? By way of conclusion, I would like to suggest some approaches to this question.

One approach might take its point of departure in the history of medicine, and, in particular, in the confusion created by the competition between the Aristotelian and Galenic theories of the human body. The differences between these two quite distinct approaches to the structure and functioning of the body were a primary concern in medical science and philosophy. Among the significant differences was the Aristotelian assumption that one part of the body—the heart—ruled the whole, as against the decentralized Galenic notion of coequal members governing separate parts of the body.[46] This disagreement might indeed underlie the different 'constitutional' images of the body that we have seen, for example, in Marsilius's *Defensor Pacis*. And when we add to this fundamental division of medical knowledge the widely-held theories of medical astrology, which linked human bodies to celestial bodies, and of medical care as the science of regulating the 'non-naturals' that surround, affect, or enter the body, we can begin to see how the particular condition of medical science between the Aristotelian revival of the thirteenth century and the various revolutions in medical knowledge in the sixteenth century could indeed have spawned such varied and conflicting images of the body, especially among non-specialists. Machiavelli's appeal to the authority of 'these doctors of medicine', to support his theory that 'mixed bodies like republics' must periodically return to their beginnings or die, gives us a hint of what may have been the considerable but unfocused and confused impact of medical science in the Renaissance images of both the body and the body politic.

A second approach to the problem might follow Bakhtin in distinguishing between the idealized body as an invention of high culture and the many other bodies (the grotesque, the sensual, the predatory, the incomplete, the vulnerable, and so on) as creations of popular culture (or cultures). Do the stories of the *Decameron*, Sacchetti's *Trecentonovelle*, Poggio's *Facetiae*, the *Mandragola*, or the paintings of a Piero di Cosimo give us a glimpse into a popular discourse of the body (akin to the manner in which Bakhtin believes that the Rabelaisian texts do)? In general, the problem of 'popular culture' remains relatively little studied for Italy and Tuscany before 1500, and we would need to know much more than we now do about how different social classes encountered, experienced, and represented the body in order to identify specifically popular images of the body. But it seems at least plausible that care of the body (from feeding, clothing, and bathing to medical treatment) as well as sexual practices and attitudes varied according to social standing, and that such differences helped to sustain the variety of images of the body.

Yet none of the texts we have looked at can reasonably be thought

---

[46] See esp. Nancy G. Siraisi, *Medieval and Early Renaissance Medicine* (Chicago, 1990), 107, and generally ch. 4, 78–114.

of as products of representatives of popular culture, if by this we
mean the social experience of peasants, labourers, or artisans.
Palmieri and Machiavelli belonged to the same social class but had
very different ideas of the body and the body politic. What accounts
for this difference may be not so much their knowledge or experience of the body as their experiences and languages of politics. This
approach to the problem asks whether and how the many and varied images of the body natural may reflect the ways in which individuals, groups, and classes processed the experience of politics
itself.[47] In a time in which so little was known with any certainty
about the body natural, did people learn to think about their bodies
in terms largely derived from the language or languages in which
they thought about politics and the various communities of which
they were a part (family, neighbourhood, guild, commune, city, and
republic)? As we noticed at the outset, the use of body metaphors in
political discourse commonly presupposed the 'realness' and 'certainty' of the human body; it was on the basis of this presupposition
that the body natural was assumed to be capable of serving as a
model for thinking about political communities. But the more we
examine the metaphor in its many variations, the more we become
aware that the Renaissance lacked a natural idea of the body natural
and, in fact, any consensus at all about the body. Discourses of the
body were thus not only cultural constructs, themselves in need of
verification and confirmation; they were also an arena of competition and conflict in which no verification was forthcoming. 'Body'
was a contested sign, just as bodies were contested territory.

   The struggles over both 'body' and bodies lead us back to politics
and to the hypothesis that the various and competing ideas of the
body natural were (and perhaps still are) always mediated (perhaps
even generated) by prior assumptions about the body social and
political. Metaphors of the body politic may thus have been less a
means for applying knowledge of the body to the cultural constructs
of politics (as those who used such metaphors often asserted) than
something very nearly like the reverse of this: devices by which the
great mysteries of the human body could at least be contained within
the relatively more secure and familiar terms of political discourse.

---

[47] An approach suggested by Mary Douglas, 'The Two Bodies', in id., *Natural
Symbols: Explorations in Cosmology* (New York, 1970; repr. 1982), 65–81.

11. Portraiture, Portrayal, and Idealization: Ambiguous Individualism in Representations of Renaissance Women

PATRICIA SIMONS

JACOB BURCKHARDT'S view of the Renaissance is summed up in the phrases 'the Development of the Individual' and 'the Discovery of the World and of Man' where the Italian 'was the first-born among the sons of modern Europe'.[1] Collectivity was replaced by autonomy, objectivity overruled interpersonal relations, secularization superseded blind faith, and mercantile imperialism extended man's dominion. This patriarchal, bourgeois, nineteenth-century vision still influences characterizations of the Renaissance; those examining visual culture, for instance, tend to associate Burckhardt's phrases with the institution of individualistic portraiture and naturalistic style. Social historians and new historicists, however, now examine Renaissance identity as a dynamic of overlapping, ambiguous, and corporate relationships.[2] As the end of our century

I am grateful to Patricia Rubin for acute comments on an earlier version of this paper, and to Thomas Willette and Cristelle Baskins for their valuable assistance in the late stages of revision.

[1] Jacob Burckhardt, *The Civilization of the Renaissance in Italy*, tr. S. G. C. Middlemore (Harmondsworth, 1990; first pub. 1860), 98, 185. William Kerrigan and Gordon Braden, *The Idea of the Renaissance* (Baltimore, Md., 1989), use Burckhardt as their point of departure for a pan-European application of his ideas, particularly individualism.

[2] Stephen Greenblatt, *Renaissance Self-Fashioning From More to Shakespeare* (Chicago, 1980); Ronald F. E. Weissman, *Ritual Brotherhood in Renaissance Florence* (New York, 1982); id., 'Reconstructing Renaissance Sociology: The "Chicago School" and the Study of Renaissance Society', in Richard C. Trexler (ed.), *Persons in Groups, Social Behavior as Identity Formation in Medieval and Renaissance Europe*

approaches, it is timely to revivify Burckhardt's interdisciplinary sense of cultural history, and to recast Renaissance art from a perspective less determined by the biases of modernism.

Modernism will here refer to certain characteristics of post-Enlightenment culture, especially the sense of the autonomy of the sphere of cultural production, allied with classificatory systems which normalized experience and maintained separation between clearly ordered categories, including that between individuals and their social milieu. The apparatus of critical theory available in a post-modern or, rather, post-structuralist age supplies a different approach to historical agency.[3] In place of the self-contained individual, there stands any number of socially conditioned actors without singular, intrinsic essences, and thus Renaissance portraits may be understood as more complex and mediated than modernist individualism will allow. Selfhood, conceived of as having multiple, insecure foundations, must be defined differently at various historical moments.[4] Like transient facial expressions themselves, identities are mobile and intertextual, dependent upon altering contexts and shifting interior landscapes. Portraits can be enunciations of cultural

(Binghamton, NY, 1985), 39–45; id., 'The Importance of Being Ambiguous: Social Relations, Individualism, and Identity in Renaissance Florence', in Susan Zimmerman and Ronald F. E. Weissman (eds.), *Urban Life in the Renaissance* (Newark, NJ, 1989), 269–80. See also Thomas C. Heller, Morton Sosna and David E. Wellbery (eds.), *Reconstructing Individualism. Autonomy, Individuality, and the Self in Western Thought* (Stanford, Calif., 1986), particularly the essays by Greenblatt and Natalie Zemon Davis.

[3] For a starting point consult Linda Alcoff, 'Cultural Feminism versus Post-Structuralism: The Identity Crisis in Feminist Theory', *Signs*, 13 (1988), 405–36; Joan W. Scott, 'Deconstructing Equality-versus-Difference: Or, the Uses of Poststructuralist Theory for Feminism', *Feminist Studies*, 14 (1988), 33–50; Joan W. Scott, 'Multiculturalism and the Politics of Identity', *October* 61 (1992), 12–19; Lisa Tickner, 'Feminism, Art History, and Sexual Difference', *Genders*, 3 (1988), 92–128.

[4] Elizabeth Cropper, 'The Beauty of Woman: Problems in the Rhetoric of Renaissance Portraiture', in Margaret W. Ferguson, Maureen Quilligan, and Nancy J. Vickers (eds.), *Rewriting the Renaissance: The Discourses of Sexual Difference in Early Modern Europe* (Chicago, 1986), 175, notes that 'portraiture . . . is not so easily defined. The image reflected in the mirror is grasped only by the self, which the face both betrays and masks.' Stephen Greenblatt, 'Psychoanalysis and Renaissance Culture', in Patricia Parker and David Quint (eds.), *Literary Theory/Renaissance Texts* (Baltimore, Md., 1986), has occasioned stimulating defences of Lacanian rather than Freudian psychoanalysis: Juliana Schiesari, *The Gendering of Melancholia: Feminism, Psychoanalysis, and the Symbolics of Loss in Renaissance Literature* (Ithaca, NY, 1992) and Elizabeth J. Bellamy, 'Psychoanalysis and the Subject in/of/for the Renaissance', in Jonathan Crewe (ed.), *Reconfiguring the Renaissance: Essays in Critical Materialism* (Lewisburg, Penn., 1992), 19–33.

display rather than of private subjectivities; they can be readable as ideological apparatuses rather than as aesthetic units reporting referential truth; as a medium of exchange between art and society, object and viewer, sitter and artist, patron and artist, sitter and spectators (frequently including the posing subjects themselves), in a rich conversation of overlaid, even competing and conflicting voices, rather than as singular objects with one universalized and static, authoritative interpreter. Portraits themselves performatively shape their world and are not passive reflectors of simple, pre-existing appearances.[5] The work of one court artist, for instance, so conditioned his audience's vision that a chancellor reported to Barbara of Brandenburg that the Florentine women greeting her husband Ludovico Gonzaga in 1460 'truly seemed to have issued from the hands of Andrea Mantegna'.[6]

The notion that Renaissance art was driven internally towards naturalistic reflection of the world, simply for its own sake, has enabled a conception of Renaissance portraiture as transparent, empirically unproblematic presentations of 'modern' individuals.[7] High Renaissance portraits thence are said to 'achieve a peak of visual realism' in which 'they do not symbolise, they *are*. They are

---

[5] Robert Schwartz, 'The Power of Pictures', *Journal of Philosophy*, 82 (1985), 711–20; E. H. Gombrich, 'The Mask and the Face: The Perception of Physiognomic Likeness in Life and in Art', in id., *The Image and the Eye* (Oxford, 1982). I here focus on single or isolated heads, as does Lorne Campbell, *Renaissance Portraits: European Portrait-Painting in the 14th, 15th and 16th Centuries* (New Haven, Conn., 1990), rather than group portraits where the interdependence of the sitters is more evident. On the latter see e.g. Patricia Simons, 'Portraiture and Patronage in Quattrocento Florence with special reference to the Tornaquinci and their Chapel in S. Maria Novella', Ph.D. thesis (Melbourne, 1985); Patricia Fortini Brown, *Venetian Narrative Painting in the Age of Carpaccio* (New Haven, Conn., 1988).

[6] Andrew Martindale, *The Triumphs of Caesar by Andrea Mantegna in the Collection of Her Majesty the Queen at Hampton Court* (London, 1979), 27 n. 3. John Shearman, *Only Connect . . . Art and the Spectator in the Italian Renaissance* (Princeton, NJ, 1992), ch. 3, argues that Renaissance portraiture was 'dramatically affected by the communicative idea' of a 'transitive relationship between sitter and spectator' (108, 124). For reports of people speaking with portraits, kissing them, eating with them, and so on, see Campbell, *Renaissance Portraits*, 107, 183, 196, 205–6, 220–5.

[7] On the religious significance of naturalism, see Leo Steinberg, *The Sexuality of Christ in Renaissance Art and in Modern Oblivion* (New York, 1984). One overly reductive case of conflating biography and portraiture is Flavio Polignano, '*Ritratto e biografia*: due insiemi a confronto, dalla parte dell'iconologia' in Augusto Gentili (ed.), *Il Ritratto e la Memoria. Materiali I* (Rome, 1989), 211–25. A more sophisticated yet problematic attitude is typified by the statement that 'a portrait is usually the most intimate record available of a sitter's personality': Campbell, *Renaissance Portraits*, 37.

Patricia Simons

not models of life, they *are* life.'[8] Although rarely using portraits as source material for biography, art historians have for a long time tended to link them to a 'cult of personality' and read them as celebrations of unique individuals.[9] A seeming Renaissance glorification of the individual has been anachronistically taken as akin to a much later positioning of the unique historical actor against his (inevitably 'his' when 'public' actions are paramount) social context, as though a modernist, ultimately Hegelian, sense of autonomy and freedom is recognizable in the different historical circumstances of the Renaissance.

Instead of reading Renaissance portraits in this way, we need to reinterpret them critically according to categories like class, gender, and age, since degrees of accessibility to Renaissance notions of fame varied. For instance, women's claims to civic recognition, familial regard, entrepreneurial success, and intellectual worth, although not impossible, were more limited than they were for men. The stress on chastity, moderation, and containment so often repeated in discussions about women (who it was feared might otherwise escape patrimonial control), was not an accurate reflection of everyone's daily experience, but the commentaries uttered deeply-felt anxieties and influential sentiments.[10] 'Woman', as an essentialized, dangerous entity, was not readily granted individualism and subjec-

---

[8] Alistair Smith, *Renaissance Portraits* (London, 1973), 31; cf. the thoughtful treatment of a historically located notion of 'likeness' in Linda Klinger, 'The portrait collection of Paolo Giovio', Ph.D. thesis (Princeton University, NJ, 1991), chs. 3–4.

[9] Jean Alazard, *The Florentine Portrait* (Paris, 1924), tr. Barbara Whelpton (London, 1948), 13: 'In the fifteenth century, which was very individualistic, it was a means of exalting the individual'; on p. 51 the 'cult of personality' appears. John Pope-Hennessy, *The Portrait in the Renaissance* (Princeton, NJ, 1966), used the phrase as the title of his first chapter. One of the best correctives to this tradition is Cropper, 'The Beauty of Women', 175–90. For a survey of social function see Enrico Castelnuovo, 'Il significato del ritratto pittorico nella società', in *Storia d'Italia*, v, pt. 2 (Turin, 1973), 1033–94; for a survey of 'social types' see Peter Burke, 'The presentation of self in the Renaissance portrait' in id., *The Historical Anthropology of Early Modern Italy* (Cambridge, 1987).

[10] For treatises see Giuseppe Zonta, *Trattati del Cinquecento sulla Donna* (Bari, 1913); Ruth Kelso, *Doctrine for the Lady of the Renaissance* (Urbana, 1956); Mary Rogers, 'The decorum of women's beauty: Trissino, Firenzuola, Luigini and the representation of women in sixteenth-century painting', *Renaissance Studies*, 2 (1988), 47–88. For the history of Renaissance women see Ian Maclean, *The Renaissance Notion of Woman* (Cambridge, 1980); Joan Kelly, *Women, History, and Theory* (Chicago, 1984); Christiane Klapisch-Zuber, *Women, Family, and Ritual in Renaissance Italy*, tr. Lydia Cochrane (Chicago, 1985); Constance Jordan, *Renaissance Feminism: Literary Texts and Political Models* (Ithaca, NY, 1990); Margaret L. King, *Women of the Renaissance* (Chicago, 1991).

tivity.[11] While a patriarch 'like a true and generous sculptor . . . carves in his offspring a living image of himself', women were only satirically granted self-creative status as sculptors or painters who defied God and acted 'against nature' by changing their body shape or adding cosmetics.[12] Femininity was stereotyped as dissimulation, artifice, and masking, contrasted with a more stable, truthful masculinity. Many women were complicit with patriarchal rules, but others took daring notice of inequalities. A sixteenth-century Dominican who wrote a play for her sister nuns had a male character defend women against misogynist accusations, concluding that they treated women as if they were 'pictures to hang on the wall'.[13] Ironically protesting objectification in the voice of a man, a nun's discourse showed subtle varieties of subversion and compliance. What follows is a contribution to a more multi-layered reading of Renaissance portraits which takes the above perspectives into account when looking at certain examples (FIGS. 11.1–11.8).

Identities and Masks

Richard Brilliant defines a portrait as 'a human image, individualized by physiognomic specifications, subjected to artistic and psychological interpretation, presented as a work of art, and affected by the changing circumstances of perception'.[14] He seeks to go beyond the definition of portraiture as a referential substitution, as a mere surrogate for the sitter, or as a mirror of reality, wanting instead to stress the deliberate artifice and the role of the artist. Thus he usefully denies the 'easy assumption of the equivalence of the Person and his [*sic*] portrait', warning that the appearance of intimacy and consequent transfer of associations from portrait to presumed sitter

---

[11] Valeria Finucci, *The Lady Vanishes: Subjectivity and Representation in Castiglione and Ariosto* (Stanford, Calif., 1992), 1–24.

[12] The first quotation is from *The Letters of Marsilio Ficino* (London, 1981), i. 69. The large literature on cosmetics includes Franco Sacchetti, *Il Trecentonovelle*, ed. Antonio Lanza (Florence, 1984), no. CXXXVI, which ironically praises Florentine women who 'sono maggiori maestri di dipignere e d'intagliare che mai altri maestri fossono, però che assai chiaro si vede ch'elle restituiscono dove la natura ha mancato' (p. 274).

[13] Elissa Weaver, 'Spiritual Fun: A Study of Sixteenth-Century Tuscan Convent Theatre', in Mary Beth Rose (ed.), *Women in the Middle Ages and the Renaissance: Literary and Historical Perspectives* (Syracuse, NY, 1986), 193: 'pitture d'appicarle ad un muro'.

[14] Richard Brilliant, 'On Portraits', *Zeitschrift für Äesthetik und Allgemeine Kunstwissenschaft*, 16/1 (1971), 11–26. For a later discussion see id., *Portraiture* (London, 1991).

is due to 'the unconscious presumptive familiarity of the human face as a centre of empathetic reaction'. Specificities are 'grafted onto a formal pattern which particularizes the type'. Although Brilliant does not focus on cultural processes and power, his attention to 'interpretation' and 'circumstances' as determinants of portraiture permits more probing studies in which descriptive individualization is considered together with conventional, performative, and political aspects of the portrait.

Castiglione claimed that his book on the ideal courtier was presented 'as a portrait of the Court of Urbino', thus grounding his treatment of courtly artifice and body management in the standards of a portraiture practice that was seemingly natural yet adorned.[15] Michelangelo emphasized his own simulation more directly when he explained his perfected portrait heads for the Medici tombs by saying that in a thousand years no one would know what the dukes looked like and that instead viewers are 'stupefied by them'.[16] Portraiture is a fictive, rhetorical device. Characters display themselves in theatrical masks, or don disguises; for instance, a woman portrayed by Piero di Cosimo was apparently praised when she appeared as the reformed prostitute Mary Magdalen.[17] Even on the literal level of physiognomic appearance, it is difficult to know what a person 'really looked like'. Variations among portraits of the same person, such as Francesco Sassetti or Isabella d'Este, can be so marked that no one work can be considered the authoritative likeness.[18] In her search in 1493 for 'painters who can perfectly counterfeit [*contrafaciano*] the natural face', Isabella did not desire a perfect copy but an impressive, beautiful visage and magnificent

[15] Baldesar Castiglione, *The Book of the Courtier*, tr. Charles S. Singleton (Garden City, 1959), 3; Wayne A. Rebhorn, *Courtly Performances: Masking and Festivity in Castiglione's 'Book of the Courtier'* (Detroit, 1987); Robert W. Hanning and David Rosand (eds.), *Castiglione: The Ideal and the Real in Renaissance Culture* (New Haven, Conn., 1983).

[16] David Summers, *Michelangelo and the Language of Art* (Princeton, NJ, 1981), 279–82.

[17] Mina Bacci, *Piero di Cosimo* (Milan, 1966), 85–6.

[18] For Sassetti see Eve Borsook and Johannes Offerhaus, *Francesco Sassetti and Ghirlandaio at Santa Trinita, Florence: History and Legend in a Renaissance Chapel* (Doornspijk, 1981); Federico Zeri with Elizabeth E. Gardner, *Italian Paintings: A Catalogue of the Collection of The Metropolitan Museum of Art. Florentine School* (New York, 1971), 133–7. The portraits said to be of Isabella d'Este are treated in David Chambers and Jane Martineau (eds.), *Splendours of the Gonzaga* (London, 1981), 159–64, with further references.

persona.[19] Since she found posing tedious, she did not always sit for a portrait, and others were also portrayed *in absentia*.[20] Renaissance theorists treated portraiture as the potent presentation of resemblance filtered through the artist's contribution of imitative, ennobling artifice.[21] Artistic discrimination idealized appearances in order to highlight the artist's share, and to respond to social and theoretical requirements for a decorum befitting, as well as actively constructing, the sitter's social identity. A pleasing portrait gave the appropriate appearance of presence, stature, and what Ludovico Gonzaga called in 1475 'grace'.[22] Recognizability was important for such purposes as family identification, state propaganda, strategic flattery, and consonance with status.

To Alberti, a key theorist of art in the early fifteenth century, a portrait indicated neither individual fame nor mere physiognomic accuracy but was a primary instance of painting's worthiness. Through portraiture, 'the absent [were made] present' to their friends, the dead were seen by 'the living many centuries later', a king's majesty caused his subjects to tremble, and so too the painter was granted 'deep admiration'.[23] The 'divine power' of painting made artists 'feel themselves to be almost like the Creator'. Artist, Art, and God are each linked in a patriarchal model of power and creativity, the same model Aretino used when he later praised Titian's brush for reviving the dead.[24] At the end of the sixteenth century, a self-portrait by Palma il Giovane immortalized the artist, whose God-like brush usurped maternal productivity and created the

---

[19] Joanna Woods-Marsden, ' "Ritratto al Naturale": Questions of Realism and Idealism in Early Renaissance Portraits', *Art Journal*, 46 (1987), 209–16; she differs from Campbell, *Renaissance Portraits*, 1 and *passim*. When desperate for a work from Leonardo, and unsuccessful in her attempts to have him send another copy of her portrait, she even suggested that his drawing of her could be converted into a head of an adolescent Christ, valuing 'that sweetness and softness of atmosphere which is the peculiar excellence of your art'; the text is in Luca Beltrami (ed.), *Documenti e memorie riguardanti la vita e le opere di Leonardo da Vinci* (Milan, 1919), 90.

[20] Campbell, *Renaissance Portraits*, 140, 178, 185, 190.

[21] Luigi Grassi, 'Lineamenti per una storia del concetto di Ritratto', *Arte Antica e Moderna*, 13–16 (1961), 477–94.

[22] Woods-Marsden, ' "Ritratto al Naturale" ', 210: 'in portraits [Mantegna] could have more grace [*più gratia*]'.

[23] Leon Battista Alberti, *On Painting and On Sculpture: The Latin Texts of 'De Pictura' and 'De Statua'*, ed. and tr. Cecil Grayson (London, 1972), 61.

[24] Pietro Aretino, *Lettere sull'arte*, ed. Fidenzio Pertile and Ettore Camesasca (Milan, 1957–60), ii, no. dcxliii: 'resuscita i morti in lo stile' (p. 419).

supreme instance of everlasting life, a Resurrection.[25] Like Aretino and Palma, Alberti focused not on personality or mimesis but on the effect of visual power in relation to status. Portraiture's commemorative function was utilized differently by the French army that invaded Italy in 1494. These troops collected in a book the likenesses of women they had raped, or prostitutes they had used, as mementos of their conquests.[26] Upper-class men, like the Duke of Milan in 1473, instead gathered portraits of beautiful women for specialized collections, or selected sites of pleasure by consulting portraits of courtesans in certain city guidebooks.[27] As possessive *memorie* and statements of sexual assessment, portraits may tell more about their artists, owners, or viewers than about their sitters.

To a sceptical Alberti, there need be no face behind the mask, no distinction between truth and deception, since people could 'transform themselves' and 'wise artifice' feigned any number of appearances.[28] Alberti's contemporaries recognized that masks or personae, at least those of the masculine variety, could be refashioned and represented. The humanist Leonardo Bruni thus wrote that citizens who temporarily act as knights defending their *patria* are individuals who 'perform two functions in turn, as if they had been turned into someone else and temporarily transformed'.[29] Reverting to a theatrical and legal metaphor from antiquity, Bruni acknowledged that 'the same man can play many parts [*persone*]' and this 'actor' declares that 'it was the dignity of the office that made me what I was not before.'[30] Not all personae or roles were false, nor were they singular and fixed. At the turn of the fifteenth century, the merchant Giovanni Morelli had advised his descendants about how to acquire

---

[25] Jane Martineau and Charles Hope (eds.), *The Genius of Venice 1500–1600* (New York, 1984), 192.

[26] Campbell, *Renaissance Portraits*, 209, 271 n. 88, quoting two separate reports.

[27] On the collections, see Campbell, *Renaissance Portraits*, 218, 220; Giulia Bologna, *Tutte le dame del re: Ritratti di dame milanesi per Francesco I re di Francia* (Milan, 1989). On tourism and guides to prostitution, see most recently *Il Gioco dell'Amore: Le Cortigiane di Venezia dal Trecento al Settecento* (Milan, 1990), 73–9.

[28] Mark Jarzombek, *On Leon Baptista Alberti: His Literary and Aesthetic Theories* (Cambridge, Mass., 1989), 159, 165, citing his *Momus*.

[29] Leonardo Bruni, *De Militia*, in C. C. Bayley, *War and Society in Renaissance Florence* (Toronto, 1961), 375; tr. in Gordon Griffiths, James Hankins, and David Thompson, *The Humanism of Leonardo Bruni: Selected Texts* (Binghamton, NY, 1987), 132.

[30] Bayley, *War and Society*, 385, 387; Griffiths *et al.*, *Leonardo Bruni*, 141–2, 144.

honour and political efficacy.[31] Here too behavioural modification was central to the refashioning of the self, all the more interesting for its vernacular context. Morelli's sons were to choose a sagacious, efficient elder and closely 'watch his modes in words, in counsel, in the ordering of his family and his things' so that they would 'resemble him'. The imitative model was very visual: 'When you do something, mirror yourself in him' and 'follow his style [*stile*]' so that 'you will always be comforted by his image [*immagine*]'. Later another father advised his daughter to remake herself in her husband's image: 'I wish you to transform yourself totally in him . . . and as a new kind of chameleon take from him the colour that he shows you'.[32]

A Renaissance portrait also presented an exemplary, normative image for admiration and imitation. No matter what the alternative assessments of a sitter might be, a portrait presented the posed body, and by extension the group that displayed it, as honourable; it represented an ideal against which the sitter and viewers measured themselves. Francesco Barbaro wrote of the 'well born' understanding that 'the image [*imagines*] of their parents is more of a burden than an honour unless they prove themselves by their own virtue worthy of the dignity and greatness of their ancestors'.[33] In 1490 the Camaldolan general Delphin wrote of his predecessor's death-mask that 'I have it daily before my eyes. Through gazing at it, I am aflame to be bound to emulation and imitation of such a father, wishing to be transformed into that same image, which this celestial being imaged when he was alive'.[34] So non-familial relations were also

---

[31] Giovanni di Pagolo Morelli, *Ricordi*, ed. Vittore Branca (Florence, 1969), 283. For an early 1480s procession in Florence for which citizens' sons 'carved their faces and countenances in masks' so that they were pleased to see 'their very selves feigned', see Rab Hatfield, 'The Compagnia de' Magi,' *Journal of the Warburg and Courtauld Institutes*, 33 (1970), 116.

[32] Pietro Belmonte, *Institutione della sposa* (1587), quoted in Jordan, *Renaissance Feminism*, 145.

[33] Margaret L. King, 'Caldiera and the Barbaros on Marriage and the Family: Humanist Reflections of Venetian Realities', *Journal of Medieval and Renaissance Studies*, 6 (1976), 33. In 1440 Poggio noted: 'If we want our own deeds to be praised and remembered by our posterity, the recollection and praise of parents must shine— as their portraits [*imagines*] would—on sons': Poggio Bracciolini, *Opera Omnia* (Turin, 1964), i. 81, tr. Renée Neu Watkins (ed.), *Humanism and Liberty: Writings on Freedom from Fifteenth-Century Florence* (Columbia, SC, 1978), 143.

[34] Richard C. Trexler, 'Florentine Religious Experience: The Sacred Image', repr. in his *Church and Community 1200–1600: Studies in the History of Florence and New Spain* (Rome, 1987), 65. The pantheon of saints and Christ were also role models to

represented in terms of patriarchal patterns of inheritance and masculine standards of achievement, centred around the transformative
power of images.

Awareness of self-fashioning was voiced in Francesco Guicciardini's assertion that 'we pay attention only to the quality of the
performance.'[35] Whilst the adoption of performative styles opened
up a multitude of possible roles, the very fluidity also gave rise to
alienation.[36] Fathers anxiously advised offspring about behavioural
routes to acceptance, churchmen recommended exemplars in the biblical and institutional past, merchants and oligarchs struggled with
the uncontrollable blows of *fortuna*, and humanists asserted idealizing ideologies—all because of the realization that the ground was
shifting in an age of political and economic transition. Renaissance
philosophers like Pico could think of themselves as 'chameleons',
others envisaged 'transformations', 'masks', or 'performances', as
images for different occasions.[37] When a Florentine portrait-cover of
about 1510 depicts a mask, with the inscription, 'To every man his
mask [*persona*]', some degree of deceit is accepted as part of the
process of visual display.[38] Further, both in texts like Alberti's treatise on the family and in many female portraits, 'losses, fears, and

be mirrored. The idea of St Francis's *imitatio Cristi* when he received the stigmata
informs an unusual panel by Macrino d'Alba, once signed and dated 1506, in which
St Francis is stigmatized whilst being venerated by a tonsured, white-robed Franciscan,
Enrico Balistrero. The donor is present in the scene by way of an illusionistically
framed and seemingly separate portrait of his head and shoulders in the hands of St
Francis's companion. As a mirror held up to reflect the saint's features, the framed
portrait enacts Enrico's pious wish to imitate his *exemplum*. See Noemi Gabrielli,
Galleria Sabauda. Maestri Italiani (Turin, 1971), 159–60 and pl. 213. For more on *imitatio* see Simons, 'Portraiture and Patronage', 90–100. For a useful overview of commemoration and role-models, see Campbell, *Renaissance Portraits*, ch. 8.

[35] Francesco Guicciardini, *Maxims and Reflections (Ricordi)*, tr. Mario Domandi
(Philadelphia, 1965), 97.

[36] On alienation see Alison Brown, 'City and Citizen: Changing perceptions in the
Fifteenth and Sixteenth Centuries', in Anthony Molho, Kurt Raaflaub, and Julia
Emlen (eds.), *City States in Classical Antiquity and Medieval Italy* (Stuttgart, 1991, Ann
Arbor, Mich., 1992), 93–111; Perez Zagorin, *Ways of Lying: Dissimulation,
Persecution, and Conformity in Early Modern Europe* (Cambridge, Mass., 1990);
Robert S. Kinsman (ed.), *The Darker Vision of the Renaissance: Beyond the Fields of
Reason* (Berkeley, 1974); and Weissman, *Ritual Brotherhood*, 'Restructuring
Renaissance Sociology', and 'Importance of Being Ambiguous', on the agonistic char-
acter of social bonds which were both supportive and competitive.

[37] Giovanni Pico della Mirandola, 'Oration on the Dignity of Man', tr. Elizabeth
Livermore Forbes, in Ernst Cassirer, Paul Oskar Kristeller and John Herman Randall,
Jr. (eds.), *The Renaissance Philosophy of Man* (Chicago, 1948), 224–5.

[38] Campbell, *Renaissance Portraits*, 254 n. 125.

anxieties are . . . played out in the figure of woman' who is limned, among other reasons, to authenticate masculine hegemony.[39]

Potential loss of power and wealth was ever-present, and artifacts such as portraits constructed visual appearances of stability, élitism, and exemplarity. In this sense, Burckhardt's vision was correct. His insistence that 'political circumstances' fundamentally shaped individualism led him to investigate that development after his first section on 'The State as a Work of Art', by which phrase he meant 'a new fact in history—the state as the outcome of reflection and calculation'.[40] It was this detachment that he also perceived at the level of conduct. The 'demeanour of individuals, and all the higher forms of social intercourse, became ends pursued with a deliberate and artistic purpose.'[41] Burckhardt's Renaissance individual was not only a 'modern man' released from communal bonds; but a work of art, a skilled, educated, élitist construction.[42] Biography and portraiture were only two formats for framing behaviour, which framing became more widespread and reflexive in an age of increasing attention to decorum, court etiquette, diplomatic rituals, family honour, bureaucratic organization, imperialist state expansion—and all the other ideological apparatuses of a display culture that focused on outward, materialist signs by which to judge and control the changing world. As the structures of power became more élitist, portraiture sought to distinguish its sitters and makers from all rivals. Alienation from the growing, abstract State, from the nostalgically valued yet now remote classical world, from a sense of ease and open honesty in an agonistic society, helped to form a culture and a self of artifice. Distance between subject and object led to a variety of visual manifestations, whether in the conscious 'rebirth' of classicism, the systematic development of perspective and idealized naturalism, the increasing assertion of the high status of the arts and of their makers, or in art's communicative address to its audience and representation of the portrait as 'mask'.

---

[39] Carla Freccero, 'Economy, Woman, and Renaissance Discourse', in Marilyn Migiel and Juliana Schiesari (eds.), *Refiguring Woman: Perspectives on Gender and the Italian Renaissance* (Ithaca, NY, 1991), 192–208, here quoted from 198.

[40] Burckhardt, *Civilization*, 98, 20.   [41] Ibid. 236.

[42] This 'Renaissance Man' is akin to his cousin depicted by New Historicists. For a criticism of the latter approach, directed primarily at Greenblatt's work, see Kerrigan and Braden, *The Idea of the Renaissance*, 223 n. 27, and David Norbrook, 'Life and Death of Renaissance Man', *Raritan*, 8 (1989), 89–110, both of whom argue that it offers a purer, more aestheticized version of Burckhardt.

The arbitrariness of social relations informed the Renaissance construction of gender, an area Burckhardt glossed over.[43] A tension between detachment and desire is especially evident in the portrayal of women, for portraits betray cultural anxieties as well as idealizing norms formulated to allay such fears. Thus in a poem written by Castiglione in 1519, his wife and son address him, when he is absent on ambassadorial duties, by responding to his portrait by Raphael so that he remained their cynosure and governor.[44] His anxieties are assuaged by the consolation offered by his loving wife who makes 'tender approaches' to the painted image, smiling and conversing with the absent man, and by a young son who babbles when greeting the father he recognizes. The animation he imagines that his image spurs in his domestic domain indicates the kind of performative viewing expected for portraits. Castiglione's attentive poise in the portrait nevertheless suggests a contained body, wrapped in its chair and within itself. Along with the air of ease and approachability that Raphael painted and Castiglione later stressed in his poem, there is an air of uncertainty, a wariness that calls for assurance which is also subsequently offered through poetic fantasy. Sensual, familial pleasures are constructed for the writer around his dignified portrait by Raphael, so that his wife remains loyal, chaste, maternal, and attentive during his travels.

Worried about wives abandoning them through adultery, or through remarriage or illicit sex after their husband's death, men could seek assurance by placing an everlasting reminder of themselves in the home.[45] The dead man's image maintained the paternal presence so that the wife was comforted and the growing children were 'afraid to shame him'.[46] In the first of my illustrations, an anonymous woman by Bernardino Licinio, painted within fifteen years after Castiglione's elegy, the portrait presents a loyal, upright

[43] Burckhardt, *Civilization*; his inaccurate claims for women's equality are at 250–3; he discusses Firenzuola's treatise on feminine beauty only as an instance of the 'universal education of the eye', 222–5.

[44] Raphael's image of Castiglione is now in the Louvre. The poem is sensitively treated by Shearman, *Only Connect . . . Art*, 135–7, where Castiglione's attention to another portrait, that of his illicit beloved, is also discussed.

[45] Klapisch-Zuber, *Woman, Family, and Ritual*, ch. 6; for Venetian women judged increasingly adulterous in their social behaviour see Guido Ruggiero, *The Boundaries of Eros: Sex Crime and Sexuality in Renaissance Venice* (New York, 1985), 163–5 and *passim*. For portraits of absent husbands see Campbell, *Renaissance Portraits*, 193.

[46] Francisco da Hollanda, *Four Dialogues on Painting*, tr. A. F. G. Bell (London, 1928), 25–6, putting words in the mouth of the female poet Vittoria Colonna.

FIG. 11.1 Bernardino Licinio, *A Woman Holding a Portrait of a Man*, Pinacoteca del Castello Sforzesco, Milan

woman touching a framed image of a man who appears to be her dead husband (FIG. 11.1).[47] The representation of a respectable woman reassures its viewers that her reputation and their honour are protected and she will not shame them. Whomever the patron, and whatever the circumstances requiring memorialization, the portrait creates the impression that the woman deserves admiration for her demeanour, that the family attracts homage for its wealth and reputation, and that the man earns respect for his judgement and authority.

Licinio's female subject is dressed in black and framed by a dark block behind her, with only her arm extending beyond that containing realm to embrace the male portrait's frame. Above his artificial

---

[47] Chambers and Martineau, *Spendours of the Gonzaga*, 164; Luisa Vertova, 'Bernardino Licinio', in *I Pittori Bergamaschi dal XIII al XIX Secolo. Il Cinquecento* I (Bergamo, 1980), 389, 425, no. 70.

representation, a landscape suggests that his proper place is more expansive than hers, although a waning light also may indicate a paradisal afterlife. She averts her eyes from the beholder, refusing to recognize another or to engage in optic dalliance. The man's eyes and head turn towards her, but in a generalized manner so that he appears aware and forever alive yet neither overly uxurious nor confined. An appropriately feminine sobriety is suggested by bearing and costume, yet her body also carries splendid gold finery and displays a bosom and neck of white flesh. Hers is still a body to be accoutred and displayed, perhaps for his family and sons, to indicate their wealth and her desirability, albeit an attractiveness which is theirs alone to enjoy. She is enclosed within their realm of display, still available to scrutiny and still a meaning-bearing sign, with her chastity reinforced by her very beauty, a beauty imbued by that containment and respectability. A woman's body is located in the paradoxical realm of desire *and* repression. A sonnet by Aretino on Titian's portrait of Eleanora Gonzaga praises its representation of both 'chastity and beauty, eternal enemies'.[48] In Licinio's portrait the husband becomes an *immagine* which lives on and will not be shamed. The figures are linked by the woman's extended gesture, yet there is also a sense of remoteness between them as their scale is so different, they exist in clearly differentiated realms of artistic representation, and her body keeps a respectful distance, mindful of her station.[49]

For the oligarchic classes who engaged in portraiture, masculinity was coded as a state of access to a range of offices and opportunities, and thence performative masks. Spatially and biologically confined, a decorous woman was also controlled by social precepts, complicit obedience and normative representations. For her, autonomy was contrasted with duty, dishonour with chastity, seduction with modesty. Such essentialist dichotomies have too often been applied by art historians who classify the subjects of female portraits

[48] Mary Rogers, 'Sonnets on Female Portraits from Renaissance North Italy', *Word and Image*, 2 (1986), 304, with the Italian and an English tr. In his elegy on the death of Simonetta Vespucci in 1476 Bernardo Pulci also wrote of 'pudica e bella . . . due gran nemiche': Achille Neri, 'La Simonetta', *Giornale storico della letteratura italiana*, 5 (1885), 144.

[49] Nearly one hundred years earlier Filippo Lippi had also presented a heterosexual couple in a dialectical relationship of distance and proximity: see Patricia Simons, 'Women in Frames: The Gaze, the Eye, the Profile in Renaissance Portraiture', repr. in Norma Broude and Mary D. Garrard (eds.), *The Expanding Discourse: Feminism and Art History* (New York, 1992), 43, with bibliography.

as either wives or courtesans, upright or licentious; indeed, the operative notion of portraiture will often not admit the possibility that a sexualized female body belongs within the conventions of that genre.[50] Yet the potential attractions as well as dangers of feminine bodies fill Renaissance texts, dreams, and paintings. The female body supplied a signifier on which could be inscribed, alongside lessons of conduct, a range of less contained imaginings, usually as examples of excess and abandon. In social discourses, fictive and otherwise, a female body was alien, controlled and fantasized, confined and displayed. The fundamental ambiguity of femininity is also evident in Renaissance portraiture.

Ambiguity and Femininity: Leonardo's Portrait of Cecilia

Combating poetry's claims to a higher efficacy than painting, Leonardo argued for the relative potency, instantaneity, and forthrightness of visual images. His contribution to the *paragone* debate engaged with Petrarchan poems written about portraits, to argue that here too painting better captured beauty, more completely satisfied love, and more fully aroused desire. Thinking like Castiglione, Leonardo claimed that 'lovers are impelled toward the portraits of the beloved, and speak to the paintings'.[51] 'More so' than the images of poets, the painter's 'very effigy of the beloved' can 'inflame men with love' and 'the lover often kisses and speaks to the picture'.[52] Leonardo supported his case by relating an anecdote about King Matthias who interrupted a poem to concentrate instead on 'a portrait of his beloved' since the painting 'serves a better sense' and he could 'hold with my two hands, offering . . . to my eyes' an image that satisfied sight, and also touch.[53] He enacted Leonardo's precept that good painting 'fills you with love for it and makes all the senses, as well as the eye, desire to possess it'.[54] For a Duke of Milan, Leonardo himself painted a portrait of a beloved, the *Lady with an*

---

[50] See Cropper, 'The Beauty of Woman', 176, who observes that portraits of beautiful women are often reduced to images of courtesans or a painter's mistress and deemed to show 'no specific identity'.

[51] A. McMahon (ed. and tr.), *Treatise on Painting by Leonardo da Vinci* (Princeton, 1956), 20 and *passim*. An informed summary of the *paragone* between poetry and painting, in relation to portraiture, is offered by Shearman, *Only Connect . . . Art*, 113 ff.

[52] McMahon, *Leonardo da Vinci*, 21–2.

[53] Ibid. 15–16.　　　　　　　　　　　　　　　　　　[54] Ibid. 29.

FIG. 11.2 Leonardo da Vinci, *Lady with an Ermine*, National Museum, Cracow

Ermine, some time around 1490 (FIG. 11.2).[55] The prominent animal puns on the name of a mistress, Cecilia Gallerani (*galée* is Greek for ermine), who entered the Sforza court as a fatherless adolescent around 1489, became an elegant presence at court, and bore the Duke a son in May 1491.[56] When Duke Ludovico forged an alliance with Ferrara by marrying Beatrice d'Este in early 1491, Cecilia was married off to a Count in July 1492, and it may be that the portrait was commissioned at this time, as a memento of her relations with the Duke, as a promise of continued affection, and/or as an assertion of her nuptial worth.

The painting itself does little to resolve the question of who was the primary male viewer, husband or Duke, but rather contains enigmatic signals which invoke multiple audiences. The multivalency is especially displaced onto the sitter's bestial attribute. The ermine functions as an emblematic pun on the woman's paternal, noble line but also as a witty physiognomic metaphor for a certain type of femininity. Sitter and symbol are alike in posture, attentiveness, elongated elegance, ovular cranial structure, and refined remoteness, and linked by the grammar of physiognomic theories relating human to animal types.[57] In the symbolic tradition of bestiaries, the ermine is a sign for purity, a significance known to Leonardo who noted that 'the ermine would die rather than besmirch itself', and thus stands for moderation which 'checks all the vices'.[58] The care the animal

---

[55] Martin Kemp's entry in Jay A. Levenson (ed.), *Circa 1492: Art in the Age of Exploration* (Washington, 1991), 272; Janice Shell and Grazioso Sironi, 'Cecilia Gallerani: Leonardo's Lady with an Ermine', *Artibus et Historiae*, 25 (1992), 47–66. A poem on the painting, discussed below and written by a man who died in 1492, gives a *terminus ad quem*.

[56] She is praised, for instance, as a 'molto gentile e dotta signora', 'eroina', poet, Muse and centre of learned gatherings in Matteo Bandello, *Novelle*, ed. Giuseppe Guido Ferrero (Turin, 1974), 62, 100, 196–8. See also Mary Garrard, 'Leonardo da Vinci: Female Portraits, Female Nature', in Broude and Garrard, *The Expanding Discourse*, 64–5; Józef Grabski and Janusz Walek (eds.), *Leonardo da Vinci (1452–1519): Lady with an Ermine from the Czartoryski Collection, National Museum, Cracow* (Vienna, 1991), 28–9; Shell and Sironi, 'Cecilia Gallerani', 55–8.

[57] For the homophonic and homomorphic relations see Paul Barolsky, 'La Gallerani's *Galée*', *Source*, 121 (1992), 13–14.

[58] Jean Paul Richter (ed.), *The Literary Works of Leonardo da Vinci* (London, 1970), ii, nos. 1234, 1263. For a drawing depicting an ermine submitting to capture, see A. E. Popham, *The Drawings of Leonardo da Vinci* (London, 1946), no. 109. A. Götz Pochat, 'The Ermine—a Metaphor in Renaissance Poetry', *Tidskrift för Litteraturvetenskap*, 3 (1973–4), 140–57 treats the tradition of the pure ermine in love poetry. In Cesare Ripa, *Iconologia*, 3rd edn. (Hildesheim, 1970), 90, fac. of 1603 edn., the ermine is a sign of Continence and the animal is not named under Chastity, but her white cloak 'denota, che la castità esser pura, & netta da ogni macchia' (67).

took to remain immaculate constructs Cecilia's reputation as unsullied, perhaps at the very moment a paramour was passed on to a husband who would not have wanted a dishonoured bride, but also recalling her position in the ducal court as an object of desire, who nevertheless had to maintain the appearance of propriety. But the animal permits further associations, including a heraldic reference to the Duke, who received the Order of the Ermine in 1488.[59] And Alciati's *Emblemata* noted that the ermine symbolized lasciviousness and sensuality.[60] Although it is unlikely that the dependent court painter Leonardo was critiquing his lord's hypocrisy, when mistresses were a common appendage for Renaissance princes, the ermine functions in the portrait as a squirming sign of contradictory aspects of the Milanese court and of Renaissance attitudes towards sexual relations. The woman's position as a creature marked with both sexualized body and feminine chastity is represented in the painting's delicate balance of suggestive offering and chaste withdrawal. Analogously, the ermine's embodiment of seeming opposites, whether as a *figura serpentinata* or as a multivalent emblem, reiterates Cecilia's bodily posture and courtly significance. In its use of *chiaroscuro* and ornamental movement as well as in the subtle balancing of apparent antithetical elements, the painting is an example of *concordia discors*, or the harmony of contraries.[61]

Not only the animal, but its temporary containment by its 'mistress' Gallerani, signals a complex passion. Her enlarged, conspicuous hand both controls and caresses a beast whose positive significance marks her as chaste but whose negative meaning suggests her own complicity in illicit relations. The heraldic surrogate for her ducal admirer appears aristocratic, fine, and watchful, so that it praises the master, whether or not he is the patron or primary viewer. The intimacy of embrace and the delicacy of touch between woman and animal suggests both the sensuousness of the human

---

[59] Shell and Sironi, 'Cecilia Gallerani', 53, referring to Carlo Pedretti's research.

[60] Ripa, *Iconologia*, 289, quotes Alciati. The emblem from the Latin edition of Alciati published in 1550 is reprinted in Arthur Henkel and Albrecht Schöne, *Emblemata. Handbuch zur Sinnbildkunst des XVI. und XVII. Jahrhunderts* (Stuttgart, 1967), col. 464; for the ermine in the editions of 1549 and later, see Andreas Alciatus, *The Latin Emblems*, ed. Peter M. Daly with Virginia W. Callahan (Toronto, 1985), I, no. 79 and II, no. 79. Grabski and Walek, *Leonardo da Vinci*, 28, briefly allude to alternative meanings.

[61] Edgar Wind, *Pagan Mysteries in the Renaissance* (Harmondsworth, 1967), ch. 5, 'Virtue Reconciled with Pleasure'; David Summers, 'Contrapposto: Style and Meaning in Renaissance Art', *Art Bulletin*, 59 (1977), 336–61.

relationship and its awkward tension. The very touch King Matthias exercised over a portrait is now transposed. A heterosexual man is still seduced by the senses of sight and touch, but these are now figured by the painting's particulars as well as by its sheer existence. The Duke may be present as the source of light and animation which enlivens Cecilia and her companion, but the painting also enacts the King's prerogative within itself.[62] Cecilia's gaze off-stage suggests modesty along with attention to her lord whilst her arms continue to enfold a sign of passion: the painted figure performs the senses of sight and touch. The painter is, however, the ultimate seducer of the male viewer since it is his artifice, 'of greater value than that of nature', which incorporates these senses within his frame.[63] The painter's mastery sets up a visual mode of homosocial bonding. Leonardo had noted that, whilst a painting stimulates all senses and elicits a desire to swallow it whole, and urges the sense of touch to 'absorb it through all its pores', ultimately 'the satisfaction of touch is lacking'.[64] But he immediately qualified this, saying that touch 'becomes an older brother', being translated from a kind of sensual 'desire' to mental 'reason' when touch is satisfied by imagination. His portrait presents both gestural touch of a soft, luscious, and pristine surface, and that secondary, or underlying, visual excitement of sensual tactility.

The Duke could enjoy his substitution within the painting, as could all his courtiers for whom the wit would have been obvious. *Both* purification and sensualization mark her body and its ambiguous location at court. The animal suggests the Duke, even if the portrait initially functioned as a nuptial present: regardless, he stays with her in pictorial terms. The future and posterity are themes running through a poem written about this same portrait by Bernardo Bellincioni, who writes as though the painting marked a farewell or parting.[65] His mention of gratitude to Ludovico for the painting, as well as to 'l'ingegno e la man' of Leonardo, suggests that the Duke

---

[62] Shearman, *Only Connect . . . Art*, 120, notes that she turns 'toward her sun or her illumination, her duke'.

[63] McMahon, *Leonardo da Vinci*, 31. [64] Ibid. 29.

[65] The poem is in Beltrami, *Documenti e memorie*, 207–8; also Rogers, 'Sonnets on Female Portraits', 300–1, and Shell and Sironi, 'Cecilia Gallerani', 49, each with a parallel translation; paraphrased in Shearman, *Only Connect . . . Art*, 120. For poems about female portraits see Giovanni Pozzi, 'Il ritratto della donna nella poesia d'inizio Cinquecento e la pittura di Giorgione', *Lettere Italiane*, 31 (1979), 3–30; Rogers, 'Sonnets', 291–305.

has commissioned the portrait. An epigram on a lost Leonardo painting of another mistress of Ludovico's instead named him as the
owner of that woman's very soul, but Bellincioni's sonnet works
with a more sophisticated sense of the relationship between poetry,
painting, spectatorship, and production.[66] Jealous Nature is assured
that the painting honours her because it lacks Cecilia's speaking likeness that only Nature represents, but the portrait will appear more
alive and beautiful in the future and thus 'Art confers immortality,
not just on the sitter, but even on Nature'.[67]

The sitter has left a tantalizing comment upon her portrait, and it
seems that Leonardo's conquest was complete since she believed
'there is no other painter to equal him in the world'.[68] Cecilia was
replying to Isabella d'Este's urgent request in April 1498 for the panel
to be sent to her in Mantua so that it could be compared with 'fine
portraits' by Giovanni Bellini. The Este princess was presumably also
impressed, because within two years she sat for her own portrait
from Leonardo.[69] Ensconced in her court and less mobile than men,
she nevertheless knew about the portrait of this mistress, probably
from her sister who had become Ludovico's bride seven years earlier, and sent out a messenger to bring the world to her door. Several
times she mentions that she wants to make a comparison between
portraitists, and Cecilia's response is to offer her own opinion that
Leonardo was without peer. Instead, Cecilia finds a fault in herself,
explaining that the image was done when she was of an 'imperfect

[66] The Latin epigram is in Richter, *Leonardo da Vinci*, ii, no. 1560; tr. M. Kemp,
Leonardo da Vinci: The Marvellous Works of Nature and Man (London, 1981), 199
('Possidet illius Maurus amans animam' or 'the soul is owned by Il Moro her lover');
discussed briefly by Shearman, *Only Connect . . . Art*, 120–1.

[67] Shearman, *Only Connect . . . Art*, 120, his summation of the poem's point. He
also points out that Cecilia's silence refers to the Petrarchan idea of the frustrated
lover who cannot induce the painting of the beloved to speak.

[68] Beltrami, *Documenti e memorie*, 5, tr. Grabski and Walek, *Leonardo da Vinci*,
10; Creighton Gilbert, *Italian Art 1400–1500: Sources and Documents* (Englewood
Cliffs, NJ, 1980), 142; Shell and Sironi, 'Cecilia Gallerani', 49–50.

[69] For the 1499–1500 portrait drawings by Leonardo see Chambers and Martineau,
Splendours of the Gonzaga, no. 108. The two portrait sketches by Leonardo satisfied
her and in March 1501 she requested a copy from his version since her husband had
given the other one away: Beltrami, *Documenti*, 65. For other instances of inter-
changes of portraits among courtly women in Renaissance Italy see Campbell,
Renaissance Portraits, *passim*; Peter Thornton, *The Italian Renaissance Interior
1400–1600* (New York, 1991), 265. More attention has been paid to portraits as items
of diplomatic dialogue between men, but women partly counteracted their courtly
immobility through the exchange and collection of portraits.

age' so that it no longer resembles her '*effigie*'. She too, then, agrees with the conceit that Nature and Art are more successfully immortalized by the portrait than is the mere sitter. Cecilia voiced some discomfort about the disjunction between the image and her current semblance, and perhaps between her past life and her more 'perfect' state as a respectable wife.

Cecilia herself is thus overshadowed by the Petrarchan ideal of an unattainable woman, whose beauty becomes a sign for poetry and painting, arts coded as masculine in terms of social practice and as phallocentric in terms of their masterful assertion. A figure for the viewer's masculine desire (Duke and husband both), and for phallic professions (poetry, painting, and connoisseurship), the portrait of Cecilia is a panegyric to her beauty but also celebrates the painter and the male viewer. The portrait's tension between plasticity and tonal sensuality on the one hand, and an abstract geometry of design and linearity on the other, embodies the contradiction between presence and absence, and the ambiguity of her position at court. Conventions of love purify her as an acceptable court lady and ideal bride, yet the visual specifics also suggest her physicality as a mistress.[70] The ermine is pure yet also signals passion, her embrace is contained yet her touch is sensual, her gaze is disengaged from the viewer's direct regard yet attentively focused on another's, her body static in its attitude of listening yet mobile as it turns. Her body and face are elegant marvels but refined to the point of abstraction, as the portrait suggests both a person's incidental specifics and the Petrarchan universals which idealize her.

Intermediary Categories: Portrayal and Anonymous Referentiality

As a figure who stands for something other than her own self, Cecilia is subsumed by cultural poetics and social conventions. A canonical

---

[70] On the central yet illicit figure of the mistress see Sergio Bertelli, Franco Cardini, and Elvira Garbero Zorzi, *The Courts of the Italian Renaissance* (New York, 1986), 10–14; Burckhardt, *Civilization*, 30; Joanna Woods-Marsden, 'Pictorial Legitimation of Territorial Gains in Emilia: The Iconography of the "Camera Peregina Aurea" in the Castle of Torchiara', in Andrew Morrogh, F. Superbi Gioffredi, P. Morselli, and E. Borsook (eds.), *Renaissance Studies in Honor of Craig Hugh Smyth* (Florence, 1985), ii. 553–64. David Alan Brown and Konrad Oberhuber, '*Monna Vana* and *Fornarina*: Leonardo and Raphael in Rome', in Sergio Bertelli and Gloria Ramakus (eds.), *Essays Presented to Myron P. Gilmore* (Florence, 1978), ii. 48, point out that 'from the point of view of Christian convention the love of the mistress is as free and illegitimate as that of a courtesan and yet for the beloved it is as exclusive, faithful and devout and therefore chaste as that of the bride'.

portrait of an upright woman can for Renaissance viewers also evoke
intellectualized generalizations and erotic fantasies, yet it is no less a
portrait for that. Between the polarities of the mundane and the
ideal, the chaste and the erotic, there lies a vast number of images
which belong to a spectrum of composites.[71] If we apply less modernist interpretations to these images, more flexible, less moralizing
and misogynist readings become possible. At the moment, art historians are often at an impasse, seeing paintings like Titian's *Venus of
Urbino* as an idealized classical goddess (for nuptial or voyeuristic
reasons), or as a courtesan's portrait, or as a portrait of a model
applied to a domesticated goddess, or even a meaningless 'pretty
girl'.[72] *Flora* images are usually seen as either purely mythological
figures, as bridal portraits, or as portraits of courtesans (nymphs
all'antica).[73] Lorenzo Lotto's portrait of a woman holding a drawing of Lucretia is taken for a wanton courtesan or a sober bride,[74]
and the list could go on. Awkwardness tends to arise with any hint
of mythological guise. The feminine body is veiled by either
respectable clothing—whence the image is deemed a portrait—or by
learned classicism and poetic ornament—whence the image becomes
an erotic idealization or allegory which can be viewed without
qualms because it has not presented any actual woman in a manner
thought indecorous. Bourgeois moral dichotomies too readily influence our readings of Renaissance images. We are hampered by a
modern, even Victorian, distinction between the separate spheres of
public and private worlds, which we translate into such binaries as
display and intimacy, chastity and sensuality, portraiture and idealization. Representations of Renaissance women who, like Cecilia

---

[71] The difficulty is noted by Campbell, *Renaissance Portraits*, 6, and Michael Hirst, *Sebastiano del Piombo* (Oxford, 1981), 93.

[72] The quotation is from Charles Hope, *Titian* (London, 1980), 82. See Hans Ost, 'Tizians sogenannte "Venus von Urbino" und andere Buhlerinnen', in Justus Müller Hofstede and Werner Spies (eds.), *Festschrift für Eduard Trier zum 60 Geburtstag* (Berlin, 1981), 129–49; David Rosand, 'Venereal Hermeneutics: Reading Titian's *Venus of Urbino*', in John Monfasani and Ronald G. Musto (eds.), *Renaissance Society and Culture: Essays in Honor of Eugene F. Rice, Jr.* (New York, 1991), 263–79; Mary Pardo, 'Artifice as Seduction in Titian', in James Turner (ed.), *Sexuality and Gender in Early Modern Europe: Institutions, Texts, Images* (New York, 1993); and further references in *Tiziano nelle Gallerie fiorentine* (Florence, 1978), 125–33.

[73] Julius Held, 'Flora, Goddess and Courtesan', in M. Meiss (ed.), *De Artibus Opuscula XL: Essays in Honor of Erwin Panofsky* (Princeton, 1961), 201–18; *Tiziano nelle Gallerie fiorentine*, 341–6, with further references.

[74] Michael Jaffé, 'Pesaro Family Portraits: Pordenone, Lotto and Titian', *Burlington Magazine*, 113 (1971), 696–702; Ost, 'Tizians', 130–6.

Gallerani, belong to social categories such as the mistress and the concubine, do not quite find their comfortable niche in traditional art history since they combine a 'public' face with 'private' desire.[75]

Similarly difficult to categorize are portraits of socially elevated women who appear respectable, which were commissioned or owned by upper-class men who were not the women's husbands. Such portraits cross a hard line drawn between moral rectitude and illicit sensuality. The captivating allure seen in another Leonardo portrait, that of *Ginevra de' Benci*, suits Bernardo Bembo's Petrarchan attitude toward a married woman twenty-six years his junior, an admiration joined by others in the Medicean circles whose poetry produced Ginevra as a publicly displayed vehicle for bonding between men.[76] Seemingly the patron of the poetry, Bernardo probably commissioned the painting and gave it to her as a keepsake of an honourable fancy. Neither the sitter, the patron, nor the owner of a female portrait in Berlin attributed to the Master of S. Spirito is known, but various inscriptions may place it in the context of mistress portraiture (FIG. 11.3). Lines surrounding a laurel-wreathed coat of arms on the reverse declare 'it was as God wished; it shall be as God shall wish. Fear of disgrace and longing for honour alone. Formerly I cried for that which I wished, and again after I had it.'[77] On the obverse underneath the portrait is inscribed 'Noli me tangere', a witty

[75] The mischaracterization of Cecilia Gallerani's portrait as that of a courtesan is made, for instance, by Philip Rylands, *Palma Vecchio* (Cambridge, 1992), 91. Much discussion has been stimulated by two images often thought to be portraits of artists' mistresses. On Parmigianino's *Antea* see Konrad Oberhuber's entry in *The Age of Correggio and the Carracci: Emilian Painting of the Sixteenth and Seventeenth Centuries* (Washington, 1986), 163–5, with further bibliography. On Raphael's images of the *Fornarina* see Brown and Oberhuber, 'Leonardo and Raphael in Rome', 37–60.

[76] John Walker, '*Ginevra de' Benci* by Leonardo da Vinci', in *National Gallery of Art, Report and Studies in the History of Art 1967* (Washington, 1968), 1–38; Cropper, 'The Beauty of Woman', 183 ff.; Jennifer Fletcher, 'Bernardo Bembo and Leonardo's portrait of Ginevra de' Benci', *Burlington Magazine*, 131 (1989), 811–16; Garrard, 'Leonardo da Vinci', 59 f., has an alternative interpretation.

[77] 'Fu che Iddio volle. Sarà che Iddio vorrà. Timore d'infamia e solo disio d'onore. Piansi già quello ch'io volli, Poi ch'io l'ebbi', from a sonnet attributed to Matteo di Meglio, a herald of the Florentine government, in 1452: D. A. Covi, 'The Inscription in Fifteenth Century Florentine Painting', Ph.D. thesis (New York, 1958), 164 n. 27, 467 no. 164; Giuseppe De Logu and Guido Marinelli, *Il Ritratto nella Pittura Italiana* (Bergamo, 1975), i. 172–5, with a usefully large illustration. The frame bears another inscription, SPECIOSVS FORMA PRE FILIIS HOMINVM. The suggestion by Cornelius von Fabriczy, 'Andrea del Verrocchio ai servizi de' Medici', *Archivio storico dell'arte*, 2nd ser., 1 (1895), 171, and others that this is the Verrocchio portrait of Lucrezia Donati (see n. 136), usually rejected on stylistic grounds, is not strengthened by the use of non-Medicean poetry.

FIG. 11.3 Master of S. Spirito, *Portrait of a Woman*, Staatliche Museen, Berlin

reference to a biblical incident where the risen Christ declared to the Magdalen, 'do not touch me'.[78] If the lines refer to a past affair, a husband or father declares anew his protective ownership of the woman, or the woman herself constructs an upright self-presentation. It could even be an ironic departing gift from the woman to her lover, declaring her honour yet forever continuing to tempt him with the image of an adored body, or a gift from him eternally recording honourable devotion. Depending on who is thought to speak the lines, to whom, and the voices may vary between the reverse and obverse, different possible allusions are made. The inscriptions and the painting itself offer a teasing, ambiguous attitude towards the past and the present.

The woman's piety is avowed, yet the desire for tactile contact is also affirmed. God's will is acknowledged on the reverse, but so too is the woman's own desire. Obedient and fatalistic, the speaker notes the desire for the attainment of honour and reputation, yet that state was balanced against the mourning for lost love. The agonies of a double standard, of the tension between desirous infamy and necessary chastity, between the wistful longing for love and the longing for burdensome vigilance, catch a feminine body between the terms of poetic sensuality and abstraction.[79] The proscription not to touch or imaginatively envisage flesh is subtly countered by the painting's surface. A dark green undergarment is visible beneath her cream bodice only at the laced opening; beneath this cream gown, lines of another undergarment plunge from either shoulder down to her waist forming a large v, echoed by the wedge of a chain which disappears into her bodice, its pendant elusively hidden. The layers of costume closer to her flesh are thus subtly marked and the alluring presence of forbidden regions is announced.

---

[78] Robert M. Durling (ed. and tr.), *Petrarch's Lyric Poems. The 'Rime sparse' and Other Lyrics* (Cambridge, Mass., 1976), no. 190, has the beloved in the figure of a doe wearing a collar inscribed 'Nessum mi tocchi' which refers to Solinus's report that stags wore collars declaring 'Do not touch me, I am Caesar's'. The Florentine poet Altissimo, in verses on ideal feminine beauty first pub. in Venice in 1525, described the woman's marmoreal throat and then, descending, he spied an inscription written by Artemis: 'nella parte sezza | pende umbre ch'in sen si vede frangere | scritto di Delia son, noli me tangere': *Opere dell'Altissimo poeta fiorentino* (Florence, 1572), 3ᵛ.

[79] For the 'penitence and remorse' felt by Lucrezia Donati, or the seclusion sought by Ginevra de' Benci, each objects of love in Laurentian circles, see Charles Dempsey, *The Portrayal of Love: Botticelli's 'Primavera' and Humanist Culture at the Time of Lorenzo the Magnificent* (Princeton, NJ, 1992), 91–7, 104–9; Walker, '*Ginevra de' Benci*', 5–6, 38.

Some female representations have been termed 'love portraits' because the usually anonymous woman portrayed is judged to be adored by a man assumed to be the patron.[80] If we define carefully the sense of 'love', so that the term does not become a romantic overlay of Platonic respectability, it may prove useful. It could acknowledge the discursive construction of femininity, as well as the homosocial bonding between men played out via a female body, and also the courtly play of heterosexual flirtation, alongside the illicitness of non-marital relations in a society where arranged marriages predominated and where adultery was a key fantasy in stories written by Boccaccio and numerous other authors. The long-recognized category of the 'courtesan portrait' has too often been conflated with the 'ideal portrait', as though the arousal of sensuality is visually embodied only when the model's profession overtly allows it or when an idealization excuses sexual fantasy. Another naturalizing assumption at work is the idea that ideal femininity is always a matter of heterosexual desirability for a male viewer. Future thinking could work at dismantling old prejudices and at forming a more rigorous historical contextualization of the purposes and effects of such images. Some of these, for instance, may have been marketed as genre-like records of a typical courtesan, using a prostitute or other available model on which to build an evocative painting for a fantasizing clientele. This possibility may be realized in the cases of painted 'beauties' which were collected in groups. Gathered because the depicted femininities were representative, exceptional, exotic, or some combination of such values, the world of imagined femininity thus formed was an archive that reflected on the objects' owner. He was a virile man at the world's centre, an aesthete of flesh and fine painting, a man of substance and dominion over all he surveyed in his gallery, a stylish bureaucrat extending his orderliness and epistemological control to these objects, a tourist-at-home who collected souvenirs of places he had not necessarily visited.

A collecting mentality could apply to a single image of a 'beauty'. Titian's *La Bella* (FIG. 11.4) is routinely cited as an instance of a woman's image severed from a connection with portraiture by virtue of a letter of 1536 from its first owner, Francesco della Rovere, referring to 'that portrait of that lady in the blue dress'.[81] The woman

---

[80] Hirst, *Sebastiano del Piombo*, 95, and Rylands, *Palma Vecchio*, 92–3, for example, employ the category.

[81] 'direte al Titiano ... che quel'retratto di quella Donna che ha la veste azura,

FIG. 11.4 Titian, *La Bella*, Palazzo Pitti, Florence

desideriamo che la finisca bella circa il Tutto et con il Timpano': Pope-Hennessy, *Portrait in the Renaissance*, 144; Cropper, 'The Beauty of Woman', 179, with an acute survey of past interpretations; Hirst, *Sebastiano*, 93; Hope, *Titian*, 82. Further references are in *Tiziano nelle Gallerie fiorentine*, 110–15, which refers to a letter of 1536 in which the Duke again requests the finishing of 'il quadro di quella donna'.

may have posed in the nude for other paintings by Titian, so her ubiquity and Francesco's disinterest in naming her makes *La Bella* 'not a true portrait but a painting of a professional model' in one assessment, or in others a case of an idealized, even 'mildly erotic', image.[82] These judgements, however, apply a restrictive notion of portraiture, one the Duke of Urbino ignored when he called it a *ritratto*, and fail to distinguish between the sitter and the painting. Describing an image he'd probably not seen, the Duke awaited an object in which the painting of the costume was as important as the face.[83] Both were represented as the finest that money could acquire and present the appearance of traditional portraits.[84]

To work effectively as a desirable object, the painting had to appear to record substantial materiality. Recognition and personal knowledge of the sitter were not necessarily important, but a sense that the woman *did* exist (she was 'quella Donna', not a generic woman), that the painting implies a naturalistic referent, probably was important. Like many pin-ups, the fantasy of power and arousal depended on the imaged figure being both anonymous *and* plausible. Representations of women acted as metaphors as well as instances of specific embodiment, and the areas overlapped since femininity stood for the general idea of physicality. A model from vernacular poetry, which began by reference to a specific woman and spun from there grand fantasies about aesthetic issues, offered authentication to a viewer's delight in images of unnamed yet existing women. So too a Neoplatonic concept of hierarchical beauty gave a rationale for the appreciation of such a portrayal. At the very court of Urbino, Castiglione's *Courtier* placed an explanation for this in Pietro Bembo's hands: 'he will no longer contemplate the particular beauty of one woman, but that universal beauty which adorns all bodies ... so in the highest stage of perfection beauty guides [the soul] from

[82] The first quotation is from the caption in Campbell, *Renaissance Portraits*, pl. 12, the latter from Hope, *Titian*, 82. Roberto Zapperi, 'Alessandro Farnese, Giovanni della Casa and Titian's *Danae* in Naples', *Journal of the Warburg and Courtauld Institutes*, 54 (1991), 168, argues that it is 'undoubtedly a portrait of a courtesan'.

[83] In the next decade, a portrait of Giulia Varano commissioned from Titian by the same court required that her costume be sent to the artist in Venice: *Tiziano nelle Gallerie fiorentine*, 144–8. Campbell, *Portraits*, 182, gives other examples where costume was painted separately.

[84] In her justifiably critical review of Lynne Lawner, *Lives of the Courtesans* (New York, 1987), Rona Goffen (*Renaissance Quarterly*, 41 [1988], 503) asks 'how is one to think of such images as Titian's *La Bella* ... whose garments are formal, whose hair is properly dressed, whose demeanour is dignified?'

the particular intellect to the universal intellect.'[85] What might be termed 'anonymous referentiality' enabled idealization to act in concert with specification rather than in opposition to it. Given the application of anxiety and fantasy to female figures during the Renaissance, the standards of portrait-like reference for images of women were more lax than they were for men. That Titian's *La Bella* is a 'portrait' of a kind of model made it no less a 'ritratto' in the eyes of its owner.

We do not yet have the language to discuss the differences and relationships among various categories of portrayal. The 'portrait' meeting a strict, modernist definition of the genre was accompanied by a range of images which are not so readily accepted now, such as an allegorical portrait; a genre scene containing a figure whose face was part of the reportage; an intentionally erotic representation; a portrait-in-guise; an image informed by the use of a model; and the image, which probably predominated, combining some or all of these. Our modern categories were not always shared by the Renaissance. Firenzuola's treatise *On the Beauty of Women*, finished in 1541, describes a woman's 'charm' (*vaghezza*) in a way that may sound contradictory, for he combined elements that modernism holds apart. To him, charm was 'a beauty that attracts and sparks the desire to contemplate it and enjoy it . . . we speak of a woman who has a certain sensual air [*un certo lascivetto*] and a certain desirability, mingled with virtue [*onestà*]'.[86] The text allocated this quality of sensual virtue to specific members of his cast, so that it was discursively attachable to living women. In a more intimate medium, Sigismondo della Stufa's letter to Lorenzo de' Medici in 1466 about the latter's *inamorata* Lucrezia Donati, employed a similar sense of allurement alongside virtue. Fresh from confession, the penitent woman had 'no fire at all, such that you never saw a thing so beautiful, with her black clothing and her head veiled, with such soft steps . . . I do not want to go on saying more, lest you fall into sin in these holy days'.[87] Between two men, a joking reference to the sensually arousing image of pious chastity crosses over the boundaries expected by modernist values. Difficulties in locating images of

[85] Castiglione, *The Book of the Courtier*, 352, 354; see Finucci, *The Lady Vanishes*, 70–2.

[86] Agnolo Firenzuola, *Opere*, ed. Adriano Seroni (Florence, 1958), 564; Konrad Eisenbichler and Jacqueline Murray (eds. and trs.), *On the Beauty of Women* (Philadelphia, 1992), 36–7.

[87] Dempsey, *The Portrayal of Love*, 98.

women often arise from modern linguistic limitations and romanti-
cizing or moralizing blinders, but the very imprecision or ambiguity
called forth by many images of women may be the heart of their
attraction for Renaissance viewers.

The distinction between the idealized woman and the eroticized
courtesan is especially blurred in Venetian images of women.
Fifteenth-century portraits of Venetian women are relatively rare and
if the collections viewed by Marcantonio Michiel in the 1520s and
1530s contained many female portraits, they were not usually
deemed to be of sufficient aesthetic, monetary, or social interest, so
were not listed.[88] Inventories throughout Italy, not only in Venice,
frequently identify paintings as heads of men or women rather than
as named portraits.[89] In a 1492 Medici inventory, for instance, we
find 'a head of a woman' behind a cover.[90] Yet by the sixteenth century, Venetian documents indicate a high preponderance of anonymous female 'portraits'. The presence of objects named as portraits,
but of unspecified women, suggests that anonymous referentiality
was to the fore. In the Contarini collection, for example, Michiel
listed not only a profile portrait of a foreigner, Emperor
Maximilian's wife, but also two images of unidentified women. 'A
panel of the woman portrayed from life' was by Giovanni Bellini,
and a painting of 'three women portrayed from life' was given to
Palma Vecchio.[91] Judged as portraits *al naturale*, yet with unnamed

[88] Rylands, *Palma Vecchio*, 93, 108 n. 23. The exceptions indicate what kind of
renown brought a woman's portrait to notice: there were four cases of international
princesses, a nun from Santo Secondo in the same frame as a named man, noted for
its precious packaging and perfection, an anonymous wife accompanied by her
unknown husband in a Flemish pendant, and the special case of the Bembo version
of Petrarch's Laura.

[89] Thornton, *Italian Renaissance Interior*, 265; John Kent Lydecker, 'The domestic
setting of the arts in Renaissance Florence', Ph.D. thesis (Johns Hopkins University,
1987), 67.

[90] Hellmut Wohl, *The Paintings of Domenico Veneziano ca. 1410–1461* (Oxford,
1980), 196, 350, for 'una tresta di una dama'. The language used by the documents in
Lydecker differs according to function, date, clerk, or other writer, and clear patterns
are not apparent. 'Testa', with or without a name following, is often used when a portrait seems indicated (such as, 'the head of a man in a red hat', 230). Of ten portraits
of named people raised in Lydecker's documents, the men are described with a word
like 'figura', 'testa' or 'impronta' rather than 'ritratto', and four are women. One is
'Mona Casandra ritrata al naturale', a grandmother known to the clerks, a second
case concerned a husband and wife pair of 'teste di terra cotta ritratte', and the last
two instances were each a 'testa e busto' of named women in the Tornabuoni household (63, 66–7).

[91] George C. Williamson (ed.), *The Anonimo: Notes on Pictures and Works of Art
in Italy Made by an Anonymous Writer in the Sixteenth Century* (London, 1903) (repr.

sitters, the latter two objects might each be 'a picture of which the subject is a woman' rather than traditional portraits.[92] Perhaps Michiel's judgement that they were portraits should be retained, and we could call them 'portrayals of examples of femininity' rather than portraits of distinct entities. A third category in Michiel's notes is closer to a generic kind of head that may be identified now as genre painting. In various collections he saw both male and female heads which were labelled, according to their attributes or actions, by their class, profession, or representativeness. So various male heads by Giorgione were called something like 'the head of a young man holding an arrow', or 'the head of the young shepherd holding a fruit', or a 'soldier, armed, but without his helmet'.[93]

Several paintings by Palma have similarly vague descriptions. In Andrea Odoni's bedroom, along with his portrait by Lotto and a bedhead with Savoldo's reclining female nude, there was a painting with 'two half-length figures of a girl and an old woman behind her', probably showing a procuress directing her charge.[94] Girolamo Marcello possessed 'a canvas of a woman waist-length, who holds in her right hand a lute and has her left hand under her head'.[95] A third painting, described as 'a nymph', may be Palma's full-length reclining nude in Dresden, the erotic suggestiveness of which is increased by having her chemise beside her as though she has just undressed.[96] None of these instances was associated with portraiture by Michiel, yet each resembles paintings sometimes thought to be portraits. Rylands argues that the descriptions of the Bellini and Palma 'portraits' are no different from, say, that given to the Lutanist, but there seem to be two important shifts: the latter examples are given no kind of attachment to portraiture or naturalism, and they are instead described by various actions or pictorial associations.[97] With regard

New York, 1969), 103; Rona Goffen, *Giovanni Bellini* (New Haven, Conn., 1989), 317 n. 10 ('el quadretto della donna retratta al naturale'); Rylands, *Palma Vecchio*, 341 ('3 donne retratte dal naturale').

[92] Goffen, *Giovanni Bellini*, 196. Hirst, *Sebastiano del Piombo*, 93, earlier suggested the category 'paintings of people'.

[93] Williamson, *Anonimo*, 93, 114, 121. The Palma inventory includes a 'testa' rather than portrait of a shepherd, the only male secular object so classified (Rylands, *Palma Vecchio*, 350 no. 15).

[94] Williamson, *Anonimo*, 99; Rylands, *Palma*, 341, see also 19, 107 n. 6, 298, 318.

[95] Adjusted from Williamson, *Anonimo*, 106; Rylands, *Palma*, 341, see also 19, 93, 100–1, 183–4, 318.

[96] Williamson, *Anonimo*, 111; Rylands, *Palma*, 341, also 19, 21, 89, 102, 184–5.

[97] Rylands, *Palma*, 93.

to women, Michiel distinguishes three categories: first, portraits of notable women or women accompanying men; second, pictures of women 'portrayed'; third, heads of women who appear in semi-genre or erotic scenes.

A similar typology is employed by whoever drew up the inventory of Palma's studio in 1529. Every male head is a 'ritratto', whether named or simply recognized as a priest, a pauper, or a Cypriot. In this sample, masculinity was coded as worldly, public, and representative. Of the eight paintings with secular female subjects, only one sitter is so identified—'1 retrato de la carampana'—that is, by reference to a district set aside for prostitution (FIG. 11.5).[98] But the seven others are not all alike. One sketch merely represented 'una donna' without any indication of portrayal or action.[99] Two others, like the local prostitute, are said to be 'uno retrato de una dona'.[100] Only two are noted as nude, one 'una nuda', the other 'una nuda retrata', and both are large so they may be reclining nudes.[101] The last two *ritratti* are described in Michiel's manner, with the participle rather than the noun: 'una dona retrata', a woman portrayed.[102] So one painting was an indefinite sketch, one was a portrait of a prostitute in a green dress with hair falling on her shoulders, two were portraits of women (displayed with items such as an apple, a red dress, plaited hair, or a hand on her breast), two were nudes (one of which was 'portrayed'), and two were of 'portrayed' women (one in poor condition so little else is indicated, the other figure held her hair in her hand). The various attributes, actions of toilette and so on, when described at all, would fit many images thought to be anonymous 'courtesan portraits', so it is difficult to see what the clerk had in mind when distinguishing, for instance, between a 'nude woman' and a 'portrayed nude woman'. Nevertheless, the linguistic distinctions employed by the scribe and by Michiel suggest that early sixteenth-century Venetians envisaged portraiture as a range of options, rather than as a singular category.

Many modern writers instead make virtually every image of a

---

[98] Rylands, *Palma*, 89, 350 no. 23. Described as an unfinished painting, with a figure dressed in green whose hair falls onto her shoulders, it may resemble Palma's *Woman in Green* in Vienna, which Rylands, however, dates to 1512–14 (152).

[99] Ibid. 26, 350 no. 40.   [100] Ibid. 350 nos. 3, 13.

[101] Ibid. 27, 350 nos. 12, 22.

[102] Ibid. 350, nos. 17, 20. Only one male head is 'portrayed', and this is as an explanatory phrase describing a painting of the Virgin in which the owner is 'portrayed' as the donor with saints, 'et lui retrato con doi sante' (no. 19).

Fɪɢ. 11.5 Palma Vecchio, *Woman in Green*, Kunsthistorisches Museum, Vienna

woman either an ideal portrait or, when there is any hint of sensuality, a courtesan's portrait.[103] A dichotomy between respectability
and sensuality, however, does not adequately comprehend the courtesan's experience. Advancement depended upon both physical allure
and the attainment of various skills such as music and poetry, akin
to those of the court lady and mistress. They negotiated with words
and images in what the courtesan poet Veronica Franco called 'the
theatre of public competition'.[104] Aretino gave the courtesan Angela
Zaffetta a backhanded compliment when he recognized the skills
required: 'you have known how to put a mask of decency on the face
of lust, procuring through wisdom and discretion both possessions
and praise.'[105] Variations depending upon audience, artist, and so on
are likely to characterize the 'courtesan portrait' which cannot be
reduced to one standard 'mask'. The relatively new phenomenon of
the courtesan stimulated a range of responses.

Men of rank in the Venetian State tried to regulate women's costume so that a clear distinction would visibly mark out courtesans
and prostitutes from the women of their own class. They addressed
class and ethnic ambiguity, tried to distinguish between the streets
and less visible arenas, and even between genders when some courtesans donned items of masculine attire. As a decree put it in 1543,
the prostitutes 'publicly frequent the streets, churches, and other
places, adorned and dressed so handsomely that often our noblewomen and our citizens are dressed in much the same way', so that
both locals and foreigners could not tell 'the good from the bad' and
a 'most pernicious example' was set.[106] Extreme edges of a binary

---

[103] Examples of the latter tendency include: Ost, 'Tizians', 129–49; Lawner, *Lives
of the Courtesans, passim*; *Gioco dell'Amore*, 81 ff., 111; Hope, *Titian*, 62, 82. Carol
M. Schuler, 'The Courtesan in Art: Historical Fact or Modern Fantasy?', *Women's
Studies*, 19 (1991), 209–22, points out problems in the moralizing historiography.

[104] Margaret F. Rosenthal, *The Honest Courtesan: Veronica Franco, Citizen and
Writer in Sixteenth-Century Venice* (Chicago, 1992), 87.

[105] Pietro Aretino, *Lettere*, ed. Francesco Flora (Verona, 1960), 367, 'la mascara de
l'onesta'; tr. George Bull as *Selected Letters* (Harmondsworth, 1976), 149. For the possibility that a Roman courtesan named Angela was given the mask of respectability
when she was portrayed in 'the guise of a gentlewoman' by Titian, see Zapperi,
'Alessandro Farnese', 163, 166 ff.

[106] Rosenthal, *The Honest Courtesan*, 59–60, see also 5–6, 68–72; David Chambers
and Brian Pullan with Jennifer Fletcher (eds.), *Venice: A Documentary History*
(Cambridge, Mass., 1992), 7, 123–7, 178–80. Casola reported in 1494 that Venetian
women 'dress very splendidly' and 'try as much as possible in public to show their
chests—I mean the breasts and shoulder—so much so, that . . . I marvelled that their
clothes did not fall off their backs': M. Margaret Newett, *Canon Pietro Casola's
Pilgrimage to Jerusalem In the Year 1494* (Manchester, 1907), 144–5, 340.

were blurring into a spectrum of confusing possibilities. Courtesans mimicked the costume of noblewomen, no matter what the laws attempted to forbid, and a similar ambiguity is evident in paintings like Titian's *La Bella* (FIG. 11.4) and Parmigianino's *Antea*, where demeanour and dress are indistinguishable from that of upper-class women. That a painting of a woman richly attired amidst sumptuous surroundings is necessarily a representation of a courtesan is thus flawed. Franco's promotion of herself constructed 'an elegant self-portrait, unconcerned with sexual pleasure and financial profit'.[107] So 'respectable' portraits of courtesans wishing to appear *oneste* may exist as traces of complex mediations by sitter, patron, and artist, with each person concerned about self-construction and advertisement. Similarly, some 'courtesan portraits' may be of wealthy women who are bedecked in finery and sensually beautiful, in line with the predominant ideology of ideal femininity. Between the 'portrait', the 'portrayed', and the 'non-portrait', the representation of female bodies occurred along a continuum. Most images leave us guessing, and this game of puzzlement and slippage may be one of their most affective, because elusive, strategies.

There are documented reasons for thinking that enticing female images were sometimes informed by a portrait-like reference, or had a resemblance factor. Palma's 'retrato' of a prostitute is one case. We know that courtesans themselves owned or commissioned portraits. Franco, for example, applied the standard format of a frontispiece portrait to her *Terze Rime* dated 1576.[108] Sometime before 1580 she also received Tintoretto's portrait of her.[109] She praised his diabolical ability to conjure a bewitching vision of her, by claiming that for a while she was not sure if the portrait was 'a painting or a ghost' (*pittura o pur fantasima*). Resisting the temptation to 'fall in love with myself', she made the portrait's hallucinatory effect redound on her own self-portraying and seducing skills. From the inventory of the courtesan Giulia Lombardo, drawn up in 1569, we know that courtesans displayed images of naked women in their bedrooms and parlours, doubtless to incite anticipation in male clients.[110] Such

---

[107] Rosenthal, *Honest Courtesan*, 111.   [108] Ibid. 51–3, 277 n. 107.

[109] Ibid. 247–8, 313 n. 32, 347 n. 93; Ann Rosalind Jones, *The Currency of Eros: Women's Love Lyric in Europe, 1540–1620* (Bloomington, Ill., 1990), 182–4; Lawner, *Lives of the Courtesans*, 57–9, 102, 200, 205 n. 12; *European Paintings in the Collection of the Worcester Art Museum* (Worcester, 1974), 480–2.

[110] Cathy Santore, 'Julia Lombardo, "Somtuosa Meretrize": A Portrait by Property', *Renaissance Quarterly*, 41 (1988), *passim*.

paintings and portraits could be outright commissions from the women or gifts from male clients. Portrayals of beautiful women could be given by courtesans, mistresses, and noblewomen to their admirers, or they could pass from one man to another. Raphael's production in 1518 of a portrait of the famed beauty Joanna of Aragon, for instance, was commissioned by Cardinal Bibbiena as a diplomatic gift to be sent to the King of France.[111] The practice of collecting images of beautiful women, whether as tourist souvenirs, signs of possessive masculinity, or marks of cultivation, could be adopted by courtesans as part of their self-promotion. When Henri III visited Venice in 1574, Franco presented this special tourist with two sonnets and her miniature portrait, later writing about the gift in a way that made it both a civic diplomatic gesture and a sign of her own learned stature and economic independence.[112] In another genre of tourism, the book of customs, Franco appeared in the *Mores Italiae* of 1575, with carefully-coiffed hair but otherwise naked, in what may be an entirely fanciful body map of her charms, accompanying other scenes of courtesanal seduction and views of the city.[113] Whether gifts, advertisements, or documentations, 'portraits' or 'portrayals' of famous, seductive women circulated through Europe. Their currency depended upon the appearance of what I have called anonymous referentiality, an understanding, in a visual and marketing sense, that the images reported particular, localized women.

Visual clues, no longer decipherable because they depended on ephemeral puns and lore, may mark some images as specific portraits. In a case like Palma's *La Bella*, an inscription might partially record the woman's name and indicate its dedication by an admirer.[114] Objects surrounding the women, such as an apple or certain clothing, may allude to professional nicknames.[115] The use of names and mythological guise enabled women to advertise their intellectual attractions. Franco named her sons Achille and Enea, and

---

[111] Roger Jones and Nicholas Penny, *Raphael* (New Haven, Conn., 1983), 163; Rogers, 'Decorum of Women's Beauty', p. 59 n. 46.

[112] Rosenthal, *Honest Courtesan*, 102–11; Jones, *Currency of Eros*, 180–2.

[113] Selections from this album in the Beinecke Rare Book and Manuscript Library, Yale University, including the Franco page, appear in several unnumbered figures in Rosenthal, *Honest Courtesan*, after 152 and Lawner, *Lives*, 69, with the Franco watercolour mentioned on 58.

[114] Rylands, *Palma*, 95–6, 186–7.   [115] Ibid. 92.

her poetry played with other proper names including her own.[116] Levels of play and wit, including some degree of mockery, could be embodied in the portraits. Noblewomen were urged to model themselves on saints or chaste exemplars like Lucretia, so their portraits could cast them in various roles, and prostitutes too could be exhorted to reform like the Magdalen. A somewhat ironic reference to Christian and classical exemplars may, for instance, imbue certain images of the Magdalen or Lucretia which could have been modelled on a courtesan's features or be portraits-in-guise.[117] Ambiguous characters like Danae, chastely enclosed yet physically penetrated by Jupiter, were adapted to depictions of sumptuous sensuality.[118] Titian's *Danae* in Naples, painted around 1545, was given the features of a favourite courtesan, Angela, for the secretive and voyeuristic delight of its patron and her client Cardinal Alessandro Farnese.[119] He kept the painting in his *camera propria* where he could fantasize about himself as the seducer and virile god.[120]

The visual, poetic conventions of portraits made in the manner of Petrarch's mistress were adapted to the sophisticated portrayal of a possibly cross-dressed courtesan in Giorgione's innovative *Laura* of 1506.[121] A painting dated around the same year, Bartolomeo Veneto's *Flora* (FIG. 11.6), may be more a literal, but at its time daring, cross-over between portraiture, allegory, sensuality, and visual poetics. Panofsky identified the subject as 'a young bride in the guise

---

[116] Rosenthal, *Honest Courtesan*, 80, 229, and *passim*.

[117] Lawner, *Lives*, 139, 167 f., 176 f.; *Gioco dell'Amore*, 88, 90.

[118] Zapperi, 'Alessandro Farnese', 159–71, with earlier references; Cathy Santore, 'Danae: The Renaissance Courtesan's Alter Ego', *Zeitschrift für Kunstgeschichte*, 54 (1991), 412–27. On courtesans' usage of the Danae myth or name see Lawner, *Lives*, 81, 82, 158, 151–9; Rosenthal, *Honest Courtesan*, 107–9, 247.

[119] Zapperi, 'Alessandro Farnese', 159–71. For the more general use of unnamed sexual professionals as nude models see, for example, Alfonso d'Este's agent's report to him in 1522 that Titian was using 'whores' as models for his *Bacchus and Ariadne*: Dana Goodgal, 'The Camerino of Alfonso I d'Este', *Art History*, 1 (1978), 177. In such cases, anonymous referentiality to prostitutes could still be titillating.

[120] Aretino appealed to a similar desire for divine aggrandizement when he invited a friend to Venice so that he could be 'moved by our assembly of goddesses, and come to enjoy the enchantments of their presence if you want your old age to grow green again': *Selected Letters*, 215.

[121] On Giorgione's *Laura*, 'taken to be a portrait of a poetess, part of a marriage or betrothal diptych or an idealized representation of Petrarch's Laura' (Campbell, *Portraits*, 6), see now Anne Christine Junkerman, 'The Lady and the Laurel: Gender and Meaning in Giorgione's *Laura*', *Oxford Art Journal*, 16/1 (1993), 49–58, which mounts a sensitive argument for its classification as a portrait of a courtesan, who was perhaps a poet too.

FIG. 11.6 Bartolomeo Veneto, *Flora*, Staedel Institute, Frankfurt am Main

of Flora . . . the happy wife of Zephyr'; while at the opposite extreme Huysmans called the image 'this implacable androgyne' and identified it as a portrait of Giulia Farnese, mistress to Pope Alexander VI.[122] Others call it a portrait of that pope's daughter Lucrezia

---

[122] Erwin Panofsky, *Problems in Titian, Mostly Iconographic* (New York, 1969), 137–8, pl. 149; independently proposed also by Egon Verheyen, 'Der Sinngehalt von Giorgiones *Laura*', *Pantheon*, 26 (1968), 223. Huysmans is quoted in Georg

Borgia, or a straightforward representation of Flora, of a courtesan, or some sort of emblematic portrait, or a representation of poetry itself.[123] New bride or newly-fertile wife, seductive noblewoman, or allegorized courtesan, the painting's subject is somewhere clustered around a conjunction of portrayed referentiality and classical allusion. *Flora* images may be portraits of specific courtesans, but they are also mythologized guises, suggesting the sitter's learning and garbing heterosexual masculine desire in such sophistication also. Both individualization and idealization at work in such paintings are sexualized strategies. The play between various indeterminates (portraiture, allegory, idealization, even sexual identity) is erotically heightened by a play between clothing and skin, between sitter's gaze and viewer's response.

The resort to classical garb and learned allusion is not restricted to courtesans alone, nor only to pictures of women. A number of heads, often identified as portraits, indicate that the practice and its pretensions were made use of by other Renaissance people anxious to assert their status.[124] Presented *all'antica* with the connotations of erudition, prestige, and commemoration of the dead, or more generally with the nostalgic aura surrounding the spreading enthusiasm for pseudo-classical dignity, the male examples predominate. Appearing in the north Italian examples only as pendants to young men, women are dressed in nymph-like scraps, although in two

Swarzenski, 'Bartolomeo Veneto und Lucrezia Borgia', *Städel-Jahrbuch*, 2 (1922), 64–5. A painting of a woman with a bared breast and pseudo-classical garb, currently attributed to Catena and dated around 1505–10, should also be considered in the context of portrayal and female nudity early in the 16th c.: Brown and Oberhuber, 'Leonardo and Raphael', 68 n. 61.

[123] Swarzenski, 'Bartolomeo Veneto', 63–72, dating the picture to the time when the artist worked for Lucrezia Borgia at Ferrara in 1505–7; Lawner, *Lives*, 80; Pope-Hennessy, *Portrait in the Renaissance*, 226; Pozzi, 'Il ritratto', 23–4; Cropper, 'Beauty of Woman', 183.

[124] In rough chronological order, north Italian examples include: a *Portrait of a Poet* with a wreath and classical tunic showing one shoulder bare, attributed to Giovanni Bellini's shop, and a less naked figure without a wreath in a *Portrait of a Humanist*, each dated around 1475–80 (Goffen, *Bellini*, 191–2); Mantegna's *Self-Portrait* relief bust in his Mantuan tomb monument; Tullio Lombardo's *Double Portrait* marble relief in Venice, dated to the early 1490s, and his later relief sometimes called *Bacchus and Ariadne* in Vienna (Alison Luchs, 'Tullio Lombardo's Ca' d'Oro Relief: A Self-Portrait with the Artist's Wife?', *Art Bulletin*, 71 (June 1989), 230–6; Martineau and Hope, *Genius of Venice*, 365–7); a bronze bust in the Museo Civico Correr, variously attributed to Riccio or Rizzo, where the youth's tunic slips off one shoulder; Palma's *Bust of a Man* and *Bust of a Woman* in Budapest, dated around 1510–11 (Rylands, *Palma*, 95, 97, 148–9).

reliefs by Tullio Lombardo they show bare breasts. Filarete earlier condemned the practice of clothing portrait sitters in 'the antique fashion' on the grounds that it misrepresents decorum, plausibility, and dignity.[125] Art historians, however, increasingly read these images of heroic youths as portraits. Costume details and bared flesh in these male portraits less often give rise to discussion of allegorical or idealized portraiture, nor does the nudity often lead to comments on sexual identity or sensual appeal.

Whilst male nudity calls forth grand allusions to heroic activity, female nudity re-dresses a woman in a poetically remote, even transcendent, time. Depending on the audience for particular images of semi-naked women, the partly stripped body can function as a sign of mourning, idealization, intimacy, and an increasingly more visibly displayed interest in illicit contact and sensual arousal. The presence in Palma's studio of 'una nuda retrata' suggests that nudity in itself did not exclude connotations of portrayal, and Giorgione's *Laura* seems to be another Venetian instance of semi-nude portrayal, albeit in a Petrarchan more than antique mode. Treatises on ideal femininity pondered whether the clothed or naked body was more beautiful and the variable answers suggest that disrobing did not necessarily demean certain sitters in the eyes of their masculine viewers.[126] The scant clothing of only a chemise or undergarment, visible in paintings by artists like Titian or sculptors like Tullio, may refer to classical nymphs and theatrical festivities, but these rhetorical and ceremonial discourses each evoked sensual pleasure, as do the images.[127] Savonarola chose to typify indecorous young women in the streets and churches of Florence by the name 'nymph', but his very attack acknowledges an increasing attraction to pastoral fantasies.[128]

Three Florentine representations of women with bare breasts

[125] Filarete, *Treatise on Architecture*, tr. John R. Spencer (New Haven, Conn., 1965), i. 306: 'When you make a figure of a man who has lived in our own times, he should not be dressed in the antique fashion but as he was. What would it look like if you wanted to portray the Duke of Milan and dressed him in clothes that he did not wear? It would not look well and it would not look like him. . . . they should be done according to their quality and their nature'.

[126] Rogers, 'Decorum of Women's Beauty', 52 ff.

[127] For differing opinions on the nymph-like costume and its connotations see Held, 'Flora', and Emma Mellencamp, 'A Note on the Costume of Titian's *Flora*', *Art Bulletin*, 51 (1969), 174–7; Dempsey, *Portrayal of Love*, 65 ff., 123, 131.

[128] Gilbert, *Italian Art*, 157; Dempsey, *Portrayal of Love*, 113, 141, 'che paiono ninfe'.

foreshadow the later northern Italian images of semi-naked, classicized women referred to above. The earliest is a marble bust, attributed to the workshop of Bernardo Rossellino and dated 1440–5.[129] A classical garment slips down to reveal fully one breast, a gesture of startling nudity probably related to generic pseudo-classical busts rather than to portraiture, although such busts usually represented masculine figures. Another is a marble relief, currently attributed to the young Verrocchio and dated 1460–5, showing a woman in profile with her hair only loosely contained and her torso released from its billowing wraps.[130] The third is Piero di Cosimo's late fifteenth-century profile head of a naked woman richly bejewelled, with a snake around her neck, set off against a landscape background (FIG. 11.7).[131] The latter two instances of solitary women, publicly naked, in the profile format that usually suggested portraiture at the time for single panels with female heads, are early instances of the combination of idealization with portrait conventions, of classical allusion with female specificity.

The later inscription on the Piero di Cosimo painting, identifying it as a portrait of Simonetta Vespucci, has attracted attention but it is probably the image of Cleopatra seen by Vasari in Francesco da Sangallo's house. Cleopatra is constructed as a figure of luxury, ambition, and sensuality, in a warning yet alluring image.[132] Even if the figure does not signify this queen, her overt nudity, extravagant coiffure, excessive jewellery, patterned fabric, and general busyness of the decoration, as well as the foreboding atmosphere, make the painting a captivating, disturbing, erotic fantasy. No matter what narrative or moralizing justification existed for the painting, the nudity, and to a lesser extent the profile format, ally it with a sixteenth-century pattern of idealizing images of 'Woman' presented in

---

[129] John Pope-Hennessy, *Luca della Robbia* (Oxford, 1980), 272 and fig. 62.

[130] John Pope-Hennessy, *Catalogue of Italian Sculpture in the Victoria and Albert Museum* (London, 1964), i. 168–9; iii. fig. 64. For Florentine profile reliefs of women in pseudo-classical garb, but with less nudity, see, for example, the entry on a Mino da Fiesole work in Cornelius C. Vermeule, III, Walter Cahn, and Rollin Van N. Hadley, *Sculpture in the Isabella Stewart Gardner Museum* (Boston, 1977), 108–9.

[131] Giorgio Vasari, *Le vite de' più eccellenti pittori scultori ed architettori*, ed. Gaetano Milanesi (Florence, 1906), iv. 144; Sharon Fermor, *Piero di Cosimo: Fiction, Invention and 'Fantasia'* (London, 1993), 93–101. Poliziano's verses on Simonetta's early death may use an image recalled by Piero: 'he saw his nymph, enveloped in a sad cloud, cruelly taken from before his eyes'. The air seemed to turn dark': tr. David Quint, *The Stanze of Angelo Poliziano* (Amherst, Mass., 1979), ii. 33–4.

[132] For a sustained discussion of Cleopatra in relation to this image see Fermor, *Piero di Cosimo*, 96–100.

Fɪɢ. 11.7 Piero di Cosimo, '*Simonetta Vespucci*', Musée Condé, Chantilly

such media as maiolica and drawings. The decorative, static presentation of a woman behind a ledge and against a sky links the panel with earlier traditions of female portraiture. Like quattrocento portraits of women, this 'Cleopatra' is feminized by her status as ornamentation, as well as by her accoutrements and profile placement, as the object of a voyeuristic masculine gaze.[133] That eroticized viewing performance is enhanced or exaggerated by the painting's deliberate excess. Like the female beauties displayed on sixteenth-century maiolica plates, this creature is a depiction of an overtly sexualized female body, idealized on the one hand, but on the other, like Eve, a vehicle for a pedagogic point about the dangers of unbridled feminine lust.

Not strictly a portrait, and more than a heavy-handed didactic allegory, Piero di Cosimo's painting exists on the borders between various categories and is all the more appealing for that. It is like some portraits in its use of the profile, in its abundance of jewellery, in its allure and erotics of beauty, and it points to ways in which femininity was envisaged in portraiture, portrayal, and idealization. The bared essence of femininity is shown as ornamental, excessive, dangerous, mysterious, yet attractive and mesmerizing. To some later viewers, including those who added the inscription, such a representation of femininity was natural and they happily recognized a sufficient degree of individualization here to regard it as a depiction of one mythologized woman, Simonetta Vespucci, rather than a type.[134] The same process occurs in other cases where indefinite portrayal of, say, courtesans is readily described as straightforward portraiture: woman is naturalized as essentially sexual, and a concomitant romanticization further ingrains this easy idea.

The Verrocchio-like profile, currently dated earlier than the Piero di Cosimo, offers a figure similarly wrapped in garments which billow out at the breasts, but a simplification allows the marble to become its own luscious medium. The pared-down decoration and refined purity of form idealize a figure whose face is nevertheless

[133] Simons, 'Women in Frames'. For the Renaissance relationship between femininity and decoration see Donald Hedrick, 'The Ideology of Ornament: Alberti and the Erotics of Renaissance Urban Design', *Word and Image*, 3 (1987), 111–37; Patricia Reilly, 'Writing Out Colour in Renaissance Theory', *Genders*, 12 (1991), 77–99, repr. in Broude and Garrard, *The Expanding Discourse*.

[134] The inscription was probably added by the Vespucci who may have owned it by the 1580s and certainly by 1841: Elisabeth de Boissard and Valérie Lavergne-Durey, *Chantilly, musée Condé. Peintures de l'Ecole italienne* (Paris, 1988), 120.

more particularized, so that here too a Florentine object experiments with the boundary between various conventions. The sixteenth-century Venetian blurring of borders is not unique to that city, nor to that century.[135] Earlier aristocratic regimes, like the burgeoning court of fifteenth-century Medicean Florence, could also position the female body as the site of heterosexual masculine pleasure and as a surface to be inscribed by social values. Like the Venetian documents, Florentine records refer to female portraits in a manner which indicates a more composite comprehension of that genre. Amongst the works done for the Medici that were listed in 1496 by Verrocchio's heirs was 'uno quadro di legname drentovi la fighura della testa della Lucherezia de Donati', 'the figure of the head of Lucrezia Donati', one of Lorenzo de' Medici's mythopoetic mistresses.[136] Although a particular woman is named, the word 'portrait' is not used.

The most evident case of early Florentine portrait-like images filtered through idealizing conventions is a group of provocative female heads by Botticelli and his school traditionally associated with Simonetta Vespucci (FIG. 11.8).[137] Compared to Botticelli's portrait in the Pitti Palace of a domesticated, dutiful woman, images of 'Simonetta' represent a more buxom, sexual woman. Predecessors to Piero di Cosimo's image, Botticelli's paintings have similarly attracted romantic musings about Giuliano de' Medici's mistress.

---

[135] For just one instance of a 16th-c. courtesan image from Florence, see Vasari's description of a work by Domenico Puglio: 'Ritrasse anco in un quadro la Barbara Fiorentina, in quel tempo famosa, bellissima cortigiana, e molto amata da molti, non meno che per la bellezza, per le sue buone creanze, e particolarmente per essere bonissima musica e cantare divinamente': iv. 465. Various paintings produced outside Venice, by Bacchiacca, Raphael, Sebastiano del Piombo, and others, less often enter the debate.

[136] Fabriczy, 'Andrea del Verrocchio', 167, 171. On Donati see Dempsey, *Portrayal of Love, passim*. The 1492 inventory of Medici possessions included a portrait in another medium, 'una testa di marmo sopra l'archo dell'uscio di chamera ritratto al naturale mona Lucretia', which may refer to an unidentified marble bust of the Donati woman, or of Lucrezia Tornabuoni, Lorenzo's mother: G. Passavant, *Verrocchio. Sculptures, Paintings, and Drawings* (London, 1969), 180. Suggested painted portraits of Lucrezia Donati include a profile panel in Detroit (Piero Adorno, *Verrocchio. Nuove proposte nella civiltà artistica del tempo di Lorenzo Il Magnifico* (Florence, 1991), 143–4, fig. 90), and the 'Noli me tangere' example discussed earlier.

[137] Ronald Lightbown, *Sandro Botticelli. Complete Catalogue* (London, 1978), ii. 116–19, 154–5, 168–9, with further references; Aby Warburg, *La rinascita del paganesimo antico*, ed. Gertrud Bing (Florence, 1966); Dempsey, *Portrayal*, 131–5; Monika Schmitter, 'The Case of the Portraits of Simonetta Vespucci: Images of Women Between Portrait and Ideal', M.A. thesis (University of Michigan, 1991).

FIG. 11.8 Sandro Botticelli, '*Portrait of a Woman*', Staatliche Museen, Berlin

Vasari did later record a profile portrait of Giuliano's unnamed 'innamorata' in the Medici collection.[138] The married woman Simonetta Vespucci, whose favour was won by the victorious Giuliano in a joust in 1475, died less than a year later, giving rise to poetry by Poliziano and others including Lorenzo de' Medici, who

[138] Vasari, *Le vite*, iii. 322.

chose his brother's beloved as an object for his own contempla-
tion.[139] The provenance of the Berlin painting from the Palazzo
Medici, and the Medici carnelian of Apollo and Marsyas she wears
in the Frankfurt example, give credence to origin in a Medici context. There is little other evidence that the images posthumously refer
in a strict, individualized manner, to the empirical Simonetta.[140] Her
untimely death, two years to the day before Giuliano's assassination,
made her a safely remote object for a process of poetic idealization,
political memorialization, and sensual fantasy in Lorenzo's circle.
Graven on his heart, this poetic portrait of perfect adoration preserved in Lorenzo's words 'the sweetest accidents both of my lady's
face and name' so his heart 'desired to keep it within itself and so
conserve it forever'.[141] The Albertian idea that painting forever com-
memorates a dead person is here put to the use of focusing on the
masculine poet's possessive, creative powers. Upon her death,
Simonetta's beauty 'appeared perhaps greater than ever it had in life',
wrote Lorenzo, who mourned through her the loss of his brother and
the loss of his own younger self, transforming absence into a regen-
erative creation through the medium of a woman's body.[142] The particular death of a woman is converted into poetic self-display to
function as a cultural myth of masculine genius and power.[143]

The 'Simonetta' images anticipate the *Flora* or *Laura* type in that
the conventions of decorous portraiture are overlaid by elements of
poetic reverie and sexual fantasy. Whereas the Pitti woman is in
strict profile, the Berlin head is slightly turned, with the whole body
closer to the viewer and more of the bare chest visible, including the

---

[139] Dempsey, *Portrayal*, chs. 3–4; Neri, 'La Simonetta', 131–47.

[140] A letter from her father-in-law Piero Vespucci to Lorenzo de' Medici's mother
Lucrezia Tornabuoni, dated 12 January 1480 may, however, document a particular
commemoration of her by the Medici (*ASF*, MAP, 88, 247). An unclear passage cor-
rupted by damage recalls that Piero and Marco tried to console Giuliano de' Medici
on Simonetta's death, then may suggest that Piero sent some of her clothes to the
Medici, and he seems to write of 'sua inmagine' also. An overconfident translation of
the relevant section was published in Germán Arciniegas, *Amerigo and the New
World*, tr. Harriet de Onís (New York, 1955), 56. I am grateful to Gino Corti and
F. W. Kent for their assistance and caution regarding this difficult passage, and to
Monika Schmitter for bringing its publication to my attention.

[141] Dempsey, *Portrayal*, 139.

[142] Ibid. 125, see also 117–18. For a more political reading of Lorenzo's writings,
see William J. Kennedy, 'Petrarchan Figurations of Death in Lorenzo de' Medici's
Sonnets and *Comento*', in Marcel Tetel, Ronald G. Witt, and Rona Goffen (eds.), *Life
and Death in Fifteenth-Century Florence* (Durham, N.C., 1989), 46–67.

[143] Schiesari, *Gendering of Melancholia*, esp. 239, 241.

swelling of the bust before the bodice begins (FIG. 11.8). But it is the unruly hair which most sets the image apart from the overdetermined restraint of traditional Florentine portraiture. A tumbling profusion of real and cosmetic blond hair spills from its few bounds, mobile and bejewelled beyond the decorous limits seen in other portraits. Like many female figures in Poliziano's *Stanze*, this vision has 'loosened hair . . . blown about by the amorous breezes'; Bernardo Pulci's elegy described Simonetta's 'rippling blond tresses' as well as 'the angelic form of her beautiful face', both standard Petrarchan hyperbole in vernacular poetry.[144] The Berlin example is the closest to previous Florentine depictions of chaste young women in isolating frames, against relatively plain backdrops, jewelled and bedecked. It may be a posthumous immortalization of Simonetta's image. More removed from traditional portraiture, and on a larger panel, the Frankfurt body appears more like a festal nymph. Her body is further twisted to display both curvaceous breasts, emphasized by braids flowing down her cleavage. Mobility is stressed by suggestions of plasticity and movement as if in a wind. Her costume is multicoloured yet predominantly the white of a nymph; her agitated hair is richly attired with pearls, feathers, and other items which exaggerate the wanton, relaxed nature of the highly decorative woman. The creature appears an idealized portrayal of Simonetta as an alluring nymph or poetic muse.[145]

The chastity of Cecilia Gallerani, Lucrezia Donati, or Simonetta Vespucci became in itself a seductive attraction. What Firenzuola called 'charm' was a sensual virtue, the penitence della Stufa observed was sinfully stimulating, and the paradox of desire was figured in poems by Lorenzo de' Medici and others where a fleeing beloved became all the more desirable.[146] The end result of the visualization of chastity reaches its paradoxical extreme—a public display of reclusion—so that purity becomes erotically charged. In the 'Simonetta' images the woman and her specifics are poetically

[144] Poliziano, *The Stanze*, tr. Quint, i, 113 (59), and *passim*; Pulci is in Neri, 'La Simonetta', 145.

[145] Warburg, *La rinascita*, 283–307; Dempsey, *Portrayal*, 71, 132. Derivations from the 'Simonetta' image, with allegorical references, are in the National Gallery, London, and the Kisters collection, Kreuzlingen: see Lightbown, *Sandro Botticelli*, ii. 118–19, 154–5; *Meisterwerke der Malerei aus Privatsammlungen im Bodenseegebiet* (Bregenz, 1965), 26 and colour pl. X.

[146] On Lorenzo de' Medici see Dempsey, *Portrayal*, 101 f.: 'Lorenzo's message to Lucrezia [Donati] is that the harder one tries to remain chaste, the more the heat of amorous passion intensifies.'

evacuated. The paintings range in closeness to portrait conventions. But the discursive process, whereby the female figure's representation is rendered ambiguous, between purity and seduction, portrait and ideal, individual and generic, is inherent in most Renaissance portraits of women. Contrary signs are in juxtaposition but, rather than negatory conflict, a poetic *concordia discors* results.

A portrait was a collection of specifics, rearranged and perfected, according to the vernacular model of the anatomizing *blason* and the classical model of Zeuxis, whose image of Helen of Troy was built upon his close observance of five naked women.[147] It is entirely plausible, then, to see Leonardo's *Mona Lisa* as a 'cumulative image developed over a number of years', whose 'prolonged gestation' was fuelled by poetic traditions and 'a meditation on the human and terrestrial bodies'.[148] The portrait's renowned 'veil of ambiguity' is essential to its appeal. That elusive existence between portrait of a woman and representation of Woman later provoked versions of a nude Mona Lisa when certain male viewers sought a more explicit portrayal for their fantasies.[149] As Leonardo realized, a necessary part of portraiture is the addition to naturalism and resemblance of layers of artifice. The art of portraiture is selection, like most Renaissance art balancing archetype and experience, norm and nature, *imitatio* with *electio*. Any portrait of a woman is a representation of femininity imbued by social and poetic norms. Individualism, in its anachronistic and fixed sense, does not illuminate Renaissance portraiture of women. Against unified, coherent selves and singular meanings, many Renaissance portrayals of women face us with ambiguity and multivalency. Neither the particular face which occasioned the art nor the social conditions of Renaissance women can be reduced to an essentialist, monochromatic picture. An open-ended slippage in our reception of these images counteracts a modernist desire for sealed categorization.

Intellectual, imaginative, and sensual meditation upon a female

---

[147] On the *blason*, see Nancy Vickers, ' "This Heraldry in Lucrece' Face" ' in Susan Rubin Suleiman (ed.), *The Female Body in Western Culture: Contemporary Perspectives* (Cambridge, Mass., 1986), 209–22. On Zeuxis: Pliny, *Natural History*, xxxv. 64, and Cicero, *De inventione*, II. i. 1–3, constantly cited by Renaissance texts on both art and feminine beauty, for example, Alberti, *On Painting and On Sculpture*, 99 ff., 135; Castiglione, *Book of the Courtier*, 83; Rogers, 'Decorum of Women's Beauty', 50 f.; Raphael's letter to Castiglione in 1516, in Erwin Panofsky, *Idea. A Concept in Art Theory*, tr. Joseph J. S. Peake (New York, 1968), 60.

[148] Kemp, *Marvellous*, 267–70, hereafter quoted from 266.

[149] Brown and Oberhuber, 'Leonardo and Raphael', 25–37 for bibliography.

ɔody did not exclude a measure of portrayal. Poetic traditions long
validated the use by the literate classes of an existing woman as the
starting point, the initiation or muse, for masculine fantasy. Dante's
Beatrice Portinari, Petrarch's Laura, Lorenzo de Medici's Simonetta
Vespucci and Lucrezia Donati—each existed at some point, always
removed by distance or death but remaining as memory images in
the poet's vision. The conventions of vernacular poetry necessitated
this initial presence of a concrete inspiration, an actuality on which
to structure abstraction, and thence perform a phallocentric translation from the feminine surface back to the masculine creative base.[150]
The Renaissance portrayal of women also required some link with a
historical personage, filtered and mediated, to a point between portraiture and entire fantasy, reference and dream, experience and
metaphor.

A continuing state of unresolved desire or indecision before these
portrayals may more closely echo the Renaissance conditions of their
production and consumption. The erotics of multiplicity, tease, and
disjunction filled Renaissance treatises written by men about ideal
women; paradoxical tension between desire and distance fuelled the
poetry; women daily negotiated a delicate existence between normative and contingent circumstances; patrons gathered a gamut of
images which their language could not describe precisely; artistic
practice was 'more flexible and unsystematic than art historians are
inclined to assume'.[151] The images were often associative rather than
definitive; performative and communicative rather than static. What
they suggested nevertheless bore meaning within the context of
patriarchal virility and possession. Women's bodies were socially
constructed as discursive markers of desire, potentially beyond normative control. Feminine images could embody or stand for fears
about change; yet in the process of visualization and fantasy, the
images were stimulating, reassuring in their authentication of viril-
ty, property rights, and masculine creativity. Solidifying the assertion of sexual difference, a female portrait visually authenticated
masculinity and bonded men in a homosocial discourse. Yet the substance of the painting and the tangibility of its fiction paradoxically
continued to present women's faces to their world.

[150] Dempsey, *Portrayal*, 15–17, also 124, 146. For the necessary presence of women,
leading to their paradoxical absence, see Finucci, *The Lady Vanishes*, ch. 1.
[151] Hirst, *Sebastiano del Piombo*, 94. For the treatises see Rogers, 'Decorum of
Women's Beauty', 64–5, 72.

12. The Italian Renaissance Tale as History

LAURO MARTINES

TWENTY years ago, coming from a historian, the title of this essay would have seemed odd indeed. Nowadays we live easily with the assumption that fiction and fictional modes have something to do with history.[1] On the one hand, historians tell 'stories'; they use narrative techniques; on the other, they deal with the stories of others, whether in state papers or private accounts. But wherever we find sustained historical testimony, there the resources of language—or of semiotic systems such as ritual—are being used not only to convey meaning but also to present a narrative structure. Can we get the early Italian tale into this wide net?

If he was to give pleasure to his readers and listeners, the Renaissance *novelliere*, from Boccaccio to Bandello, had to fill his accounts with all sorts of realistic touches.[2] Italian tales of the period from the later fourteenth to the mid-sixteenth centuries are persistently realistic in setting, details, tone, motivation, and language. For audiences then sought the terrain of the real world in their preferred tales; they sought particulars or anecdotes that pertained to their own experience; and this is where the historian may have an entry into fiction and may, by means of negotiation and analysis, turn any Renaissance tale into a fount of historical evidence.

In the *Decameron* tale (VIII. 7) about the good-looking Florentine widow and the scholar trained in Paris, we have a drama ingeniously centred on the Petrarchan amatory metaphors of ice and fire: all very 'literary'. But other ingredients in the tale, such as the esteem for

---

[1] The theoretical breakthrough came with Hayden V. White, *Metahistory: The Historical Imagination in Nineteenth-Century Europe* (Baltimore, Md., 1974).

[2] The best general work on the Italian Renaissance tale is still Letterio di Francia, *Novellistica: Dalle origini al Bandello*, i (Milan, 1924). On the degrees of realism involved, see Lauro Martines, *An Italian Renaissance Sextet: Six Tales in Historical Context*, tr. M. Baca (New York, 1994).

learned men, the courting of young widows, their slippery honour, the smooth traffic between town and country, the alleged credulity of women, the art of revenge, and the hint of savagery in urban human relations all belong to the quotidian landscape of cities such as Florence, Siena, Bologna, Lucca, and Perugia. Moreover, more than Boccaccio, fifteenth-century *novellieri* cast their fictions around many of the views that went to guide and regulate daily life. In fact, revealingly, they did not even draw distinctions between invented anecdotes and stories taken from life: all were grist to their mill.

How many professional historians of the period know that if you were going to have guests to a meal in a Renaissance city, you were more likely to invite them to a heavy breakfast than to a dinner or supper; that such a meal was apt to be more formal than a dinner; and that you were more likely to conduct business at the late morning repast? Close friends, therefore, when having meals together, tended to do so after sunset.[3]

But is this not scrappy knowledge for novelists rather than historians? Yes and no. In so far as practices concerning food are looked upon as isolated titbits, they are little more than patches of colour for adding verisimilitude to a narrative. But in so far as they mark the organization of the day and bear upon the lineaments of class, business, gender, and other human relations, they must interest students of the history of social organization, ritual, and private life. One can spend thirty years doing research in archives and never acquire any sense of when and how and what people ate, as if this were trivial—and of course it was, for the kind of historical writing long dominant in the profession. Recently, a contrary trend has been set by study of the so-called history of private life;[4] but I am suggesting that the historian's interest in food may go beyond the arbitrary—in part artificial—distinction between private and public life and pass fully over to matters of nutrition, social structure, and social attitudes, such as in the occasional urban contempt for root vegetables, which were often viewed as peasant fare.

Yet if we are working *as* historians, we cannot read the writers of tales without having first steeped ourselves in the more conventional

---

[3] Note meal times in e.g. Boccaccio's *Decameron* (any edn.); Gentile Sermini, *Novelle*, ed. Giuseppe Vettori, 2 vols. (Rome, 1968); Giovanni Sercambi, *Il Novelliere*, ed. Luciano Rossi, 3 vols. (Rome, 1974); and Sabadino degli Arienti, *Le Porretane*, ed. Bruno Basile (Rome, 1981).

[4] Best represented perhaps by Philippe Ariès and Georges Duby (eds.), *A History of Private Life*, 3 vols. (Cambridge, Mass., 1987–9).

documentation of the period. We must not be taken in by the freedom of Boccaccio's mixed company of raconteurs. Among the upper classes in Florence, unmarried and unchaperoned young women and men did not breakfast or dine together. All congress of this sort was forbidden by the ideals of chastity and corporal honour imposed on such women; and this taboo, in turn, came forth from the social require-ments of property, patrilineages, politics, the legitimacy of heirs, and womens' dowries.[5] Here too was why upper-class families moved down socially in their choice of godmothers, for lateral godparenting, involving male and female equals, would have brought too many 'hon-ourable' women into closer contact, and hence into dangerous social relations with *uomini da bene*, respected men of substance.[6]

My caveat about Boccaccio suggests that the fledgling historian should not begin with the study of Renaissance tales, or at least not without some strict guidance. Unaided, he or she would sink in that vast stretch of quicksand, in the desperate effort to distinguish fictions from former realities, for the two do not come separated in Renaissance fiction; they are perfectly fused. Which is only a special reminder—is it not?—of the fact that every historical document has to be negotiated before it can be inserted into a meaningful framework.

In this connection, let us take as an example the theme of the lubricious friar or sexy priest, who turns up continually in the tales of the period. Conventional historical scholarship and diocesan visi-tations confirm that members of the regular and secular clergy were not seldom guilty of sexual misconduct.[7] In the absence of pertinent

---

[5] The expanding literature on this cluster of themes is effectively represented by David Herlihy and Christiane Klapisch-Zuber, *Tuscans and their Families* (New Haven, Conn., 1985); Julius Kirshner, 'Pursuing Honor while Avoiding Sin; The Monte delle Doti of Florence', in *Studi senesi*, lxxix (1977), 117–258; Christiane Klapisch-Zuber, *La Maison et le nom: Stratégies et rituels dans l'Italie de la Renaissance* (Paris, 1990); Anthony Molho, *Marriage Alliance in Late Medieval Florence: A Study of Ruling Class Endogamy* (Cambridge, Mass., 1994); Thomas Kuehn, *Law, Family, and Women: Toward a Legal Anthropology of Renaissance Italy* (Chicago, 1991), chs. 8–10; and the recent dissertation by Jane Fair Bestor, *Kinship and Marriage in the Politics of an Italian Ruling House: The Este of Ferrara in the Reign of Ercole I (1471–1505)*, 2 vols. (Chicago, 1992).

[6] As demonstrated in the suggestive study by Christiane Klapisch-Zuber, 'Au péril des commères: L'alliance spirituelle par les femmes à Florence', in *Femmes, Mariages-Lignages: XII–XIV siècles*, ed. Georges Duby (Brussels, 1992).

[7] Thus Denys Hay, *The Church in Italy in the Fifteenth Century* (Cambridge, 1977), 49–71; Gene Brucker, 'Ecclesiastical Courts in Fifteenth Century Florence and Fiesole', in *Medieval Studies*, 33 (1991), 229–57; and *Storia d'Italia: Annali 9*, ed. Giorgio Chittolini and Giovanni Miccoli (Turin, 1986).

quantitative historical studies, can we base any historical considerations on the image of the lecherous cleric in Renaissance fiction? A
computer-based inquiry might miss the range and tangle of attitudes
connected with the sexuality of the clergy. Present in tale after tale,
let us call one of the attitudes 'cynicism': that is to say, the viewpoint
associated with the clerics or nuns who are chronic seekers of sex
and who treat themselves to it grossly, systematically, and without
any prickings of conscience or contrition.[8] Their holy vows and supposed religious beliefs seldom, if ever, trouble them. In a tale doing
the rounds in the 1460s, and written down for Lorenzo de' Medici
by Marabottino Manetti, the nobly-born curate of a country parish
near Florence has propositioned every woman in the village.[9]

What are we to make of this cold cynicism? Was it purely in the
mind of the storyteller and his communicant audience, rather than
in those to whom it was by implication ascribed? And so, do the
appropriate tales document a virulent strain of anti-clericalism? Or,
are they devious expressions of toleration for the carnal needs of the
clergy? More simply, therefore, are the storytellers, at least in this
matter, being reporters and effectively chronicling an outlook and a
reality? These questions draw us away from literary concerns to a
preoccupation with an inner social consciousness—inner and social
because the involved attitudes were both conflicted and community-
grounded.

In many a tale the scandalous friar or priest gets his comeuppance:
a beating, castration,[10] humiliation, expulsion from the community,
the loss of his benefice, or even death. Sin is punished; hence there is
intolerance. The fact that ecclesiastical authority often seems to be
indulgent with wayward clerics doubtless stirred up anti-clericalism
and intolerance. At the same time, however, owing to the literary frequency and banality of the sexual antics of men in holy orders, there
is a degree of tolerance in the *novellistica*. Coldly lascivious clerics

---

[8] Some examples: Boccaccio, *Decameron*, iii. 1, 4, 8; vii. 3; viii. 2, 4; ix. 2;
Sercambi, *Novelliere*, 11, 13, 30, 33, 35–6, and *passim*; Sermini, *Novelle*, 2, 9, 17, 19,
23; Matteo Bandello, *Novelle*, ed. Giuseppe Guido Ferrero (Turin, 1974), i. 30; ii. 7,
45, 48; iii. 61; Masuccio Salernitano, *Il Novellino*, iii, in G. G. Ferrero and M. L.
Doglio (eds.), *Novelle del Quattrocento* (Turin, 1975), 323–6.

[9] Marabottino Manetti, *Novella* (Lucca, 1858).

[10] The penalty once used by Bernabò Visconti, lord of Milan, as narrated by Franco
Sacchetti, *Il Trecentonovelle*, no. xxv, ed. Antonio Lanza (Florence, 1984), pp. 49–50.
Sacchetti's moralizing at the end of the incident makes it clear that the priest was cas-
trated for heterosexual misdeeds, not sodomy. On another castration tale see Agnolo
Firenzuola, *Opere*, ed. Delmo Maestri (Turin, 1977), 162–71.

are routinely taken for granted; the storyteller colludes with the angry or prurient desires of his lay audience; and it is this contradictory play of acceptance and censure which verges on turning the image of the lustful cleric into a true record. The great preacher, San Bernardino of Siena, was made uneasy by regular contact between widows and their confessors: he trusted neither his confrères nor widows.[11]

The cynicism of the contemporary layman who countenanced priestly lubricity, and of the man in holy orders who climbed easily into bed with his penitents or parishioners, summons forth the contrary theme of credulity: the creed of the man or woman who believes too simplistically in the word of clerics, in relics and miracles, and in the sacraments. Once the alleged hypocrisy of the priesthood had become a commonplace in the culture of the age, when people spoke of religious belief and of all the things avowed by the clergy, how were they to draw a line between credulity or gullibility on the one side and a sensible, solid faith on the other? Renaissance tales teem with accounts of the cruel tricks played on credulous individuals. One of the classics in this repertory is Lorenzo de' Medici's *Giacoppo*,[12] the story of a Sienese upper-class simpleton who succumbs to the belief, under the influence of his confessor, a wicked Franciscan, that because he has seduced the wife of a young Florentine—in fact she is a clever prostitute in disguise—his own wife must now be mounted by the Florentine, if he is to save his soul from eternal damnation. A game of tit for tat is mockingly made the vehicle of Giacoppo's salvation.

By means of this lively dialectic between cynicism and gullibility, or between anti-clericalism and an uncritical stance, Renaissance fiction takes us into a divided consciousness, a conflict which often, I suspect, characterized the condition of particular individuals.[13] We may enter into this mental world by other, more traditional, historical means; but fiction brings the entire problematic out into the

---

[11] San Bernardino da Siena, *Prediche volgari sul Campo di Siena 1427* (Milan, 1989), nos. xxii and xxiii, 622–5. The Dominican Lombard Congregation ruled that confession was to be heard only by elderly friars and that these 'are to be frequently changed', Hay, *The Church in Italy*, 61.

[12] In *Scritti scelti di Lorenzo de' Medici*, ed. Emilio Bigi, 2nd edn. (Turin, 1965).

[13] As seen, for instance, in the suicide of the poet, Saviozzo of Siena (*c.*1360–*c.*1420). The evidence is in his verse and culminates in his ritualized suicide poems: Simone Serdini da Siena, *Rime*, ed. Emilio Pasquini (Bologna, 1965), 68–75, 215–17.

open. It raises questions for historians, provides diverging points of view, offers possible solutions, and gets a fix on things in ways that are ordinarily denied to prosaic documentation.

Credulous laymen cuckolded by local priests and priests moved by a sense of impunity were not mere figments of the literary imagination. They were factions (fact-fictions). As images or character types, they drew their vitality and resonance from the counterpoint of meanings in the consciousness of Renaissance readers and listeners, who lived in cities where privileged space was the setting for a society of anointed men with their own courts and civil constitutions.

Accused of arrogance, friars and priests were proud men. They occasionally struck poor folk or workers with their own hands.[14] They often came from or hobnobbed with members of the upper classes. And modest laymen, out of respect, stood up for them.[15] Consequently, the ensuing social strains were perhaps exaggerated in sexual metaphor; but the strains, the resentments, and the sexual misconduct were real and were all represented along the line of contact between storyteller and audience. Fiction and reality were brought constantly together along this line, as the storyteller both invented some things and adduced others that were at once verified by the lived experience of his readers. In this mysterious but yet quotidian place of alliances between real and imagined structures, we have a region as yet largely unexplored by historians,[16] although the so-called new historicists have often claimed it for literary and semiological analysis.

Having glanced off lewd priests, food, and the fiction–reality conundrum, I turn to five other questions, with a view to identifying more of the many areas of contact between history and Renaissance tales. The questions involve:

1. the personal pronoun as social indicator;
2. dress and social structure;
3. social identity and urban space;
4. relations between city and countryside; and
5. genre itself as a mode of historical testimony.

---

[14] Ronald F. E. Weissman, *Ritual Brotherhood in Renaissance Florence* (New York, 1982), 20.

[15] e.g. Antonio Manetti, *La Novella del Grasso Legnaiuolo*, tr. Martines, *Italian Renaissance Sextet*, tale VI, where the woodcarver immediately stands up for the parish priest of Florence's Santa Felicita.

[16] I have treated the problem alluded to here in my *Society and History in English Renaissance Verse* (Oxford, 1985).

Unlike practice in modern English or even modern Italian, Renaissance Italian usage called on the pronouns *voi* and *tu* (you and thou) to shadow forth a complex world of patriarchal, vertical, and hierarchical relations. It was always a matter of social negotiation between high and low, command and obedience, or tribute expected and tribute paid. Consequently, the two pronouns were also highly subject to rhetorical manipulation. The more we understand the use of pronouns of address in, say, the fifteenth-century tale, the more accurately we come to see the ways in which people saw themselves, saw others, and saw the man-made world. For in their uttering of 'you' or 'thou', they were drawing lines and sketching in a network of lateral and vertical social relations: practice which no historian of Renaissance Italy has ever bothered to examine in sustained inquiry.

Priests, we know, addressed their penitents with the familiar pronoun.[17] Spiritual monitors and advisors, they held the commanding position. They gave the *tu*, in first encounters, to men and women of the lower classes. But at what point, in movement up the social scale, did such immediate familiarity and delineating break down? They also employed the *tu* sooner with the women than with the men of the respected classes.

Pronouns in private letters tell us much about social proximities and distances. In the late fourteenth century, Margherita Datini's early letters to her husband show a steady use of the deferential *voi*, but even the later ones dither back and forth between this and the familiar pronominal form.[18] He, I suspect, Marco, always used the familiar pronoun with her. More generally, men of the ruling class employed the *tu* with members of the lower classes, such as workers and artisans; and in the country, they used it regularly with their own tenant farmers or sharecroppers. However, neither in town nor country did humble folk respond to their social superiors with any but the deferential form, *voi*. Although older men often used the *tu* when addressing younger men of the same social class, I cannot say how general such usage was. We also come on startling exchanges, and being startled, realize that we had failed to understand the mysteries of late-medieval and early-modern social structure. In Antonio

---

[17] As attested by just about any tale of the period showing exchanges between confessors and penitents. A detail like this, in the expectations of the period's reading audience, had to be realistic.

[18] *Le lettere di Margherita Datini a Francesco di Marco, 1384–1410*, ed. Valeria Rosati (Prato, 1977).

Manetti's *Novella del Grasso Legnaiuolo* (Story of the Fat Woodcarver),[19] we find that in exchange between the two intimate friends, Filippo Brunelleschi and Manetto the woodcarver, one trained as a sculptor and the other trained to work in wood, Filippo, late in the tale, addresses Manetto as *tu* but receives the *voi* in return. The woodcarver is somehow the social inferior. Since the story was penned about seventy-five years after the reported events (1485 vs. 1409), one of two things occurred: either the author felt that the famous Brunelleschi deserved the pronoun of respect from a 'lowly' craftsman, despite the fact that they were very close friends, that both had been apprenticed to work with their hands, and that the sculptor–architect was only six to eight years older than the woodcarver; or, even in the midst of friendship, Brunelleschi's superior family background and education rightly entitled him to the deference of the craftsman, so that the social divide in Florence cut right through the intimacies of republican friendship. Was the Florentine social world so measured, subtle, and opaque? I have no doubt it was.

Relations between dress and social structure follow naturally from my remarks regarding the uses of the personal pronoun. In reading the *novellieri*, I have come to realize that clothing was much more an indicator of social station than most historians have been led to think by the ordinary runs of documentation.[20] We all know that Jews and prostitutes were normally meant to wear distinguishing insignia, that the rich often wrapped themselves in silk and fur, that Venetian noblemen wore a black gown, that high office called for official dress, that men at the princely courts wore shorter and closely tailored garments, and that sumptuary laws aimed both to curb conspicuous consumption and to preserve visual (dress) distinctions among the various social classes. But my sense is that everyday dress in Italian Renaissance cities told a more complete story by representing social differences in finer detail, with the result that people were able, at a glance, to pick out married women, maidens, and widows, as well as merchants, attorneys (*notai*), shopkeepers such as apothecaries, and the varieties of craftsmen and workers, not to speak of peasants. When in a verbal exchange with a stranger, how

---

[19] I offer a sustained analysis of this story in my *Italian Renaissance Sextet*.
[20] For an apposite reading of Boccaccio, see Elissa Weaver, 'Dietro il vestito: la semiotica del vestire nel *Decameron*', in Enrico Malato (ed.), *La Novella italiana* (Rome, 1989), 701–10.

would you know which pronoun of address to use, if not by the way in which the other was dressed? You did not use the deferential forms—*voi, signore*—with everyone, for they were not polite forms, as they are with us, but rather terms of social identification and of tribute paid to status. There is a Genoa-based story which suggests, interestingly, that the Genoese were among the first to sheer dress away from judgements regarding verbal deference.[21]

Tales of the period show that personal identity, ambition, and fraud were often deliberately linked in some fashion with the social markers of dress. The visibility of social identities traced the lineaments of society in perception and consciousness; and all the transactions of everyday life, from greeting people to marketing, accorded with the signifiers of the dress worn. Tricksters and swindlers, therefore, sought to wear the appropriate raiment.

Pronouns, dress and social identities—or words, visual matter, and what people felt themselves and others to be: we are seeing a world in which social signification is at the core of existential understanding; and it is certainly at the core of the Renaissance tale, which is always an urban production. For either the setting is a city, or the characters are *cittadini* (urban denizens) on some business or pleasure jaunt in the country, or the tale is depicting *contadini* (rustics) strictly from the viewpoint of the domineering city. The representation of princes apart, seldom do we find departures from our three situations.

Naturally enough, therefore, as if in response to the current interest in the social uses and gendering of space, Renaissance tales have much to say about this. It is clear, for example, that night-time was male time out of doors; that the places where men often collected in the evenings, to gossip and retail anecdotes, such as the Mercato Nuovo in Florence, were exclusively male enclaves; that government squares, with their companies of armed men, were also places pre-eminently for the male—and even the immediately-adjoining churches were more likely to be frequented by men than by women. Cathedrals too were nearly always male arenas, owing to their central locations, mammoth proportions, and suitability as metropolitan meeting places. *Par contre*, evidence from Venice indicates that local churches (not necessarily the parish church) were the out-of-doors places for women, particularly for 'honourable'

---

[21] Sercambi, *Novelliere*, ii. 35–41 (tale 64).

women.[22] But what if a church was in the care of a suspected lecher? And speaking of movement out of doors, did women from the propertied classes do their own occasional marketing? Therefore, were fruit and vegetable markets neutral territory? The *novellistica* suggests that while servants often shopped for well-off widows, in families of substance, husbands did much or all of the important buying of food, cloth and other dress materials and household objects. Hence it is most likely that upper-class women, say, up to about the age of thirty,[23] regarded markets as male space. But this is subject-matter which is fully open to study.

Back at home, meanwhile, window space was feminine space. Although proverbs, preachers, and parental advice warned women against being at windows, fiction associates them with that very space, not only because here were points for the making of eye-contact which led to love but also because, being more often indoors and under parental or marital surveillance, women rightly saw windows as the eyes to the world outside.

But we must beware of overemphasizing the blanket gendering of space. Individual women could throw down challenges. In Gene Brucker's *Giovanni and Lusanna* (1986), one of the claims made against Lusanna was that she dared to look men in the face when walking through the streets of Florence. Under her bold eyes, masculine space became problematic terrain.

In trying to get at the semiotics of place and locale, we must also consider the ways in which space was apportioned and understood among rich and poor, political citizens and disenfranchised, or among the well-connected and the people of no name, no family name. The way a man 'read' the spatial units of Italian Renaissance cities had everything to do with who and what he was. The deeper study of urban space has to be predicated, therefore, on the study of social identities. In middle- and upper-class society, identity was derived from property, trade, kinship or neighbourhood ties (*parenti, amici e vicini*), and emotional attachment to a locality—all

---

[22] Elisabeth Crouzet-Pavan, '*Sopra le Acque Salse*': *Espaces, pouvoir et société à Venise à la fin du Moyen Âge*, 2 vols. (Rome, 1992), ii. 579–606.

[23] Generally speaking, women were seen as beginning to be old by their early thirties, the decisive factor here being marriage and childbearing. In Florence, after the age of thirty, women married or remarried with ever more difficulty. See David Herlihy, 'Vieillir à Florence au Quattrocento', *Annales ESC*, 24 (1969), 1338–52; D. Herlihy and C. Klapisch-Zuber, *Les Toscans et leurs Familles: Une étude du catasto florentin de 1427* (Paris, 1978), 202–3, 404.

often summed up by dress as a statement. Donatello would not wear a red cloak with a covering mantle given to him by Cosimo de' Medici because it denoted too grand a social identity.[24] He was thinking of the figure he would cut in the streets of Florence: public space elicited true identity. In a comic tale by Giovanni Sercambi,[25] at the point of joining a large crowd of naked men in a public bath, the Lucchese furrier, Ganfo, having peeled off his clothing (and hence the outer marks of his inner tradesman's identity), suddenly feels that his nakedness may bring the loss of all sense of himself; whereupon he sticks a bit of straw to his right shoulder, to serve as his identifying mark. When later on it floats away and sticks to another man, he is overwhelmed by fear and confusion. In effect, in public and in matters of identity, dress is all for him: it has all the markings of class, group, and individual. Identity is also, in some sense, the visible continuum which belongs to 'me'—clothing in this case, but in other cases,[26] it might be tools, a house, or a bed, thus making for a most physical view of the social world.

In Piero Veneziano's story, *Bianco Alfani*,[27] Bianco, descended from an illustrious but now ruined Florentine family, cannot accept his humble circumstances and has turned into a loud-mouth. This grave social sin, prating, committed in public streets and squares, brings about his psychological mutilation and downfall at the hands of the men around him. In other words, he is destroyed by a society which is witness to the inconsistencies among his hail of words, his modest social standing, and his claimed prestigious identity. For at the very least, in the manners and mores of the story, descent from a distinguished lineage imposes discretion and know-how in the use of words, but especially in public areas such as squares and market-places, where men of standing are most in evidence.

The most disturbing story of the age, Antonio Manetti's *Novella del Grasso Legnaiuolo*, hinges on the pitiless challenge to a man's identity, a plot to make him think that he is not who he thinks he is. The company of conspirators, close friends and acquaintances of the victim, see to it that he is denied all contact with the society of his ordinary round of everyday activities. By hiving him off into the

---

[24] Vespasiano da Bisticci, *Vite di uomini illustri del secolo XV* (Florence, 1938), 280.

[25] Sercambi, *Novelliere*, i. 26–9.

[26] Such as in Manetti's *Grasso Legnaiuolo*, a point discussed in my *Italian Renaissance Sextet*, VI. 2.

[27] In *Novelle del Quattrocento*, ed. Aldo Borlenghi (Milan, 1962), and tr. in my *Italian Renaissance Sextet*, IV.

dark (night, jail, shadows, and an alien neighbourhood), they are able to substitute their small company for the large, true, validating society. In effect, they counterfeit Florentine society so as to usurp its power to assign identities to people by the mere act of recognizing them. The counterfeiters then recognize Grasso as someone else, and for thirty-six hours—save for a period of drugged sleep—he is hounded by the terror of having become another.

The historical lessons of this story reside in the ways and in the extent to which personal identity in Italian Renaissance cities was a continuing function, and purely a function, of the society and transactions that circumscribed the individual, meaning chiefly his trade, family, and everyday street and shop routines. Take away the mirror of society, or let that mirror reflect another you, and in fact you become someone else.

There are other lessons here as well. City society in Renaissance Italy put its mark on you, so that you then 'read' its streets and squares accordingly and with much less leeway or choice than is available to us. When carried back into the fifteenth century, our modern and ready distinction between public and private life breaks down, for the public dimension then was far more overarching, and occupied more of the deeper consciousness of people, than is the case today.

But if the social pressures on men were as strong as we have seen them to be, we may begin to appreciate what they must have been on women, whose field of action was very much more restricted and who were more subject to moral constraints, stereotypes, and outright coercion. This is why Renaissance fiction bristles with tales of crafty, imaginative, and highly practical female characters. If women were in reality to get a better deal—the better to soothe the conscience of contemporaries (and conscience did needle them[28])—then tricks, ingenuity, and common sense had to provide the ways and means.

My elusive point about relations between urban space and social identity may be seen more fixedly in literature that broaches relations between *cittadini* and *contadini*.[29] In prose fiction and poetry from the fourteenth to the sixteenth centuries, but most especially perhaps

[28] As in complaints against the arranged marriage of girls who were often twenty and even thirty years younger than their husbands; hence the many verse laments of the *malmaritata*, the unhappily married girl.

[29] French literary scholarship has been at the forefront of work on citizen–peasant relations. See André Rochon (ed.), *Ville et campagne dans la littérature italienne de la Renaissance*, 2 vols. (Paris, 1976); and Michel Plaisance, 'Les rapports ville campagne dans les nouvelles de Sacchetti, Sercambi et Sermini', 61–73, in *Culture et société en*

in Tuscany, city people have their opposite in country folk. The peasant is the other: dirty, dishonest, coarse, unlettered, and uncivil—unworthy of citizens and unworthy to live in the city. No Arcadia here. In so far as sex is demeaning or base, it is summed up in metaphor which smacks of the country. When people are ugly or barbarous, they are countrified. And when stupidity is the sin, the disparaging metaphors again bring in the peasantry. It is as if the citizen in literature, *his* literature, is able to define himself only by conjuring up the peasant as foil. The citizen is everything that the peasant is not, and *vice versa*. The one belongs in the walled-in city, with all its mansions and amenities, while the other belongs in the country with his coarse food, root vegetables, and barnyard animals. Yet the traffic between city and country was absolutely essential. No big city could have survived without the food, immigrants, and labour that came in from the rural hinterland; and much urban wealth, often the larger part, was the agricultural wealth of the absentee landlords domiciled in the city.[30]

In this commerce between urban landlords and peasants, so advantageous for the city, we have the historical setting for much that is going on in fiction: an aspect of the literary enterprise revealing some of the ways in which *cittadini* organized their mental world. The fact that citizens enjoyed remarkable material and political advantages over the neighbouring peasantry did not incline them towards seeing country people in a better light. On the contrary, as if to square things with the needs of conscience, their literature rather demeaned the other. It made the social inferiority of the peasant into something that was also moral and cultural; and we find this policy of abasement not only in poetry and fiction, but also in letters, family log books, and collections of advice.

I am broaching a variety of themes, with a view to pointing out some of the diverse connections between history and fiction. But let it not be imagined that themes alone here are the bridge. There is also the evidence of genre, language, metaphor, and voices.

By voices I mean the presence of a kind of chorus or social buzz

Italie du Moyen-Âge à la Renaissance: hommage à André Rochon (Paris, 1985); and again Plaisance, 'Città e campagna', in *Letteratura italiana*, v. 583–634, ed. Alberto Asor Rosa (Turin, 1986).

[30] Herlihy and Klapisch-Zuber, *Les Toscans*, ch. 9; Philip Jones, *Economia e società nell'Italia medievale*, tr. C. S. Jones and A. Serafini (Turin, 1980), 17–47, 178–89; Giovanni Cherubini, *Signori, Contadini, Borghesi: ricerche sulla società italiana del basso medievo* (Florence, 1974), 73–99.

in many tales, such as by Sermini and Sercambi, a buzz produced usually by different interlocutors and by characters cast as ideal or stock types. These are the voices of a lively oral culture: the serried urban community is here having its say. Proverbs and platitudes, but also neighbours, idealized ladies, merchant types, and go-betweens all introduce the axioms by which the society lives and flourishes. And the historian is wrong not to listen, just as the student of literature is mistaken to steal the social buzz away from its vital sources by regarding it as mere literary occurrence.

By metaphor—apart from technical definitions—I mean the way in which judgement and value sneak through trope into the language of description and supposed neutral statement, to reveal the imprint of class, group, gender, locality, or creed. And, speaking of language, I would also note the ways in which turns of phrase, register, and everyday speech also allow us to break into the circuit of undercover societal presences. By these means, we come to see how practical, basic, and group-oriented the civilization of the Renaissance city was, and—for all its religious impregnation—how earthy were its chronic cares in being fixed on the jejune physicality of sex, on the external trappings of personal identity, the fear of neighbourhood censure, and on money, food, looks, maladies, odours, and sights and sounds. If the language of the Renaissance tale ties country people to the earth, to smells, animals, and crass movements, it binds the citizens of the middle and upper classes to values that are less earthy but no less earthly, for even the lofty honour of families and girls is pinned to money, property, concrete political office, dowries, maidenheads, and visually attested behaviour.

By genre I mean the different kinds of tales: amatory, misogynistic, malicious, jokey, anti-clerical, *fortuna* governed, anti-peasant, and so on. Keyed to contemporary experience and revealing remarkable spontaneity, these forms are testimony to the input of historical time and place. I shall take one genre, the sort of tale built around the prank or practical joke (*beffa*, *natta*), and illustrate the way in which form itself may be teased out into a mode of historical documentation.

One of the most popular of all genres was constructed around the machinery of the prank or sustained practical joke. There was a very large number of such tales.[31] Typically character X is led by one or

---

[31] My sampling includes Boccaccio, Franco Sacchetti, Giovanni Sercambi, Gentile Sermini, Giovanni Sabadino degli Arienti, Antonfrancesco Grazzini (il Lasca), Matteo Bandello, and a scattering of anonymous and lesser writers.

more people to perform a given action or to expect certain events. Manipulated by friends, a spouse, acquaintances, a confessor, or confidence men, the victim is persuaded that the outcome will be good for him or her. He or she is then cheated, swindled, cuckolded, or made the butt of scathing derision. The intention is comic; no pity is shown; the goal is to provoke laughter, and the more hilarious the better. Boccaccio's Calandrino fits the recipe of the dupe. The same may be said of Sercambi's goodlooking widow, Antonia de' Virgiliesi of Pistoia, of Sermini's upstart son of a peasant (Mattano), of Piero Veneziano's Bianco Alfani, of Giovanni Sabadino degli Arienti's Friar Puzzo and of Lorenzo de' Medici's Giacoppo.[32]

Now we may wish to stress the universality of the kind of story founded on the trick, joke, or deception. But universality does not do away with time and place. Although the love poem, for example, is universal, its multifarious forms, strategies, accents, and so forth, anchor it to different times, places, and needs, and—in Italy—even to different cities.[33]

The practical joke as tale had a particular and enduring relevance for certain Italian cities of the late medieval and Renaissance periods. In Florence, for example, as we learn from R. F. Weissman's analysis of the city's 'agnostic' society, neighbourly one-to-one relations were fraught with a contradictory mix of amity and hostility.[34] In response, 'Judas the Florentine' looked for ways of transcending his aggressions and suspicions in the spiritual brotherhood of religious confraternities, and Florence had a hundred of these.[35] But the anxieties of parish and neighbourhood did not go away, owing to the pull of political faction, powerful patron–client networks,[36] nagging traditions of civil conflict, and the city's confining (walled-in) spaces. Thus the trick or *beffa* as tale, with its union of amity and

[32] On the designated victims, see Boccaccio, *Decameron*, viii. 3, 6; ix. 3; Sercambi, *Novelliere*, tale 29; Sermini, *Novelle*, ii, tale 25; *Bianco Alfani*, in Ferrero and Doglio (eds.), *Novelle del Quattrocento*, 629–52; and Lorenzo de' Medici's *Giacoppo*, in *Scritti scelti*. The last two of these stories, in translation, are in my *Italian Renaissance Sextet*.

[33] Lauro Martines, 'The Politics of Italian Renaissance Love Poetry', in Janet L. Smarr (ed.), *Historical Criticism and the Challenge of Theory* (Urbana, Ill., 1993); also my 'Amour et histoire', forthcoming in *Annales ESC* (1995).

[34] Weissman, *Ritual Brotherhood*.

[35] On Florentine confraternities, see John Henderson, 'Le Confraternite religiose nella Firenze del tardo medioevo: patroni spirituali e anche politici?', *Ricerche storiche*, 15 (1985), 77–94.

[36] For succinct study of the main one, see Anthony Molho, 'Cosimo de' Medici: Pater Patriae or Padrino?', *Stanford Italian Review*, 1 (1979), 5–33.

animosity, of trust and perfidy, captures—and is the very form or paradigm of—the everyday hostilities and loyalties in, say, Florence, Bologna, Lucca, Siena, and Perugia. The woodcarver, Grasso,[37] was liked by his friends and perhaps even loved by the most treacherous of them, Brunelleschi; and yet they rounded on him; they could not keep from teaching him a lesson so cruel that it drives him to an act of ritual suicide. Grasso abandons Florence altogether, in a self-imposed exile from a city where for two centuries exile had been one of the most severe of all penalties levelled against serious political dissent or disobedience. In this feature of the story—teaching by means of punishment—we have a second narrative element which links the trick as tale to the society of the Renaissance city. The victim is always guilty of a social sin or two: simplicity, vanity, eccentricity, or religious gullibility. That is to say, in our fiercely practical, alert, suspicious, and conformist city society, the individual has an intense street and neighbourhood life. Hence he must beware of being overly trusting, odd, or foolishly vain, because this is to get neighbours and surroundings wrong. It is to misunderstand a society which punishes such obtuseness by means of tricks, humiliation, and laughter. Friends and neighbours are spurred on to teach the social sinner a harsh lesson; and that which we, with our modern sensibilities, consider cruel, they considered comical, necessary, and just.

Narrative as the account of a prank has yet a third feature which relates it to the urban milieu. It is the best kind of anecdote for word-of-mouth transmission. This is to say that it both renews, and takes animation from, the community's oral traditions. To the extent that the energy of storytelling resides in the social topography of a community, it lies outside any given tale. Or to say the same thing differently: in so far as the ingenuity of a tale depends upon effective storytelling, and therefore upon a primed and ready audience, neither tale nor ingenuity can be cut away from the community's oral culture.

Franco Sacchetti, in the late fourteenth century, tells a story about a rich Florentine citizen, Antonio, who hides thirty eggs in his under-breeches (*brache*), just before entering Florence, to avoid paying customs at the city gate.[38] Secretly betrayed by his servant, he is then offered a glass of wine by the customs officials and forcefully invited to sit down, whereupon there is what seems the sound of cracking

---

[37] In A. Manetti, *Novella del Grasso.*
[38] Sacchetti, *Trecentonovelle*, no. CXLVII, 304–8.

glass; all the eggs are shattered, and his stockings begin to ooze orange. Heavily fined, Antonio then adds a generous gratuity and swears the officials to secrecy, out of fear that an account of the incident will get out to do the rounds. And indeed this story is about the vivacity of the city's oral and gossipy life. For when Antonio reaches home and his wife sees his drawers, he has to tell her what happened and she is horrified. Knowing perfectly well that the *gabelle* officials would dine out on the incident, and associating it with matter for popular songs and tales, she screams furiously at him, saying that the story would race through the city, that he would be forever disgraced, that she would never again be able to appear among women without shame.

Sacchetti refuses to give the surname of the egg-breaker because, he claims, he wants to avoid further infamy to the family. In other words, he purports to be chronicling a real incident, and like so many other stories in his *Trecentonovelle*, it may indeed have taken place, but we are unlikely ever to know with any certainty. No matter, for the point here has to do with the liveliness and pedagogic malice of Florentine oral civilization and with the viability of its streets and squares as oral conductors. No rich man, no well-placed family, no distinctive figure or personality could escape having a place in the public consciousness. Moreover, the trick as tale, like gossip, flourished best at the expense of such people and in such a setting. In the name of literary understanding as a kind of knowledge, the *beffa* may be divorced from its social milieu, but in their search for entries to an opaque mental world, historians must look for the marriage.

Having touched, perhaps, too many points, I close with my principal plea. The Renaissance tale is both literature and historical document. The first of these may be the willed act of the writer; the second is an unavoidable condition. If, as history, the tale is to surrender its holdings to us, then we have to work on it, just as we work on any historical source. No document, however forthright or simple, ever speaks for itself. But whereas the conventional historical document comes to us with an *a priori* affidavit of reality, of its being the carrier of some quondam transaction in the real world, the literary product appears as something imagined, invented, or even brainspun. And so it more or less is. But in so far as it is not, it has historical information to impart; and even where it is largely imagined, its departures from reality have a great deal to tell us about the construction of alternate imaginary realities, and therefore about problems in the real world. The Renaissance love poem, almost never addressed to a spouse, is a response to—and an act of revenge against—the utilitarian, strictly arranged, upper-class marriage of convenience. Study the one, and you throw light on the other. Certainly, no less so than poetry, Renaissance storytelling engaged with life and aimed to pivot on contemporary experience, thereby mixing invention and reality at will. This means that the historical study of Renaissance fiction requires more strategies, nous, and professional experience—in short, more work—than the prosaic document. But the prizes to be had are inestimable, for they come forth from underlying oral traditions and from the society's conflicted consciousness: that is, from those parts of a mental world that are likely to be flatly represented, or ignored altogether, in the ordinary runs of historical documentation.

Index

Bold type refers to illustrations.